must try to get hold of one
Novels; -it would [illegible] e
ke our Heroine read it, and
e as Isabella Wardour in the
History of the Hartz Demon
' I believe, upon recollection,
bye, my dear Edward, I am
ur Mother mentions in her
o be missing is monstrous!
at Steventon lately, & therefore
ng them; -two strong twigs
own, would have been some
er that any theft of that
ful to me. What should I
spirited Sketches, full of
I possibly join them on to
[illegible] hich I work.

I must try to get hold of on

Novels;—it would be a fine

ake our Heroine read it aloud

ll as Isabella Wardour in th

. History of the Hartz Demon

o' I beleive, upon recollection,

bye, my dear Edward, I am

our Mother mentions in her

to be missing is monstrous

at Steventon lately, & therefore

ing them;—two strong twigs

own, would have been som

ver that any theft of that

eful to me. What should I

spirited Sketches, full of

. I possibly join them on to

which I work,

WRITERS REVEALED

WRITERS REVEALED

TREASURES FROM THE BRITISH LIBRARY AND THE NATIONAL PORTRAIT GALLERY, LONDON

By Catharine MacLeod & Alexandra Ault

NATIONAL PORTRAIT GALLERY

BRITISH LIBRARY

CONTENTS

FAME

WRITING TO CHANGE THE WORLD

P. Heron
1949

INTRODUCTION

Catharine MacLeod & Alexandra Ault

How much can a manuscript draft tell us about an author's writing process? What does a writer's portrait say about the person it depicts? What do the letters between novelists and their publishers uncover about how a book came to be? And does an author's identity or life story matter at all to our understanding or enjoyment of a text? *Writers Revealed* brings together some of the greatest treasures of two British national institutions – the National Portrait Gallery and the British Library – to address these questions and reveal more about the lives and works of famous and favourite authors.

From the frontispiece portraits of the sixteenth century to the ubiquitous 'author photograph' and potted biography on the back covers or flyleaves of books published today, there is plenty of evidence that readers have always had a fascination with writers' lives and appearances. The huge value put on original manuscripts and first editions is also testament to this phenomenon. Manuscripts, letters and documents in an author's own hand shed light on intentions, ways of thinking and writing processes. They enable us to feel, perhaps, that we are entering into a kind of conversation with the author, bearing witness to private moments and experiencing a deeper engagement with the works that we love. Original manuscripts seem somehow imbued with an essence of the writer while printed editions made during the author's lifetime appear to give us a better understanding of the world in which they worked. Meanwhile, we seek out portraits that give us an idea of an author's physical appearance, a key to their tastes and a flavour of the times they lived in, which seem to flesh them out as recognisable human beings whom we feel closer to knowing.

The premise of this book is that the juxtaposition of authors' portraits with texts written by them provides valuable insights into their lives and works – often in exciting and surprising new ways. Since ancient times, writing and art – usually more specifically poetry and painting – have been compared and contrasted. They have been weighed up in terms of their value, the ways they are enjoyed and what they can reveal about life. The competitive comparison of these two art forms, known as 'ut pictura poesis' (as is painting, so is poetry), takes on a particular character in relation to portraits of authors. Philosophers, artists, writers and readers have enquired as to what reveals most about the mind of an author: their writing or their portrait. In England, the question took its most explicit form in the late sixteenth and early seventeenth centuries, when portraits of authors first began to be in demand. When the First Folio of collected plays by William Shakespeare (1564–1616; p.180) was published in 1623, it included an engraved frontispiece portrait of the author facing a poem by his friend and contemporary, Ben Jonson (1572–1637; pp.25 and 182). In the poem, Jonson takes up this very issue, posing the engraver's challenge as 'a strife / with Nature, to out-doo the life'.[1] But he goes on to say that a portrait cannot convey Shakespeare's wit, and therefore advises, 'Reader, looke / Not on his Picture, but his Booke'.[2] Not unnaturally, since he was himself a writer, Ben Jonson concludes that Shakespeare's words reveal more about him than his portrait; inevitably, the writer has the last word. The debate continues.

A more symbiotic and less competitive relationship between writing and the visual arts was often expressed in later periods. This is apparent in the reciprocal sequence of inspiration between the poet William Wordsworth (1770–1850; p.91) and the painter Benjamin Robert Haydon (1786–1846), who wrote and painted in response to each others' works (pp.91–3). More broadly, visual representation of various kinds has been a preoccupation for many writers. Derek Walcott (1930–2017; p.105) described painterly techniques to convey atmosphere, while Jane Austen (1775–1817; p.189) compared writing to the art of painting a miniature. Sir John Harington the Younger (bap. 1560–1612; p.128) praised artists, while the creation of certain characters, such as Winnie-the-Pooh, was as reliant on the images by E. H. Shepard (1879–1976) as it was on the words of A.A. Milne (1882–1956; p.218). Similarly, performance has provided dynamic, visual representations of literature that draw out new layers of meaning. From Shakespeare through to Harold Pinter (1930–2008; p.102), texts, written or adapted for performance, are consumed and understood in different ways on the page and when performed by others.

Texts are not, of course, unmediated expressions of authorial intent. While, in one sense, it is undoubtedly true that writers' works are windows into their ways of thinking, values and experiences, these are always filtered, or even disguised, in a myriad of ways. Prose fiction, poetry, drama, even autobiography: all require imaginative creation and re-creation, as well as selective choices, in which omissions are often as revealing as inclusions. Moreover, books are almost always productions that involve more people than just the author. Those involved in making a book include publishers, who at an early date were also the printers; the printers, who included foremen, punch cutters, typesetters and inkers; paper mills; ink suppliers; proof-readers; advertisers; artists and illustrators; professional readers, copy-editors and editors; designers; and binders. Additionally, the critic and audience, two key elements in the popularity of a work, could have an influence not just on the production of subsequent editions, but also on the content of later works by the same author. Even Jane Austen was conscious of the impact of her readers and collected their opinions on her novels. Since the Romantic movement in the early nineteenth century, readers have increasingly focused on the idea of writing as a solo enterprise, which has meant that the economics of book production are often ignored. Yet, from an early date, writers were acutely aware of the business of printing and publishing, often making notes on their manuscripts to show the printer where their text should be placed, or asking publishers for guidance as to what they should write.

Portraits, like written works, are also the product of a selection process and what we are shown is a careful construct, affected by various factors and individuals. Even what might appear to be the most casual of photographs involves choices. The sitter, the artist and the intended viewer or viewers of the portrait all influence the appearance of the finished work. The person paying for the portrait might be another individual with a say in the matter. Many portraits are produced by groups of artists in a studio or involve collaborations with other specialists. Some portraits are created specifically to celebrate the sitter's identity as an author; others contain no references to writing and pertain to other aspects of the author's life and identity. Some are intended for a select audience; others are made and reproduced multiple times through processes like engraving or photography, for as many viewers as possible. So, 'reading' what a portrait tells us about a sitter is not a straightforward process.

The texts and portraits that are in this book have also been shaped by the history of publishing and printing. Books were originally made by writing in ink on paper or parchment (animal skin) and binding the leaves or pages together. Even when printed books began to appear in the fifteenth century, people continued to write books in manuscript form, circulating historical, political, religious and philosophical texts, stories, poems and drama. While nowadays we think of the manuscript as reserved for writing and drafting, in the seventeenth century and before, works were often published in manuscript, with scribes making multiple copies; examples in this book include works by John Donne (1572–1631; p.21) and Andrew Marvell (1621–1678; p.234). This kind of publication meant that literary works circulated among a limited audience. Such publications were particularly suited to those authors who did not want to be associated with the commercial side of writing, which might be regarded as socially degrading, or to those who were concerned about negative judgments on the basis of their subject matter or, in the case of women, their sex. While books in manuscript form appeared up to and throughout the seventeenth century, by the eighteenth century the practice was largely defunct as printing took over.

Printing with moveable type had been developed in Europe in the 1450s. William Caxton (*c.*1422–*c.*1491) set up the first printing press in England in the grounds of Westminster Abbey, London, in 1476 and from this point, the print trade developed in Britain. Printing and publishing were increasingly formalised in the seventeenth and eighteenth centuries, with authors and publishers signing contracts agreeing the number of books to be printed, the types of paper to be used and whether further editions would be produced. As the trade expanded and developed so too did the kinds of book available. The evolution of the novel, or prose fiction, occurred at this time in the context of a growing demand for literature. Increasing literacy and new circulating or lending libraries meant that more people had access to reading material.

By the nineteenth century paper- and ink-making and printing technologies became streamlined and mechanised. Mass production contributed to decreasing costs of materials. Continuing increases in literacy and the production of more widely affordable reading material, as well as serialised novels, made reading a far more accessible pastime than it had been even a century before. The survival of manuscript material in the context of this increased mechanisation remained a matter of chance, just as it had been in the preceding centuries. A fair copy manuscript of *Jane Eyre* (1847) by Charlotte Brontë (1816–1855; p.139) was carefully preserved by her publisher, whereas Charles Dickens (1812–1870; p.197) saw no reason to retain many of his manuscripts and the only reason for their fragmented survival is because other people, including a foreman of his printers, chose to rescue them. The survival of letters, also in manuscript, relied on their recipient preserving them. In some cases, manuscripts, both letters and literary drafts, were deliberately destroyed, such as those of Lord Byron (1788–1824; p.193) by his publisher John Murray (1778–1843), in an attempt to control the public perception of the author.

The spread of author portraits grew more slowly than the expansion of printing. In medieval Britain, illuminated books – those including illustrations or decorations painted in colour pigments – sometimes included a portrait of the author presenting the work to a patron. These portraits focused the reader and recipient of the work on the gratitude of the writer, and the hope of future patronage. Printed frontispiece portraits began appearing occasionally in books in the sixteenth century. At this time in Britain, painted portraits were associated largely with the wealthier and well-educated ruling classes, so such images lent the author a degree of status and gave their work additional authority. Sometimes they were based on an existing oil painting, but at other times they were made from drawings commissioned by the author or publisher of the book specifically for the frontispiece. In many early cases, a frontispiece portrait is the only known likeness of an author. Frontispiece portraits became more common as painted portraiture began to spread beyond the very wealthiest in society to the professional classes. The enormous popularity of the theatre in the late sixteenth and early seventeenth centuries, and the growth in the status of playscripts – which until the publication of *The Workes of Benjamin Jonson* in 1616 had largely been regarded as ephemeral – also created a new demand for frontispieces as further collections of plays were published.

Throughout the seventeenth century, portraiture in oils, including those of authors, became increasingly popular among the more prosperous classes. Most oil paintings of professional authors – as opposed to wealthy individuals who also wrote – took the relatively modest form of head-and-shoulder depictions with few, if any accessories, which had been established at the beginning of the century in portraits such as those of Ben Jonson (fig.7) and William Shakespeare (fig.103). Such simplicity may have been considered socially appropriate for individuals whose social status was not particularly high, but it also focused the viewer's attention on the individuality of sitters: their faces, as opposed to signifiers of wealth, rank or often even profession. This approach reflected a growing interest in individual identity and directed the attention of the viewer to what they could 'read' of the sitter's virtue, intellect and creative genius in their face.

Increasingly, in the eighteenth and nineteenth centuries, portraits of authors, whether in books or independent images, were used to convey an important and sometimes obvious message about the nature of their work or character in order to promote or to celebrate their writing. Contemplative poses suggested deep thought, sometimes with the head resting on the hand, eyes often turned away from the viewer. Landscape backgrounds or piles of books alluded to the subject of their writing or the depth of their learning. In the case of the British African abolitionist writers Ignatius Sancho (*c.*1729–1780; p.237) and Olaudah Equiano (*c.*1745–1797; p.241), simply their formal presentation and inclusion in portraiture conveyed a powerful argument to their contemporaries in support of their cause (see figs 136 and 137). Conversely, as some writers became celebrities, the popularity of their books promoted the sale of their portraits; for example, Sir Joshua Reynolds (1723–1792) painted the newly popular Laurence Sterne (1713–1768; see fig.46) as a speculative venture, in order to profit from the sale of prints based on the painting. Lord Byron's appearance was as important to his popularity as his poetry, as he well knew, but although he tried to control his portraiture, he had no real control over the thousands of images that circulated of him during his lifetime, including prints, painted copies and imagined portraits.

The story of female authors and their portraits followed a different trajectory from that of their male counterparts, reflecting a very different authorial journey. For many centuries, most British women were not able to experience the same level of education as men, and literacy rates among them lagged considerably behind. When women were lucky enough to be educated, their writing, like their lives, was often circumscribed by societal conventions. In the sixteenth and early-seventeenth centuries, translating religious material, or some dramas, was regarded as a suitable literary activity for women, along with writing certain kinds of poetry, but being published was not encouraged. In the late seventeenth century, Aphra Behn (1640–1689; p.82) took advantage of the high level of demand from the public theatres, and an unprecedented liberal atmosphere emanating from Charles II's (1630–1685) court, to make a public career as a professional playwright, but she was continually censured for doing this and became a target of often ribald verbal abuse. Subsequent women writers who published largely hid behind pseudonyms during the eighteenth and nineteenth centuries. This gave them the possibility of writing what they chose and being judged – and paid – on equal terms with men. Inevitably, in this context, when they were portrayed, female writers were almost always depicted simply as fashionable women, not as authors.

Colonialism, the expansion of empires, the transatlantic slave trade and long-term, widespread racism have also significantly shaped the demography of authors writing in English over time. Writers of colour faced significant challenges, resulting in few opportunities to write or publish in the English language until the twentieth century. That Ignatius Sancho's eighteenth-century manuscript letters survive and were published is remarkable, as is the fact that he sat for a portrait. Although the slave trade was abolished in the UK in 1807, it was not until the activism of figures including C. L. R. James (1901–1989; p.159) and John La Rose (1927–2006; p.165) that new opportunities really opened up. This has led to a growing interest in, and appreciation of, writing by authors of colour, including those from former British colonies. The twentieth and twenty-first centuries have also seen a dramatic increase in new styles and approaches, both in writing and in portraiture, as well as an expansion of participation in these activities by previously – and often still – under-represented groups of people.

The authors' texts in this book are a selection of handwritten and typewritten drafts, legal documents, printed editions and letters, all of which cast light on the writers, their lives, work and the times in which they lived. Similarly, the portraits, including paintings in oil or acrylic, photographs, drawings, engravings and sculpture, all have their own stories to tell, which help to open up the world of writing and image-making to their viewers. These works have been arranged into five thematic sections, which consider different issues that have affected authors across time, providing a focus for a deeper exploration of their lives, words and images. Together, texts, portraits and biographies offer a unique opportunity for a closer encounter with some of the most talented writers of the last 500 years.

IN SEARCH OF THE AUTHOR

In our persistent desire to understand more about the authors we admire, we seek out their likenesses and their manuscripts, and study their biographies. This chapter looks at what is revealed and what is hidden when life, writing and portraiture intersect. Portraits of writers and original manuscripts allow us to explore different facets of their lives and can also illuminate otherwise hidden stories behind the finished literary product. A widely published book or portrait might make us feel that we are closer to knowing an author. And yet, a book may, in various ways, obscure the author's identity, and a portrait may give very little away about the character or profession of the sitter. This is particularly the case with women writers. The portraits of Fanny Burney and Virginia Woolf celebrate only their beauty and fashionable appearance, leaving their texts to reveal more about the work for which they became renowned. Other items that at first seem to belong to more private realms, such as manuscript drafts, could be made in or for more open spaces, such as the theatre, created as part of a collaborative process, or intended to be circulated more widely. Meanwhile, a unique and seemingly intimate portrait might have been created for, or end up in, a very public setting.

In some cases, there seems to be little to distinguish the public and private lives of an author, with their portraits and texts providing an impression consistent with what is known of their lives. John Donne's portrait depicts him as a melancholy lover, as does much of his poetry. J. R. R. Tolkien's warm letters to his grandson, complete with maps, and his photographic portrait among tree roots evoke something of the fantasy world of his novels. Mervyn Peake's startling self-portrait could be mistaken for a character in one of his own books, or in his illustrations for the 1949 edition of Robert Louis Stevenson's *Treasure Island*.

Something of the depth of feeling expressed both in his poetry and his life is conveyed in the posthumous portrait of John Keats by his friend Joseph Severn. Andrea Levy's drafts for *Small Island* (2004), and her character notes, together with the photograph of her outside the flat she grew up in, remind readers of the aspects of her personal experience woven into her writing.

In other cases, the juxtaposition of portrait and text underlines the difference between public perception and private reality. T. S. Eliot's modernist portrait by Patrick Heron seems, at first glance, to echo the difficult, hard-edged imagery of his poetry, but, closer inspection yields a surprise: the outline of a cat above the poet's right shoulder. The affectionate letter containing one of his playful cat poems similarly reminds the reader that there was more to Eliot than the despair of *The Wasteland* (1922). Augustus John's portrait of the infamously heavy-drinking and chaotic Dylan Thomas shows the poet as almost cherubic, and Thomas's meticulous approach to the content and even the typesetting of his poetry reflects a very different side from his public reputation. Ted Hughes's portrait in bronze by his friend Leonard Baskin depicts his stern features and the subjects of some of his most famous works, but the tender, painful, deeply personal drafts of his poetry addressed to his late wife Sylvia Plath reveal thoughts, feelings and actions kept private until shortly before his death.

While the objects in this chapter yield revelations and insights, ultimately these are only partial glimpses into the creative and complex lives of talented authors.

THOMAS WYATT

Sir Thomas Wyatt (*c.*1503–1542) is the author of the oldest manuscript to feature in this book. 'The Book of Sir Thomas Wyatt' is one of the earliest examples of an English poet gathering their work together as a collection. It reveals many aspects of Wyatt's life as a diplomat and courtier serving Henry VIII (1491–1547) and illustrates something of his huge achievement as a writer. The first English poet known to have written sonnets, a poetic form he brought to England from Italy, he also produced a larger and more varied *oeuvre* than any other writer of the early Tudor period. Wyatt originally employed scribes (or amanuenses) to copy his poems in the book, but he edited many of these in his own hand and also went on to write out others in their entirety himself.

Some of the poems in this volume are concerned with love and historically were thought to be about Anne Boleyn (*c.*1501/7–1536), the second wife of Henry VIII with whom Wyatt was alleged to have had an affair. Whether or not the affair took place, in May 1536 Wyatt was imprisoned in the Tower of London along with other men accused of being Anne's lovers. Five men were executed on 17 May, followed by Anne herself on 19 May, but Wyatt, probably at the behest of the powerful politician Thomas Cromwell (*c.*1485–1540), escaped death and was later released.

Between 1537 and 1539 Henry VIII sent Wyatt to Spain as an ambassador. He appears to have written some of the poems in this volume during his travels, as the location 'Spayne' has been written above a number of them. The volume also served as a working notebook, which Wyatt used to record his thoughts as well as his poems. After his death, the volume passed to his son, Thomas Wyatt the Younger (1521–1554). Another owner was the writer Sir John Harington the Younger (1560–1612; see p.128).

As well as love poems, the verses within this volume include Wyatt's 'Penitential Psalms' and their 'Introductory Poem'. Penitential psalms were parts of the Bible designated by the church as being particularly appropriate for prayer during contemplation of personal failings and sin, and for seeking forgiveness. Many people wrote their own penitential psalms by way of offering contrition to God. In 1541, after the downfall of Cromwell, Wyatt was imprisoned in the Tower for a second time, again under charge of treason. It is likely that he wrote his 'Penitential Psalms' and 'Introductory Poem' after he was released later that year, following

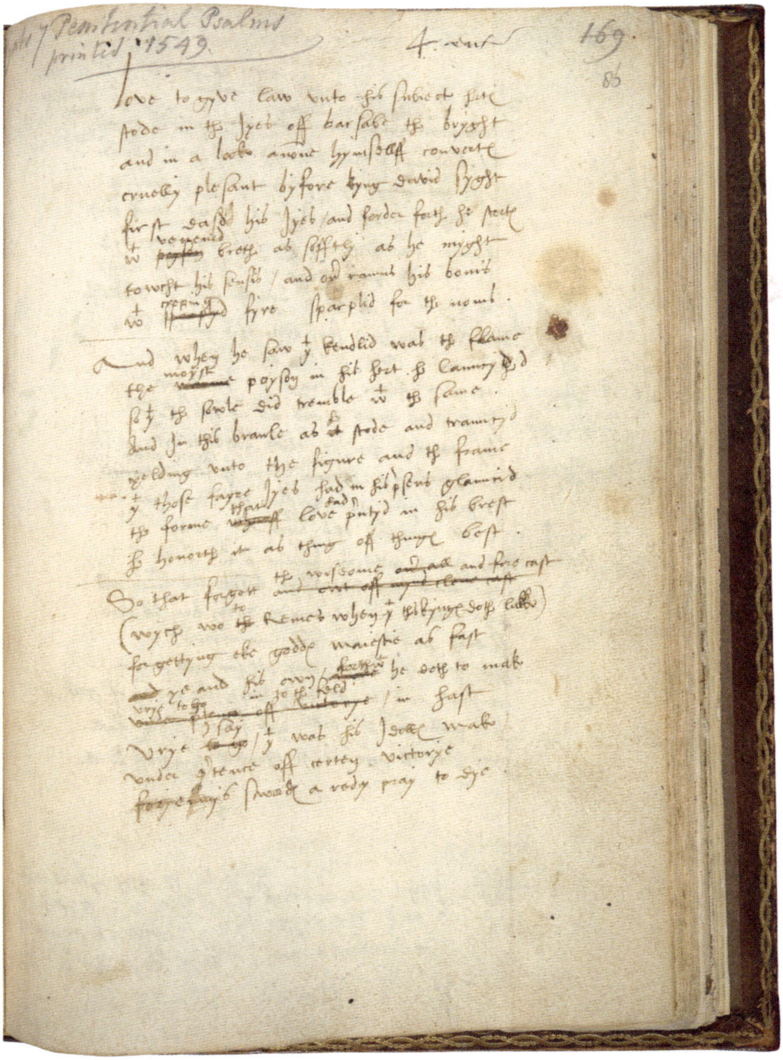

FIG. 1
The Book of Sir Thomas Wyatt
By Sir Thomas Wyatt
c.1538–42
Iron gall ink on laid paper
British Library
Egerton MS 2711, f.86r

an intervention by the queen, Katherine Howard (*c.*1524–1542). Some readers have suggested these verses reflect Wyatt's uneasy relationship with Henry VIII and were a way of the poet addressing both the king and God on his own terms.

Wyatt transcribed his 'Penitential Psalms' directly into the volume himself and continued editing and amending them. Shown here is the beginning of the prologue to the psalms (fig.1), which begins 'Love to give law unto his subjects hearts'. This section has been understood to show Wyatt paralleling the sin and repentance of the Biblical King David with his own life.

The German artist Hans Holbein the Younger (*c.*1497–1543) was employed by Henry VIII first in 1527 and then officially as the king's painter from 1535. He drew and painted many courtiers and people associated with the court during his two periods in England from 1526 to 1528 and 1532 to 1543. The Wyatt family seem to have been important patrons of the artist. Holbein painted portraits of Sir Henry Wyatt, the poet's father (1460–1536) and his daughter Margaret, Lady Lee (*c.*1506–*c.*1543), and he designed a metalwork book cover to celebrate the marriage of Wyatt's son, Thomas Wyatt the Younger to Jane Haute (*c.*1522–*c.*1600) in 1537.

Holbein portrayed the poet Thomas Wyatt at least twice, both times during the period Wyatt was writing and compiling his collected works. The earliest portrait, now in the Royal Collection at Windsor Castle, probably dates from about 1535. The second portrait, now lost, is believed to have been the basis for this National Portrait Gallery painting (fig.2). The unusual circular format may suggest that it was intended for a particular setting. It is possible that the informal clothing, without a hat, reflects Wyatt's situation in 1540 when he had retreated from court after an unsuccessful diplomatic mission. **AA, CM**

FIG.2
Sir Thomas Wyatt
After Hans Holbein the Younger
Sixteenth century, based on a work of *c.*1540
Oil on panel
National Portrait Gallery
NPG 2809

JOHN DONNE

John Donne (1572–1631) was a writer and clergyman, whose eventful and complicated life yielded some of the most admired poems in the English language. Writing many of these during the 1590s, he often combined clever wordplay with romantic imagery and sometimes sexual innuendos. Donne's ability to describe the nuances of love and passion has meant that his writing remains meaningful today.

It was around 1595 that the portrait of Donne 'taken in the shadows' was made by an unknown artist (fig.3).[1] This arresting image shows him as a young man, presenting himself as a melancholy lover. Looking away from the viewer, his face and hands emerge from the darkness. Within the image, the Latin words '*llumina Tenebr(as) Nostras domina*' can be seen. This translates as 'O Lady, lighten our darkness', which is a play on the line found in Psalm 17 of the Latin Bible: '*Deus meus illumina tenebras meas*' (O Lord lighten my darkness). Donne is issuing a plea to a lover, rather than to God. The role of melancholy lover was one Donne also played in much of his poetry during this period in his life.

By 1597 Donne was working as a secretary for the senior courtier Sir Thomas Egerton (1540–1617), remaining in this role for five years. It was here that he met his future wife, Anne More (1584–1617), a niece of Egerton. As Donne knew Egerton was unlikely to give his blessing to any union, he and More married in secret in 1601. This bold move meant that Donne was banished from his role in Egerton's household and briefly imprisoned. With no money or any prospect of employment, the newly weds were forced to live in relative poverty, surviving on donations from patrons and friends. Despite this hardship, Donne wrote both poetry and prose during this time. His career took a different turn when he took holy orders and was ordained on 23 January 1615, subsequently becoming Dean of St Paul's Cathedral, London, on 22 November 1621. He became famous for his powerful sermons, which large crowds gathered to hear in the courtyard of St Paul's.

A significant proportion of Donne's writing was not published in print during his lifetime. Rather, it was written down and copied in manuscript form by friends and admirers. Such groups of friends who circulated private poetical works were known as a 'coterie', and Donne himself was known as a coterie poet. While only one full manuscript poem in Donne's hand survives, more copies or transcriptions of his work were made

FIG.3
John Donne
By an unknown artist
*c.*1595
Oil on panel
National Portrait Gallery
NPG 6790

FIG.4
The Melford Hall Manuscript
By John Donne
c.1620
Iron gall ink on laid paper
British Library
Egerton MS 3884, f.34r

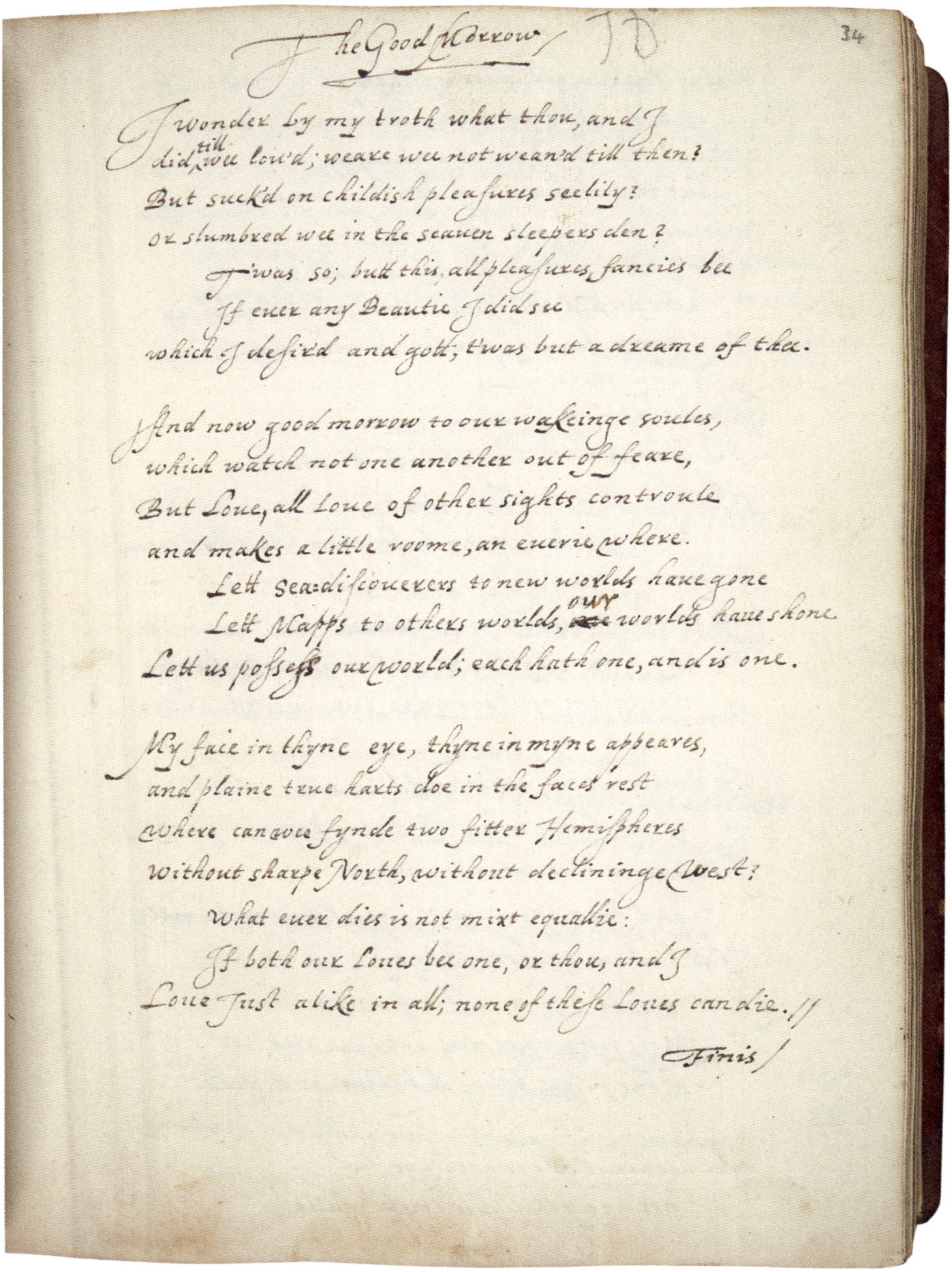
The Good Morrow JD 34

I wonder by my troth what thou, and I
did, till wee lov'd; weare wee not weand till then?
But suck'd on childish pleasures seelily?
or slumbred wee in the seauen sleepers den?
T'was so; but this, all pleasures fancies bee
If euer any Beautie I did see
which I desir'd and gott; t'was but a dreame of thee.

And now good morrow to our wakeinge soules,
which watch not one another out of feare,
But Loue, all loue of other sights controule
and makes a little roome, an euerie where.
Lett sea:discouerers to new worlds haue gone
Lett Mapps to others worlds, our worlds haue shone
Lett us possess our world; each hath one, and is one.

My face in thyne eye, thyne in myne appeares,
and plaine true harts doe in the faces rest
Where can wee fynde two fitter Hemispheres
Without sharpe North, without declininge West?
What euer dies is not mixt equallie:
If both our Loues bee one, or thou, and I
Loue Just alike in all; none of these Loues can die. //

Finis /

than of any other poet from the sixteenth and seventeenth centuries. In some cases, copies were expensive and luxurious productions, usually for those within Donne's circle, and based either on his original manuscripts or orations. While many copies were made during his lifetime, others were made after his death.

The discovery of the Melford Hall Manuscript in 2018 was a surprise to Donne scholars. Discovered in the private library of Melford Hall, a country house in Suffolk, England, this hitherto unknown volume represents the second largest collection of Donne's work and was almost certainly made during his lifetime. The volume was written by one or two hands and is expensively bound. There are small corrections to the text, which show that the accuracy of the wording was important to its owner. It is likely that it was produced for someone within Donne's inner circle. The manuscript contains 145 poems, elegies and satires by Donne, including some of his most famous love poems such as 'Songe' (Go and Catch a Falling Star) and 'The Good Morrow', which would have been composed at a similar time to the brooding portrait (fig.4). 'The Good Morrow' is about both the intimate nature of love and its ability to open up new worlds to those experiencing it. While much of Donne's work might be divided into private (poetry) and public (sermons), all of his writing walks the fine line between bodily and spiritual, open worlds and closed rooms, and public voice and private thought. **AA**

BEN JONSON

Probably the most famous and highly regarded poet and playwright of his day, Ben Jonson (1572–1637) lived a colourful life that included periods as a bricklayer and then a soldier, before turning to the theatre in the 1590s. Real success as a playwright arrived in 1598 with *Every Man in his Humour*, but this year also saw Jonson imprisoned and narrowly escape hanging for killing an actor in a duel. Other spells in prison related to offence caused by his plays but, in spite of this, his career flourished and after the accession of James VI and I (1566–1625) to the English throne in 1603, Jonson became the most important writer associated with the court. An unlikely courtier in terms of background and lifestyle, he was the leading provider of the elaborate court entertainments known as masques, in addition to writing plays, poetry and prose works.

The publication in 1616 of Jonson's collected works (fig.5) was a milestone in establishing plays – previously regarded as ephemeral scripts, which belonged to theatre companies rather than the authors – as lasting, serious works of literature. The book also established a new sense of the significance of authorial identity and ownership. Jonson regarded his poetry as his greatest achievement, but he is best known now for his comic plays *Volpone* (1607) and *The Alchemist* (1610). This copy (fig.6) of the first edition of Jonson's play *Volpone* was given by the author to his friend John Florio (*c*.1553–1625), a tutor, translator and dictionary writer of Italian descent. The inscription reads:

> 'To his loving Father & worthy Friend
> M^r^. John Florio:
> The ayde of his Muses
> Ben: Jonson seales this testemony
> of Friendship, & Love'[2]

Florio probably helped Jonson with the Italian aspects of his play. His knowledge of Italian Renaissance literature and his language skills helped to make European texts accessible to English writers. He was an important figure in the flourishing of literature during the late Elizabethan and Jacobean periods. Florio was employed by the queen, Anne of Denmark (1574–1619), during her time in England.

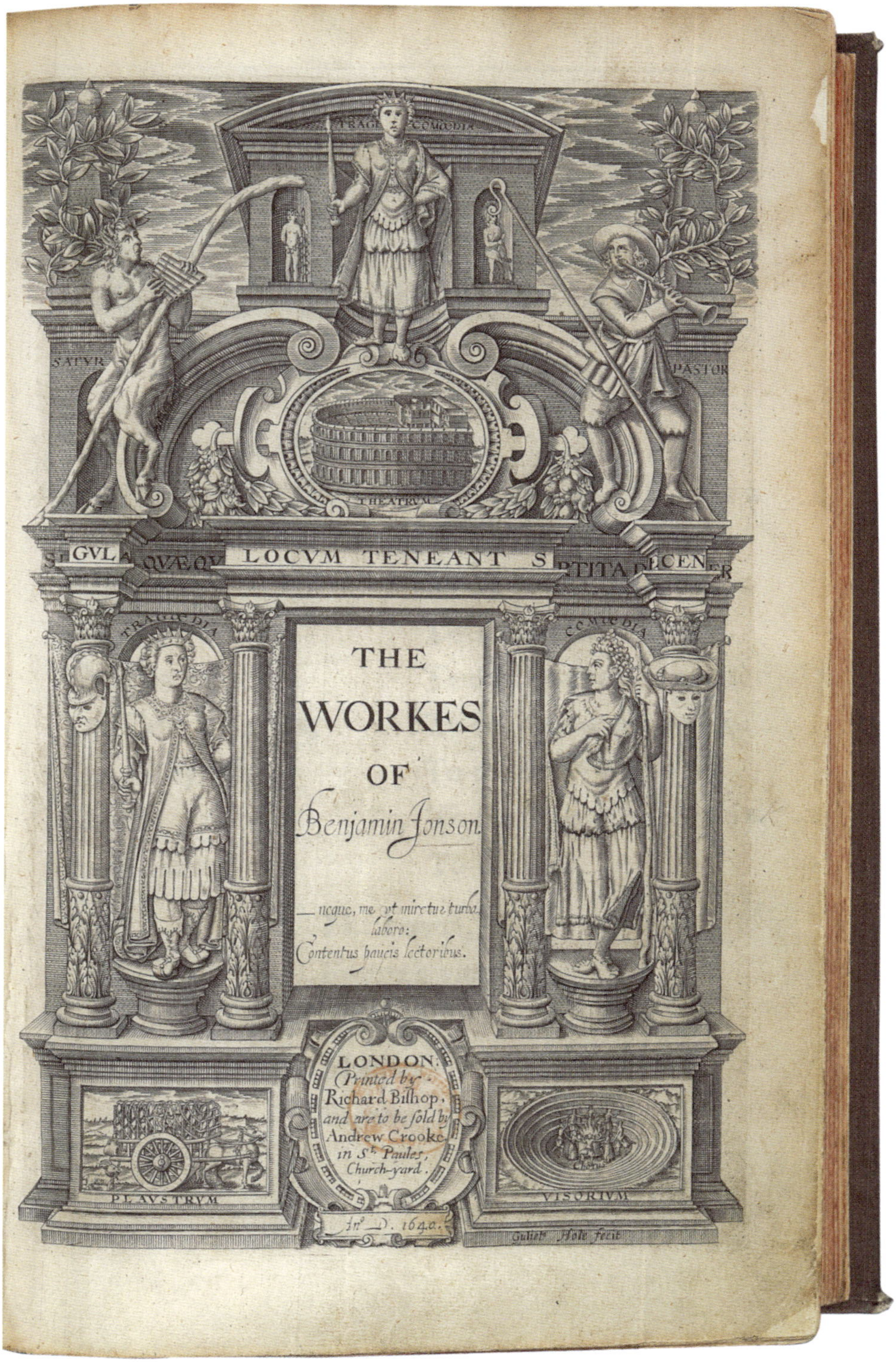
SATYR
PASTOR
THEATRVM
LOCVM TENEANT
THE
WORKES
OF
Benjamin Jonson.
—neque, me ut miretur turba, laboro:
Contentus paucis lectoribus.
LONDON.
Printed by
Richard Bishop,
and are to be sold by
Andrew Crooke
in St. Paules
Church-yard.
An. D. 1640.
PLAVSTRVM
VISORIVM
Guliel. Hole fecit

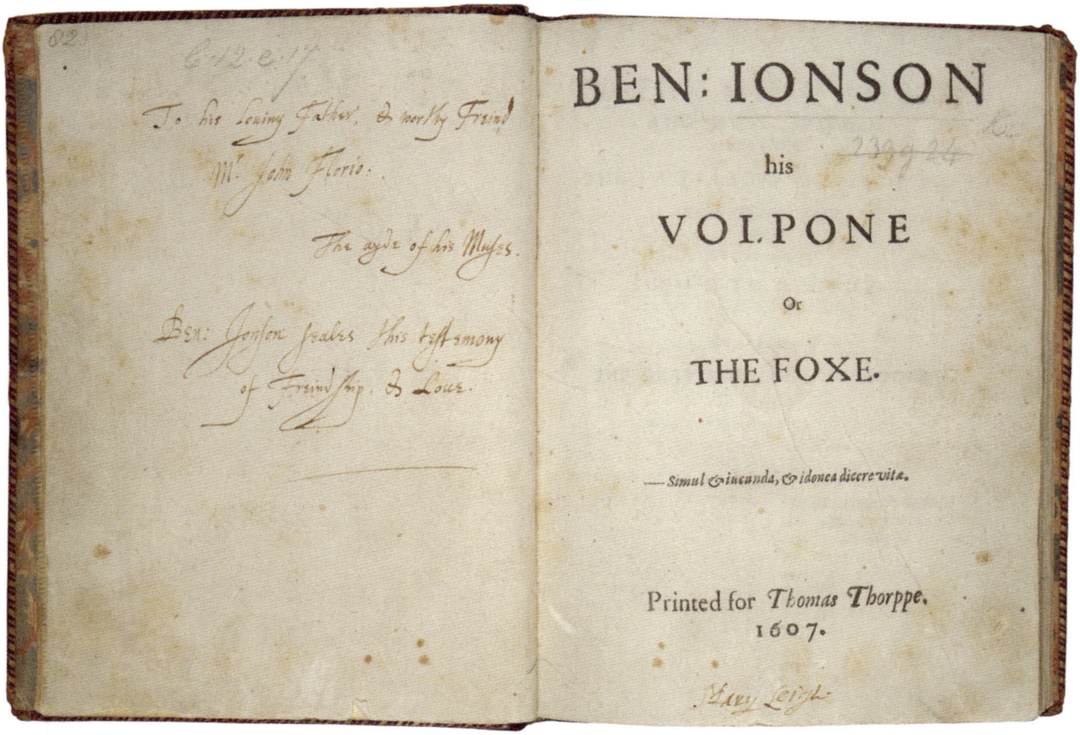

FIG.5
Workes
By Ben Jonson
(Richard Bishop, London, 1640)
British Library
c.28.m.11.

FIG.6
Volpone
By Ben Jonson
(Thomas Thorpe, London, 1607)
British Library
c.12.e.17.

Jonson's close association with the queen – who commissioned him to write several masques for her – would have brought the two writers into the same literary circles.

Jonson's portrait (fig.7) was painted by the Flemish artist Abraham van Blyenberch (1575/6–1624), who was in London from about 1617 to 1621/2. Van Blyenberch painted portraits of a number of aristocratic courtiers in a broad, vigorous style that differed strikingly from the precise, smooth painting that characterised most British portraits of this period. He also produced this lively, direct image of Jonson, whom he shows not as an elegant courtier but as the robust character who had lived an often far-from-elegant life. Jonson described himself at this time as having a 'Mountaine belly, and ... rockye face'.[3] **CM**

FIG.7
Ben Jonson
By Abraham van Blyenberch
*c.*1617
Oil on canvas
National Portrait Gallery
NPG 2752

FANNY BURNEY

The novelist Frances 'Fanny' Burney (1752–1840) was born into a close-knit and creative middle-class family. Until the publication of her first novel, *Evelina*, in 1778, her life revolved around her work as assistant to her father, the musician and writer Charles Burney (1726–1814), and the family's social and musical activities. As a child she had written a novel as well as plays and poems, but she had burned all her literary manuscripts on her fifteenth birthday, perhaps at the urging of her father or stepmother. She probably wrote most of *Evelina* in 1776, in secret, fearing the disapproval of society at large and particularly of her father: disapprobation both of the novel as a genre and of her as a female writer. With the help of younger relatives, particularly her brother Charles (1757–1817) and her cousin Edward Francisco Burney (1760–1848), she submitted the first instalments of her manuscript novel anonymously, in disguised handwriting, to the bookseller and publisher Thomas Lowndes (1719–1784) in 1776. Shown overleaf is a letter from Burney to Lowndes asking whether the bookseller would consider reading and potentially publishing a book whose author he had never met (fig.8). Lowndes replied in the affirmative through the younger Charles Burney, who, in order to disguise his identity, had called himself 'Mr King'.

Fanny Burney wrote more of the book in the following year and *Evelina* was published anonymously in January 1778, becoming an immediate bestseller. Burney's identity as the author was revealed later in the year, much to her embarrassment. Many readers were astonished that a woman could write such a compelling combination of social comedy and realism. She was fêted by literary London and became particularly friendly with the influential writer Samuel Johnson (1709–1784). Burney went on to write other novels, plays and extensive, detailed diaries, which, along with her letters, are important sources of information about the society in which she lived.

Burney's portrait was painted twice by her cousin, Edward, a painter and illustrator to whom she was particularly close. Edward had acted as a go-between during the publication of *Evelina* in the guise of 'Mr Grafton'. The portrait shown here is the second of the two works by Edward (fig.9). In it, he depicts Burney as a fashionable, wealthy woman of her day, wearing a spectacular hat known as a 'Lunardi'. There is no indication of her profession or literary interests, probably

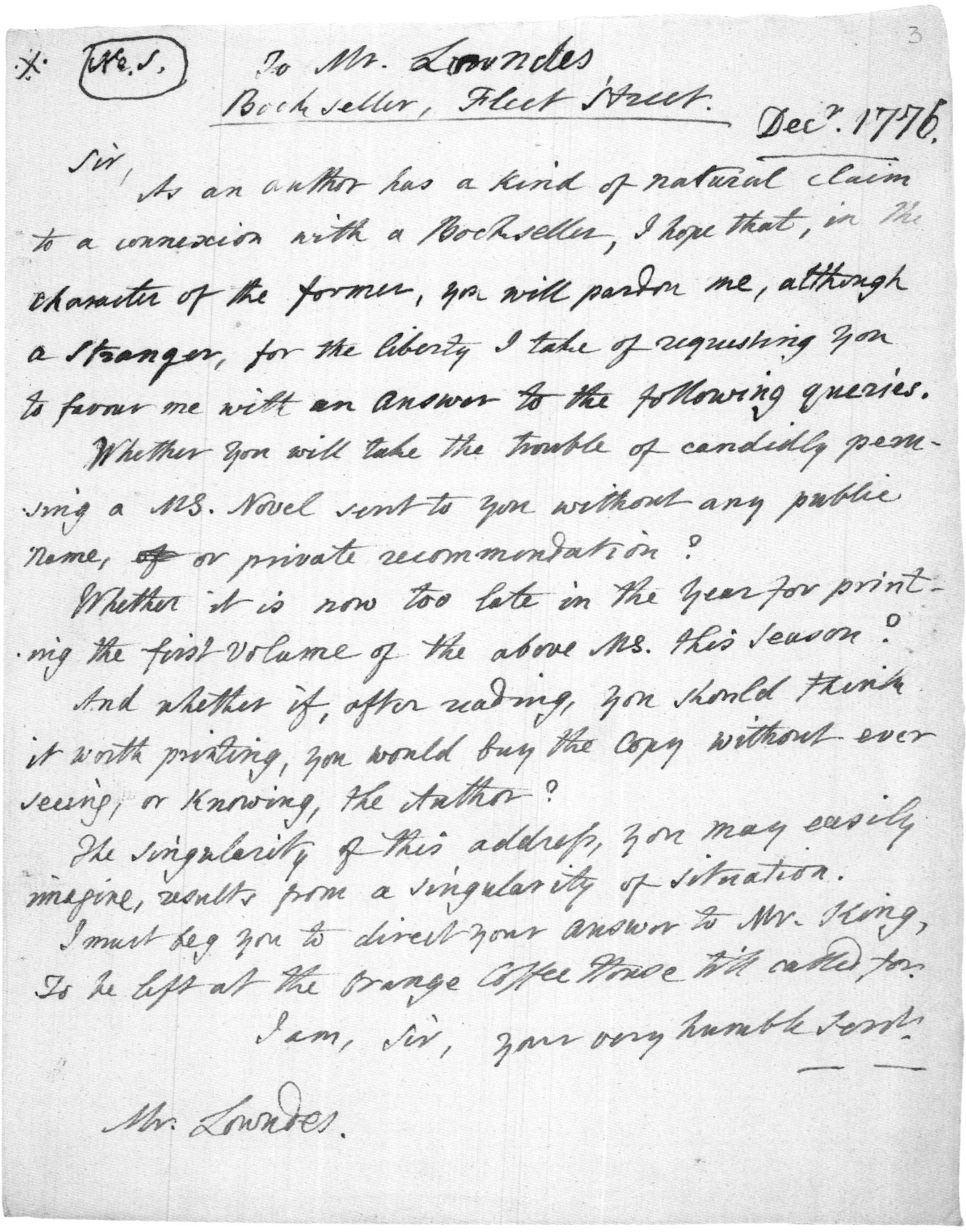

No. 1, To Mr. Lowndes
Bookseller, Fleet Street. Dec.r 1776.

Sir,
As an author has a kind of natural claim to a connexion with a Bookseller, I hope that, in the character of the former, you will pardon me, although a stranger, for the liberty I take of requesting you to favour me with an answer to the following queries.

Whether you will take the trouble of candidly perusing a MS. Novel sent to you without any public name, ~~of~~ or private recommendation?

Whether it is now too late in the year for printing the first volume of the above MS. this season?

And whether if, after reading, you should think it worth printing, you would buy the copy without ever seeing, or knowing, the Author?

The singularity of this address, you may easily imagine, results from a singularity of situation.

I must beg you to direct your answer to Mr. King, To be left at the Orange Coffee House till called for.

I am, Sir, your very humble servt.

Mr. Lowndes.

FIG.8
Letter to Thomas Lowndes
From Frances Burney
December 1776
Iron gall ink on laid paper
British Library
Egerton MS 3695, f.3r

FIG.9
Portrait of Frances (Fanny) Burney
By Edward Francisco Burney
*c.*1785
Oil on canvas
National Portrait Gallery
NPG 2634

reflecting the fact that, despite her success, the life of a professional writer was still not regarded as entirely suitable for a woman. In fact, around the time this was painted, and in spite of her successful literary career, Burney was offered, and felt compelled to accept for five years, a prestigious position as an attendant on Queen Charlotte (1744–1818). This both interfered with her writing and caused her ill-health. Burney's friends, including the philosopher Edmund Burke (1729–1797) and the painter Sir Joshua Reynolds (1723–1792), put pressure on her father, Charles, to allow her to leave the post, which she eventually did, resuming her writing and her position in London's literary world. **CM**

SAMUEL TAYLOR COLERIDGE

Samuel Taylor Coleridge (1772–1834) was a poet and critic, now most famous for writing 'Kubla Khan' (1797; published 1816) and 'The Rime of the Ancient Mariner' (1798). With the poet William Wordsworth (1770–1850; p.91), Coleridge is considered one of the founders of English Romanticism, whose premise was that painting, writing and music should focus on expression, nature, emotion and individualism. Born in Devon, Coleridge was sent to Christ's Hospital School in London at the age of eight, where he wrote and studied poetry and became friends with the writer and critic Charles Lamb (1775–1834). Between 1791 and 1794 Coleridge studied at Jesus College, Cambridge, where he met the poet Robert Southey (1774–1843). It was here that Coleridge and Southey devised a utopian scheme for an egalitarian society that they described as a 'Pantisocracy'.

Coleridge's first volume, entitled *Poems on Various Subjects*, was published in 1796. It was in this same year that this portrait by the printmaker, painter and draughtsman Robert Hancock (1730–1817) was made (fig.10). The portrait was commissioned by the Bristol bookseller and publisher Joseph Cottle (1770–1853), who had met Coleridge in about 1794. He also commissioned portraits of Wordsworth, Lamb and Southey, all of whom were at the beginning of their careers as published authors. The portrait shows a youthful and fresh-faced poet with his writing career just developing, and years away from the opium addiction that was to dominate his later life. Cottle later said of it:

> 'The image was much admired at the time, and has an additional interest from having been drawn when Mr C's spirits were in a state of depression on account of the failure of his *Watchman* [Coleridge's radical journal].'[4]

Between 1797 and 1798 Coleridge lived in Nether Stowey, Somerset, near Wordsworth and his sister, Dorothy (1771–1855). This fuelled an intense and productive period of collaboration and writing. Coleridge and Wordsworth published their famous book *Lyrical Ballads* in 1798, funded by Cottle, which contained 'The Rime of the Ancient Mariner'. In 1800 Coleridge settled in the picturesque Lake District in England, again living near the Wordsworths. From 1804 to 1808 he travelled

FIG.10
Samuel Taylor Coleridge
By Robert Hancock
1796
Black, red and brown chalk and pencil
National Portrait Gallery
NPG 452

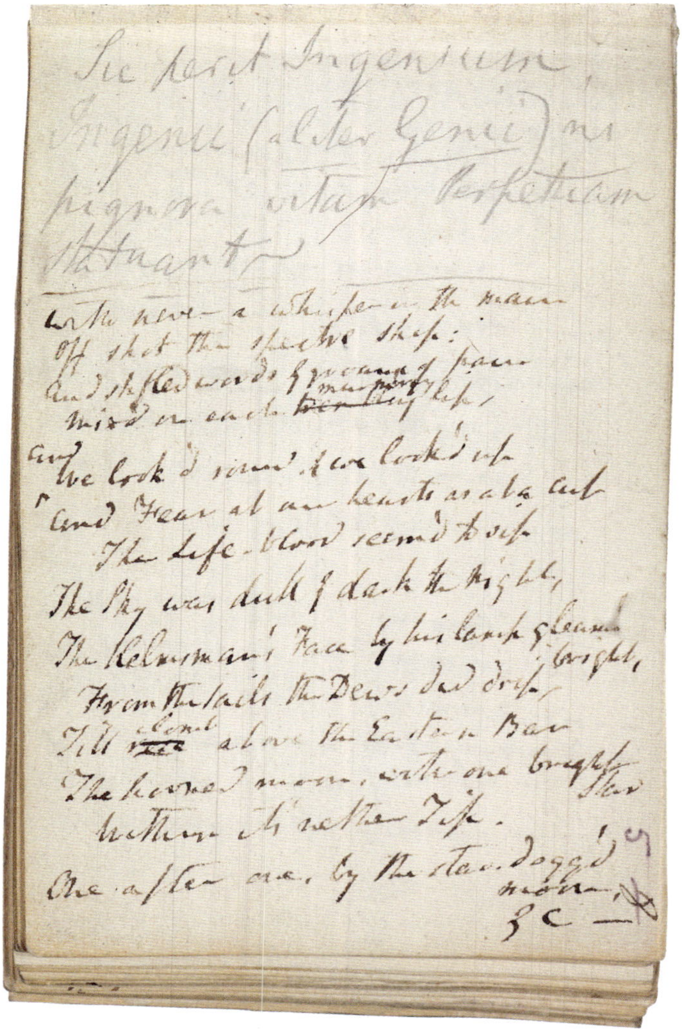

FIG.11
Lines 201–12 of 'The Rime of the Ancient Mariner'
By Samuel Taylor Coleridge
1806–10
Pencil and black ink on wove paper
British Library
Add MS 47508, f.5r

between England, Malta, Sicily and Italy, and it was during the latter part of his travels that his use of opium intensified to the point of addiction.

Throughout his life, Coleridge wrote in a series of notebooks, of which 72 survive. Shown here is notebook 11, which he used between 6 September 1806 and 25 November 1810 (fig.11). Many of the notebooks are uniform in size, and Coleridge wrote in different inks and pencils, making a variety of notes and recording verse within them. Shown here is an ink autograph transcription of lines 201–12 of 'The Rime of the Ancient Mariner' that he had originally written between 1797 and 1798 and published in 1798. The lines begin 'With never a whisper in the main / off shot the spectre ship'. This manuscript shows changes to the lines that were published, meaning Coleridge continued to work on the poem, even after publication. For him, publishing did not mean a work was finished and he ultimately went on to write 18 different variants of the poem. **AA**

JOHN KEATS

John Keats (1795–1821) was one of the most famous and admired of the Romantic poets of the late eighteenth and early nineteenth centuries. His brief and tragic life story echoed the imaginative tales popular with the Romantic movement. Orphaned at a young age, Keats trained to be a physician and surgeon but increasingly felt that he was thwarting his natural inclinations. After some success publishing his poems, at the age of 21 he eventually abandoned medicine altogether and turned to poetry. Over the next four years he produced a remarkable *oeuvre* of increasingly mature and sophisticated poetry, often considered some of the most influential and important works of English literature. Affected but undaunted by bad reviews, Keats continued to write until his early death from tuberculosis at the age of 25.

Keats's life, image and poetry were closely entwined. A central tenet of Romanticism was that art should flow from genuine emotion. The difficult circumstances of Keats's life – the loss of his parents and one of his younger brothers, Tom (1799–1818); his thwarted love affair with a neighbour, Fanny Brawne (1800–1865); and his own terminal tuberculosis – informed his passionate poetry. His friends described him, especially after his death, as having had an intense look and a compelling physical presence, which was clearly seen by them as indicative of the extraordinary creative forces within.

'The Eve of Saint Mark' (1819; fig.12) is an unfinished poem by Keats that was seen as a sequel to his much-admired 'The Eve of St Agnes' (published 1820). This draft of the poem is part of a manuscript volume of Keats's verse that was owned by his brother George (1797–1841). Keats regularly sent manuscript copies of his poems to George, a businessman and civic leader in America. Usually these were completed works, as Keats described when he wrote to George on 14 February 1819: 'In my next packet ... I shall send you the Pot of Basil, St Agnes eve, and, if I should have finished it, a little thing called the "eve of St Mark".'[5] The poem was never finished but Keats seems to have sent the draft anyway. George clearly valued it and had it bound into the volume, along with other works sent by John Keats, and copies that George had made of his brother's poems.

Joseph Severn (1793–1879), a friend of the poet, painted several portraits of Keats following the latter's death. In 1821, at the age of 25, Keats died in Severn's arms while the two were in Rome. When this painting, showing Keats in his home in Hampstead (fig.13), was bought

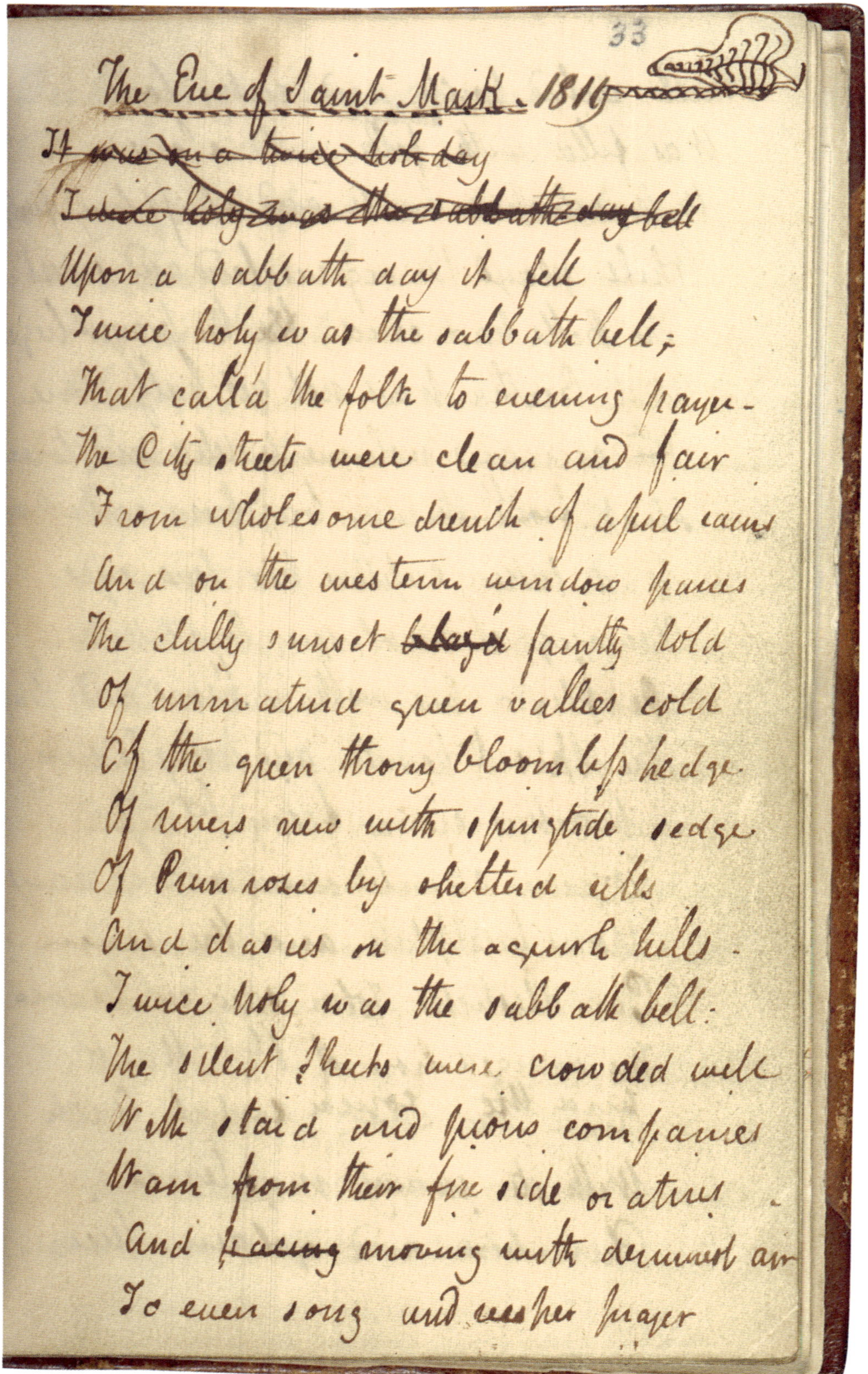
33

The Eve of Saint Mark. 1819

~~It was on a twice holy day~~
~~Twice holy was the sabbath day bell~~
Upon a sabbath day it fell
Twice holy was the sabbath bell;
That call'd the folk to evening prayer.
The City streets were clean and fair
From wholesome drench of april rains
And on the western window panes
The chilly sunset ~~blaze~~ faintly told
Of unmatur'd green vallies cold
Of the green thorny bloomless hedge.
Of rivers new with springtide sedge
Of Primroses by shelter'd rills
And daisies on the aguish hills.
Twice holy was the sabbath bell:
The silent streets were crowded well
With staid and pious companies
Warm from their fire side oratries.
And ~~pacing~~ moving with demurest air
To even song and vesper prayer

FIG.12
'The Eve of Saint Mark'
By John Keats
1819
Ink on wove paper
British Library
Egerton MS 2780, f.33r

FIG.13
John Keats
By Joseph Severn
1821–3
Oil on canvas
National Portrait Gallery
NPG 58

by the National Portrait Gallery in 1859, Severn wrote to the director, George Scharf (1820–1895), explaining its genesis:

> 'After the death of Keats the impression was so painfull on my mind that I made an effort to call up the most pleasant remembrance in this picture, which is posthumous. This was the time he first fell ill & had written the Ode to the Nightingale (1819) on the mor.[ning] of my visit to Hampstead I found him sitting with the two chairs as I have painted him & was struck with the first real symptoms of sadness in Keats so finely expressed in that Poem.'[6]

Severn later seems to have used a life-mask of Keats made by Benjamin Robert Haydon (1786–1846; see pp.91–3) to complete the face to his satisfaction. **CM**

WILKIE COLLINS

Wilkie Collins (1824–1889) was an English novelist and playwright who produced early detective fiction and 'sensation novels', such as *The Woman in White* (1860) and *The Moonstone* (1868). In 1850 Collins published his first novel, *Antonina, or the Fall of Rome* and, in the spring of 1851, he was introduced to Charles Dickens (1812–1870; see p.197) who became his collaborator, friend and mentor. They first acted together in 1851 in the play *Not So Bad as We Seem* by Edward Bulwer-Lytton (1803–1873), the performance of which was attended by Queen Victoria (1819–1901) and Prince Albert (1819–1861). Collins wrote *The Lighthouse* (1855) and *The Frozen Deep* (1856), both of which were produced by Dickens's acting company. In 1856 Collins joined the staff of Dickens's magazine *Household Words*.

This portrait by Sir John Everett Millais (1829–1896; fig.14) was made around the same time that Collins met Dickens. It depicts the writer deep in thought and shows the large congenital bump on Collins's forehead – thought at the time to be a sign of intellect. Although painted on a small scale, the portrait is dramatic and shows Collins as both serious and pensive; the inclusion of a coat of arms reflects the artist's interest in fifteenth-century Netherlandish portraiture. Millais was good friends with Wilkie Collins's brother, the painter and writer Charles Allston Collins (1828–1873). The artist painted Collins at the time he was writing the novel *Mr Wray's Cash Box* (1851). Millais also designed the frontispiece for this novel, showing how the worlds of art and literature overlapped.

Much of Collins's work was first published in magazines or as serials (in parts), so that what we now experience as a novel was originally read in sections, on a weekly or bi-weekly basis. Writing over 30 novels, Collins also produced numerous articles and over 12 plays. In many cases, his stories were also adapted for the theatre. To experience a story on stage would have been different from reading an entire novel in one volume. Reading a serialised version would yield a different experience with suspense, scandal and unease prolonged between each part. Popular and academic focus on the novel has meant the importance of theatre and serials have often been overlooked in assessments of Collins's work.

The playscript for *The New Magdalen* was written at the same time as the serialised novel of the same name. The serial appeared between October

FIG.14
Wilkie Collins
By Sir John Everett Millais
1850
Oil on panel
National Portrait Gallery
NPG 967

1872 and July 1873 in *Temple Bar* magazine and between October 1872 and June 1873 in *Harper's New Monthly Magazine*. The play opened at the Olympic Theatre in London on 19 May 1873, two days after the novel was published. Whole sections of speech are identical between playscript and novel, showing Collins conceived the story as working both on stage and page. The play is set within a limited interior space – in a frontier cottage located within a battleground during the Franco-German war of 1870, and in a manor house in London. Duality is a key theme. The play was produced by Ada Cavendish (1839?–1895) who played the central part of Mercy Merrick, a former prostitute turned wartime nurse who adopts the identity of 'Grace Roseberry', a penniless but respectable young woman presumed dead. It received much attention, and some audiences were left shocked by the story.

The playscript in Collins's hand shows the speed at which he worked, writing quickly and crossing out lines repeatedly (fig.15). Collins probably wrote with a metal nib on relatively inexpensive paper. This has caused the acidic ink to 'eat' through the cheap paper in places. The manuscript reveals a less composed aspect of Collins, as compared with Millais's portrait. It also shows other titles Collins considered for the story including 'Vice and Virtue', 'A Creature from the Streets', 'Sarah the Sinner' and 'An Outrage on Society'. Collins often worked on his playscripts during rehearsals and the actor Sir Arthur Pinero (1855–1934) witnessed him amending one during rehearsals for *Miss Gwilt* in 1875: 'I remember his appearances at rehearsal very clearly. He used to sit, his manuscript before him, at a small table near the footlights, and there he made such additions and alternations'.[7] **AA**

FIG.15
Playscript draft for *The New Magdalen*
By Wilkie Collins
*c.*1872
Black ink on paper
British Library
Add MS 89175, f.50r

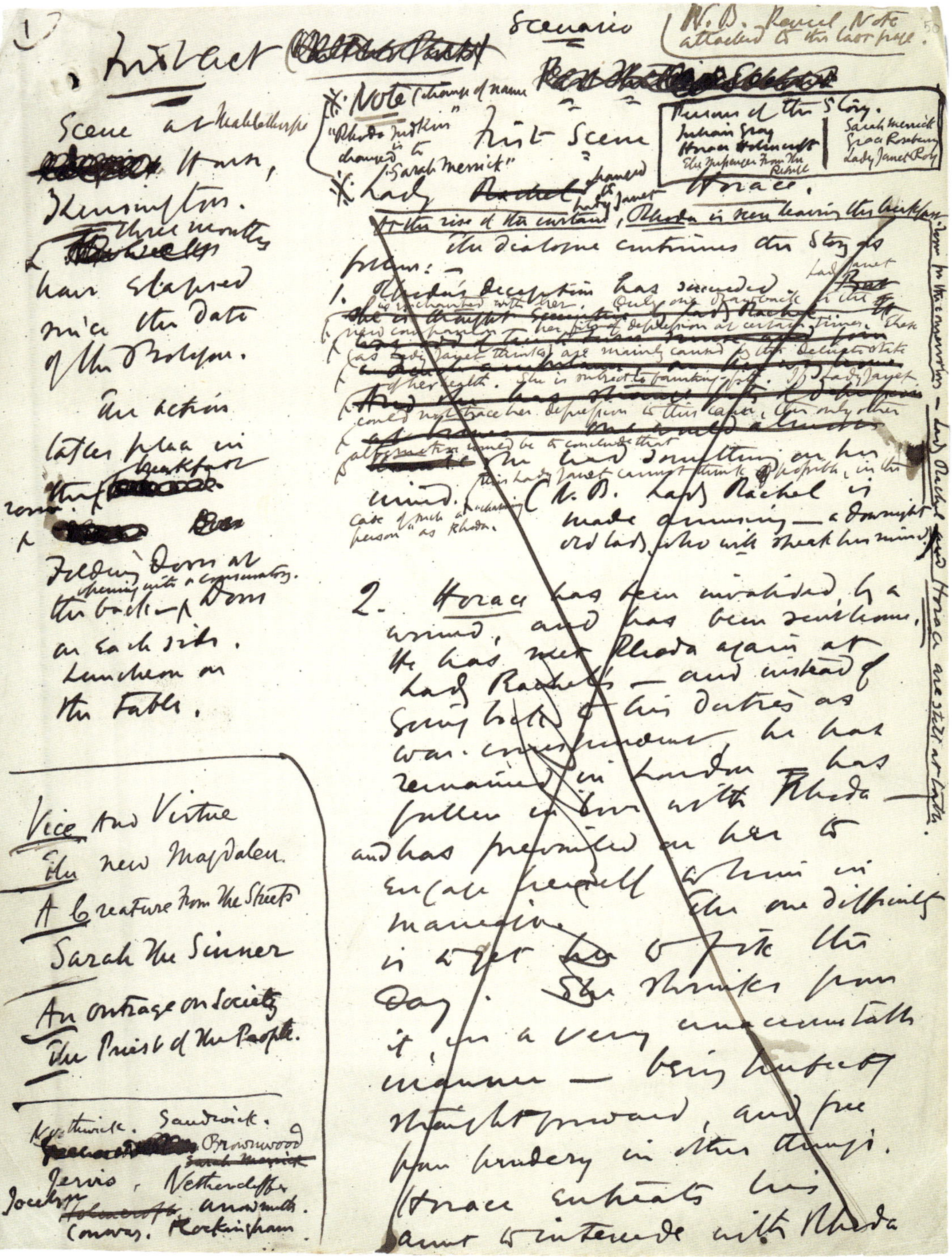

1

1st Act [struck]

Scenario

(N.B. Revised Note attached to the last page.)

Scene at Mablethorpe [struck] House, Kensington.

[struck] Three months have elapsed since the date of the Prologue.

The action takes place in the breakfast room [struck]

Folding Doors at the back [opening into a conservatory]. Doors on each side. Luncheon on the Table.

* Note (change of name) "Rhoda Judkins" changed to "Sarah Merrick"

First Scene

* Lady [struck: Rachel] named Lady Janet

Horace.

Persons of the Story.	
Julian Gray	Sarah Merrick
Horace Holmcroft	Grace Roseberry
The Messenger from the Rebels(?)	Lady Janet Roy

At the rise of the curtain, Rhoda is seen leaving the breakfast-room for the conservatory — Lady Rachel and Horace are still at table.

The dialogue continues the story as follows:—

1. Rhoda's deception has succeeded. Lady Janet is enchanted with her. Only one drawback to the new companion — her fits of depression at certain times. These (as Lady Janet thinks) are mainly caused by the delicate state of her health. She is subject to fainting-fits. If Lady Janet could not trace her depression to this cause, the only other alternative would be to conclude that she had something on her mind. [this Lady Janet cannot think possible, in the case of such a charming person as Rhoda.] (N.B. Lady Rachel is made amusing — a downright old lady who will speak her mind.)

2. Horace has been invalided by a wound, and has been sent home. He has met Rhoda again at Lady Rachel's — and instead of going back to his duties as war-correspondent he has remained in London — has fallen in love with Rhoda and has prevailed on her to engage herself to him in marriage. The one difficulty is to get her to fix the day. She shrinks from it in a very unaccountable manner — being perfectly straightforward, and free from prudery in other things. Horace entreats his aunt to intercede with Rhoda

Vice and Virtue

The new Magdalen

A Creature from the Streets

Sarah the Sinner

An outrage on Society

The Priest of the People.

Kirkwick. Sandwick. [struck] Brownwood

[struck: Sarah Merrick]

Jervis. Netherclyffe.

Jocelyn [struck: Holmcroft] Arrowsmith.

Conway. Rockingham.

VIRGINIA WOOLF

The writer and publisher Virginia Woolf (née Stephen; 1882–1941) was born into a large, complex and privileged literary and artistic family in London. Her father was an editor and 'man of letters' while her mother managed the home and occasionally posed as a model for artists and photographers. Both parents had been married and widowed before. Along with four children from their earlier marriages, Woolf's parents went on to have four further children of their own, making them a family of ten. While the large family enjoyed happy times at their summer home in Cornwall, a location that inspired several of her novels, Woolf's childhood was impacted by tragedy. Suffering the loss of her mother when she was just 13, the subsequent death of her half-sister and sexual abuse at the hands of her half-brothers, Woolf went on to experience the first in a series of episodes of mental illness in 1895. Such illness was to afflict her for periods throughout her life, culminating in her suicide at the age of 59.

While her brothers were given a formal education, Woolf was not permitted to go to school. This was an exclusion she felt keenly, and her awareness of the imbalance between the sexes was a theme she later wrote about in *A Room of One's Own* (1929). After the death of her father in 1904, the family moved to the bohemian Bloomsbury district in London. She became part of the 'Bloomsbury Group', which comprised intellectuals, writers and artists including Woolf's sister, the artist Vanessa Bell (née Stephen; 1879–1961), art critic Duncan Grant (1885–1978), and Woolf's husband-to-be Leonard Woolf (1880–1969).

Between 1906 and 1912 Woolf wrote her first novel, *The Voyage Out* (published 1915). Marrying Leonard in 1912, she was supported by him in her writing projects, as well as through her episodes of ill health. During their marriage, Woolf engaged in an affair with Vita Sackville-West (1892–1962), which was to last over ten years. In 1917, the Woolfs set up The Hogarth Press, which published their own works and those by emerging and significant writers. Rejecting Victorian narrative fiction, Woolf demonstrated that the modern novel need not be shaped by dramatic events and that an ordinary day, with the exploration of interior moments, could be a worthy subject. Her most famous works are *Mrs Dalloway* (1925), *To the Lighthouse* (1927), *Orlando* (1928) and *The Waves* (1931).

FIG.16
Virginia Woolf
By George Charles Beresford
1902
Platinum print
National Portrait Gallery
NPG P222

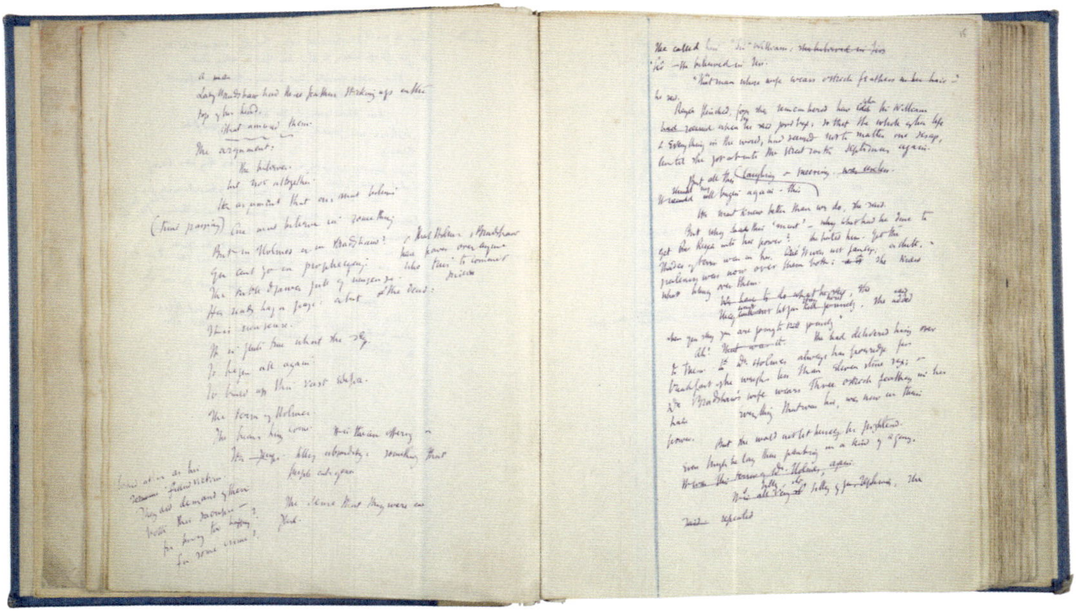

FIG.17
Draft for *Mrs Dalloway*
By Virginia Woolf
1924
Blue ink on laid paper, ruled with blue crayon
British Library
Add MS 51046, ff.14v–15r

This portrait of 1902 was taken by the studio photographer George Charles Beresford (1864–1938; fig.16). From 1902 to 1932 Beresford had a studio in Knightsbridge, London, where he produced platinum prints of figures from society, and writers, politicians and artists. His portraits were often published in magazines and journals including the *Illustrated London News* and *Tatler*. Beresford apparently took 14 photographs of Woolf during this sitting, as well as photographs of her father and sister, Vanessa. His technique, using platinum paper, produced delicate and precise images that capture Woolf's wistful expression but give no clue that she would soon emerge as one of the most complex and talented writers of the twentieth century.

Woolf's fourth novel, *Mrs Dalloway* (1925), is set on a Wednesday in mid-June 1923 and follows Clarissa Dalloway as she navigates her way through the day. The final, published version of 1925 is markedly different to the manuscript held by the British Library. This manuscript (fig.17), dated 31 July 1924, is open at the point just before one of the central characters dies. Very little of this text appears in the final printed version. Despite the 'stream of consciousness' narrative, which apparently replicates the spontaneous flow of the character's thoughts, this manuscript demonstrates that Woolf thought carefully about the construction of the text. On the left-hand side, she has made notes as to how she wished to depict the scene, including the phrase 'time passing', a hint at the overall theme of the novel, which was originally called *The Hours* on account of its time-based structure. **AA**

T. S. ELIOT

The poet and playwright Thomas Stearns (T. S.) Eliot (1888–1965), was born in America to a middle-class family, but gained British citizenship in 1927. Eliot attended Harvard University from 1906, and it was here that he was inspired to pursue a career in writing. In 1910 Eliot began writing 'The Love Song of J. Alfred Prufrock' (1915), which became one of his most famous poems. In 1914 he left America for a travelling fellowship in Europe, where he first visited Germany and then enrolled at Merton College, Oxford. In 1915 he met Vivienne Haigh-Wood (1888–1947), and they married later that year. This union meant that Eliot remained in England at the outbreak of the First World War; residing in the London flat of the philosopher Bertrand Russell (1872–1970). Through Russell, Eliot was able to join London's intellectual and artistic society, socialising with members of the Bloomsbury Group. It was during this time that he took up the post of literary editor to the avant-garde magazine *The Egoist*, thus solidifying his position as writer, editor and critic.

In 1921 Eliot suffered a period of psychological distress and went to stay by the sea in Margate, Kent, for three months. It was here that he composed the bleak and intellectual modernist poem *The Waste Land* (1922), one of the most important poems of the twentieth century. *The Waste Land* was first published in Eliot's literary journal, *The Criterion*, a quarterly publication that printed works by other writers such as Virginia Woolf (1882–1941; see p.42) and W. H. Auden (1907–1973; see p.262). In 1925 Eliot was made literary editor at the publishing house Faber and Gwyer, which later became Faber & Faber.

Although a serious writer, Eliot also produced more light-hearted work, including his *Old Possum's Book of Practical Cats* (1939). This series of poems about cats, all with distinctive names and personalities, was developed initially in a series of letters to the Tandy Family. Geoffrey Tandy (1900–1969) was a marine biologist and broadcaster, who wrote a 'Broadcasting Chronicle' for *The Criterion*. Eliot was also good friends with Tandy's wife, Doris, (known as Polly, née Ellis, 1894–1971), and wrote to her and her daughters Alison (b.1930) and Anthea (1935–1989). In his typewritten letters, often under *The Criterion* letterhead, Eliot described the characters of the cats and sent various verses to the Tandys. Writing on 10 November 1936 to Alison Tandy, Eliot described the 'Old Gumbie Cat' (fig.18). On 9 December 1936 Eliot wrote to Polly Tandy about cats

THE

CRITERION

A QUARTERLY REVIEW

EDITED BY T. S. ELIOT

TELEPHONE: MUSEUM 9543
TELEGRAMS: FABBAF, WESTCENT, LONDON

24 RUSSELL SQUARE,
LONDON, W.C.1

10th November 1936: such a long time
after Guy Fawkes' Day.

My dear Alison,

The last Cat I wrote about, was such a Boastful Brutal Beastly Bloody Bad Pirate, that you may think that I am a kittenthrope, or Hater of Cats: but such is not the Case. On the contrary. So I hasten to tell you about another Kind of Cat, to my knowledge, that is wholly admirable. It is

THE OLD GUMBIE CAT.

I have a Gumbie Cat in mind, her name is Jennyanydots;
Her coat is of the tabby kind, with tiger stripes and leopard spots.
All day she sits upon the stair or on the steps or on the mat;
She sits and sits and sits and sits and that's what makes a Gumbie Cat!

But when the day's hustle and bustle is done,
Then the Gumbie Cat's work is but hardly begun.
And when all the fambly's in bed and asleep,
She tucks up her skirts and downstairs will creep.
There she must every night attend to the mice -
Their behaviour's not good and their manners not nice;
And when she has got them lined up on the matting,
She teaches them music, crocheting and tatting.

I have a Gumbie Cat in mind, her name is Jennyanydots;
Her equal would be hard to find, she likes the warm and sunny spots.
All day she sits beside the hearth or on the bed or in my hat:
She sits and sits and sits and sits and that's what makes a Gumbie Cat!

But when the day's hustle and bustle is done,
Then the Gumbie Cat's work is but hardly begun.
As she finds that the mice will not ever keep quiet,
She is sure it is due to irregular diet.
And believing that nothing is done without trying,
She sets straight to work with her baking and frying.
She makes them a mouse-cake with bread and dried peas,
And a beautiful fry of lean bacon and cheese.

FIG.18
Letter to Alison Tandy
From T.S. Eliot
10 November 1936
Typewritten and ink on paper
British Library
Add MS 71002, f.45r

FIG.19
Design for the dust jacket of *Old Possum's Book of Practical Cats*
By T.S. Eliot
1939
Proof reproduction
British Library
Add MS 71003, f.37r

in more general terms, and in a way that demonstrated he clearly found the animal amusing:

> 'When a cat adopts you, and I am not superstitious at all I don't only mean Black cats, there is nothing to be done about it except to put up with it and wait until the wind changes, and perhaps it will go away of its own accord and never be heard of again ... you must at present provide liver and rabbit, and a comfortable seat by the fire.'[8]

Eliot designed the dustjacket for the *Old Possum's Book of Practical Cats*, and he sent Polly Tandy a copy of the design together with a letter on 9 September 1939 (fig.19):

> 'I have now completed my autumn publications: I send you herewith O.P's design for the jacket of that book; the small figures in the upper hand corner however are to be enlarged and go on the back instead of the front as you might suppose.'[9]

Eliot often signed his letters O.P (Old Possum) or T.P (Tom Possum). It was Geoffrey Tandy who first recited the poems on BBC radio, and the subject matter continues to be popular to this day with a number of adaptations, including Andrew Lloyd Webber's musical *Cats*.

With the Second World War on the horizon, *The Criterion* ceased publication in 1939. In 1943 Eliot published *Four Quartets*, four interlinked poems considered equal in importance to *The Waste Land*. Despite not producing poetry after the Second World War, Eliot wrote critical essays and plays. In 1948 he was awarded the Nobel Prize in Literature.

This portrait by the influential artist and critic Patrick Heron (1920–1999) was painted the year after Eliot won the Nobel Prize (fig.20). The artist had written to Eliot in January 1947 asking him if he would sit for a portrait. When Heron first visited Eliot, the painter was at the very start of his career, while the writer was at the height of his. Heron attended Eliot's offices at Faber & Faber, where the poet was now a director. An electricity outage had meant the Faber offices were cold and Eliot greeted Heron wearing a blue overcoat, part of which can be seen on the left-hand side of the portrait. An outline of a cat can be seen in the upper left-hand corner. The artist's experimental, semi-abstract style is particularly appropriate for a depiction for a writer of innovative, complex poetry. Heron said of the meeting that he found himself, 'looking into the grey eye of this greatest of living writers and feeling that I was looking into the most conscious eye in the universe'.[10] **AA**

FIG.20
T. S. Eliot
By Patrick Heron
1949
Oil on canvas
National Portrait Gallery
NPG 4467

J. R. R. TOLKIEN

John Ronald Reuel (J. R. R.) Tolkien (1892–1973) is best known for his enormously popular fantasy books, *The Hobbit* (1937) and *The Lord of the Rings* (1954–5). Born in South Africa and brought up in London, he had lost both his parents by the age of 12. In spite of this difficult start, he excelled at school and gained a scholarship to read classics at Oxford University, where he took a particular interest in ancient Northern European languages and mythology. An academic career followed, first in the English department at the University of Leeds, and then, from 1925, as the Professor of Anglo-Saxon at Oxford University. Throughout his career, Tolkien created imaginary worlds, stories and languages in his spare time. Within his elaborate mythology, a continuing theme was the extraordinary bravery and ingenuity of apparently ordinary characters, inspired by his experiences fighting in the First World War. His imaginary worlds first came to public attention with the publication of *The Hobbit*, after a former student showed the manuscript to an employee of the publishers George Allen & Unwin. Such was the enthusiasm of its reception that the publishers asked for a sequel. This was to be *The Lord of the Rings*.

Tolkien wrote *The Lord of the Rings* over many years, during which time he often read parts of it aloud at meetings of 'The Inklings', a group of writer friends based in Oxford. This group included the writer and academic C. S. Lewis (1898–1963), whose encouragement was of particular importance to Tolkien. *The Lord of the Rings* met with mixed reviews when it was published, partly because it was not clear to critics where it belonged in terms of genre. Tolkien had not intended it, or *The Hobbit*, specifically for children, although *The Hobbit* began as a bedtime story for his own children, and the books clearly appealed to young people as well as to adults. Both books sold exceptionally well and inspired numerous imitations, creating a new and continuing appetite for 'heroic fantasy' in literature and in other media.

In 1916 Tolkien had married Edith Bratt (1889–1971), his childhood sweetheart. The stable family life they created – in contrast to his own early life and the lives of many of his literary contemporaries – was the background to his entire career in both academia and fiction writing. He frequently wrote warm and affectionate letters to family members, including a number to his grandson Michael George (b.1943), son of his second son, also Michael (1920–1984). The letters are often about

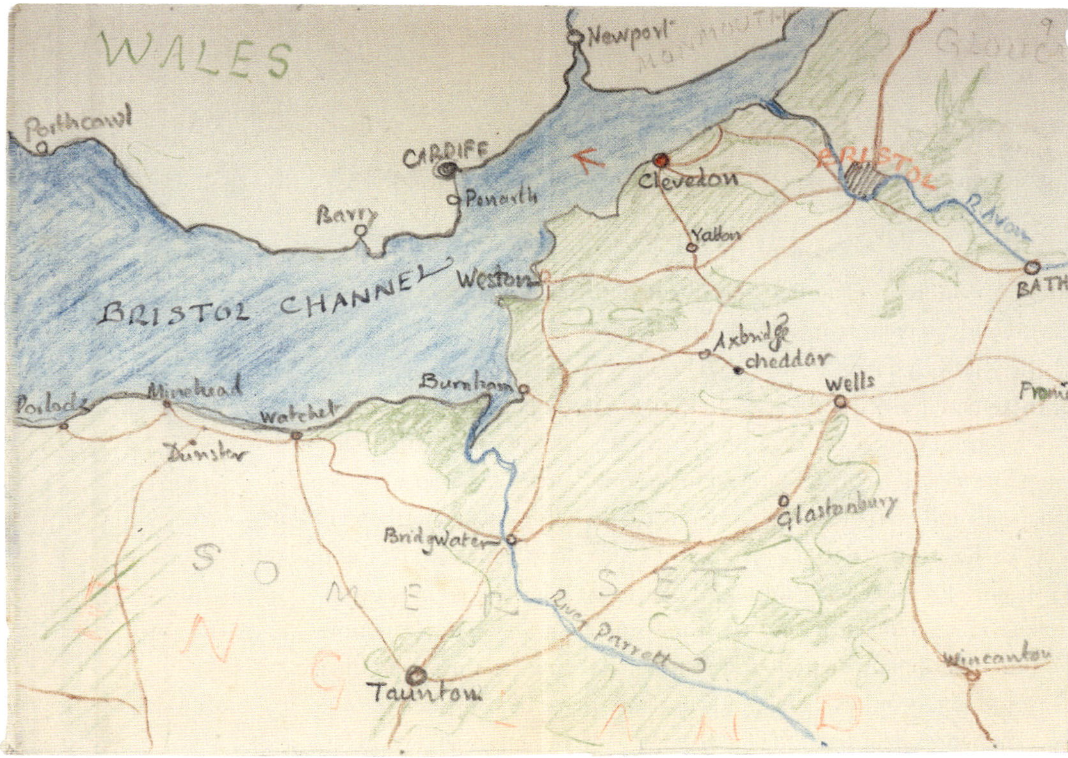

FIG.21
Map of Somerset
By J.R.R. Tolkien
24 September 1952
Graphite, blue, red and green pencil on paper
British Library
Add MS 71657, f.9r

mundane family matters, but the world of Tolkien's books also intrude. In one early letter to Michael George, written in 1952 when his grandson was nine, the author included a map of Somerset on which he marked where he was staying, in Clevedon, the places he had visited in the county and even the direction that his window faced (figs 21 and 22). Although simpler in form, this recalls the maps he made for his books, and his explanation that when writing:

> 'I wisely started with a map, and made the story fit (generally with meticulous care for distances). The other way about lands one in confusions and impossibilities, and in any case it is weary work to compose a map from a story.'[11]

In later letters he discussed with Michael his work on medieval literature and also mentioned the frustration of being besieged by fans and the publication of pirate copies of *The Lord of the Rings*.

In retirement, the Tolkiens moved from Oxford to the suburbs of Poole, near Bournemouth, which was Edith's wish. It was here, in 1971, that Lord Snowdon (1930–2017), the society photographer, and at the time husband of Princess Margaret (1930–2002), photographed the author (fig.23). Snowdon recalled:

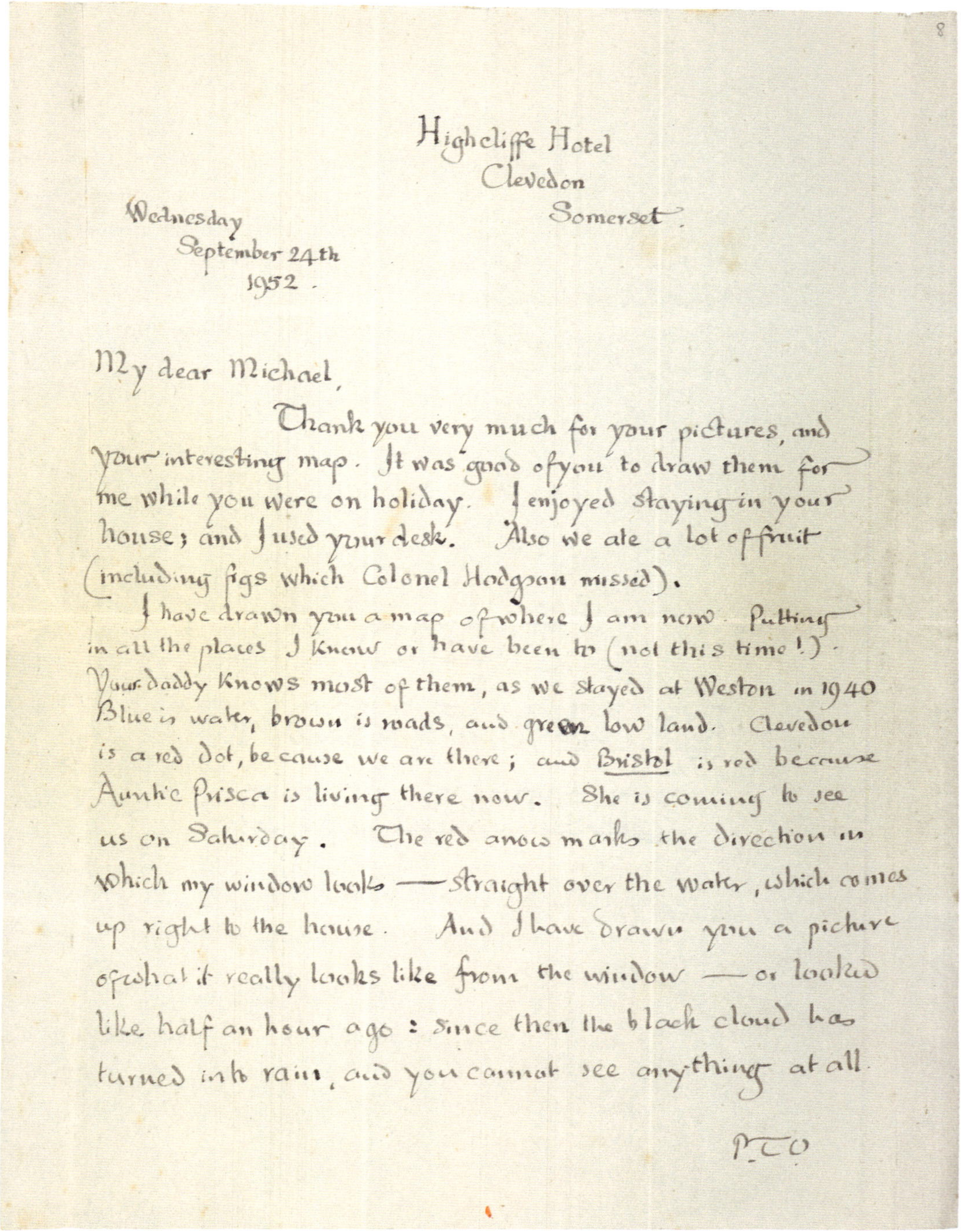

8

Highcliffe Hotel
Clevedon
Somerset.

Wednesday
September 24th
1952.

My dear Michael,

Thank you very much for your pictures, and your interesting map. It was good of you to draw them for me while you were on holiday. I enjoyed staying in your house; and I used your desk. Also we ate a lot of fruit (including figs which Colonel Hodgson missed).

I have drawn you a map of where I am now. Putting in all the places I know or have been to (not this time!). Your daddy knows most of them, as we stayed at Weston in 1940. Blue is water, brown is roads, and green low land. Clevedon is a red dot, because we are there; and Bristol is red because Auntie Prisca is living there now. She is coming to see us on Saturday. The red arrow marks the direction in which my window looks — straight over the water, which comes up right to the house. And I have drawn you a picture of what it really looks like from the window — or looked like half an hour ago: since then the black cloud has turned into rain, and you cannot see anything at all.

P.T.O.

'When I arrived at Tolkien's house I found it curiously characterless. Before I met him, I had spent hours near his home looking for places that might reflect *The Lord of the Rings*, but had found nothing. When we went for a walk before lunch, we came upon this bit of wood.'[12]

FIG.22
Letter to Michael Tolkien
From J. R. R. Tolkien
24 September 1952
Black ink on paper
British Library
Add MS 71657, f.8r

FIG.23
J. R. R. Tolkien
By Lord Snowdon
May 1971
Gelatin silver print
National Portrait Gallery
NPG P843

Tolkien himself wrote in a letter to a cousin that he had found Snowdon 'a very thin almost "elvish" figure ... we had much in common – especially a devotion to trees'.[13] The tree roots protruding from the ground recall Tolkien's own illustrations for *The Lord of the Rings*, particularly his watercolour of Fangorn Forest. Both the photograph and Tolkien's letters suggest that, despite the author's suspicion of and annoyance with his international fame and the accompanying fan base, he still felt a deep imaginative connection to the fantasy worlds he had created. **CM**

MERVYN PEAKE

Mervyn Peake (1911–1968) was a writer and artist who created fantastical works in word and image. Born in China to missionaries, Peake attended grammar school in Tianjin before the family left for England in 1922. At the age of ten, Peake wrote and illustrated his first story, 'Ways of Travelling', which was published in the London Missionary Society magazine. He went on to study art at the Croydon School of Art and the Royal Academy Schools in London. A talented painter and draughtsman, he was commissioned to produce theatre sets and costume designs, illustrations for journals and newspapers, and he regularly exhibited work in galleries. Peake's self-portrait in oils was painted in 1932, a year after he was accepted into the Royal Academy (fig.24). It shows a young man, with large eyes and unkempt hair, not dissimilar to the characters in his illustrations and books. Peake was able to work comfortably in oils as well as pencil, crayon and watercolour. In 2019 this portrait was given to the National Portrait Gallery by the artist's estate, having remained with the family since his death.

From 1935 until 1939 Peake taught life drawing at the Westminster School of Art, where he met Maeve Gilmore (1917–1983), whom he married in 1937. The Peakes went on to have two sons and a daughter, whom Peake often used as models for his illustrations. Serving in the Royal Artillery and the Royal Engineers during the Second World War, he suffered a psychological decline and left the military in 1943. During this time, he made illustrations for Samuel Taylor Coleridge's (1772–1834) 'The Rime of the Ancient Mariner' (see p.32). Best known for his *Gormenghast* series of fantasy novels (1946–59), which he illustrated himself, Peake also illustrated modern editions of other famous works, including *Alice in Wonderland* by Lewis Carroll (1832–1898; see p.200) and *Bleak House* by Charles Dickens (1812–1870; see p.197). Peake felt a great responsibility when asked to illustrate the work of others, saying he should 'subordinate myself totally to the book, and slide into another man's soul'.[14]

As a child in China, one of Peake's favourite books was *Treasure Island* (1883) by Robert Louis Stevenson (1850–1894), and he recalled lying in the shade on hot days, committing every line to memory. Peake illustrated *Treasure Island* for the 1949 Eyre and Spottiswoode edition. It features his

FIG.24
Self-Portrait
By Mervyn Peake
1932
Oil on canvas
National Portrait Gallery
NPG 7074

illustrations throughout, together with a depiction of the duplicitous Long John Silver on the cover. *Treasure Island* tells the story of Jim Hawkins, a boy who finds a map that indicates the location of treasure buried by Captain Flint. Therein a search for Flint's treasure begins, with Jim as a cabin boy aboard the *Hispaniola*, captained by Long John Silver. Mutiny, murder, plotting and piracy drive the story. Peake used his children as models for the illustrations.

His son, Sebastian (1940–2012), said:

> 'I was drawn, sketched and "gouache'd" many, many times, and I always loved the results. I became a leaping athletic hero with pistols in both hands up in the rigging of the *Hispaniola*, or hiding in an apple barrow listening to the murderous plot nearby.'[15]

These original illustrations show how Peake developed his images for *Treasure Island*. Beginning with a loose ink sketch, he mapped out the figures and props, before producing a second, more detailed sketch. Shown here is the development of an illustration to Chapter 11, 'What I heard in the apple barrel' (figs 25 and 26). This image was one for which Sebastian Peake undoubtedly posed and shows Jim hiding in the barrel as he hears that the crew of the *Hispaniola* are pirates. Peake then used a thin paper on which to trace the first image, developing a more detailed picture before sending it to the printer so proofs could be made, on which he could comment. Peake's intense and dramatic illustrations and self-portrait reveal something of the Gothic nature of his imagination, also evident in his writing. **AA**

FIGS 25 & 26
Illustrations for *Treasure Island* by Robert Louis Stevenson
By Mervyn Peake
1949
Pen and wash on paper; printed proof and black ink on paper
British Library
Add MS 89724/17/1/3 f.2r; f.16r

DYLAN THOMAS

Perhaps the most famous of all Welsh poets, Dylan Thomas (1914–1953) has gained enormous admiration for his rich, complex and evocative use of the English language. His most well-known works include the poems 'Fern Hill' (1945) and 'Do not go gentle into that good night' (1951), and the radio play *Under Milk Wood* (1954). Thomas's father, an English teacher in Swansea, named him 'Dylan' after a character in the *Mabinogion*, a collection of medieval Welsh stories. At that time, the name was virtually unknown; its subsequent popularity, including its adoption by the singer-songwriter Bob Dylan (b.1941), was all due to Dylan Thomas's renown.

Thomas left school at 16 and briefly worked as a journalist, while filling notebooks with his poetry. By the age of 20 he had written more than 200 poems. Of the 90 poems he published in his lifetime, over half were written during this period. His poem 'And death shall have no dominion' was published in 1933, when he was still 18, and 'The Force that through the Green Fuse Drives the Flower' a few months later, shortly after his nineteenth birthday. These works brought him to the attention of the London literary scene; both T. S. Eliot (1888–1965; see p.45) and the poet Stephen Spender (1909–1995) wrote to him, and in 1934 his first book of poetry, *18 Poems*, was published.

By the mid-1930s Thomas was living in London much of the time, although returning regularly to Wales. It was during this time that he met the painter Augustus John (1878–1961), a fellow-Welshman who, like Thomas, had shown precocious talent in his youth. By this stage, John was a celebrated artist and also a heavy drinker. The two met in the Fitzroy Tavern in London, cementing their friendship there and in the nearby Marquis of Granby pub. In 1936 John introduced Thomas to Caitlin Macnamara (1913–1994), a family friend and, at that time, John's lover. She and Thomas began their turbulent, chaotic and alcohol-fuelled marriage the following year. John painted this portrait (fig.27) in late 1937 and early 1938 while the Thomases were visiting Caitlin's mother, who lived near John's house in Hampshire. The artist said: 'I got him to sit for me twice, the second portrait being the more successful: provided with a bottle of beer he sat very patiently.'[16] It is not clear which of the two portraits, this one or one in the National Museum of Wales, was the second. Thomas was at this time still only 23; the portrait captures his cherubic, youthful appearance and something of his vulnerability.

FIG.27
Dylan Thomas
By Augustus John
*c.*1937–8
Oil on canvas
National Portrait Gallery
NPG 7049

A couple of years earlier, in 1935, Thomas had met the Welsh poet Vernon Watkins (1906–1967) when Watkins was working in Lloyds Bank in Swansea, Wales. They became lifelong friends, despite Thomas's failure to turn up to Watkins's wedding in October 1944, at which he was supposed to be best man. Thomas valued Watkins's advice enormously, and he sent many of his poems to him for his opinion before publishing them, including 'Vision and Prayer'. The visual structure of the poem on the page was part of its meaning, and as Thomas pointed out in a note to Watkins on the back of the poem (fig.28), the person who had typed it out for him had got this wrong. Each verse in the first part of the poem was to take a diamond shape; each verse in the second part was to be the opposite shape, a kind of angular hourglass. Watkins evidently had some

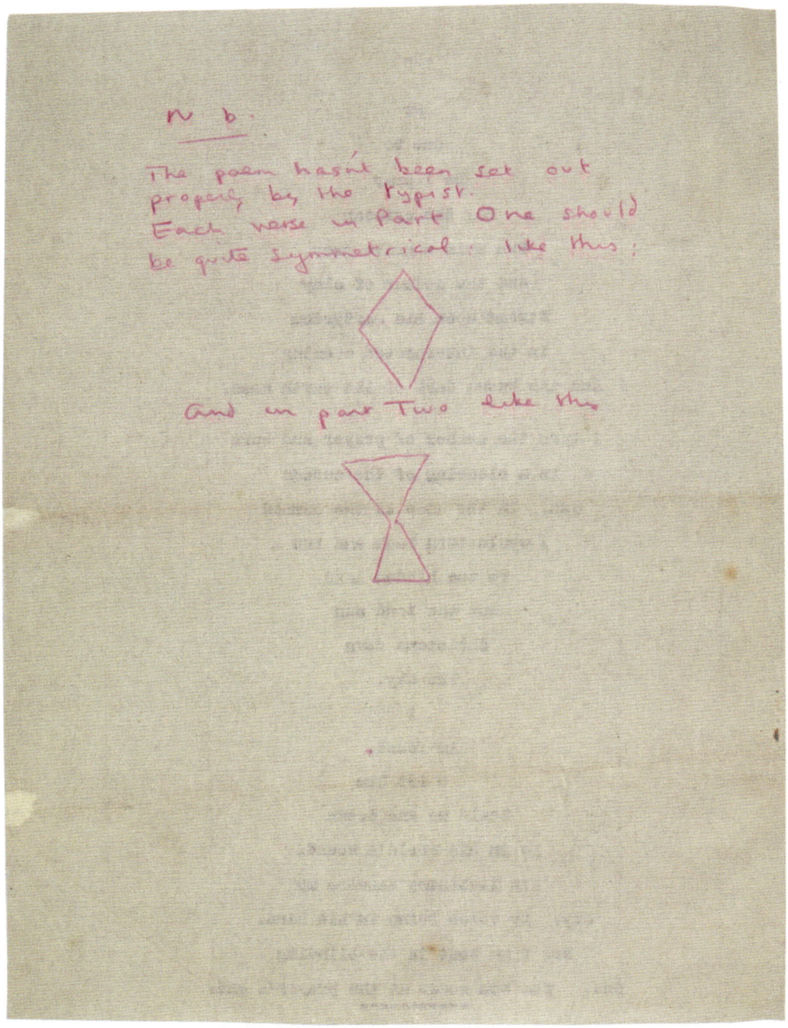

FIG.28
Notes for the draft of 'Vision and Prayer'
By Dylan Thomas
1944
Pink ink on paper, with typewritten poem on verso
British Library
Add MS 52612, f.167v

initial reservations about the shape of the poem but came round to it. Thomas noted in the letter:

> 'I am so glad you liked the "Vision & Prayer" poem, and that the diamond shape of the first part seems no longer to you to be cramped & artificed. I agree that the second part is, formally, less inevitable, but I cannot alter it, except, perhaps, in detail. I will read the very last line again ...'[17]

The poem was first published in the literary review magazine *Horizon* in January 1945 and then included in Thomas's volume *Deaths and Entrances* in 1946. Thomas's correspondence with Watkins, along with his worked and re-worked manuscripts, reflect a meticulous, painstaking side to the poet's character very different from his chaotic public reputation. **CM**

JAN MORRIS

Jan Morris (1926–2020) was a Welsh writer and historian who travelled extensively and wrote prolifically, particularly about the places she visited. In relation to her authorial identity, Morris stated that she considered herself a writer who travels, rather than a travel writer. She regarded her trilogy about the British empire, *Pax Britannica* (1968–78) to be her most important work, but it is her books about places that remain her most well-known works. *Venice* (1960; fig.29) typifies her engaging, personal and sometimes whimsical style, and has been described as one of the best travel books ever written. Opposite the title page in the first edition are line drawings of small Venetian boats by Gerry Facey (1919–1999).

Morris first came to public attention as a journalist for *The Times*, who accompanied the first successful Everest expedition in 1953. The writer famously communicated the conquest of the summit by Edmund Hillary (1919–2008) and Tenzing Norgay (1914–1986) in a coded message that reached the UK on the morning of the coronation of Queen Elizabeth II (1926–2022). In 1972 Morris underwent gender reassignment surgery,

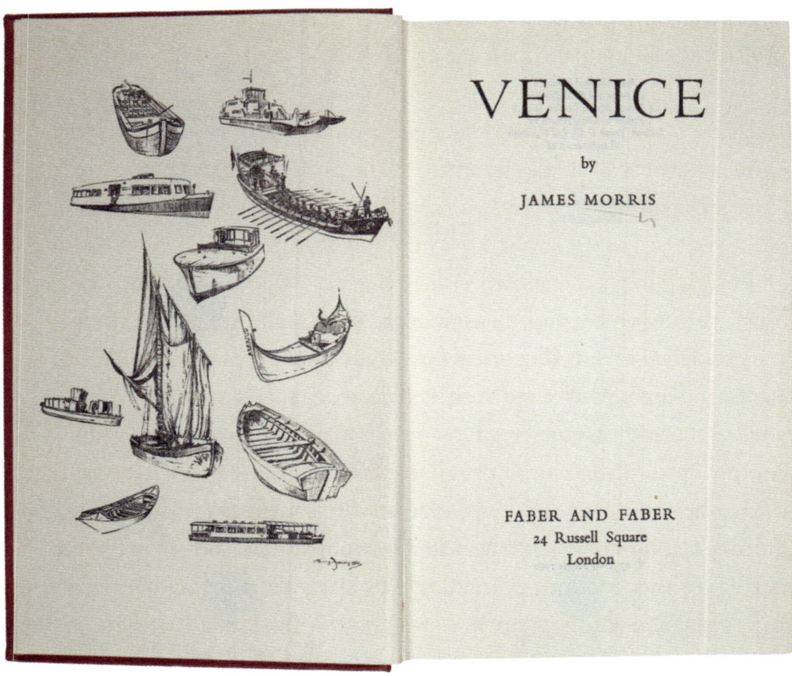

FIG.29
Venice
By Jan Morris
(Faber & Faber, London, 1960)
British Library
10060.bb.2.

FIG.30
Jan Morris
By Arturo Di Stefano
2004–5
Oil on canvas
National Portrait Gallery
NPG 6722

becoming one of the most prominent transgender figures in Britain. She wrote about her identity in *Conundrum* (1974), but made it clear that her work, rather than her gender should define her.

Although Morris was born and brought up in England, her father was Welsh and she identified strongly with Wales, settling there in the 1960s with her wife, and later civil partner, Elizabeth Tuckniss (1924–2024), and their four children. She was a committed Welsh Nationalist and wrote a number of books about the country and its history.

In this painting, commissioned by the National Portrait Gallery, the artist Arturo Di Stefano (b.1955) includes references to Morris's life and writing in ways that Morris herself specified (fig.30). She insisted on the inclusion of her Norwegian cat, Ibsen, and suggested what she described as, 'an allegorical landscape of the imagination'.[18] The landscape includes Wales, Venice, Trieste, Manhattan and Everest, all places of significance to the writer. Morris's involvement in the composition of the portrait perhaps reflected the struggles she had during her life to establish the identity she sought for herself, both as a woman and as a writer. She recorded that she thoroughly enjoyed sitting for this portrait, describing it as 'life enhancing' and 'one of the happiest experiences of my life'.[19] **CM**

TED HUGHES

The poet Ted Hughes (1930–1998) is generally considered one of the most original and influential British poets of the twentieth century. A prolific writer of prose as well as poetry, his best-known works focus on wildlife and the countryside, in which his observations of the raw brutality of nature are used to explore elemental, universal and human themes. Born and brought up in Yorkshire, England, he first came to international attention when his collection of poems, *The Hawk in the Rain*, won a competition in New York in 1957. It was then published and widely praised for its extraordinarily original style and content. Drawing on nature and legends, Hughes created his own mythology, expressed in powerful and complex language. Other collections include *Crow* (1970), and he also wrote children's stories, including *The Iron Man* (1968). Hughes was Poet Laureate from 1984 until his death. In later life he gave extensive public readings, especially to schools, and did much charity work, particularly for environmental causes.

Hughes met the American artist Leonard Baskin (1922–2000) in the 1950s when he and his first wife, the American poet Sylvia Plath (1932–1963; see p.108), were living, briefly, in the US. They struck up a lifelong friendship that was to have important creative consequences for them both. Baskin and Hughes collaborated on a number of works beginning in 1959 with the poem 'Pike', printed by Baskin's Gehenna Press. It was under Baskin's influence that Hughes started exploring the use of the crow as a literary vehicle, and Baskin illustrated Hughes's volume *Crow: From the Life and Songs of the Crow*, along with other works. In 1974 Baskin and his family moved to the UK, settling in a house near Hughes's home in Devon. This facilitated other important collaborations. Baskin's relief sculpture portrait (fig.31) of Hughes makes clear references to their work together, including images of the crow and pike. It is inscribed, along with Hughes's name and age, '*Amicus Meus*' (My Friend).

For much of his professional life, Hughes's poetic achievement was partially overshadowed by the public's interest in the tragedies of his personal life. Sylvia Plath had suffered from severe bouts of depression since her university years, and in 1963 she took her own life. Subsequently, his partner Assia Wevill (née Gutmann; 1927–1969) killed both herself and their child in 1969. Hughes was intensely private about these events, but suspicion, rumour and blame circulated among his critics. The publication

FIG.31
Ted Hughes
By Leonard Baskin
1978
Bronze relief
National Portrait Gallery
NPG 6259

in 1998 of *Birthday Letters*, his final collection of poetry, months before he died of cancer, was therefore met with surprise. It comprises a series of poems, written over the course of more than 25 years, addressed to Plath, exploring their relationship. This early draft of 'Fingers' (fig.32) is one of the lighter poems, which traces his joy in Plath's fingers and their legacy in their daughter Frieda's fingers. After his lifetime of public silence about their relationship and her death, the poems were seen as an extraordinarily frank, honest and often painful examination of their marriage, its disintegration and his feelings and actions. It won the Whitbread (now Costa) Prize for Poetry, among other prestigious prizes. **CM**

FIG.32
Draft for 'Fingers'
By Ted Hughes
Before 1998
Black ink on lined paper within
a school exercise book
British Library
Add MS 88918/1/7, f.251r

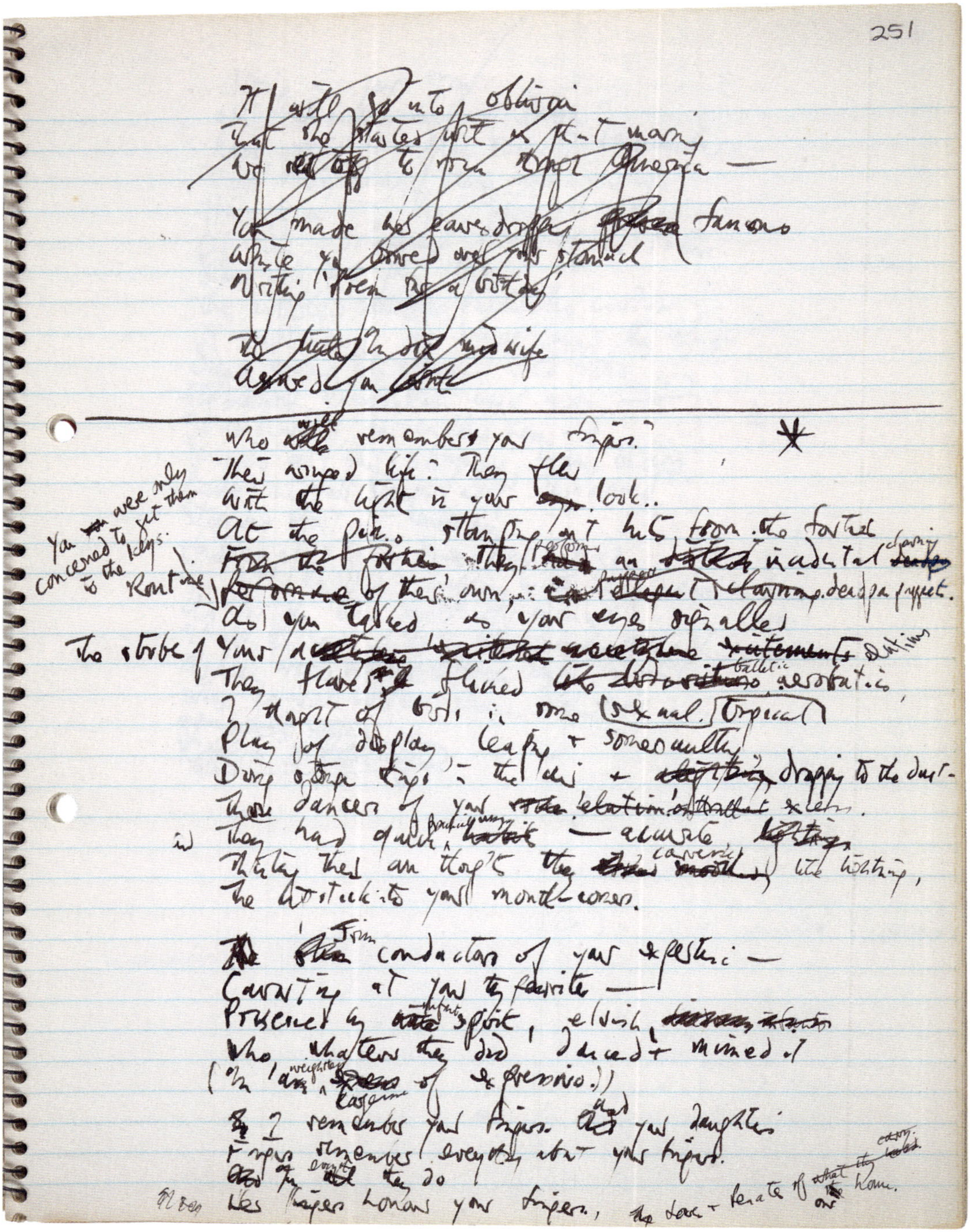

HANIF KUREISHI

The playwright, screenwriter and novelist Hanif Kureishi (b.1954) began writing novels at school and found success with plays as a young adult. He rose to fame through his Oscar-nominated screenplay for the film *My Beautiful Laundrette* in 1985. The film was regarded as ground-breaking for its frank exploration of a gay relationship between a young British Pakistani man and a young white man who is part of a far-right racist group. Like Kureishi's later work, it resisted the typical racial, social and sexual stereotypes prevalent in writing at the time. It also explored the dichotomy inherent in the notion of identity: the tension between self-perception and how people are perceived by others. Kureishi's mother was white British, and his father was from a wealthy Indian family who moved to Pakistan during the Partition of India (1947). Kureishi described himself as 'an English writer, a British writer, let's say, with an Indian background'.[20]

The success of *My Beautiful Laundrette* gave the author the confidence to write the novel he had always wanted to write. He later said: 'If people were not writing books about people like me, I'd write one myself, spitting out all the painful things, rudely, lightly. Someone said to me, write your pleasure. I did.'[21] Kureishi's first novel, *The Buddha of Suburbia*, was published in 1990, and won the Whitbread Prize for a first novel (fig.33). It was originally called *Streets of the Heart*, underlining the importance of the location to the narrative. The protagonist is a biracial teenager, and the novel apparently draws extensively on Kureishi's own life. He has commented: 'All first novels are letters to one's parents, telling them how it was for you, an account of things they didn't understand or didn't want to hear.'[22]

This photograph (fig.34) was taken in 1989, the year before *The Buddha of Suburbia* was published. Although Kureishi was 35 at the time, the photographer Jillian Edelstein (b.1958) captures something of the rebellious schoolboy in the author's pose, rocking back in his chair and fixing the viewer with a defiant stare. Born and brought up in South Africa, Edelstein has described the act of portrait photography as a collaborative process: 'I am dependent on the other person. It is a bit like a dance, albeit a brief one.'[23]

Kureishi's novels, screenplays, short stories and non-fiction works often explore the theme of the relationships between fathers and sons, the conflicts that play out and the implications for identity, be they religious, sexual, social or political. He recently observed of his own work:

Chapter One.

-1-

It was the most exciting time there could have been, perhaps because everything was in flux. Movement and change and the new were in everything. It was also a gullible age and people were looking for something to believe in, to worship, to follow - someone to tell them how to live and not be unhappy. Yes, if there was one thing that charactised the age, it was people's determination not to be unhappy, though as a family we were unhappy in our own way. But that particular unhappiness wasn't to last, though I didn't know it.

So I'll start with an ordinary day and an ordinary though cheering event: my father coming home to the suburbs from his office in the city. I could smell the train on him as he put his briefcase away behind the front door and took off his raincoat, hanging it at the bottom of the stairs. He kissed me and my mother. But instead of flopping into his chair and watching the television news and waiting for my mother to bring him his supper, he went into hsi room and stripped to his vest and underpants. He told me to fetch the big pink towel from the bathroom. He spread it on the floor. He fell onto his knees - and he was by means a flexible man - placed his arms beside his head, and kicked himself into the air.

"I must practise," he said, in a stifled voice.

"Practice for what?" I asked him.

Now he was standing on his head on the pink towel. His stomach sagged down. His balls and prick fell forward in his pants. The considerable muscles on his arms swelled up and he breathed energetically. Like most Indians he was a tiny man but he was elegant and handsome, and beside him most Englishmen looked like

FIG.33
Second draft of *Buddha of Suburbia*
By Hanif Kureishi
1987–8
Typewritten, pencil and black ink
British Library
Add MS 89091/6/3, f.1r

FIG.34
Hanif Kureishi
By Jillian Edelstein
1989
Gelatin silver print
National Portrait Gallery
NPG x34146

'Reading the first paragraph of *The Buddha* now, I'm surprised to notice that the hero, Karim Amir, announces his nationality three times. I guess he was insecure. Like David Bowie, he was eager to find an identity, throw it away, and start again next day with another one, brand new.'[24]

In late December 2022, Kureishi suffered a fall in Rome, which left him paralysed. Since then, he has published thousands of words on social media about his thoughts and feelings, dictated to members of his family. His memoir of this experience, *Shattered*, was published in 2024. CM

ANDREA LEVY

The author Andrea Levy (1956–2019) is best known for her novel *Small Island* (2004), which won the Orange Prize for Fiction (now the Women's Prize for Fiction), the Whitbread Book of the Year and the Commonwealth Writer's Prize. One of four children, she was born in London to Jamaican parents and grew up on a council estate. Her father had come to England on the ship HMT *Empire Windrush* in 1948 and her mother had arrived later that year. Levy studied textile design at art college, later working as a costume assistant at the Royal Opera House and at the BBC, before becoming a graphic designer. It wasn't until she was loaned books by her friends that she really found a love of reading. Inspired by African American writers like Toni Morrison (1931–2019), Levy realised she wanted to read novels about the lives of Black British people, reflecting her own family's experiences and those of her contemporaries. Building on the work of earlier Caribbean writers who had made England their home, such as Sam Selvon (1923–1994; see p.165), Levy included the experience of families, women and children.

In 1989 Levy enrolled in a creative writing class at City Lit, a London college providing classes to adults in a vast range of subjects. Despite encouragement from her tutor and her partner, Levy found publishers were unwilling to invest in stories about Black British families, which they felt would not have a large readership. When she visited Jamaica in 1996 and met many of her relatives, she really felt the importance of her history, embracing it as rich and valid, and one in which to feel pride, rather than shame. She once said she had grown up thinking she was worthless and that the story of the Caribbean was worthless; her experience in Jamaica reinforced her determination to bring her writing to a wider public.

Small Island is about Jamaica and England: two small islands, joined, yet thousands of miles apart. The manuscript for *Small Island* (fig.35) shows notes on the left-hand page opposite a more developed scene on the right. This page is from an early section in the book, when one of the main characters, Hortense, first arrives in London from Jamaica and is horrified by her husband Gilbert's rooms in the home of the white landlady, Queenie. Here, Levy is exploring the character of Queenie in her notes. She writes: 'So Queenie is racist but also takes in these people and befriends them.' Levy said she often developed characters

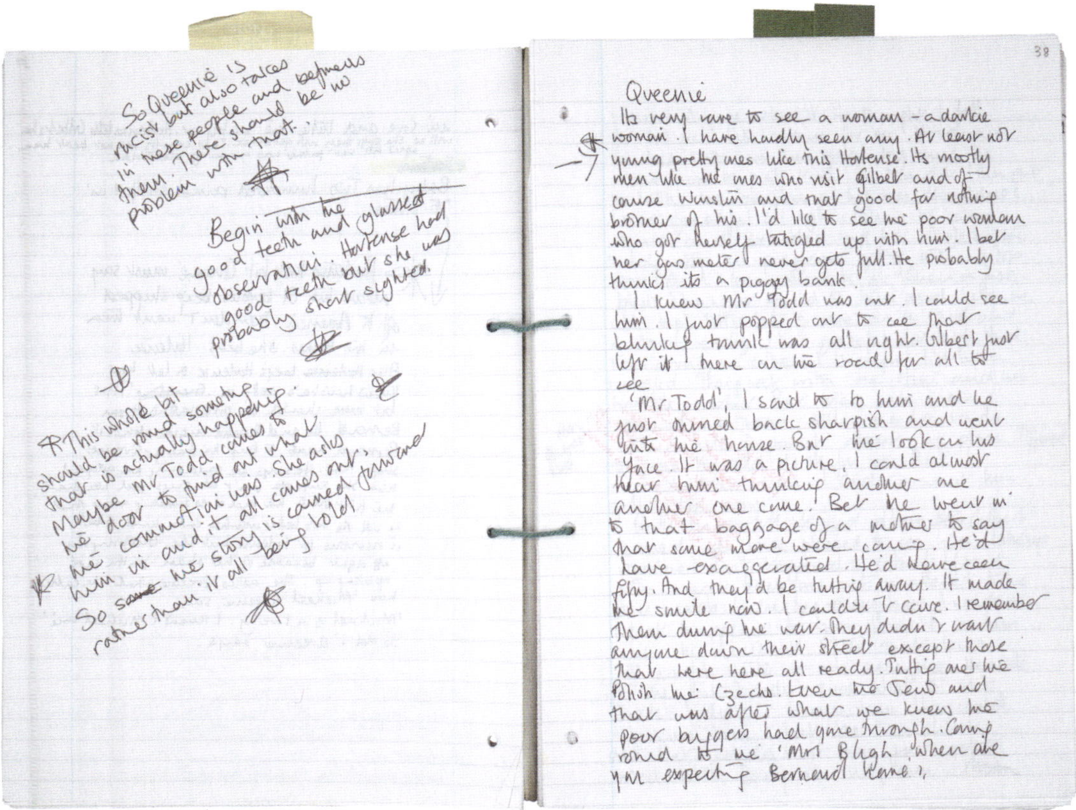

FIG 35
Draft for Small Island
By Andrea Levy
Before 2004
Black ink on lined paper
British Library
Add MS 89736/1/2, ff.37v–38r

based on people and experiences she knew, as well as undertaking significant historical research. In an interview in 2014 with the British Library, Levy said she had the idea for *Small Island* after talking to and making tapes of both her Jamaican mother and her mother-in-law, who was from the Midlands in England. She said she was struck by the difference between the two women. Her mother-in-law was open and spoke about her heritage, while her mother was closed and guarded. She said her mother lived with a landlady when she first moved to England from Jamaica and Levy began thinking about what would happen if her mother-in-law was the landlady and the two women met. This became the basis for the story of *Small Island*. Levy based other characters on her father and uncle.

Levy was surprised by the success of *Small Island*, which was her fourth novel. As well as winning a number of prizes it became a set text for school children. She said the interest in the novel emboldened her to write about the heart of the Caribbean story, which was slavery. This photograph of Levy (fig.36) shows the author standing in front of the flat where she was born. It was taken in August 2004, six months after *Small Island* was published. Levy had always dreamt that her portrait might hang in the National Portrait Gallery. The photograph was taken by Mary Dunkin (d.2008), who, like Levy, faced a battle with cancer. Pride in and exploration of her heritage and ancestry, both British and Jamaican, are at the crux of what made Levy such a humane, popular and talented writer. **AA**

FIG.36
Andrea Levy
By Mary Dunkin
31 August 2004
Chromogenic print
National Portrait Gallery
NPG x126690

105

THE JOURNEY TO SUCCESS

2

Writers' journeys to success are as varied as the authors themselves. Over time, the routes to recognition and achievement have changed as publishing has evolved. Official appointments and personal patronage have become less important, while competitions and awards offer new opportunities to be seen. Portraits play a part in this journey, in some instances celebrating successes, in others, revealing something of the struggles. This chapter looks at the ways these journeys are reflected in manuscripts and books, as well as in letters, contracts and portraits.

While readers are naturally focused on a writer's published output, the journey to publication requires an author to engage with different people and processes to bring their work to readers. The economics of writing are very much part of an author's journey to success. The contract for John Milton's *Paradise Lost* (1667) is the earliest surviving agreement in Britain between a writer and a publisher and shows how the author needed to consider not just writing, but also the details of printing his work. Alexander Pope's manuscript for his translation of Homer's *Iliad* was written on the backs of letters, and his contract with the printer show his business acumen. William Wordsworth's manuscript for the poem 'I wandered lonely as a cloud' (1807) shows a writer who was keen to control the order and layout of his book. Rudyard Kipling's precise drawings and carefully corrected proofs testify to his involvement with the publication process. By contrast, the portraits of Pope, Wordsworth and Kipling focus not on the business side of authorship but on the elements of thought, inspiration and imagination that go into writing.

Yet before contracts could be signed and publication arranged, writers had to find the time and the means to write. From the sixteenth to the eighteenth century, at a time when literacy rates across the population at large were relatively low, most early writers had privileged backgrounds, but some, including Aphra Behn, came from ordinary families, making their achievements particularly extraordinary. In recent times, university and creative writing courses have often been a route to literary success, but some writers, such as Harold Pinter, had different journeys, approaching play writing from experience inside the theatre.

Some of the material in this chapter illustrates the difficulties writers have found in making the first step on their journey to literary success. A letter from Thomas Hardy to a publisher records his desperation for news about his first, and ultimately unpublished, novel 'The Poor Man and the Lady'. An early letter from Kazuo Ishiguro to *Granta* magazine plaintively suggests that perhaps a lack of response from them was due to his story being lost in the post. Meanwhile, a 19-year-old Zadie Smith, submitting stories to an established writer for her opinion, comments that by virtue of her age she has very little 'old stuff' to send.

Nonetheless, many of these writers' portraits mark moments of success: Thomas Hardy's portrait was painted at the end of his career when he was probably the most famous living author in Britain. Ishiguro's portrait was commissioned by the National Portrait Gallery between his winning the Booker Prize and the Nobel Prize in Literature. Smith's photograph was taken as part of the promotion of her immensely successful first novel, *White Teeth* (2000). Such prizes have both fuelled and marked the success of the careers of authors, including Hilary Mantel, Derek Walcott and Wole Soyinka.

JOHN MILTON

John Milton (1608–1674) is perhaps best known for his epic poem, *Paradise Lost* (1667). Born in London, Milton joined St Paul's School some time around 1620 before enrolling at Christ's College, Cambridge, in 1625. Here he acquired the nickname 'The Lady', which the ancient Roman poet Virgil (70–19 BCE) had also been called. It was during his time in Cambridge that this portrait was painted (fig.37). In about 1681 the antiquarian and biographer John Aubrey (1626–1697) recorded it in the collection of Milton's widow: 'His widow has his picture drawne when a Cambridge scholar. He was so fair that they called him the Lady of Christ's Coll[ege].'[1] This image of Milton differs significantly from later portraits, which show him with long hair, approaching middle age, or as an old, blind man. This youthful portrait shows a lesser-known side of the famous writer: at the beginning of his career – young, fair and not yet afflicted by sight loss.

After Cambridge, Milton took up private study for five years, later travelling around France and Italy. In 1645 he published a collection of poems written during his youth. By this time the poet was beginning to lose his sight and by 1652 he was permanently blind. Hugely idealistic and critical of the church and monarchy, Milton supported the Parliamentarian side during the English civil wars (1642–51) and was later employed by the Republican government. In 1658, shortly after the death of his second wife, Milton began to dictate *Paradise Lost*. This was interrupted by the Restoration of the monarchy in 1660 and Milton's arrest and imprisonment in the Tower of London. Later released, he married for a third time and continued to compose and dictate the poem until 1663. The narrative considers the story of the Fall of Adam and Eve, and the role of Satan, whose character is often seen as an anti-hero. The poem inspired many later writers including William Blake (1757–1827; see p.243).

A number of events caused a delay to the publication of *Paradise Lost*, including the Great Plague (1665) and the Great Fire of London (1666). The printer Samuel Simmons (1640–1687) purchased *Paradise Lost* for £5, and his original publishing contract with Milton is shown here (fig.38). This is the earliest surviving contract between a writer and publisher and shows how the economics of writing were formalised. The contract states that Milton would receive another £5 if 1,300 copies of the poem

FIG.37
John Milton
By an unknown artist
*c.*1629
Oil on canvas
National Portrait Gallery
NPG 4222

FIG.38
Contract for *Paradise Lost*
27 April 1667
Iron gall ink on laid paper
British Library
Add MS 18861

were sold, and another £10 should two further editions of 1,300 copies be issued. Milton only earned £10 for *Paradise Lost* as he died in 1674. From his early days at Cambridge to the publication of *Paradise Lost*, this portrait and the contract represent the beginnings through to the end of a complicated and eventful literary career. **AA**

JOHN DRYDEN

John Dryden (1631–1700) was the first official British Poet Laureate, and one of the most influential writers of the seventeenth century. Admired today for his political and satirical poetry, and for his translations, during his lifetime he was better known for his prolific writing for the theatre, which also provided him with his main source of income. The best known of his plays are probably the comedy *Marriage A-la-Mode* (first performed 1671) and the tragedy *All for Love* (first performed 1677), although they are rarely performed today. However, poems such as *Mac Flecknoe* (1682) and *Absalom and Achitophel* (1681) had a more lasting impact stylistically and greater historical significance, as they engaged with the political, philosophical and often personally spiteful debates that were central to literary London at the time. Dryden was also a great scholar of classical literature and produced some of the most admired and influential translations of ancient texts, notably the works of Virgil (70–19 BCE). Today, he is regarded as a master of the English language, both in prose and poetry.

Dryden was born into a prosperous Northamptonshire family that was Puritan in religious practice and Parliamentarian in political inclination during the English civil wars (1642–51). During the Republic, he took a post in the civil service under the Lord Protector, Oliver Cromwell (1599–1658). Records of 1658 show that Dryden walked in Cromwell's funeral procession along with the poets John Milton (1608–1674; see p.76) and Andrew Marvell (1621–1678; see p.234). Dryden's second published poem (after an elegy for a deceased school friend) was 'Heroique Stanzas, Consecrated to the Glorious Memorie of his most Serene & Renowned Highness Oliver Late Lord Protector of this Common-Wealth, & written after the Celebration of his Funeralls', printed in 1659. The manuscript for this poem is one of very few surviving literary manuscripts of Dryden's work in his own hand, and one of the most important, in showing his typical punctuation and spelling (fig.39).

It may seem surprising that one of the next poems Dryden was to publish was in praise of Charles II (1630–1685). His religious and political allegiances changed more than once during his lifetime, and this led to criticism by his contemporaries that he was driven by ambition rather than conscience. While many supporters of the Republic concluded that a return to the monarchy was inevitable and right in 1660,

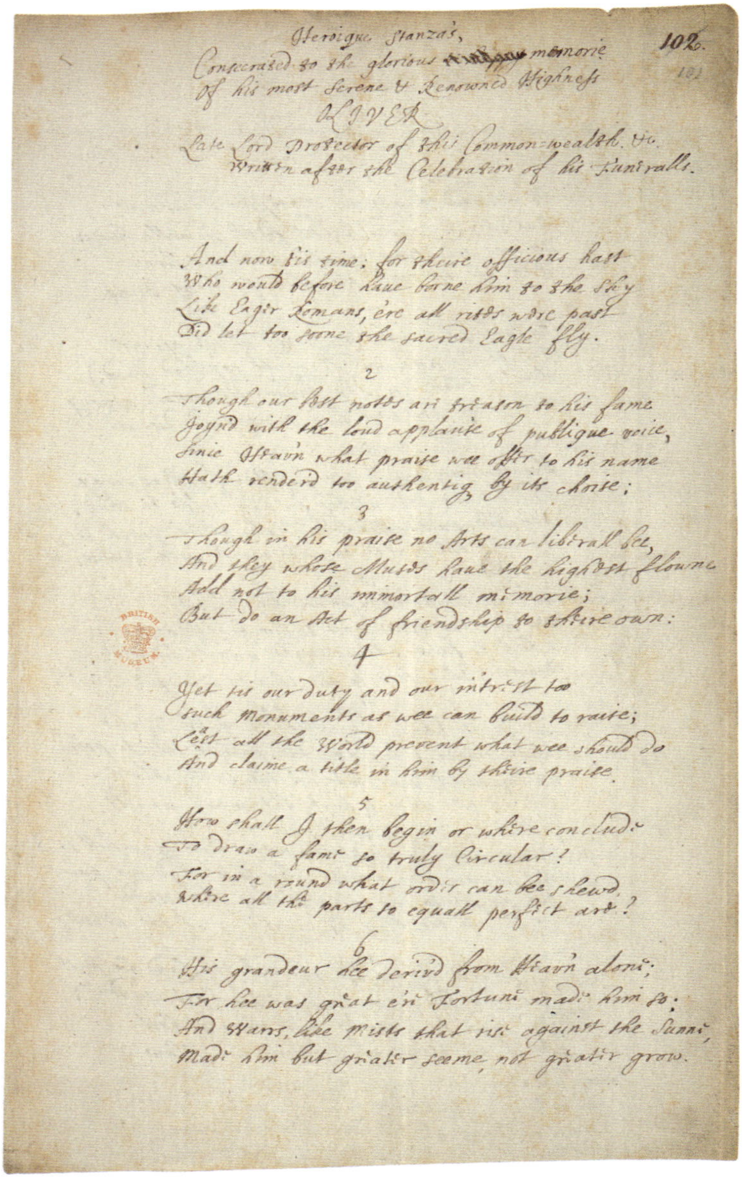

102

Heroique Stanza's,
Consecrated to the glorious memorie
Of his most Serene & Renowned Highness
OLIVER
Late Lord Protector of this Common-wealth, &c.
Written after the Celebration of his Funeralls.

And now 'tis time; for theire officious hast
Who would before have borne him to the Sky
Like Eager Romans, ere all rites were past
Did let too soone the sacred Eagle fly.

2

Though our best notes are treason to his fame
Joyn'd with the loud applause of publique voice,
Since Heav'n what praise wee offer to his name
Hath render'd too authentiq by its choise;

3

Though in his praise no Arts can liberall bee,
And they whose Muses have the highest flowne
Add not to his immortall memorie;
But do an Act of friendship to theire own:

4

Yet 'tis our duty and our int'rest too
Such monuments as wee can build to raise;
Lest all the World prevent what wee should do
And claime a title in him by theire praise.

5

How shall I then begin or where conclude
To draw a fame so truly Circular?
For in a round what order can bee shew'd,
Where all the parts so equall perfect are?

6

His grandeur hee deriv'd from Heav'n alone;
For hee was great ere fortune made him so:
And Warrs, like mists that rise against the Sunne,
Made him but greater seeme, not greater grow.

FIG.39
'Heroique Stanzas on the Death of Oliver Cromwell'
By John Dryden
1658
Iron gall ink on laid paper
British Library
Lansdowne MS 1045/69, f.101r

Dryden was undoubtedly ambitious and set out to gain royal patronage. By 1668 he was fully associated with the new regime and was appointed the first official Poet Laureate.

The portrait by John Michael Wright (1617–1694) celebrates not just Dryden's appointment to the Laureate, but also the establishment of the office itself (fig.40). It is not known who commissioned the painting, but it seems possible that it was Dryden himself. The numerous quotations from classical literature would seem to suggest that he had a strong sense of his own abilities and value, and the importance of the role of Poet Laureate. The Latin inscriptions on the lower part of the cartouche are short extracts

FIG.40
John Dryden
By John Michael Wright
*c.*1668
Oil on canvas
National Portrait Gallery
NPG 6854

from six Roman poets: Virgil, Horace, Martial, Juvenal, Ovid and Statius. All of them refer to the celebration of poets with wreaths of various leaves – oak, ivy, laurel and olive – and these leaves are all included in the wreath painted around the portrait. The main inscription, '*Par omnibus Vnus*', can be translated as 'one [poet] a match for [them] all'.

In 1685 Dryden converted to Catholicism. His critics saw this as another cynical ploy to attract favour from the monarch; Charles II, had converted to Catholicism on his deathbed in 1685 and James II (1633–1701), his brother and successor, was openly Catholic. Dryden continued in his post as Poet Laureate under the new monarch. However, as was the case with other royal appointments, the laureateship was probably more useful in attracting the patronage of others, than it was lucrative in itself. In 1688 James II fled the country after the invasion of William of Orange. With the coronation of the Protestant William and his wife Mary, as William III (1650–1702) and Mary II (1662–1694), Dryden lost the Poet Laureateship and turned back to writing for the theatre as a source of income. **CM**

APHRA BEHN

One of the first professional women writers in Britain, Aphra Behn (1640–1689) was successful and admired in her lifetime. However, like other early women writers, she fell out of fashion in the eighteenth and nineteenth centuries as the expectations surrounding the behaviour of women changed, only to be rediscovered with the growth of feminism in the twentieth century. Her adventurous and unconventional life story is echoed in the lives of some of her characters. She seems to have deliberately obscured her early life, which was apparently a relatively humble one in Kent. Around 1663–4 she spent some time in Suriname, then an English colony. Here, she may have operated as a spy, possibly following similar work during the Interregnum. In 1666, having married and perhaps been widowed, she was sent as a government agent to Antwerp. Left in debt as a result of this venture, on her return to England she turned to writing, in her own words 'forced to write for Bread and not ashamed to owne it'.[2] Having been closed for 18 years during the English civil wars and Interregnum (1649–1660), the public theatres were reopened by Charles II (1630–1685) following the Restoration of the monarchy in 1660. In addition, for the first time, the king had made it legal for women to act on the public stage. In this atmosphere of new theatrical possibilities for women, Behn chose the theatre as the arena in which to forge a new career.

Behn's first play, *The Forc'd Marriage*, was performed on 20 September 1670. She went on to write at least 18 more plays, as well as prose fiction and poetry; her most popular play was *The Rover* (1677). Unlike earlier and later women writers, she did not usually disguise her identity or gender on printed editions of her work. As a woman writing for the theatre, she was still regarded as a novelty and faced criticism for her political propaganda – she was an ardent royalist and supporter of the succession of the Catholic James II (1633–1704) to the throne – and for her frank depictions of sex. She was often accused of plagiarism and bawdiness and addressed these charges in various publications, pointing out that men writing as she did would not be criticised in the same way.

In the 1680s the merger of two big London theatre companies, the Duke's Company and the King's Company, led to a fall in demand for plays, and Behn turned increasingly to prose fiction. In this genre her most famous work was *Oroonoko* (1688), the story of an African prince sold into slavery (fig.41). It was later turned into a play (1695) and later

FIG.41
Oroonoko
By Aphra Behn
(Will Canning, London, 1688)
British Library
1052.a.32.

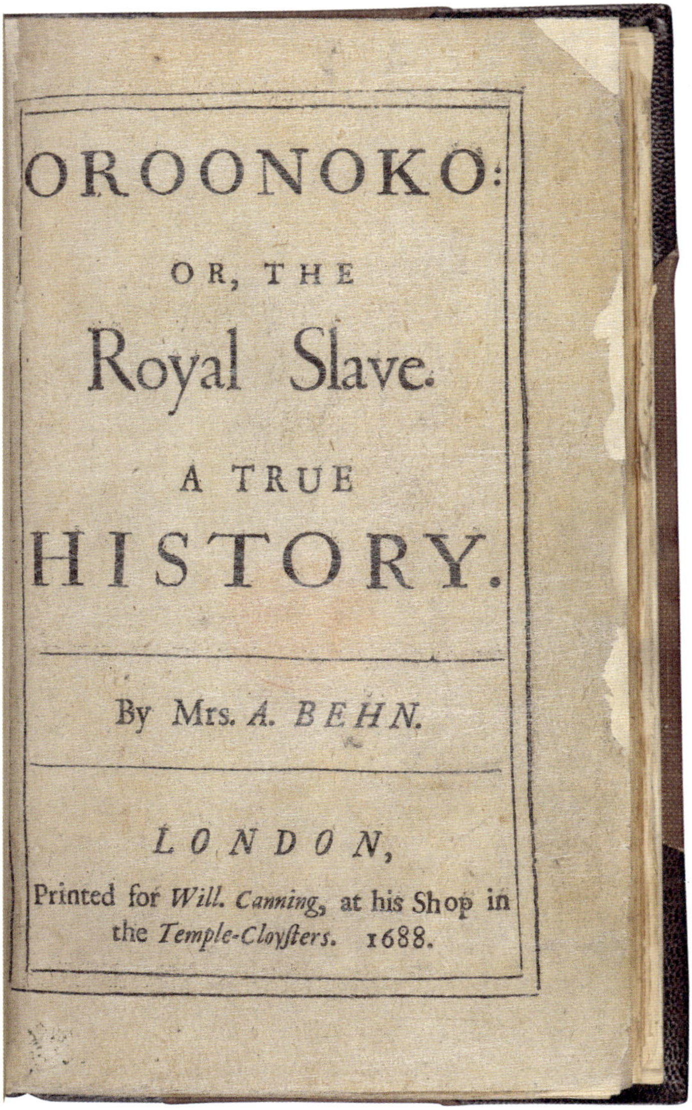

still, adapted and used in support of the anti-slavery campaign. In its original seventeenth-century form, it reveals an ambiguous attitude, expressing horror at the cruelty but acceptance of the concept of enslavement. In this respect, Behn was a woman of her time.

During her lifetime and after her death, Behn proved a divisive figure with other women writers. Some acknowledged her influence and their debt to her in establishing their own careers. Others, such as her contemporary Katherine Philips (1632–1664; see p.136), were compared to Behn at Behn's expense. Where Philips was seen as chaste and respectable, Behn was regarded as degenerate and transgressive. This print (fig.42) was made for the 1718 edition of Behn's *Poems upon Several Occasions*, first published in 1684. In 1718 her identity as a woman was still

FIG.42
Aphra Behn
By Robert White after
John Riley
1718
Line engraving
National Portrait Gallery
NPG D9483

clearly regarded as a selling point for the volume and it was therefore reinforced with an image of her displaying conventional, courtly beauty. Social attitudes were changing, however, and her work was increasingly criticised for its 'unfeminine' sexual explicitness. By the nineteenth century she was largely ignored, until she was gradually brought back to literary prominence in the twentieth century. Virginia Woolf (1882–1941; see p.42) memorably said of her, in *A Room of One's Own* (1929): 'All women together ought to let flowers fall on the tomb of Aphra Behn ... for it was she who earned them the right to speak their minds'.[3] **CM**

ALEXANDER POPE

Alexander Pope (1688–1744) became one of the most admired and influential poets of the eighteenth century, overcoming major social and physical disadvantages to do so. He was born in London into a Catholic family at a time of strong anti-Catholic discrimination by the government and the majority Protestant population. He taught himself languages by translating poems and began an epic poem, *Alcander, Prince of Rhodes* (later destroyed), at the age of 12. Pope suffered from Pott's disease (tuberculosis of the spine), which restricted his growth and led to respiratory problems. Much of Pope's literary output was influenced by ancient Greek and Roman writers, whose work was regarded as the pinnacle of literary achievement and was the basis of education at this time. In 1711 Pope wrote 'An Essay on Criticism', which contains many famous sayings we use to this day, including 'Fools rush in where angels fear to tread' and 'To err is human; to forgive, divine'. This was followed by *The Rape of the Lock* in 1712 (published between 1712 and 1717), a mock heroic epic that parodied long, narrative poems by Classical poets.

In 1711 Pope began translating the *Iliad* by the ancient Greek writer Homer. Set during the last year of the legendary Trojan War, it centres on

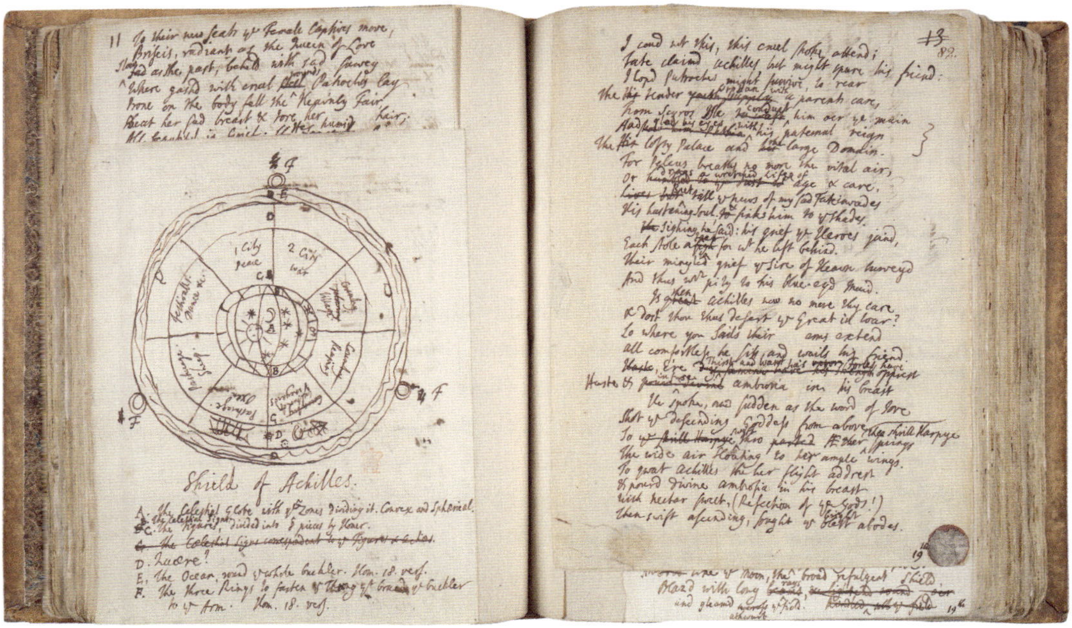

FIG.43
Homer's *Iliad*
By Alexander Pope
1712–24
Iron gall ink and pencil on laid paper
British Library
Add MS 4808, ff.81v–82r

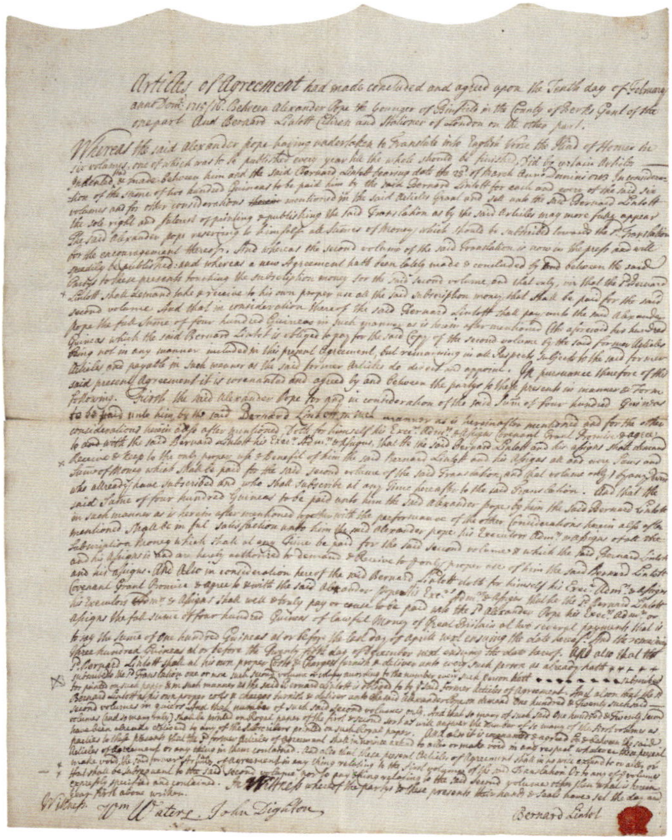

Articles of Agreement had made concluded and agreed upon the Tenth day of February anno Dom. 1715/16 Between Alexander Pope the Younger of Binfield in the County of Berks Gent of the one part And Bernard Lintott Citizen and Stationer of London on the other part.

FIG.44
Contract for the translation of Homer's *Iliad*, Volume 2
Between Bernard Lintot and Alexander Pope
1716
Iron gall ink on laid paper
British Library
Egerton MS 1951, f.3r

the siege of Troy. Pope planned that his translation should be published in parts, by subscription, between 1715 and 1720. This method of publishing was innovative for the time, with money from subscribers funding each volume. The translation took Pope six years. Shown here is Pope's sketch of the shield of the warrior Achilles, which appeared in Volume 5 (fig.43), along with part of Achilles' lament upon the death of his friend Patroclus, who was killed during battle while wearing Achilles' armour. Much of Pope's epic poem was drafted on the backs of personal letters.

Pope earned £1,275 from the book's publisher Bernard Lintot (1675–1736) and subscriptions raised this sum to £5,000, enough to allow him to exist as a professional writer. Pope was later to write 'But (thanks to *Homer*) since I live and thrive'.[4] The contract for Volume 2 of Homer's *Iliad* (fig.44), dated 10 February 1716, states that Pope will sell to Lintot the sole right to print and publish his translation. It further sets out that that Pope will be paid 200 guineas for each volume written and Lintot will print the first 120 issues of Volume 2 on the fine Royal paper, often called 'writing Royal paper', to match the initial 120 copies of Volume 1. The detail of the contract shows the level to which writer and publisher formalised their agreement.

FIG.45
Alexander Pope
Attributed to Charles Jervas
*c.*1713–15
Oil on canvas
National Portrait Gallery
NPG 112

The portrait of Pope, attributed to his friend Charles Jervas (1675–1739), shows the author seated in a pose used typically for writers and intellectuals in the period, with his head resting on his hand, clearly lost in thought (fig.45). At the upper left-hand corner is a portrait bust of Homer. It is not certain who the female figure on the right of composition is. She may be an allegorical figure, or perhaps it is a portrait of Martha Blount (1690–1762), a close friend of the writer with whom he was in love. As with Pope's other portraits, the painting's iconography was probably very carefully controlled by him. There is no hint at his physical difficulties; he is depicted here as a successful author, challenging the writers of the ancient world. **AA**

LAURENCE STERNE

For most of his life Laurence Sterne (1713–1768) was known primarily for his ecclesiastical role as a vicar in Yorkshire, in the north of England. However, with the publication of his novel, *The Life and Opinions of Tristram Shandy, Gentleman* (1759–67), he gained almost immediate widespread recognition and acclaim. He thus fulfilled his aim in writing, which he later said was 'not to be fed, but to be famous'.[5] The first two books of what was to become a nine-volume novel were published in December 1759. Sterne carefully orchestrated its London reception, organising, for example, for the famous actor and theatre manager David Garrick (1717–1779) to receive the first edition of the first two books. The second edition, which came out in April 1760, was dedicated to the Prime Minister, William Pitt the Younger (1759–1806). The anarchic and often bawdy comedy, experimental structure and stream-of-consciousness narrative was enjoyed and reviled in equal measure, particularly after it was revealed that the author of *Tristram Shandy* was a clergyman. Sterne wrote to a friend, 'One half of the town abuse my book as bitterly, as the other half cry it up to the skies'.[6]

The portrait of Sterne by Joshua Reynolds (1723–1792; fig.46) was painted between the publication of the first and second editions of the first two volumes of *Tristram Shandy*, at the height of Sterne's new-found celebrity. In early March 1760 Sterne negotiated a lucrative deal with the leading London publisher Robert Dodsley (1704–1764). Reynolds was at that time one of the most successful and fashionable painters in London. His sitter books record the Sterne sittings, with the first on 20 March and another seven sessions up to 21 April 1760. On 22 April an edition of Sterne's sermons, entitled *The Sermons of Mr Yorick*, was advertised 'with a portrait of the editor [Sterne], engraved from a portrait by Mr Reynolds'.[7] This volume was published on 22 May, with an engraved frontispiece by Simon François Ravenet (1706–*c*.1774) based on the portrait by Reynolds. The timing and circumstances around the publication of this print, along with the fact that Reynolds was never paid for the portrait, suggest that it may have been painted by the artist as a speculative venture, rather than commissioned by either the sitter or one of his supporters. Reynolds portrays Sterne in his clerical robes but with an expression that suggests both the intensity of his observation and the amusement with which he regards the world around him.

FIG.46
Laurence Sterne
By Sir Joshua Reynolds
1760
Oil on canvas
National Portrait Gallery
NPG 5019

Laurence Sterne.

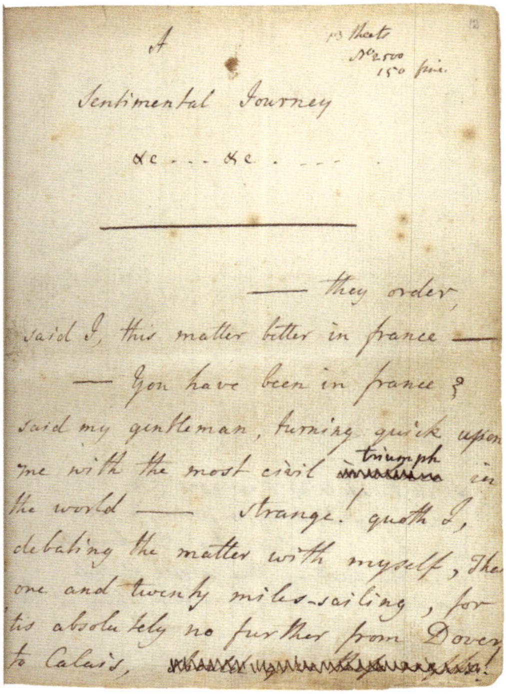
A
Sentimental Journey
&c... &c. ...

— they order, said I, this matter better in france —
— You have been in france? said my gentleman, turning quick upon me with the most civil triumph in the world — strange! quoth I, debating the matter with myself, That one and twenty miles sailing, for tis absolutely no further from Dover to Calais,

FIG.47
A Sentimental Journey
By Laurence Sterne
Before 1768
Iron gall ink on laid paper
British Library
Egerton MS 1610, f.12r

Sterne's second novel, *A Sentimental Journey through France and Italy*, was published in late February 1768, just three weeks before the author died of tuberculosis. Its narrator is the Reverend Yorick, a character who also appears in *Tristram Shandy* and is a thinly disguised version of Sterne himself. The novel is written more conventionally and elegantly than *Tristram Shandy*, with less bawdy humour. However, it still has satirical elements, including a character 'Smelfungus', based on the Scottish writer Tobias Smollett (1721–1771), whose own travel writing Sterne regarded as inappropriately negative and grumbling. *A Sentimental Journey* also reflects Sterne's interest in experimental structure, starting in the middle of a conversation and ending in the middle of a sentence. Inspired by Sterne's travels in France and Italy (although Rev. Yorick never actually gets to Italy), it was immensely influential, triggering an outpouring of travel literature, with a new focus in such works on 'sentiment'. This was understood to mean the travellers' individual subjective, emotional responses to what they came across, including the manners and morals of the people they met, as opposed to more objective accounts of buildings and famous sites. This manuscript volume for the first part of *A Sentimental Journey* is a fair copy in Sterne's hand, which he sent to the publisher (fig.47). It is one of the earliest surviving examples of a manuscript for an English novel written in the hand of the author. The layout of the text shows Sterne was considering how the words would appear on the page when printed. Even at this late stage in the writing process he appears to have moved some chapters around and continued to correct his text. **CM**

WILLIAM WORDSWORTH

The famous Romantic poet William Wordsworth (1770–1850) was born to a middle-class, professional family. One of five children, he was particularly close to his sister, Dorothy (1771–1855). He grew up in the Lake District, an area of outstanding natural beauty in the north of England. Wordsworth enjoyed spending time in nature, reading widely and watching local people go about their daily lives.

In 1797 William and his sister Dorothy moved to Somerset, and found a house near to where his friend, the poet Samuel Taylor Coleridge (1772–1834; see p.32), was staying. The two poets spent a significant amount of time together, walking in the hills and sharing ideas. In 1798 Wordsworth and Coleridge's jointly written volume of poetry, *Lyrical Ballads,* was published, a volume that is now seen as marking the beginning of the English Romantic movement. Dorothy and William settled in Grasmere in the Lake District in 1799, where they were joined by Mary Hutchinson (1770–1859), after her marriage to William in 1802.

While the more prominent biographical narrative about Wordsworth was one of him immersed in nature, developing radical ideas and collaborating with Coleridge, the presence of his sister and wife also had a profound impact on his work. Wordsworth's most famous poem is probably 'I wandered lonely as a cloud', sometimes called 'Daffodils', written between 1804 and 1807. It was inspired by a walk in the Lake District taken by William and Dorothy and was published in 1807 in *Poems in Two Volumes*. The poems for this book were written out by William, Dorothy and Mary on individual sheets and grouped in packets to be sent to the publishers Longman, Hurst, Rees & Orme between 1806 and 1807. While William copied out some poems, he dictated others, and this particular poem is either in the hand of his sister or wife (fig.48). At the top of the page are instructions to the printer showing where Wordsworth wanted the poem to sit within the book. Some lines have been changed at the last minute, most notably the first line from 'I wandered like a lonely' to 'I wandered lonely as a cloud'.

In contrast to this practical, collaborative aspect of Wordsworth's life, the portrait by Benjamin Robert Haydon (1786–1846), shows the poet as a lone figure, at one with the natural backdrop of the Lake District (fig.49). Painted when Wordsworth was 72, it was made to commemorate a sonnet the poet composed about Haydon's 1839 picture *The Duke of Wellington*

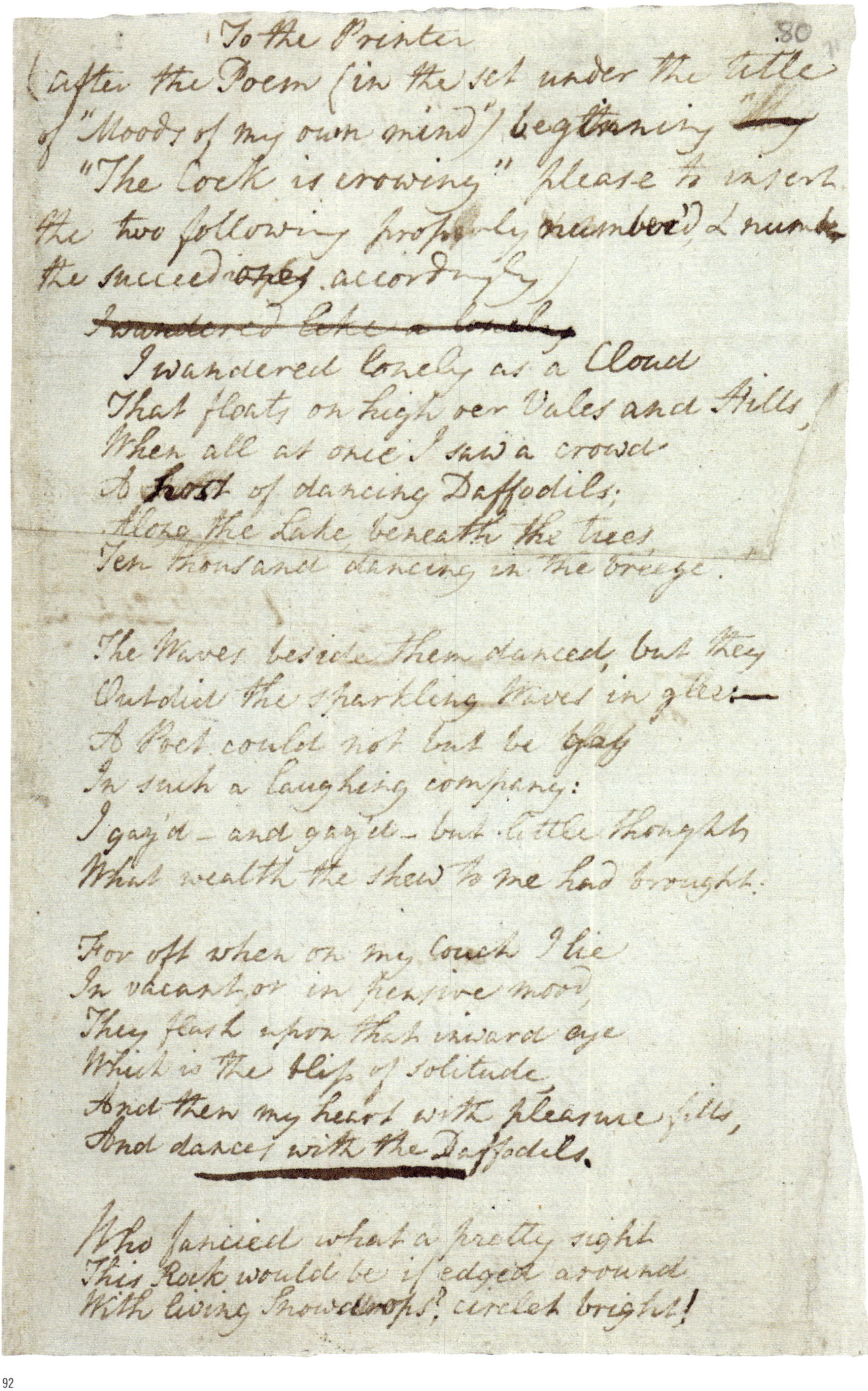
To the Printer
(after the Poem (in the set under the title of "Moods of my own mind") beginning "The Cock is crowing" please to insert the two following properly number'd & number the succeeding ones accordingly)
~~I wandered like a Cloud~~
I wandered lonely as a Cloud
That floats on high o'er Vales and Hills,
When all at once I saw a crowd
A host of dancing Daffodils;
Along the Lake beneath the trees
Ten thousand dancing in the breeze.
The Waves beside them danced, but they
Outdid the sparkling Waves in glee—
A Poet could not but be gay
In such a laughing company:
I gaz'd—and gaz'd—but little thought
What wealth the shew to me had brought.
For oft when on my couch I lie
In vacant or in pensive mood,
They flash upon that inward eye
Which is the bliss of solitude
And then my heart with pleasure fills,
And dances with the Daffodils.
Who fancied what a pretty sight
This Rock would be if edged around
With living Snowdrops? circlet bright!

FIG.48
'I wandered lonely as a cloud'
By William Wordsworth
1804–7
Iron gall ink and pencil on laid paper
British Library
Add MS 47864, f.80r

FIG.49
William Wordsworth
By Benjamin Robert Haydon
1842
Oil on canvas
National Portrait Gallery
NPG 1857

Surveying the Field of Waterloo. Haydon had sent Wordsworth a print after the painting and Wordsworth composed the sonnet, 'By art's bold privilege', while climbing Helvellyn, a mountain in the Lake District. Wordsworth wrote of the event:

> 'Haydon has just sent me a spirited Etching of his Portrait of the Duke of Wellington taken 20 years after the Battle of Waterloo, from the Life. He is represented upon the field; but no more of the Picture – take my Sonnet which it suggested the other day. The lines were composed while I was climbing Helvellyn … I was seven hours on my feet without being at all tired …'[8]

Wordsworth sat for Haydon in London in 1842, and the background of the portrait was painted from imagination. The artist inscribed on the back of the canvas, 'High is our calling FRIEND!'. The portrait of Wordsworth in turn inspired a sonnet by Elizabeth Barrett Browning (1806–1861; see p.249). **AA**

THOMAS HARDY

Novelist and poet Thomas Hardy (1840–1928) was born in Dorset and first worked as an architect, writing poetry in his spare time. Before he was able to turn his hand to writing professionally, he drafted 'The Poor Man and the Lady', a story about a young architect who marries a woman from an aristocratic background. Hardy shared an early draft with the publisher Alexander MacMillan (1818–1896) and was anxious to hear his thoughts. In a letter dated 10 September 1868 (fig.50), Hardy wrote: 'I almost feel that I don't care what happens to the book, so long as something happens.'[9] MacMillan felt that the criticism of the upper classes in Hardy's draft was an unsuitable subject for a first novel and 'The Poor Man and the Lady' was never published. However, Hardy used parts of it in other works, such as his serial *Desperate Remedies,* published anonymously in 1871. Hardy's name finally appeared in print between 1872 and 1873 when he published the novel *A Pair of Blue Eyes*, in serial. It was only then that he felt able to turn to writing full time.

Hardy's first acknowledged success was *Far from the Madding Crowd*, published first in serial and then as a novel by Smith, Elder & Co. in 1874. The story is set in fictional Wessex – a county closely based on the rural Dorset Hardy knew so well. He went on to publish *Tess of the d'Urbervilles* in 1891, which focuses on the rural lower class and follows the fortunes of the eponymous central character who is born into poverty. Hardy's powerful, tragic narrative reveals the vulnerable position of women of Tess's class.

Hardy initially had trouble finding a publisher that would accept *Tess* as some deemed the story immoral. After much revision and editing, *Tess* was first published in a serialised form in *The Graphic* in 1891. However, these edits were reversed when the story was printed as a novel that same year by the Edinburgh based firm R. & R. Clark. It was hugely popular and was adapted for the stage in 1897. There were requests to make it into a motion picture during Hardy's lifetime. Shown here is a page from the original manuscript for *Tess*, in Hardy's hand (fig.51). Although this was the finished version sent to the printers, Hardy made corrections to the text. Throughout the manuscript the names of the compositors, the people who set the letters or 'type' to be printed, can be seen, demonstrating the working life of a manuscript. The name 'L'[aw] rence' is written in the upper left-hand corner. Also visible on this page are the edits in blue ink for the serialised version. This part of the story is

FIG 50
Letter to Alexander MacMillan
From Thomas Hardy
10 September 1868
Black ink on paper
British Library
Add MS 54923, f.3r

FIG.51
Tess of the d'Urbervilles
By Thomas Hardy
1889–91
Black and blue ink and pencil on wove paper
British Library
Add MS 38182, f.83r

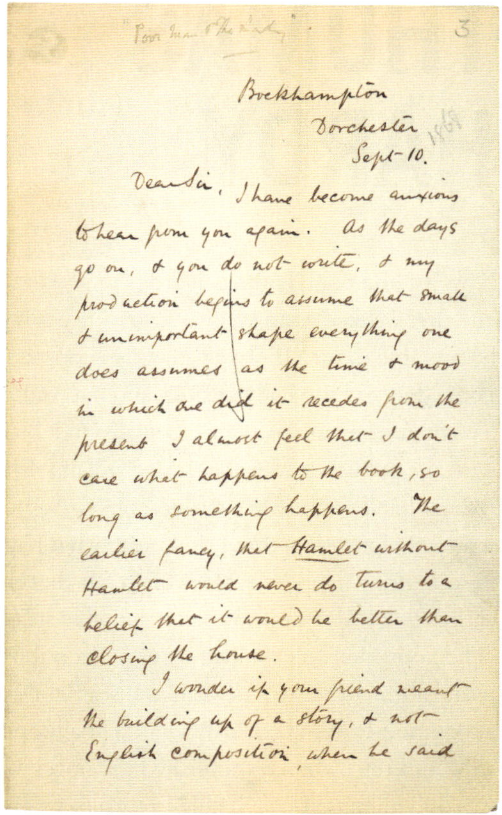

"Poor Man & the Lady" 3

Bockhampton
Dorchester
Sept 10.

Dear Sir. I have become anxious to hear from you again. As the days go on, & you do not write, & my production begins to assume that small & unimportant shape everything one does assumes as the time & mood in which one did it recedes from the present I almost feel that I don't care what happens to the book, so long as something happens. The earlier fancy, that Hamlet without Hamlet would never do turns to a belief that it would be better than closing the house.

I wonder if your friend meant the building up of a story, & not English composition, when he said

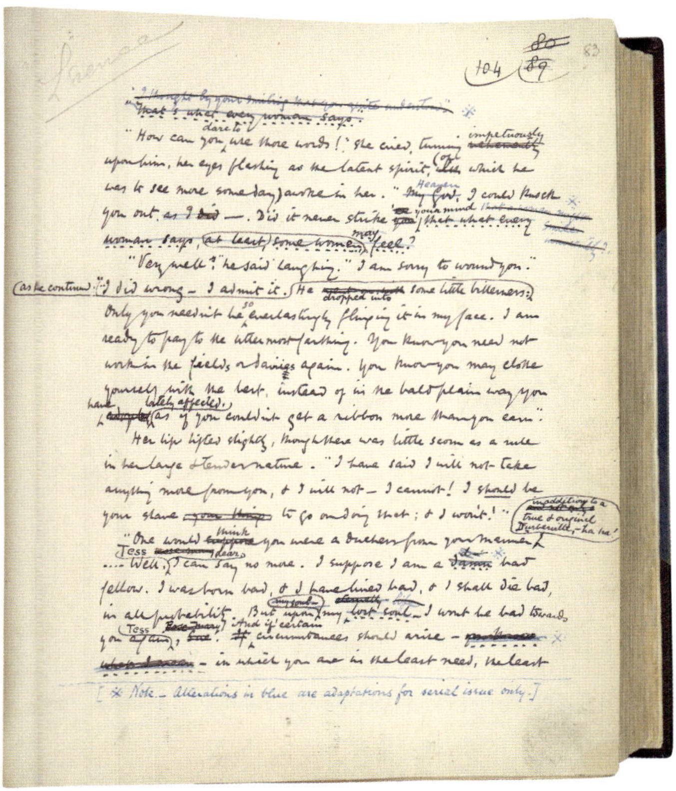

104 89

"How can you dare to use those words!" she cried, turning impetuously upon him, her eyes flashing as the latent spirit (of which he was to see more some day) awoke in her. "My God! I could knock you out as I did —. Did it never strike your mind that what every woman says, some women may feel?"

"Very well," he said laughing. "I am sorry to wound you. I did wrong — I admit it." (He dropped into some little bitterness:) "Only you needn't be so everlastingly flinging it in my face. I am ready to pay to the uttermost farthing. You know you need not work in the fields or dairies again. You know you may clothe yourself with the best, instead of in the bald plain way you have lately affected, as if you couldn't get a ribbon more than you earn."

Her lip lifted slightly, though there was little scorn as a rule in her large & tender nature. "I have said I will not take anything more from you, & I will not — I cannot! I should be your slave to go on doing that; & I won't!"

"One would think you were a duchess from your manner, in addition to a true & original D'Urberville,— ha ha! ... Well, Tess dear, I can say no more. I suppose I am a bad fellow. I was born bad, & I have lived bad, & I shall die bad, in all probability. But upon my lost soul — I won't be bad towards you again, Tess. And if certain circumstances should arise — in which you are in the least need, the least

[* Note – Alterations in blue are adaptations for serial issue only.]

FIG.52
Thomas Hardy
By Reginald Grenville Eves
1923
Oil on canvas
National Portrait Gallery
NPG 2498

from Chapter 9 and occurs shortly after d'Urberville has assaulted Tess. Thomas Hardy donated this manuscript to the British Museum Library in 1911. It was the first time the library had acquired a manuscript by a living author. With the success of *Tess*, Hardy was able to return to writing poetry, and he published his first collection, *Wessex Poems*, in 1898.

Hardy sat for a number of portraits, including one by Augustus John (1878–1961) and several by Reginal Grenville Eves (1876–1941). This portrait (fig.52), painted in 1923 by Eves, was one of a series painted over three years, based on a number of sittings. There are currently 12 portraits of Hardy by Eves that have been traced, and a further five whose whereabouts are unknown. Hardy's wife, Florence Dugdale (1879–1937), wrote on 14 September 1923 that her husband had reacted to a recent portrait saying, 'If I look like that, the sooner I am underground the better.'[10] While it is not clear to which portrait Hardy was referring, it is likely to be one of those by Eves. Yet critics seemed to provide a more favourable response; when the National Portrait Gallery first displayed the portrait a critic writing for the *Evening Standard* observed that it 'did stern justice to the lineaments of the greatest of our Stoics'.[11] **AA**

RUDYARD KIPLING

Rudyard Kipling (1865–1936) was a writer, journalist and poet, probably most famous for *The Jungle Book* (1894) and the *Just So Stories* (1902). Kipling was born in Mumbai (formerly Bombay), India, but attended school in England, before returning to India in 1882 to begin a career in journalism. From 1884 he began to publish other, non-journalistic material, which often described British life in India. Many of Kipling's works have imperial themes, and he actively promoted what he considered the merits of Britain's vast empire in the late nineteenth century. He was profoundly attached to India but believed that it benefited from what he saw as the benevolent, paternalistic rule of the British.

When he returned to England in 1889, Kipling was already a famous writer. In 1892 he married Caroline Balestier (1862–1939) and together they settled in Vermont, US. where their first child Josephine (Effie) was born in 1893, followed, three years later, by Elsie. They returned to England in 1896, and their third child, John, was born in 1897. In 1899 the Kiplings travelled to New York, where Rudyard and Effie fell dangerously ill with pneumonia. While Kipling battled for his life, Effie succumbed to the illness and died on 6 March 1899. News of Effie's death was published in the papers the very next day but was kept from Kipling while he recovered.

The *Just So Stories* had begun their life as tales Kipling told to Effie in their home in Rottingdean, East Sussex, England. The title came from Effie herself. Kipling said:

> '[I]n the evening there were stories meant to put Effie to sleep, and you were not allowed to alter those by one single little word. They had to be told just so; or Effie would wake up and put back the missing sentence. So at last they came to be like charms ...'[12]

Three of the tales were published in the children's journal *St. Nicholas* from 1897 onwards, the first in December of that year in time for Effie's fifth birthday. In 1902, three years after Effie's death, Kipling prepared the tales for publication as a single collected volume of 12 stories and 12 poems. In the book, many of the tales begin by addressing the reader as 'O My Best Beloved', reminding us they were stories once told to a dearly loved child.

FIG.53
Illustration for 'The Elephant's Child' in the *Just So Stories*
By Rudyard Kipling
1902
Pen, black ink and wash on paper
British Library
Add MS 59840, f.33r

FIG.54
Corrected proof for 'The Elephant's Child' in the *Just So Stories*
By Rudyard Kipling
1902
Printed proof with ink and pencil
British Library
Add MS 55863, f.32r

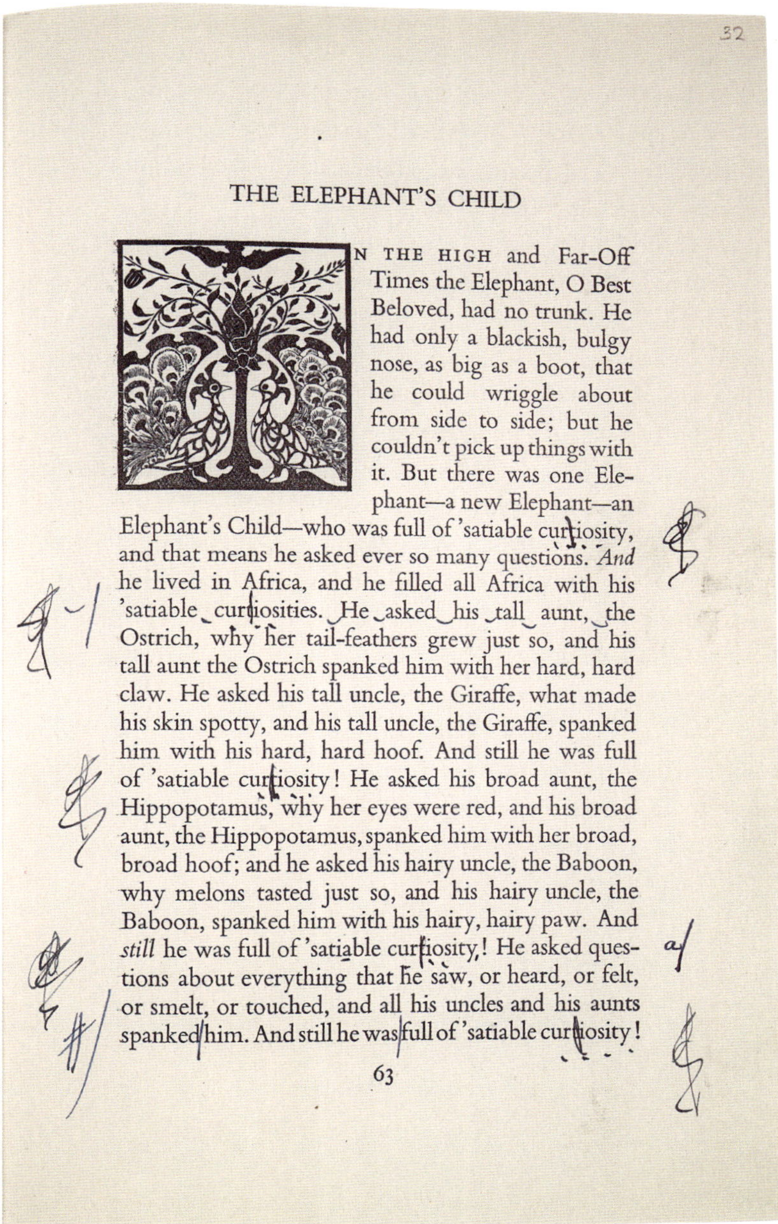

THE ELEPHANT'S CHILD

IN THE HIGH and Far-Off Times the Elephant, O Best Beloved, had no trunk. He had only a blackish, bulgy nose, as big as a boot, that he could wriggle about from side to side; but he couldn't pick up things with it. But there was one Elephant—a new Elephant—an Elephant's Child—who was full of 'satiable curtiosity, and that means he asked ever so many questions. *And* he lived in Africa, and he filled all Africa with his 'satiable curtiosities. He asked his tall aunt, the Ostrich, why her tail-feathers grew just so, and his tall aunt the Ostrich spanked him with her hard, hard claw. He asked his tall uncle, the Giraffe, what made his skin spotty, and his tall uncle, the Giraffe, spanked him with his hard, hard hoof. And still he was full of 'satiable curtiosity! He asked his broad aunt, the Hippopotamus, why her eyes were red, and his broad aunt, the Hippopotamus, spanked him with her broad, broad hoof; and he asked his hairy uncle, the Baboon, why melons tasted just so, and his hairy uncle, the Baboon, spanked him with his hairy, hairy paw. And *still* he was full of 'satiable curtiosity! He asked questions about everything that he saw, or heard, or felt, or smelt, or touched, and all his uncles and his aunts spanked him. And still he was full of 'satiable curtiosity!

63

These tales came to be read and admired around the world. The *Just So Stories* are so-called 'origin stories' explaining how animals came to appear as they do, such as how the camel acquired its hump or the leopard its spots. Kipling illustrated the stories himself, including the pictures of the animals as well as the smaller, decorative images. Shown here is his original pen and wash illustration for 'The Elephant's Child' (fig.53). Once Kipling had submitted his manuscript and illustrations to be printed, he was sent proofs to check and amend. The proofs for 'The Elephant's Child' along with his corrections (fig.54) show how Kipling edited the text, including correcting spelling mistakes and formatting spaces.

In 1899 Kipling sat for the artist Sir Philip Burne-Jones (1861–1926), who was his cousin (fig.55). Son of the famous Pre-Raphaelite artist, Sir Edward Burne-Jones (1833–1898), Philip exhibited works at the Royal Academy, including a portrait of his father, now held at the National Portrait Gallery. Writer and painter had collaborated previously in 1897 when Kipling wrote a poem called 'The Vampire' to accompany a painting by Philip Burne-Jones, exhibited at the New Gallery, London. This portrait of Kipling was made just a few months after Effie had died and after the Kiplings had returned to their home in Rottingdean, the same house where Kipling had conceived the *Just So Stories* and read them to his daughter. The author is depicted sitting at his desk in the study, surrounded by all the ephemera of writing, gazing out of an unseen window. **AA**

FIG.55
Rudyard Kipling
By Sir Philip Burne-Jones
1899
Oil on canvas
National Portrait Gallery
NPG 1863

HAROLD PINTER

From a working-class, Jewish background in east London, and without the benefit of a university education, Harold Pinter (1930–2008) became one of the most significant playwrights of the twentieth century. Inspired by an English teacher at his secondary school, he began writing as a teenager but decided on a career as an actor. After brief spells at the Royal Academy of Dramatic Art (RADA) and then at the Central School of Speech and Drama, he toured in provincial theatres for most of the 1950s, while also writing poetry and plays. His breakthrough as a writer came with *The Room*, written in 1957 for the drama department at Bristol University at the invitation of a school friend. This was seen by the theatre producer Michael Codron (b.1930), who agreed to produce Pinter's next play, *The Birthday Party* (first performed 1957). Although reviews were mixed, Pinter continued writing for the stage, television and the theatre, gradually becoming admired particularly for his distinctive, often repetitive, poetic use of everyday language, and his explorations of power in relationships.

The Homecoming (1964) was written in the middle of a very productive period for Pinter in the 1960s, which started with the great success of *The Caretaker* in 1960. Pinter went on to write television plays, including *The Lover* (1963); film screenplays, including *The Servant* (1963), starring Dirk Bogarde (1921–1999) and other works for the theatre. *The Homecoming* was first performed in 1965 by the Royal Shakespeare Company at the Aldwych Theatre in London and was a great success. Many other dramas and screenplays followed and in 2005 Pinter was awarded the Nobel Prize in Literature. In this context he was described as one 'who in his plays uncovers the precipice under everyday prattle and forces entry into oppression's closed rooms'.[13] In his acceptance speech he explained his writing process, using *The Homecoming* as an example, stating that 'most of the plays are engendered by a line, a word, or an image'.[14] In the case of *The Homecoming* this was the line: 'What have you done with the scissors?', the opening words of the play. He explained that his understanding of the characters only came gradually, as the dialogue formed itself in his mind. Initially labelled as 'A' and 'B', the characters had progressed in this draft (fig.56) to be identified as 'Father' and 'Son 3'.

The artist Justin Mortimer (b.1970) had won the BP Portrait Award at the National Portrait Gallery in 1991 at the age of 21, and part of his prize was the commission to paint a portrait of Harold Pinter, by then a

FIG.56
Draft playscript for *The Homecoming*
By Harold Pinter
Before 1965
Typewritten and black and red pen on paper
British Library
Add MS 88880/1/21, f.51r

51.

I.

Evening

Son 3 jotting notes on sports page. Enter Father.

F. - What have you done with the scissors ?
p.
I want the scissors.
3. - What for ?
F. - What have you done with them ?
3. - What do you want the scissors for ?
F. - I want to cut something out. I want to cut something out the bleeding paper. You bastard.
p
3. -I'm reading the paper.
F. - Not that paper.
F. sits.
F - I think I'll have a fag.
p.
Theres an advertisement in the paper about flannel vests. Cut price. Navy wear. I could do with a few of them. Give me a fag.
p.
Give me a cigarette !
3. - Why should I give you a cigarette ? I've got enough to do.
F. - Look what I'm landed with. A pair of bastards. Well, you can drown in your own blood, anyway. You can drown in your own blood. As far as I go. And the other one. All these tough boys. You and your bleeding bastard brother. Louzy stinking prostitutes.
p.
I'm getting old, my word of honour. You think I wasnt a tearaway ? I could have taken care of you, twice over. I'm still strong. You ask your uncle Sam what I was. I was a villian. Atthe same time I always had a kind heart. I used to knock about with a man called Berkowitz. I called him Berki. Come on Berki, where you going tonight ? Coming up West tonight ? Go round the back doubles, do a few snooker halls, run in a couple of tarts. I still got the scars. We used to walk back to back, Berki and me. The terrible twins they used to call us. He was six feet tall. But even his family called him Berki. He had a big family, mind you. But even his old man called him Berki. Of course the old man was a Berkowitz too. They were all Berkotitzs, it goes without saying. But he was the only one they called Berki. His other brothers we called Berks. Anyway, he's dead. One of his sisters died in prison. The other one died in hospital. We went to see her. She was dead whenx by the time we got there.
p.
Mind you, your mother was a good woman, even though she was too honest. Even though she made me sick she wasnt a bad bitch. Not that you two care a fart about your mother. Where did you put those bastard scissors ?
3. - Why dont you shut up ?

well-established, celebrated playwright (fig.57). Years later, Mortimer said: 'Everyone warned me he was a gruff old bastard, but we used to sit round sipping champagne and laughing. I was only 21 at the time, a nipper. He looked after me.'[15] Pinter commented on his relaxed feeling sitting for the portrait, and the difficulty of interpreting his own expression, which he thought was probably 'pensive'. He observed: 'When I saw the painting of my head I said to him, "I sometimes smile, you know". "You can't have everything", he said.'[16] Pinter also commented that his study was full of piles of papers and books like those shown in the background of the portrait. **CM**

FIG.57
Harold Pinter
By Justin Mortimer
1992
Oil on canvas
National Portrait Gallery
NPG 6185

DEREK WALCOTT

Poet and playwright Derek Walcott (1930–2017) was born on the island of St Lucia, at that time a British colony in the Caribbean. Walcott's father, a talented painter whose works hung in the family home, died when Derek was just one year old, and his absence was felt keenly. Walcott's mother, a schoolteacher and amateur actress, often recited poems and dramatic speeches, including those from the character of Portia in *The Merchant of Venice*. by William Shakespeare (1564–1616; see p.180) Walcott said he grew up with the desire to write something good enough for his mother to want to recite and to follow in his father's footsteps. Although he had been taught to paint by a friend of his father, Walcott settled on writing as a career. Publishing his first piece in a newspaper when he was just 14, he went on to borrow $200 from his mother in order to publish his first book of poems five years later. A subsequent collection, *In a Green Night: Poems 1948–1960*, celebrates the Caribbean and at the same time considers the impact of colonialism. His most famous work, the epic poem *Omeros* (1990), which follows the lives of fishermen on St Lucia, partially echoes the *Iliad* by the ancient Greek poet, Homer. Walcott enjoyed a distinguished career, winning the Nobel Prize in Literature in 1992 'for a poetic *oeuvre* of great luminosity, sustained by a historical vision, the outcome of a multicultural commitment'.[17]

Much of Walcott's written work references artworks and he described writing as a similar craft to painting, making the image or scene he was describing as visual as possible. His poem 'Lampfall' was written in April 1964 and uses painterly imagery throughout. Three drafts for the poem, which was originally titled 'At Lampfall', are each written in a different coloured ink. His first draft is in green biro, the second – the first page of which is shown here (fig.58) – is in blue biro and the final draft is in thick, black ink (fig.59). He made significant changes to the format and content of the poem. Always working with what he called the 'moth-lamp metaphor', Walcott started the poem with the words 'No light, we drew nearer at lampfall' in the first draft.[18] As he drafted and redrafted, the line changed from 'Draw nearest at lampfall', to 'Nearer by Lampfall', 'Closest at lampfall' and finally to 'Drawn closest by lampfall'. In his notes for the poem, he uses the painting by Joseph Wright of Derby (1734–1797), *A Philosopher Giving*

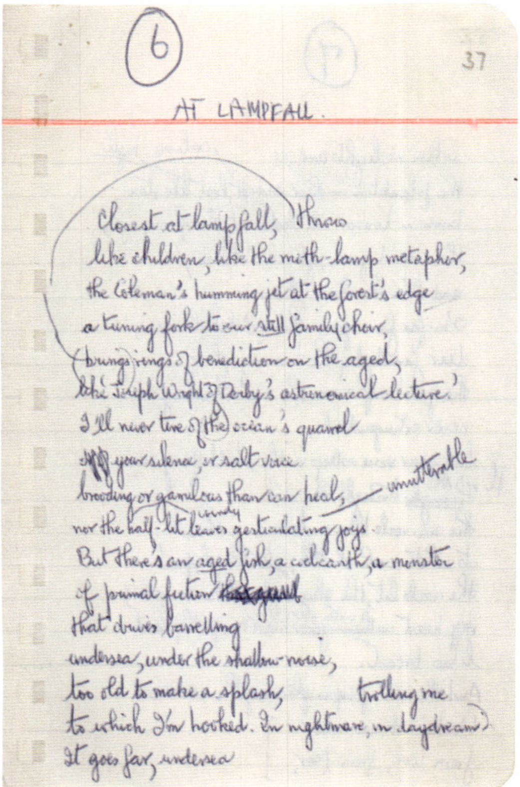

6

37

AT LAMPFALL.

Closest at lampfall, I know
like children, like the moth-lamp metaphor,
the Coleman's humming jet at the forest's edge
a tuning fork to our still family choir,
brings rings of benediction on the aged,
like Joseph Wright of Derby's astronomical lecture.
I'll never tire of the ocean's quarrel
your silence, or salt voice
brooding or garrulous than can heal, unutterable
nor the half-lit windy leaves gesticulating joys
But there's an aged fish, a coelacanth, a monster
of primal fiction
that drives barrelling
undersea, under the shallow noise,
too old to make a splash, trolling me
to which I'm hooked. In nightmare, in daydream
It goes far, undersea

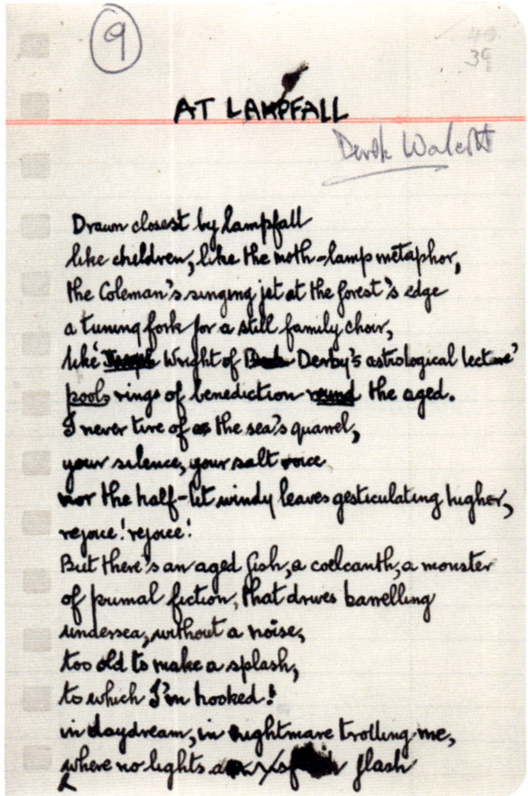

9

39

AT LAMPFALL

Derek Walcott

Drawn closest by lampfall
like children, like the moth-lamp metaphor,
the Coleman's singing jet at the forest's edge
a tuning fork for a still family choir,
like Joseph Wright of Derby's astrological lecture'
pools rings of benediction round the aged.
I never tire of the sea's quarrel,
your silence, your salt voice
nor the half-lit windy leaves gesticulating higher,
rejoice! rejoice!
But there's an aged fish, a coelacanth, a monster
of primal fiction, that drives barrelling
undersea, without a noise,
too old to make a splash,
to which I'm hooked!
in daydream, in nightmare trolling me,
where no lights [illegible] flash

That Lecture on the Orrery in Which a Lamp Is Put in Place of the Sun (1764–6), to conjure the sense of chiaroscuro, or light and dark.

This 2003 portrait by Horace Ové (1939–2023) shows Walcott at the age of 73 (fig.60). Ové was a Trinidad-born London filmmaker and photographer who documented many of the artistic and political figures from the Black diasporic community in London. His portrait of the writers Sam Selvon (1923–1994), Andrew Salkey (1928–1995) and John La Rose (1927–2006) can be seen on page 165. This image shows Walcott looking away from the camera against a natural backdrop. The simplicity of the image focuses attention on Walcott's gaze and challenges the viewer to imagine what he is thinking. **AA**

FIGS 58 & 59
Drafts for 'Lampfall'
By Derek Walcott
Blue ballpoint pen on lined notepaper; black ink and blue ballpoint pen on lined notepaper
*c.*1963–4
British Library
Add MS 52594, f.37r; f.39r

FIG. 60
Derek Walcott
By Sir Horace Ové
2003
Giclée print
National Portrait Gallery
NPG x126732

SYLVIA PLATH

Sylvia Plath (1932–1963) was an exceptional poet and novelist of the later twentieth century. Her work, which is largely autobiographical, explores with sharp and sometimes searing honesty her own mental and emotional state, her relationships with her parents and her husband, the poet Ted Hughes (1930–1998; see p.62), and her shifting sense of self. During her lifetime she struggled to forge a career, contending with serious mental illness, writers' block and juggling her roles and her perception of herself as wife, mother and writer. She was admired by other writers but not well-known outside literary circles. Her early death by suicide and subsequent revelations about her turbulent relationship with Hughes meant that she became better known posthumously, but interest in her biography sometimes overshadowed that shown in her work.

Born and brought up in Massachusetts, US, Plath was precocious and ambitious, publishing her first poem when she was eight years old, and numerous poems and short stories in magazines during her early college years. A series of prizes for her writing provided stepping stones towards a literary career. She was awarded a Fulbright Scholarship in 1955, which brought her to England to study at the University of Cambridge. She met Ted Hughes in 1956 at a party to launch a literary magazine. The two were instantly and passionately attracted to one another and were married four months later. The following year, Plath was appointed to a teaching post at Smith College in Massachusetts, where she had previously studied. She and Hughes emigrated to the US, but the depression from which Plath had suffered as a student returned during this time. She and Hughes moved to an apartment in Beacon Hill, Boston, where this photograph by Rollie McKenna (1918–2003; fig.61) was taken. Plath undertook psychoanalysis, and by the spring of 1959, her health had improved considerably. McKenna published this photograph as part of a series of photographs of modern poets in 1963, and it became the Plath estate's preferred professional photograph of her.

At the end of 1959, Plath and Hughes moved back to England where she published her first volume of poetry, *The Colossus*, in 1960. It was well received but again she struggled to write, contending with writer's block, depression and new motherhood. The poem 'Insomniac' is a powerful evocation of her experience of the recurring insomnia she suffered at this time. She submitted it in 1961 to the annual poetry competition held by

FIG.61
Sylvia Plath
By Rollie McKenna
1959
Gelatin silver print
National Portrait Gallery
NPG P1679

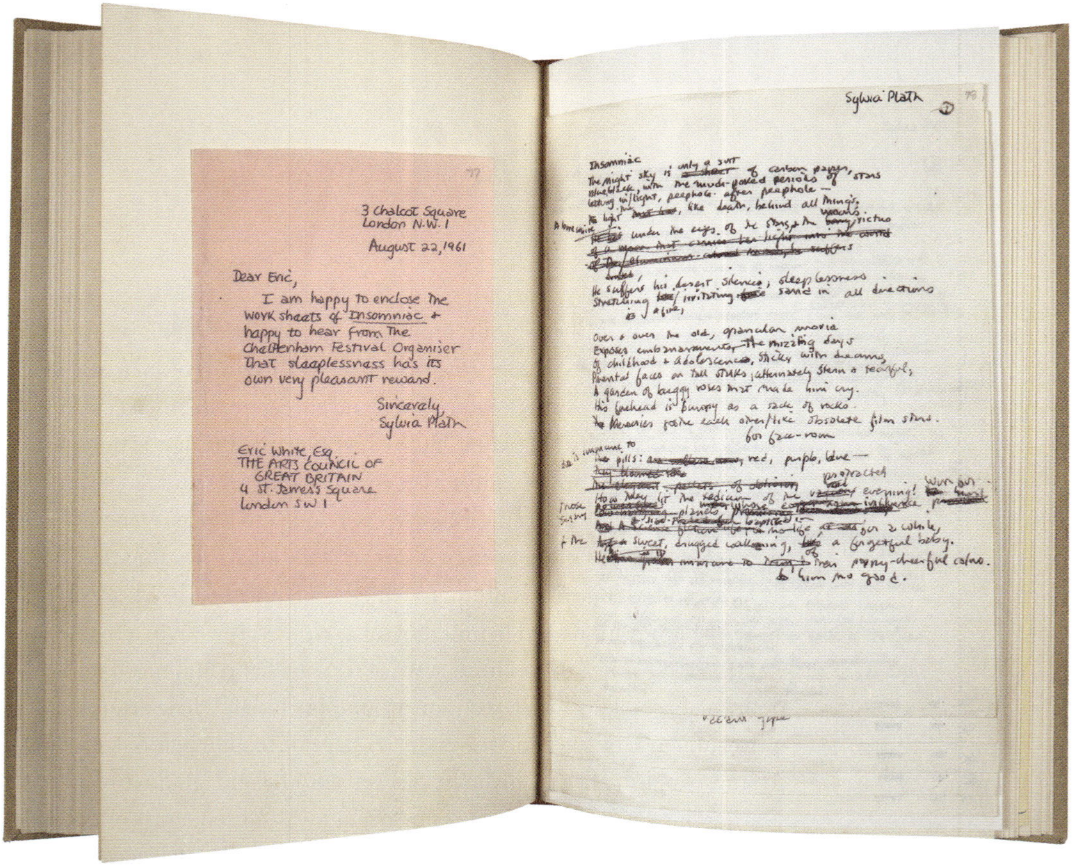

the Cheltenham Literary Festival and it won the first prize of £75. She also sent an early draft (fig.62) to the Arts Council as part of a scheme to preserve the manuscripts of contemporary poets; these were subsequently donated to the British Library. At this time, she also began *The Bell Jar* (1963), her semi-autobiographical novel.

Plath's later years were plagued by mental illness and problems in her relationship with Hughes. They separated in 1962, and a period of frenetic writing was ended by her suicide in February 1963. Hughes oversaw the publication of her volume *Ariel* in 1965, further volumes, *Crossing the Water* and *Winter Trees* in 1971 and her *Collected Poems* in 1981. The latter won the Pulitzer Prize and established Plath's place among the most important twentieth-century poets. Hughes said of her writing:

> 'This language, this unique and radiant substance, is the product of an alchemy on the noblest scale. Her elements were extreme: a violent, almost demonic spirit in her, opposed a tenderness and capacity to suffer and love things infinitely, which was just as great and far more in evidence. Her stormy, luminous senses assaulted a downright practical intelligence that could probably have dealt with anything.'[19] **CM**

FIG.62
Draft for 'Insomniac' with a submission letter for the poem to The Arts Council of Great Britain
By Sylvia Plath
1961
Black ink on pink paper; black ink on white paper
British Library
Add MS 52617, ff.77v–78r

WOLE SOYINKA

Wole Soyinka (b.1934) is a poet, novelist, playwright and essayist. His work often tackles themes of tyranny and oppression, and his writing has questioned the Nigerian government, and Britain's colonial rule in Africa. He has been exiled, imprisoned and threatened with execution. Soyinka was born in Abeokuta, south-west Nigeria during the period of colonial rule by Britain. His father was a headmaster and Anglican minister, and his mother was a shopkeeper and activist for women's rights. Soyinka was influenced by a mix of traditions, including tales and legends from the Yorùbá culture to which his family belonged, as well as Christian sermons and hymns. Soyinka said he 'grew up in a really exciting atmosphere of political activism on one hand and more staid political discussions which went on around my father'.[20] He attended Government College and University College in Ibadan before travelling to study English at the University of Leeds in England, graduating in 1957. During this time, he wrote several plays and was subsequently employed by the Royal Court Theatre, London, where his play *The Invention* was first produced in 1957, prophetically depicting the cracks of the apartheid system in the future setting of Johannesburg in 1976. Returning to Nigeria in 1960, Soyinka went on to study African drama and teach at various universities, as well as writing plays and poetry.

In 1967, Soyinka's volume *Idanre and Other Poems* was published. This volume contains the eponymous poem, 'Idanre', a draft of which can be seen here (fig.64). The poem was written specifically for the Commonwealth Arts Festival of 1965, and its narrative is inspired by creation stories associated with the Yorùbá deity Ògún, the god of war, iron, the road and the hunt. Soyinka said that the poem originated from two separate events that he merged: a walk through the hills in the city of Idanre, and a thunderstorm in Molete, in the city of Ibadan.

In 1965 Soyinka was arrested for speaking out against Nigeria's dictatorship and again in 1967 for protesting against the civil war brought on by Biafra's attempted secession. Placed in solitary confinement for 22 months of his jail sentence (with imprisonment totalling 29 months), he spent much of his time composing poems on scraps of paper. Following his release in 1969, he became head of the department of Theatre Arts at the University of Ibadan, a post that he held until 1994.

FIG.63
Wole Soyinka
By Maggie Murray
1986
Gelatin silver print
National Portrait Gallery
NPG x202638

This photograph by Maggie Murray (b.1942) was taken in 1986 for Format Photographers Agency, London, when Soyinka was 52 (fig.63). Founded by Murray and Val Wilmer (b.1941), the British women-only agency offered a platform for female photographers and sought to document the world from a different viewpoint, focusing particularly on important political events and people who were not always featured in mainstream media (see also p.161). This photograph shows Soyinka mid-speech, fingers outstretched. Behind him, the bookshelf shows works including *A Dance of Masks* (1978) by Jonathan A. Peters (b.1943), which looks at African self-identity in mask imagery in the plays of Soyinka, the poetry of Léopold Sédar Senghor (1906–2001) and the fiction of Chinua Achebe (1930–2013). Murray said of the session: 'As well as the interview we had quite an animated discussion especially as he knew Val Wilmer; and because I had worked as a photographer in a number of African

FIG. 64
'Idanre'
By Wole Soyinka
1965
Typewritten and black ink, blue pencil and graphite on paper
British Library
Add MS 53785, f.2r

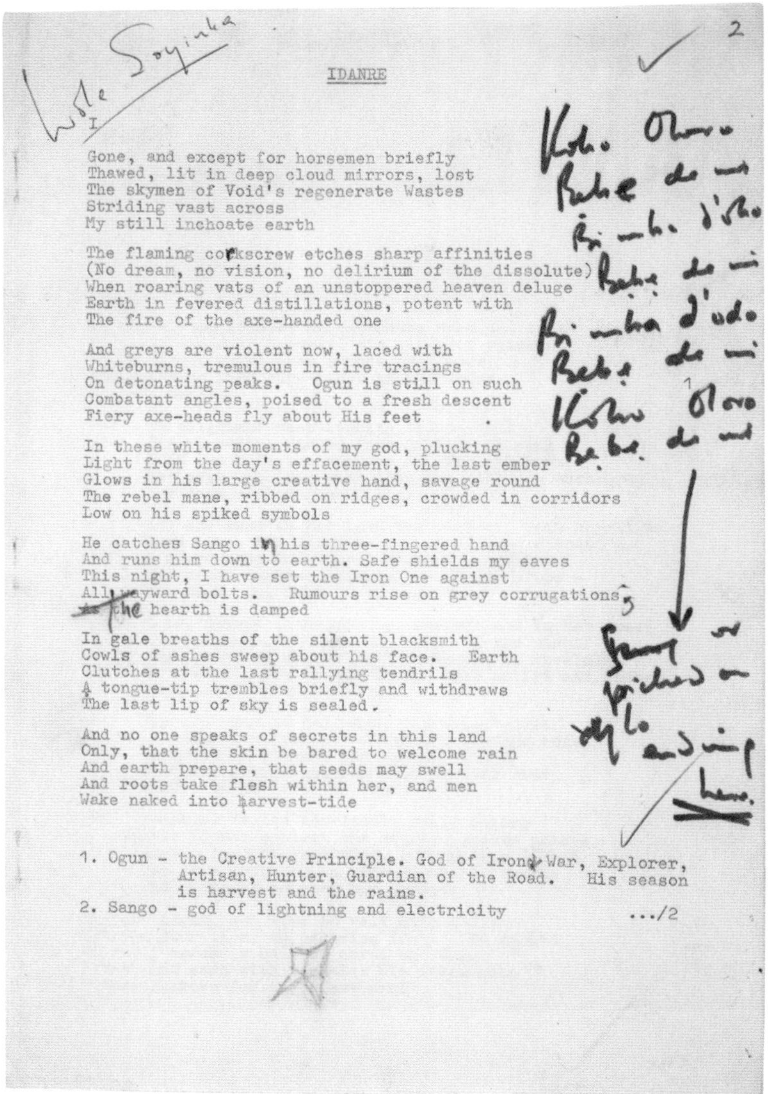

Wole Soyinka

2

IDANRE

I

Gone, and except for horsemen briefly
Thawed, lit in deep cloud mirrors, lost
The skymen of Void's regenerate Wastes
Striding vast across
My still inchoate earth

The flaming corkscrew etches sharp affinities
(No dream, no vision, no delirium of the dissolute)
When roaring vats of an unstoppered heaven deluge
Earth in fevered distillations, potent with
The fire of the axe-handed one

And greys are violent now, laced with
Whiteburns, tremulous in fire tracings
On detonating peaks. Ogun is still on such
Combatant angles, poised to a fresh descent
Fiery axe-heads fly about His feet

In these white moments of my god, plucking
Light from the day's effacement, the last ember
Glows in his large creative hand, savage round
The rebel mane, ribbed on ridges, crowded in corridors
Low on his spiked symbols

He catches Sango in his three-fingered hand
And runs him down to earth. Safe shields my eaves
This night, I have set the Iron One against
All wayward bolts. Rumours rise on grey corrugations
The hearth is damped

In gale breaths of the silent blacksmith
Cowls of ashes sweep about his face. Earth
Clutches at the last rallying tendrils
A tongue-tip trembles briefly and withdraws
The last lip of sky is sealed.

And no one speaks of secrets in this land
Only, that the skin be bared to welcome rain
And earth prepare, that seeds may swell
And roots take flesh within her, and men
Wake naked into harvest-tide

1. Ogun - the Creative Principle. God of Iron, War, Explorer, Artisan, Hunter, Guardian of the Road. His season is harvest and the rains.
2. Sango - god of lightning and electricity ..../2

nations.'[21] The photograph was published in the *New Statesman* as well as in *South Magazine*, a pioneering monthly publication that highlighted issues of international relations, development and politics in the 1980s.

Soyinka was forced to flee Nigeria in 1994 when the military head of state confiscated his passport and sentenced him to death. After he published *The Open Sore of a Continent: A Personal Narrative of the Nigerian Crisis* in 1996 he was charged with treason. It was not until civil rule was restored that Soyinka was able to return to Nigeria in 1999. Despite imprisonment, exile and threats, he is considered Nigeria's foremost man of letters, and he has received significant awards in recognition of his work. Winning the Nobel Prize in Literature in 1986, Soyinka was the first sub-Saharan African to be honoured in that category. **AA**

HILARY MANTEL

Dame Hilary Mantel (1952–2022) was a novelist whose work accorded her numerous awards and honours. Born in Derbyshire to a Catholic family, Mantel gained a degree in the theory of law from Sheffield University. In 1975 Mantel began drafting the novel *A Place of Greater Safety*, a process that was to take four years. The book is set in France during the Revolution of 1789–99, a subject that had interested Mantel since school. Speaking to the British Library over a series of sessions between 2008 and 2009, she explained her first steps in becoming a writer and producing her first novel:

> 'I picked up one or two biographies ... I began to look for more and more books and I began to take notes and one day stopped myself and said "what actually are you doing?" and the answer was "you are writing a novel" ... Nothing like the kind of thing people are supposed to produce as their first novel. And I think then at about the age of 22 I channelled all of my ambition into my book ... I suppose it seemed like the one certainty in life. I would finish it. It would be published. The path to publication was far more tortuous than I could have imagined. But, of course, the day that it was published I was able to shake hands with my 22-year-old self.'[22]

Mantel completed the draft for *A Place of Greater Safety* in 1979, but it was rejected by publishers who assumed it would be an historical romance (fig.66). The novel was not published until 1992, by which time Mantel had already published *Every Day Is Mother's Day* in 1985, *Vacant Possession* in 1986 and *Eight Months on Ghazzah Street* in 1988. *A Place of Greater Safety* went on to win the Sunday Express Book of the Year Award. Other awards followed, with Mantel's highly acclaimed trilogy about the life of Thomas Cromwell, Earl of Essex (*c*.1485–1540). Both *Wolf Hall* (2009), the first novel in the trilogy, and *Bring Up the Bodies* (2012), the second novel, won the Booker Prize. The third novel, *The Mirror and the Light* was published in 2020 and nominated for the Booker Prize. Mantel's writing is powerful in its evocation of characters and events. To be immersed in the worlds she creates is a sensory experience, filled with sound, smell and intricately described objects.

FIG.65
Hilary Mantel
By Nick Lord
2013
Oil paint, acrylic, and alkyd resin on canvas
British Library
BLWA 141

In 2013, just one year before *Bring up the Bodies* was published, Mantel sat for the portrait artist Nick Lord (b.1989) as part of the televised Sky Portrait Artist of the Year competition (fig.65). Lord was a graduate of Kingston University, London, and just 25 years old at the time he took part in the ten-month competition.

FIG.66
A Place of Greater Safety
By Hilary Mantel
(1st edition, Viking, London, 1992)
British Library

Following Mantel's sitting for him he said:

> 'It has been an absolute privilege to paint Hilary, and important to me that I captured the essence of her in this portrait – her kindness, success and intelligence ... When I first met her and asked how she wanted to be portrayed, she said she hadn't really thought about it. But, when I showed her a few of the photos I had taken of her, she was clear how she wanted to be captured, which really helped me.'[23]

Sky TV donated the portrait to the British Library and at the time, it was the only portrait of a living writer to hang on the walls of the St Pancras Building in London. Mantel passed away in 2022. The posthumous book *A Memoir of My Former Self* was published a year later and includes some of her essays, lectures and unfinished works. **AA**

KAZUO ISHIGURO

The novelist Sir Kazuo Ishiguro (b.1954) was born in Nagasaki, Japan, and moved with his parents to the UK at the age of five. His childhood outside the home was very British, but at home he led a Japanese life, with parents who regarded themselves as visitors rather than immigrants, and who planned for many years to return to Japan. The perspective that this gave Ishiguro on British life has been important to his writing and he has described creating an image of Japan from memory and imagination, which particularly influenced his early novels.

Having initially wanted to be a singer-songwriter, in 1979 Ishiguro was awarded a postgraduate place on the creative writing course at the University of East Anglia, founded and run by the author Malcolm Bradbury (1932–2000). In preparation for the course, he wrote two short stories the preceding summer; he wrote a third, 'Getting Poisoned', in the autumn of 1979. Bradbury encouraged him to submit 'Getting Poisoned' to the literary magazine *Granta*, which was undergoing a relaunch. Ishiguro sent the story to the editor Bill Buford (b.1954) in late 1979. Buford evidently didn't reply, as in the follow-up letter sent by Ishiguro in 1980 (fig.67), the author queries if the story got lost in the post. In fact, by this time, Ishiguro had also submitted the three stories, including 'Getting Poisoned', to Robert McCrum (b.1953) at Faber & Faber, and here he found more success. McCrum published all three stories in 1981, along with a selection by other young authors, in *Introduction 7: Stories by New Writers*. This volume was quickly followed by the publication of Ishiguro's first novel, *A Pale View of Hills*, in 1982, which launched his career as a novelist. Further novels followed, including his most well-known work, *The Remains of the Day* (1989), which won the Booker Prize, and was adapted into a film of the same name in 1993.

The Welsh artist Peter Edwards (b.1955) won the National Portrait Gallery's BP Portrait Award in 1994; part of his prize was a commission to paint Ishiguro (fig.68). Edwards read the author's novels and created a portrait that consciously responded to Ishiguro as a writer. The artist later said:

> 'I almost felt like I was approaching the portrait like a novel. I was sort of putting it together and almost trying to imitate the way he writes his meticulous novels. And the one thing you will

Dear Mr Buford,

Last November I sent you a short story, 'Getting Poisoned', in hopes that it may be of interest for your GRANTA magazine. I would like to say that I am just as keen as in November to be considered for GRANTA, but would be most grateful if you would let me know your decision in the near future. It may well be the case that the story got lost in the post, in which case I would be very grateful if you could contact me and tell me you have never heard of such a story, nor its author. Should it be the case however that you are interested in the story, would you please contact Robert McCrum at Faber and Faber (01 278 6881) before finalizing plans - although there should be no great problems in this quarter. Best wishes for your magazine. Many thanks.

Yours sincerely,

Kazuo Ishiguro

FIG.67
Letter to Bill Buford at *Granta* magazine
From Kazuo Ishiguro
1980
Typewritten and black ink on pale blue notepaper
British Library
Granta Archive Deposit 11183 Box 118 Lin11

FIG.68
Kazuo Ishiguro
By Peter Edwards
1995
Oil on canvas
National Portrait Gallery
NPG 6332

get from standing in front of this painting, much more so than just seeing it in reproduction, is all the many layers and the way the texture is being built up, and none of this was just purely going through some well-trodden technique, this was very much unique to this portrait.'[24]

Ishiguro recognised this correspondence between the painting technique and his books, saying in 1999 that:

> '[The portrait is] relatively small and remarkably knobbly. If you lay it down, it's like a three-dimensional landscape. Close up, it looks complex and strange. It's only when you step back that it becomes a very elegant, simple portrait. This is deliberate, I think. I put in a lot of complicated things in my books, yet I want the end result to seem simple. Peter did read my books very thoroughly.'[25]

Ishiguro has continued to produce novels, including *Never Let Me Go* (2005), as well as screenplays and song lyrics. Recurrent themes in his work include time, memory and regret; his language is characterised by precision and restraint. He has been awarded national honours in the UK, France and Japan, and in 2017 he was awarded the Nobel Prize in Literature, being recognised as someone 'who, in novels of great emotional force, has uncovered the abyss beneath our illusory sense of connection with the world'.[26] Further public recognition in the UK came with his appointment as a Knight Bachelor for services to literature in 2018. **CM**

ZADIE SMITH

Born in Willesden, London, to a Jamaican mother and white British father, Zadie Smith (b.1975) became a phenomenon in the British literary world shortly after she graduated from the University of Cambridge. While at university, Smith had shown some of her writing to the mother of a college friend, the writer Lisa Appignanesi (b.1946); in this letter of 1995 to Appignanesi (fig.69), Smith refers to the older writer's request to send her 'old stuff', but points out 'as I am a tender 19, "old" stuff amounts to adolescent rambling that I am now pretty ashamed of'. She goes on to say: 'It's just that I'd rather send no stuff if it 'aint good stuff. Sorry for not coming up with enough stuff.'[27] Smith did, however, send two stories with the letter, including 'The Newspaper Man'. Appignanesi evidently liked what she saw, and Smith's story 'The Newspaper Man' was published in an anthology of student writing, *The May Anthology of Oxford and Cambridge Short Stories 1996*, guest edited by the writer Penelope Fitzgerald (1916–2000). A second story, 'Mrs Begum's Son and the Private Tutor' was in the following year's *May Anthology* and led to an approach by a publisher. Appignanesi advised Smith to get an agent.

Smith began her first novel, *White Teeth*, while she was still an undergraduate. On the basis of about 80 pages, it became the subject of a publishers' bidding war, which was won by Hamish Hamilton, part of Penguin Books. The book was published in 2000, winning numerous awards including the Whitbread Book Award for the best first novel. Before *White Teeth* was published, Smith had come to public notice as the bidding war and rumours of the size of the advance she had been paid captured media attention. There was a fascination not just with her talent but with her youth, her beauty, her mixed ethnic background and working-class origins. A demand for photographs followed and this portrait (fig.70) was one of several professional images taken of her at the time. Roderick Field (b.1965) is a London-born photographer who has taken many photographs of authors for Penguin Books; his portrait of Zadie Smith was one of the first of these. A variant of this photograph was used inside the first edition of *White Teeth.*

Smith has gone on to write five more critically acclaimed novels, as well as a play, short stories and non-fiction, including critical essays and articles. From 2010 to 2020 she taught on the creative writing course

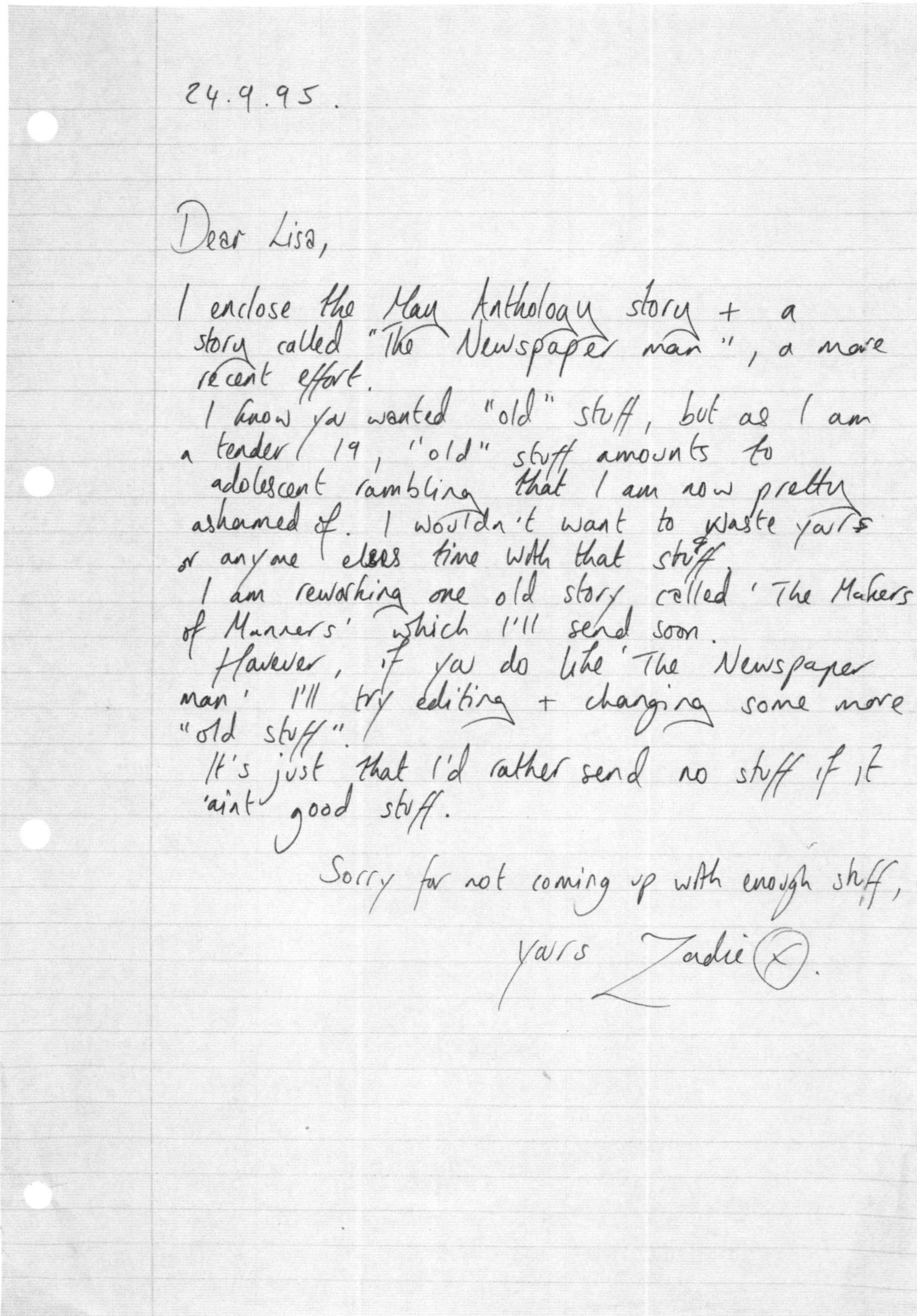

24.9.95.

Dear Lisa,

I enclose the May Anthology story + a story called "The Newspaper man", a more recent effort.

I know you wanted "old" stuff, but as I am a tender 19, "old" stuff amounts to adolescent rambling that I am now pretty ashamed of. I wouldn't want to waste yours or anyone elses time with that stuff.

I am reworking one old story called 'The Makers of Manners' which I'll send soon.

However, if you do like 'The Newspaper man' I'll try editing + changing some more "old stuff".

It's just that I'd rather send no stuff if it 'aint good stuff.

Sorry for not coming up with enough stuff,

yours Zadie (x).

at New York University. She often tackles themes of race, class and cultural identity. Her work has been praised for its confidence, freshness and originality, but she acknowledges her debts to earlier writers, her great love of reading and the importance of studying earlier texts as preparation for writing new fiction. **CM**

FIG.69
Letter to Lisa Appignanesi
From Zadie Smith
24 September 1995
Black ink on lined paper
British Library
Lisa Appignanesi Archive, Deposit 11141

FIG.70
Zadie Smith
By Roderick Field
9 September 1999
Gelatin silver print
National Portrait Gallery
NPG X88501

SUPPRESSION, CENSORSHIP & SECRECY

3

While a public appetite for new writing that challenges the status quo has always existed, some writers have had to overcome huge barriers in order to make their voices heard. This chapter considers authors whose work has been suppressed by a variety of means over the centuries. It looks at the censorship of written work on political and social grounds, and considers instances when an author's very identity has been a barrier to publication. It explores how authors have sought to bypass such obstructions by disguising their identity or publishing through other channels, and it reflects on moments when suppression has represented heroism in the public consciousness.

The written word has always had the potential to pose a threat to power structures, and indeed, some writers have seen it as their duty to do this. Censorship, in its most basic form, is a weapon against social and political change. Early examples of the censorship of texts in Britain were linked to threats to religious orthodoxy or political systems, between which there was often significant overlap. Through persistence and advocacy by activists and the writers themselves, more works by a wider range of authors became available in Britain in the second half of the twentieth century. Over the last century, censorship in Britain has focused particularly on obscenity, a concept that has changed greatly over time and around which, in British law, there has often been considerable room for personal interpretation.

Throughout this chapter are authors whose writing offended by its graphic descriptions of sexual acts. The ways in which these authors and their texts were treated reflects the times in which they lived. Sir John Harington the Younger was reputedly forced by Elizabeth I to translate the whole of the epic poem *Orlando Furioso* (1532) by Ludovico Ariosto, as a punishment for translating an explicit section of the tale.

John Wilmot, 2nd Earl of Rochester, was banned from court by Charles II for his obscene poetry and bad behaviour, although he was later allowed to return. In the early twentieth century, when a number of writers felt that literary integrity required more explicit treatment of sexual themes than had been customary hitherto, they came up against legal challenges. Books and plays were banned but authors found ways of publishing anyway, printing books privately or publishing abroad. Famous examples include works by James Joyce and D. H. Lawrence.

In some instances, the gender or sexuality of an author has been the bar to publication. In the early modern period, Katherine Philips was not unique among seventeenth-century women writers to have negative feelings about her work being printed and publicly available. In the nineteenth century, the Brontë sisters chose to write under male pseudonyms, both to protect their privacy and to ensure fair treatment. The exposure of Oscar Wilde's private life as a gay man led to the end of his writing career, and Radclyffe Hall's openly lesbian novel was banned, not for graphic descriptions of sex but for suggesting that homosexuality was natural and acceptable.

Britain's history of aggressive colonisation and involvement in the transatlantic slave trade has left a legacy of racial prejudice, which has also hindered publication by British people of Asian, African or Caribbean origin. This struggle came into a clearer focus in the mid-twentieth century when immigrants from the Caribbean to Britain included a number of gifted writers, who were frequently treated with suspicion and their work rejected on the grounds of irrelevance to wider audiences.

JOHN HARINGTON

Sir John Harington the Younger (bap. 1560–1612) was a writer and courtier whose godmother was Elizabeth I (1533–1603). Born in London, Harington attended the University of Cambridge before taking possession of his family estate in 1583 on the death of his father. During the 1580s, he undertook the momentous task of translating *Orlando Furioso*, an epic poem in Italian by Ludovico Ariosto (1474–1533), which first appeared in 1516 and was finally published in its complete form in 1532. The story, whose central character is the knight Orlando, is set during a fictional war between the Christian emperor Charlemagne and Agramente, a Saracen king from Africa. The tale, divided into 46 cantos, or sections, is concerned with love, war, fantasy and tragedy.

According to legend, Harington's translation came about as a punishment by Elizabeth I. He had translated a scandalous and sexually explicit section of canto 28, which he shared with the queen's ladies-in-waiting. This allegedly led to his banishment from court and the queen's insistence that he translate the entirety of *Orlando Furioso* into English. In the preface to his translation, Harington warns readers of the lasciviousness of certain sections, and even suggests they avoid the canto for which he was banished from court: 'Turne o'er the leafe, and let this tale alone.'[1] Of course this instruction to self-censor would have drawn readers' attention particularly to this part of the text. Such ostentatious secrecy was a distinctive feature of Elizabethan court life and was particularly associated with the power play between the queen and her courtiers.

Harington sent this manuscript for *Orlando Furioso* to the printer, Richard Field (bap. 1561–1624; fig.71). He added significant commentary to his translation, and his manuscript shows how he made changes to the text. This folio shows him praising the skill of Italian artists such as Giovanni Bellini (1430–1516) and Leonardo da Vinci (1452–1519). Originally, Harington also included praise for the miniaturist Nicholas Hilliard (*c*.1547–1619), who painted portraits of Elizabeth I and other members of court. Harington wrote: 'Allso owe Englyshe Hillyard by desart / Doe meryt in this prayse to have a part.' Although he crossed out this line he later wrote about Hilliard in the notes to his translation.Harington continually inserted his voice into the text, showing how far Ariosto's original Italian story was adapted for an English audience.

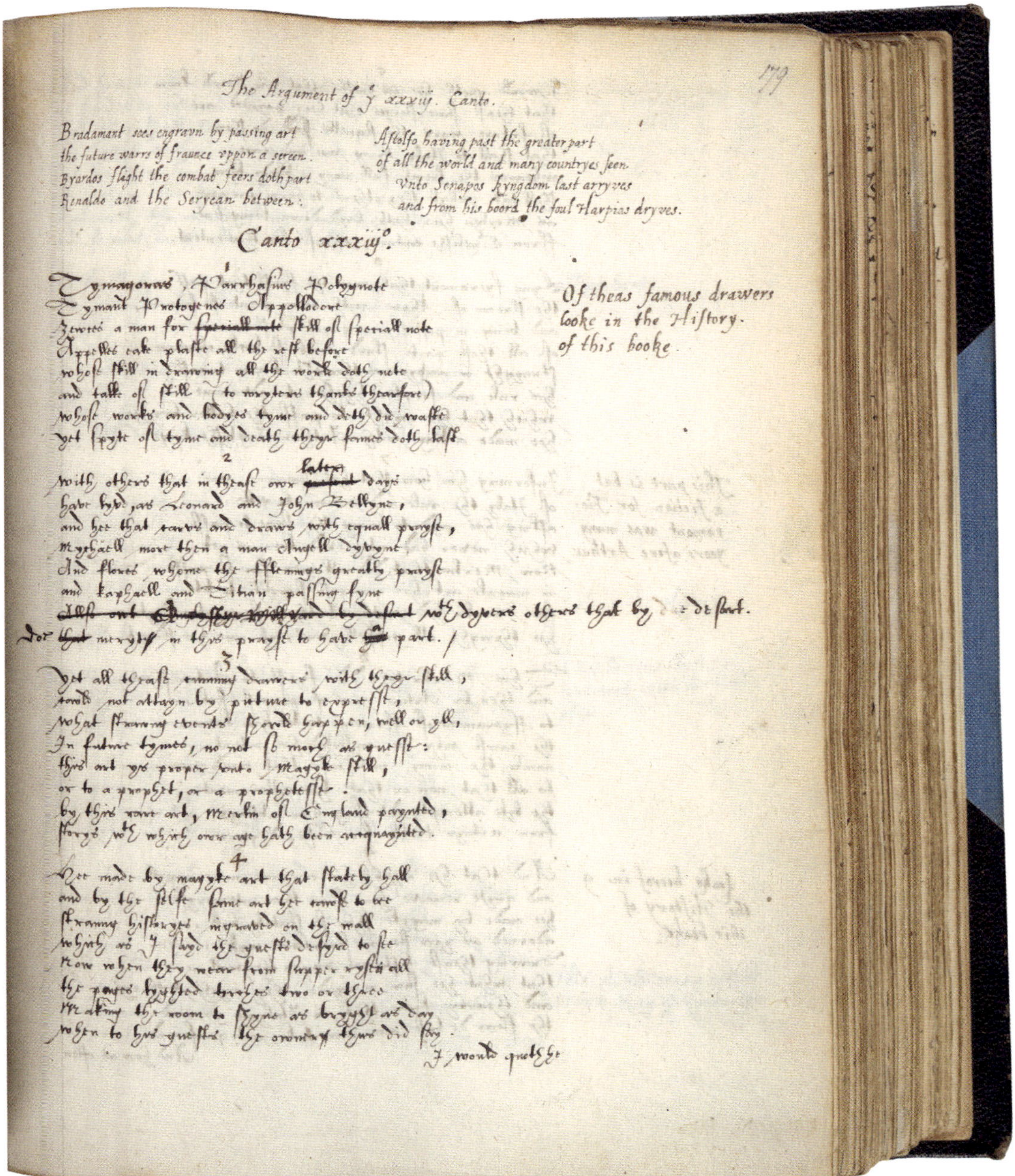
179

The Argument of y^e xxxiij. Canto.

Bradamant sees engravn by passing art
the future warrs of Fraunce uppon a screen.
Byardos flight the combat feers doth part
Renaldo and the Serycan between.

Astolfo having past the greater part
of all the world and many countryes seen.
Vnto Senapos kyngdom last arryves
and from his boord the foul Harpias dryves.

Canto xxxiij°.

Of theas famous drawers looke in the History. of this booke.

FIG.71
Translation of Ludovico Ariosto's *Orlando Furioso*
By Sir John Harington the Younger
c.1590–1
Iron gall ink on laid paper
British Library
Add MS 18920, f.179r

When *Orlando Furioso* was printed, Harington was closely involved in the personalisation of copies for friends and important contacts at court. This copy (fig.72) was made for William Cecil, 1st Baron Burghley (1520–1598) and contains manuscript corrections in the hands of Harington and a scribe. Throughout the volume are engraved illustrations about which Harington said 'they are all cut brasse, and most of them by the beste workemen in that kinde ... have bene in this land

XXVIII
Roma.
Valenza
Acquamorta
Lion
ROD
Fausto
Fausto
REX
ROD
HOSTO

FIG.72
Illustration to Canto XXVIII, *Orlando Furioso* by Ludovico Ariosto. Translated by Sir John Harington the Younger
After Girolamo Porro
(Richard Field, London, 1591)
British Library
c.57.h.1.

FIG.73
Sir John Harington
By an unknown artist
*c.*1590–5
Oil on panel
National Portrait Gallery
NPG 3121

this manie yeares: yet I will not praise them too much, because I gave direction for their making'.[2] Within this volume the erotic illustrations in Canto XXVIII have been inked over (upper right), showing how censorship could be tailored to individual copies of a publication.

Harington had his portrait painted in oils at least twice. The engraved frontispiece portrait of him by Thomas Cockson (Coxon; bap. 1569–before 1641) that appeared in his translation of *Orlando Furioso* may have been based on a lost miniature portrait of him by Hilliard, or on one of the oil paintings. This portrait of the writer by an unknown artist shows Harington in clothing that can be dated to around the time his translation of *Orlando Furioso* was published (fig.73). All Harington's portraits – like all other portraits of courtiers who were also writers at this period – show him with the attributes of a gentleman rather than a writer. While writing was part of many courtiers' lives, in a visual context it was a part of their identity to be disregarded rather than celebrated. **AA**

JOHN WILMOT, 2ND EARL OF ROCHESTER

The court of Charles II (1630–1685) was famous for behaviour unconstrained by conventional morality, but even in this context, the poet John Wilmot, 2nd Earl of Rochester (1647–1680) set new standards, both in his life and his writing. Rochester's father, the 1st Earl, had been a conspicuously loyal and brave supporter of Charles I (1600–1649), and for this reason, following the Restoration of the monarchy in 1660, Charles II took a particular interest in the 2nd Earl. This enabled Rochester to avoid the kind of punishment he would have suffered at almost any other time in the seventeenth century for his sometimes libellous and often scurrilous verse, but even so, one contemporary claimed that the king dismissed him from court at least once a year.

At the age of 13 – which was unusually young even for that time – Rochester went to study at the University of Oxford. Here he began to develop both the skill in writing and the love of drinking that characterised his later life. He was only there for a year, leaving in 1661 to travel with a governor on the Continent for three years, with all expenses paid for by the king. On his return, the king encouraged Rochester to marry an heiress, Elizabeth Malet (1651–1681). She was not willing, and Rochester's response was to kidnap her, apparently with the intention of forcing her to marry him. Caught and sent to the Tower of London, he was released in a few weeks after writing a grovelling letter to the king. He then went to sea as a volunteer in the second Anglo-Dutch War (1665–7) – one of a series of naval conflicts stemming from naval conflicts over trade and overseas colonies. In this role he distinguished himself by his bravery. After a second stint at sea in 1666, Elizabeth Malet finally agreed to marry him in January 1667.

Rochester's life then followed a pattern of residence in London during the Parliamentary sessions, and in the country with Malet at other times. While he was in London, Rochester had relationships with many women, notably the actress Elizabeth Barry (*c.*1658–1713), with whom he had a daughter. He later described himself as having been continuously drunk for five years. It is not entirely clear which five years these were, but during the late 1660s and 1670s his life in London was marked by a number of dramatic incidents. These included the destruction of a precious sundial in the Privy Garden of Whitehall Palace; beating the playwright Thomas Killigrew (1612–1683) in the presence of the king,

FIG.74
Letter to Elizabeth Wilmot, Countess of Rochester
From John Wilmot, 2nd Earl of Rochester
Undated
Iron gall ink on laid paper
British Library
Harley MS 7003, f.262r

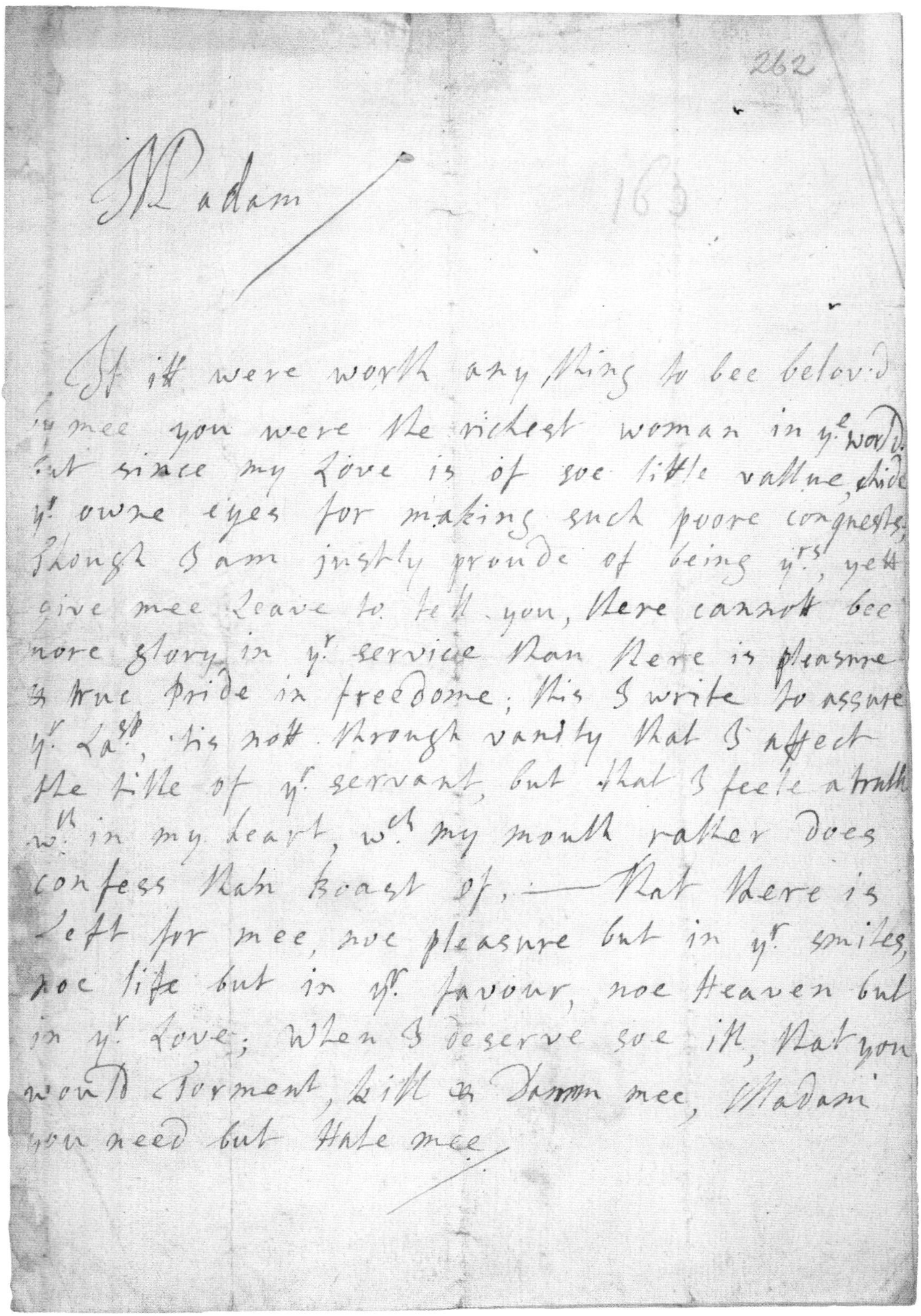

262

Madam 163

If itt were worth any thing to bee belov'd
by mee you were the richest woman in ye world.
but since my Love is of soe little vallue, chide
yr owne eyes for making such poore conquests,
though I am justly proude of being yrs, yett
give mee Leave to tell you, there cannott bee
more glory in yr service than there is pleasure
& true Pride in freedome; this I write to assure
yr Ladp, tis not through vanity that I affect
the title of yr servant, but that I feele a truth
wth in my heart, wch my mouth rather does
confess than boast of, — that there is
Left for mee, noe pleasure but in yr smiles,
noe life but in yr favour, noe Heaven but
in yr Love; When I deserve soe ill, that you
would torment, kill & damn mee, Madam
you need but Hate mee

which was regarded as treason; and a drunken episode in Epsom, Surrey, that resulted in the death of one of Rochester's friends – for which he was indirectly responsible. In the midst of all this, Rochester's letters seem to express genuine love for both his wife and Elizabeth Barry. This undated letter to his wife (fig.74) is an assertion of his love for her, concluding: 'there is left for mee, noe pleasure but in y^{r}. smiles, noe life but in y^{r}. favour, noe Heaven but in y^{r}. Love; when I deserve soe ill, that you would Torment, kill & Damn mee, Madam you need but Hate mee.'[3]

During this time Rochester was producing witty, satirical, sometimes lyrical or passionate, often startlingly explicit poetry for circulation among his friends – not for publication in printed form. From the start, his poetry was condemned for obscenity, libel, blasphemy and more surprisingly plagiarism, but his extraordinary skill was recognised even by those, like the Poet Laureate John Dryden (1631–1700; see p.79), who despised him personally. Like the writers in the early twentieth century who were censured for writing graphically about bodily functions including sex, Rochester asserted that he was writing honestly about the reality of human life, and that in terms of language, 'Expressions must descend to the nature of things expressed'.[4] Rochester's poetry could in some ways be seen as pushing at the boundaries of conventional literature just as others at the time were pushing at the boundaries of philosophy and science.

Rochester's attitude to himself as well as to other poets seems to be reflected perfectly in this portrait (fig.75). While clearly valuing his ability to write, he also mocked it, as he did almost everything. Here he crowns a monkey with the laurels of the poet, while the animal tears pages out of a book and offers them to him. His dress alludes to Roman armour and may be intended to refer to his military service, or his classical learning, or both. It is not known who commissioned this portrait, but it seems likely that the unusual iconography was specified by Rochester himself. The portrait exists in several versions, apparently by more than one artist; it is not clear which, if any, was the 'original'.

In the spring of 1680 Rochester fell ill, probably with a sexually transmitted infection, exacerbated by the effects of alcoholism. After several agonising months, during which he repented of his previous lifestyle and asserted his faith in God, ordering 'all his profane and lewd Writings ... and all his obscene and filthy Pictures, to be burned', he died at the age of 33.[5] Volumes of his poetry were published without a licence immediately after his death, but his work was not available in unexpurgated editions until the late twentieth century. **CM**

FIG.75
John Wilmot, 2nd Earl of Rochester
By an unknown artist
*c.*1665–70
Oil on canvas
National Portrait Gallery
NPG 804

KATHERINE PHILIPS

The poet Katherine Philips (née Fowler; 1632–1664), admired by a small literary circle during her lifetime, found fame only after her death, partly as a result of her own sense of propriety for a woman of her social standing. Born in London into a prosperous merchant family, she was a precocious child and voracious reader, reputedly having read the whole Bible by the age of four. She was educated at home and at boarding school in London, and at 16 was married to a Welsh landowner, James Philips (*c.*1624–1674). James was a supporter of Oliver Cromwell (1599–1658) during the Commonwealth period, and Katherine was a royalist, but both had moderate views, and their political differences do not seem to have caused particular marital dissent. He served as an MP in both Cromwell's republican parliament of 1653 and that of Charles II (1630–1685) in 1662. Philips was based at the marital home in Cardigan, Wales, for most of her adult life, with periods in London and a year's stay in Dublin, Ireland, from 1662–3.

While her affluent upbringing secured an education for Philips, which fed and stimulated her own poetry, her social status as well as her gender, limited the literary opportunities open to her. About 120 poems by Philips are known, along with a number of translations from French and Italian. Philips's translation of *La Mort de Pompée* (1644) by the French playwright Pierre Corneille (1606–1684), which she wrote in 1662, was first performed on stage in Dublin in 1663, the first play by a woman to be performed in a public theatre in the British Isles. Philips's poetry, however, was not intended for such a wide public.

Philips often addressed the theme of friendship in her poems. She seems to have established a Society of Friendship among her associates, giving her friends and herself classicising names, which she used both in poems and in her correspondence; she herself was 'Orinda' and her husband was 'Antenor'. Many manuscript collections of her poems still exist and testify to the way she circulated poetry among her friendship group. Her most passionate friendship poems are addressed to women friends and there has been much debate over the extent to which she might be regarded as a lesbian poet.

Most of Philips's poems are personal in nature, but at the time of the Restoration of Charles II to the throne in 1660, she, along with many others, addressed poems to members of the royal family. The poem 'To

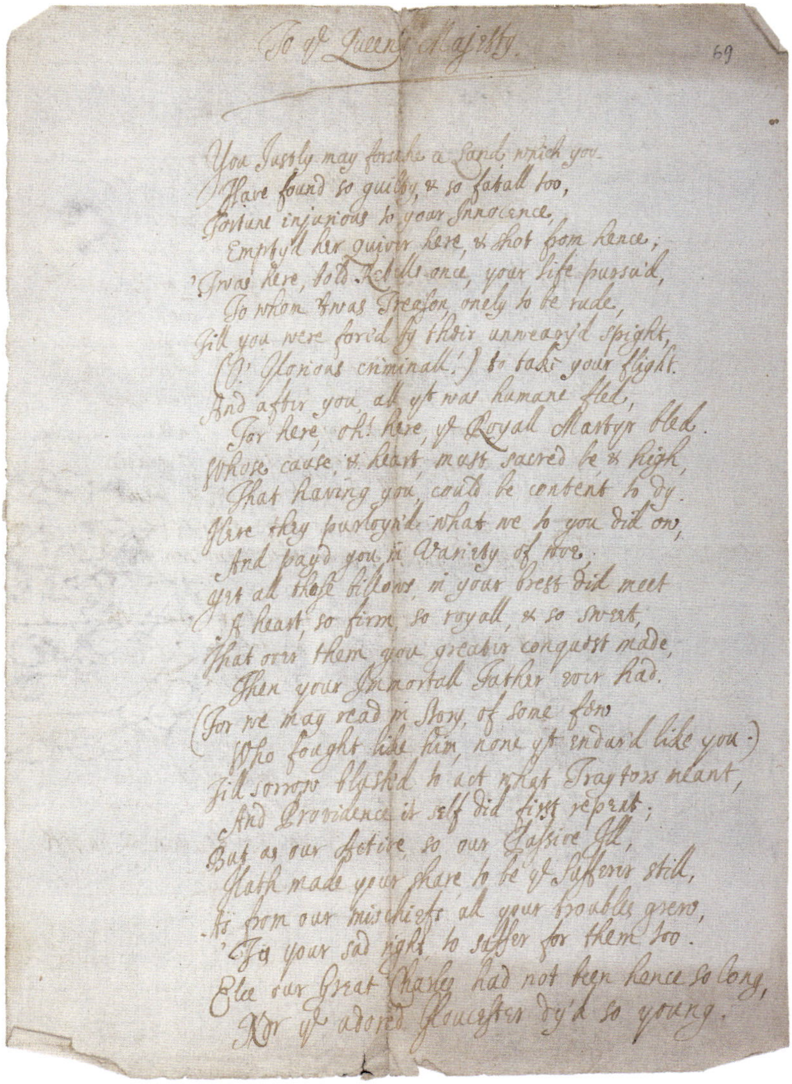
To ye Queens Majesty. 69

You justly may forsake a Land which you
Have found so guilty, & so fatall too,
Fortune injurious to your Innocence,
Emptyd her quiver here, & shot from hence;
'Twas here, bold Rebells once, your life pursu'd,
To whom 'twas Treason onely to be rude,
Till you were forc'd by their unweary'd spight,
(O glorious criminall!) to take your flight.
And after you all yt was humane fled,
For here, oh! here, ye Royall Martyr bled.
Whose cause & heart must sacred be & high,
That having you, could be content to dy.
Here they purloyn'd what we to you did ow,
And payd you in Variety of woe.
Yet all those billows in your brest did meet
A heart so firm, so royall, & so sweet,
That over them you greater conquest made,
Then your Immortall Father ever had.
(For we may read in Story, of some few
Who fought like him, none yt endur'd like you.)
Till sorrow blush'd to act what Traytors meant,
And Providence it self did first repent;
But as our Active, so our Passive Ill,
Hath made your share to be ye Sufferer still,
As from our mischiefs all your troubles grew,
'Tis your sad right to suffer for them too.
Else our Great Charles had not been hence so long,
Nor ye adored Gloucester dy'd so young.

FIG.76
'To the Queen's Majesty'
By Katherine Philips
1660–1
Iron gall ink on laid paper
British Library
Add MS 78233, f.69r

the Queen's Majesty' (fig.76), later published as 'To the Queen-mother's Majesty' and dated to 1 January 1661, was addressed to Henrietta Maria (1609–1669), the widow of Charles I (1600–1649). It commiserates with her over the way England has treated her, not just by executing her husband and causing her to flee during the civil wars, but also by causing the deaths of her son Henry, Duke of Gloucester (1640–1660) and her daughter Mary, Princess of Orange (1631–1660), both of whom died of smallpox within a short time of one another during the latter part of 1660.

A few of Philips's poems were published in collections during her lifetime, with her agreement. However, much to her dismay, in 1664 an unauthorised edition of 75 of her poems was published in London under the title *Poems. By the Incomparable Mrs. K. P.* Her objections were that she could be perceived as publishing simply for the money, and that her private

FIG.77
Katherine Philips
By William Faithorne
1667
Line engraving on paper
National Portrait Gallery
NPG D21622

thoughts might be exposed to those outside her social circles. Philips was convinced by her friend, the courtier and translator Sir Charles Cotterell (1615–1701), that there was no way of retrieving the unauthorised text, and that the best way to deal with this was to agree to publish an authorised version. However, having travelled to London, she contracted smallpox and died in June 1664, at the age of 32. The authorised volume did not come out until 1667. It secured her admiration and fame for the following century. It had an engraved frontispiece portrait of her as a classical bust (fig.77) by William Faithorne (*c.*1620–1691), presenting her not only in the tradition of the great writers of classical antiquity, but also as a woman of the period with a fashionable hairstyle. Unfortunately, Cotterell, who arranged the publication of the volume and genuinely admired Philips, somewhat counteracted the effect of the portrait with his comments in the preface:

> 'Some of them [the poems] would be no disgrace to the name of any Man that amongst us is most esteemed for his excellency in this kind, and there are none that may not pass with favour, when it is remembered that they fell hastily from the pen but of a Woman.'[6] **CM**

THE BRONTË SISTERS

The Brontë sisters: Charlotte (1816–1855), Emily (1818–1848) and Anne (1820–1849), are famous both for their powerful and passionate writing and their largely isolated and tragic lives. Remarkably, each sister made equally important literary contributions that continue to inspire readers to this day. They lived a sheltered existence in the village of Haworth, Yorkshire and, as children, created imaginary worlds in miniature books with their brother, Branwell (1817–1848). Their lives were short, with Emily and Anne dying from tuberculosis at the ages of 30 and 29 respectively. Charlotte lived the longest, dying three weeks before her thirty-ninth birthday, while in the early stages of pregnancy. Branwell also died young, of a combination of tuberculosis and alcoholism.

The sisters wrote and published some of the most famous novels of the nineteenth century. Yet their true identities were hidden when they first published their works. Emily, Anne and Charlotte jointly published *Poems by Currer, Ellis, and Acton Bell* in 1846 with the first edition selling only two copies. The literary world continued to be dominated by male writers and publishers at this time, and it was generally thought that using a masculine pseudonym would ensure publication and a wider readership. In 1847 Charlotte published *Jane Eyre,* Anne then published *Agnes Grey* and Emily published *Wuthering Heights*, all under their respective pseudonyms. *Jane Eyre* was an instant bestseller. *Agnes Grey* sold modestly. *Wuthering Heights* initially sold poorly, with critics considering it strange. The sensation around *Jane Eyre* increased the attention on Anne and Emily's novels. There was enormous public speculation as to the identity of the authors with conjecture around Charlotte's identity beginning even before her sisters' works were published. One critic believed a single author was posing as the three writers, an idea which amused the sisters. Another, when speculating on the identity of Currer Bell, thought them to be a man, or a 'very coarse woman'.[7] Shown here is the first page of the original manuscript for *Jane Eyre* on which Charlotte Brontë has written 'by Currer Bell' beneath the title (fig.78). Writing to the critic George Henry Lewes (1817–1878) on 1 November 1849, Charlotte went some way to explaining why she did not want to be identified as a female writer:

FIG.78
Jane Eyre
By Charlotte Brontë
1847
Black ink on wove paper
British Library
Add MS 43474, f.1r

FIG.79
Letter to William Smith Williams
From Charlotte Brontë
20 April 1848
Black ink on wove paper
British Library
Ashley MS 166, f.2r

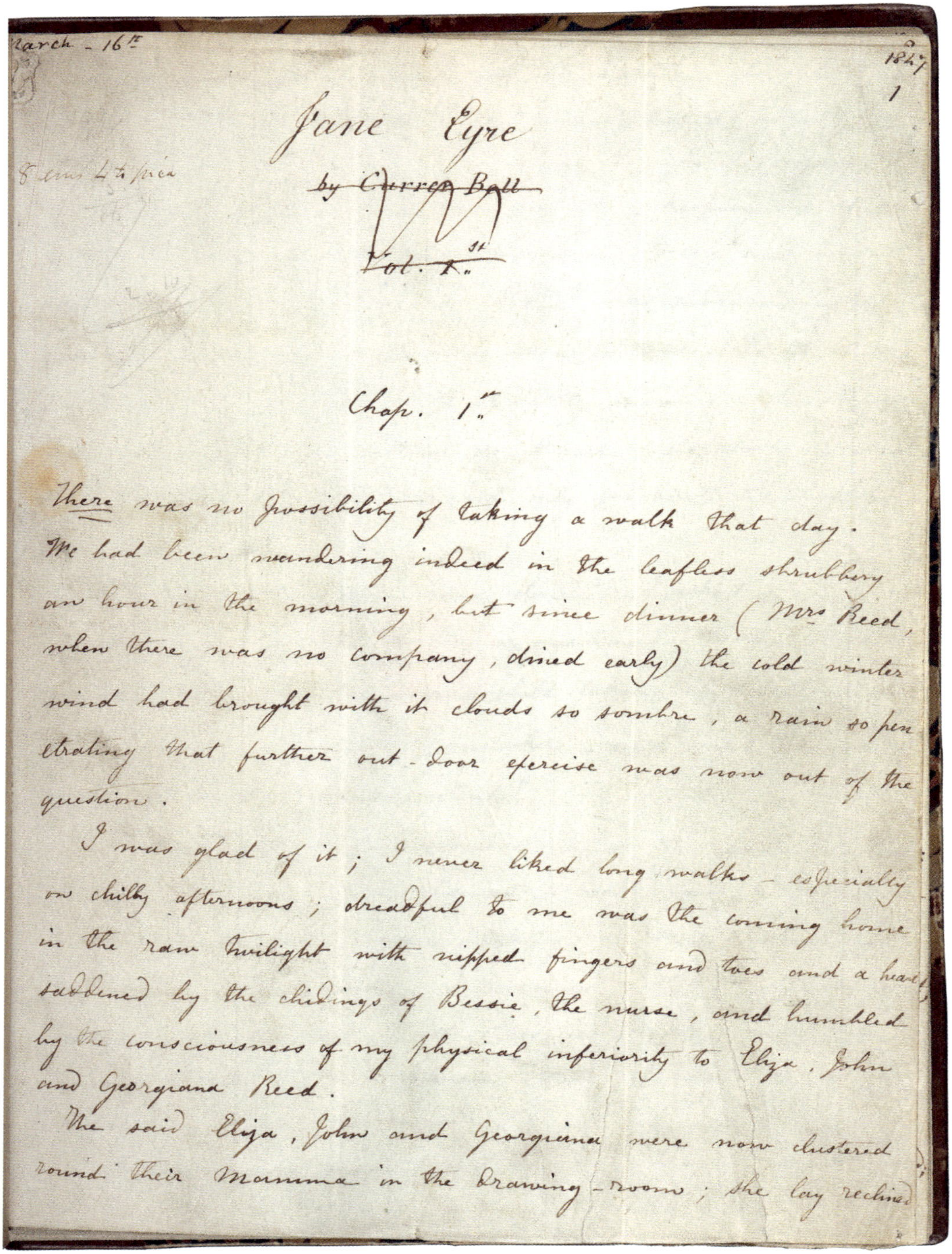

March - 16th

1847

1

Jane Eyre

~~by Currer Bell~~

~~Vol. 1st~~

Chap. 1st

There was no possibility of taking a walk that day. We had been wandering indeed in the leafless shrubbery an hour in the morning, but since dinner (Mrs Reed, when there was no company, dined early) the cold winter wind had brought with it clouds so sombre, a rain so penetrating that further out-door exercise was now out of the question.

I was glad of it; I never liked long walks – especially on chilly afternoons; dreadful to me was the coming home in the raw twilight with nipped fingers and toes and a heart saddened by the chidings of Bessie, the nurse, and humbled by the consciousness of my physical inferiority to Eliza, John and Georgiana Reed.

The said Eliza, John and Georgiana were now clustered round their Mamma in the drawing-room; she lay reclined

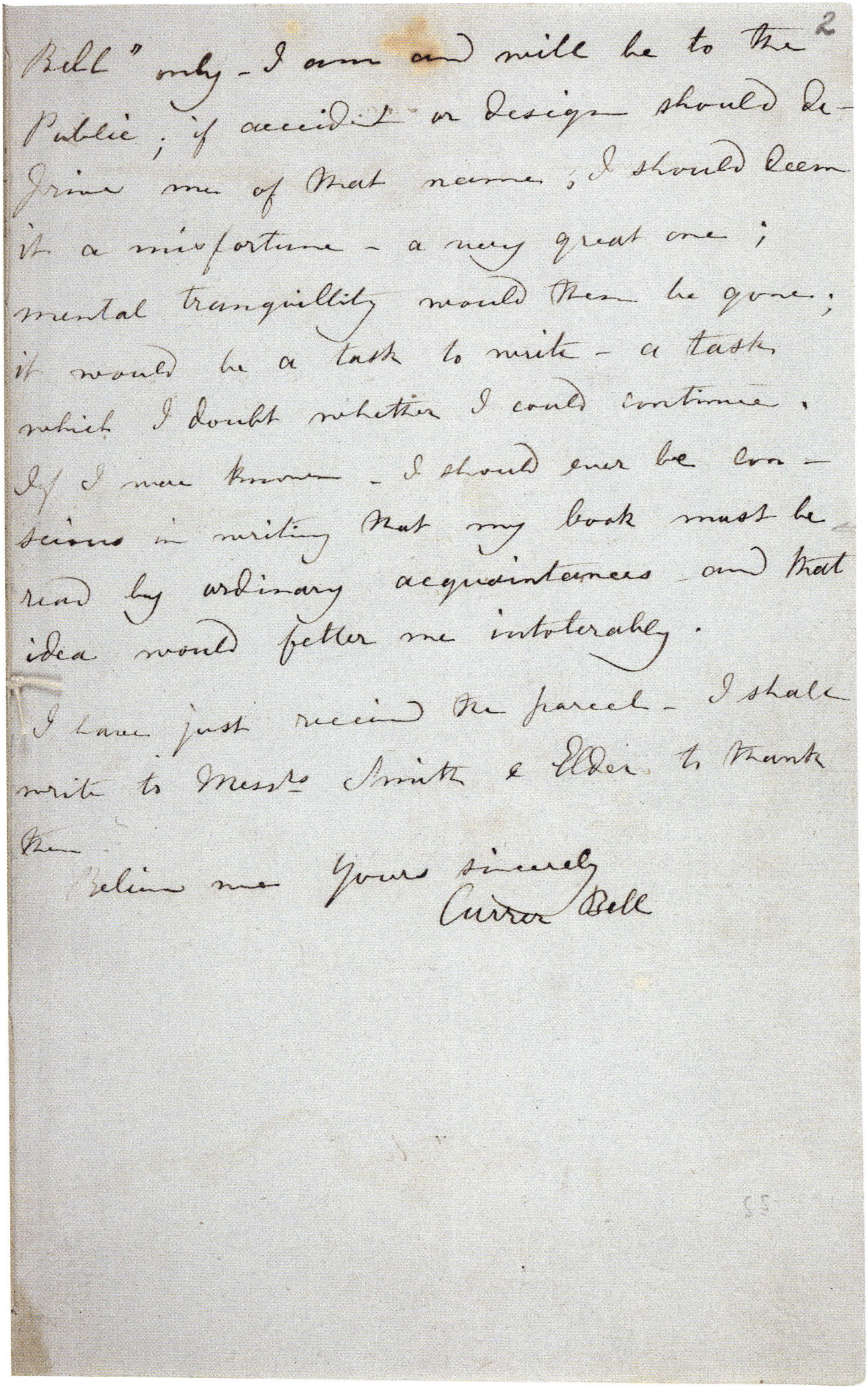

2

Bell" only – I am and will be to the Public; if accident or design should deprive me of that name, I should deem it a misfortune – a very great one; mental tranquillity would then be gone; it would be a task to write – a task which I doubt whether I could continue. If I were known – I should ever be conscious in writing that my book must be read by ordinary acquaintances and that idea would fetter me intolerably.

I have just received the parcel – I shall write to Messrs Smith & Elder to thank them.

Believe me Yours sincerely
Currer Bell

> 'I wish you did not think me a woman. I wish all reviewers believed "Currer Bell" to be a man. They would be more just to him. You will – I know – keep measuring me by some standard of what you deem becoming to my sex ...'[8]

FIG.80
Charlotte, Emily and Anne Brontë
By Branwell Brontë
*c.*1834
Oil on canvas
National Portrait Gallery
NPG 1725

While Charlotte clearly felt that being identified as a woman would somehow jeopardise the reception of her works, there were other reasons why she suppressed her identity. In an earlier letter of 20 April 1848 to William Smith Williams (1800–1875; fig.79), literary advisor to the publishers Smith, Elder & Co., Charlotte said:

> 'It is very kind and right in you to answer "Currer Bell" to all queries reflecting the authorship of "Jane Eyre": that is the only name I wish to have mentioned in connection with my writings. "Currer Bell" only – I am and will be to the public; if accident or design should deprive me of that name, I should deem it a misfortune – a very great one; mental tranquillity would then be gone; it would be a task to write – a task which I doubt whether I could continue. If I were known – I should ever be conscious in writing that my book must be read by ordinary acquaintances and that idea would fetter me intolerably.'[9]

That Charlotte also hid her identity both for mental peace and to prevent those she knew identifying themselves in her works is clear.

Themes of secrecy and obscurity emerge in the remarkable group portrait of the Brontë sisters by their brother, Branwell, painted around 1834 (fig.80). The portrait was documented by Elizabeth Gaskell (1810–1865), Charlotte's biographer, in 1857:

> 'I have seen an oil painting ... it was a group of his sisters, life size, three-quarters length ... the likenesses were, I should think, admirable ... Emily's countenance struck me as full of power; Charlotte's of solicitude; Anne's of tenderness'.[10]

The painting was believed lost when the literary critic and editor of Gaskell's work, Clement Shorter (1857–1926), visited the home of Charlotte's widower, Rev. Arthur Bell Nicholls (1819–1906), in Banagher, Ireland, in 1895. Nicholls did not tell Shorter of the existence of the portrait. Charlotte also had clearly not wanted the

portrait known as she told William Smith Williams in 1850 that she had no portrait of her sisters. It was only eight years after Nicholls's death that his second wife, Mary Anna Bell (1831–1915) discovered the painting, which had been removed from its stretcher, folded and placed on top of a cupboard.

The portrait is painted in a relatively crude, naive style; Branwell was only 17 when he made it and was trying to turn his hand to portraiture. A fourth figure is just visible at the centre of the painting; it appears to be a self-portrait of Branwell, which he subsequently painted out, and which has become increasingly visible as the overpaint has become transparent with time. Why Branwell decided to erase himself is unclear, although it has served to add to the intrigue surrounding the painting. Unusually, the National Portrait Gallery decided to leave the painting unrestored, with the creases visible and the paint losses left untouched, testifying to the fascinating story of its loss and rediscovery, and to the elusiveness of the three novelists, of whom this is one of a very few existing portraits. **AA**

OSCAR WILDE

Oscar Wilde (1854–1900) is considered one of the most talented writers of the late nineteenth century, yet he was imprisoned and repudiated by society, which led to his work being censored and suppressed. Wilde's work spanned poetry, plays, novels, essays and criticism, and much of it continues to be read and performed today. Posthumously, Wilde became a rallying point for campaigners seeking the legalisation of homosexuality; it was clear that a brilliant literary career had been destroyed by society's values and the law. He is best known for his novel *The Picture of Dorian Gray* (1890), his plays including *The Importance of Being Earnest* (performed 1895) and the poem *The Ballad of Reading Gaol* (1898), written after he was imprisoned for gross indecency for homosexual acts, which were illegal in Britain until 1967.

Born in Ireland, Wilde studied at Trinity College, Dublin and Magdalen College, Oxford. In 1879 he settled in London where he frequented the theatre, adopted the principles of aestheticism ('art for art's sake') and joined a vibrant artistic society. Known for wearing knee-breeches, bow ties and large hats, Wilde was soon parodied in the press and on the stage. The comic opera by Gilbert and Sullivan, *Patience* (performed 1881), satirised Wilde and the aesthetic movement. Wilde responded to the attention by renting a box in the theatre for the opening night. In 1882, when *Patience* was due to tour North America, Wilde began a lecture tour so that North Americans could see the subject of the opera at first hand. He landed in New York on 2 January 1882 where he is alleged to have said to a customs agent, 'I have nothing to declare except my genius'.[11]

Shortly after his arrival, Wilde was photographed by the society photographer, Napoleon Sarony (1821–1896). Sarony took full advantage of the fascination with the theatre in the aftermath of the American Civil War (1861–5). His affordable images were produced in their thousands and collected by fans, while also boosting publicity for the actors they depicted. The photographs Sarony took of Wilde show him dressed in the 'aesthetic' style (fig.81). Wilde wore the same outfit during his lecture tour, which comprised a jacket and vest of velvet, silk knee breeches and stockings, and slippers featuring grosgrain bows. Sarony's studio was at 256 Fifth Avenue, New York, and it was here that famous actors and celebrities sat for their portraits. In this photograph, Wilde is shown with his head resting on his hand, holding a book in another, 'acting' the part of thinker, writer and aesthete.

In 1891 Wilde wrote the play *Salomé*. However, it was banned from performance in London by the Lord Chamberlain due to its infringement of an old law that prevented the depiction of Biblical characters on stage, although it was performed in Paris in 1896. After *Salomé*, Wilde wrote four plays, which were popular social satires: *Lady Windermere's Fan* (first performed 1892), *A Woman of No Importance* (first performed 1893), *An Ideal Husband* (first performed 1895) and *The Importance of Being Earnest*, which opened in February 1895. Shown here is a draft for the latter play, corrected by Wilde (fig.82). While *Earnest* was instantly successful, it was forced to close after 86 performances due to the scandal surrounding Wilde himself.

Although he had married Constance Lloyd (1858–1898) in 1884 and fathered two children, Wilde was found to be engaging in homosexual relationships. By 1893 Wilde and Lord Alfred Douglas (1870–1945; known as 'Bosie') were having a tempestuous affair, to which Bosie's father, John Douglas, 9th Marquess of Queensberry (1844–1900), wholeheartedly objected. On 18 February 1895, the Marquess of Queensberry left a calling card for Wilde at his club, labelling him a 'somdomite [*sic*]', to which Wilde responded by suing Queensberry for libel. Queensberry hired detectives to trail Wilde. The trial commenced on 3 April 1895, during which details of Wilde's private life were laid bare. Queensberry was found not guilty of libel and Wilde was left bankrupt and also proven to be breaking the law. Wilde was arrested for gross indecency on 6 April 1895, and he was sentenced to two years' hard labour, ultimately ending up in Reading Gaol. During imprisonment he wrote *De Profundis* and on his release *The Ballad of Reading Gaol*, two of his most famous works that addressed his relationship with Bosie and his time while incarcerated. Prison greatly affected Wilde, and he fled to France as soon as he was released, living in poverty and exile until his death in 1900. **AA**

FIG.81
Oscar Wilde
By Napoleon Sarony
1882
Albumen silver print
British Library
Add MS 81785, f.5r

FIG.82 (overleaf)
Draft playscript for *The Importance of Being Ernest*
By Oscar Wilde
1894
Typewritten with red and black ink and pencil
British Library
Add MS 81624, ff.14v–15r

256 FIFTH AVENUE,
NEW YORK

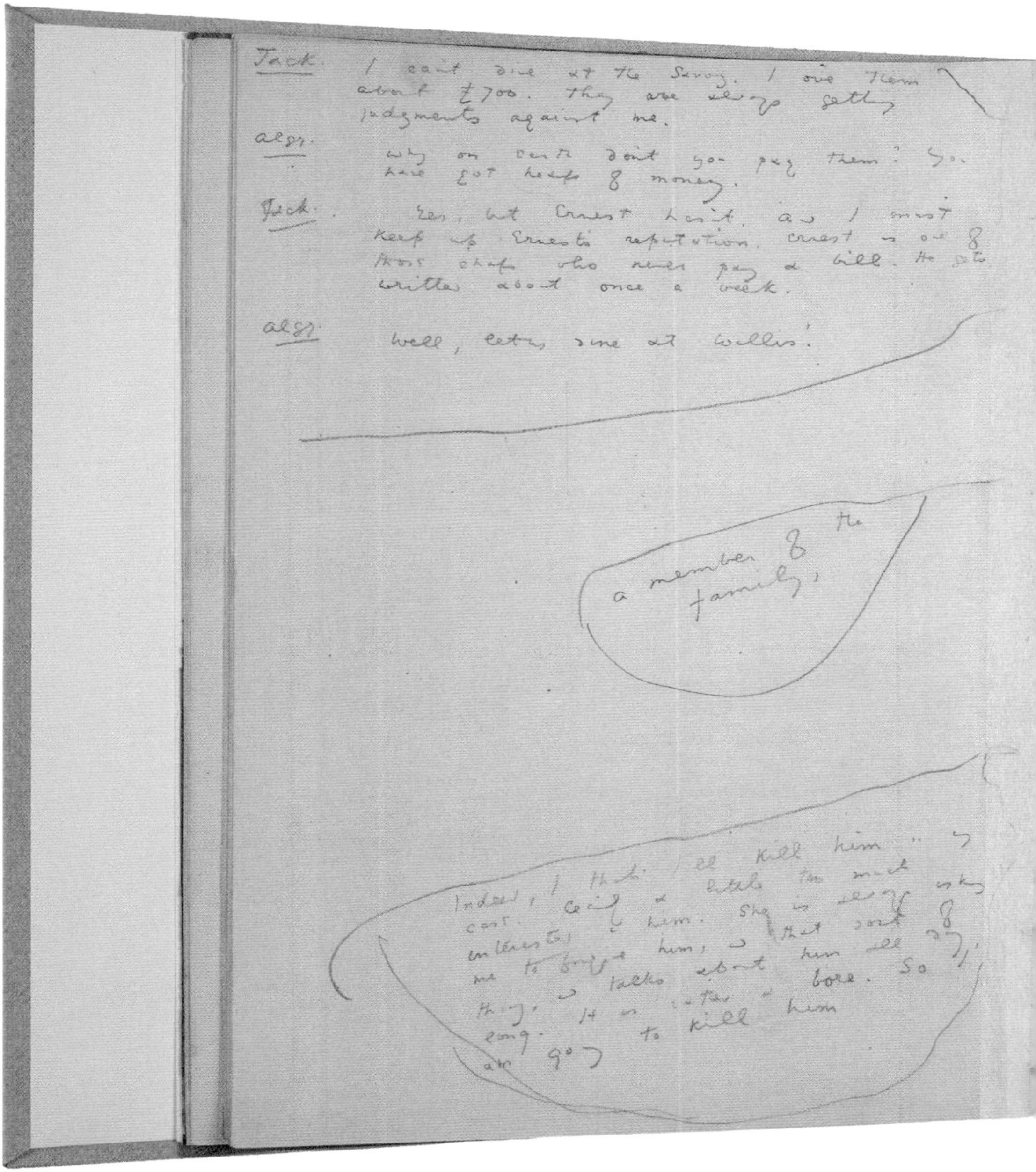

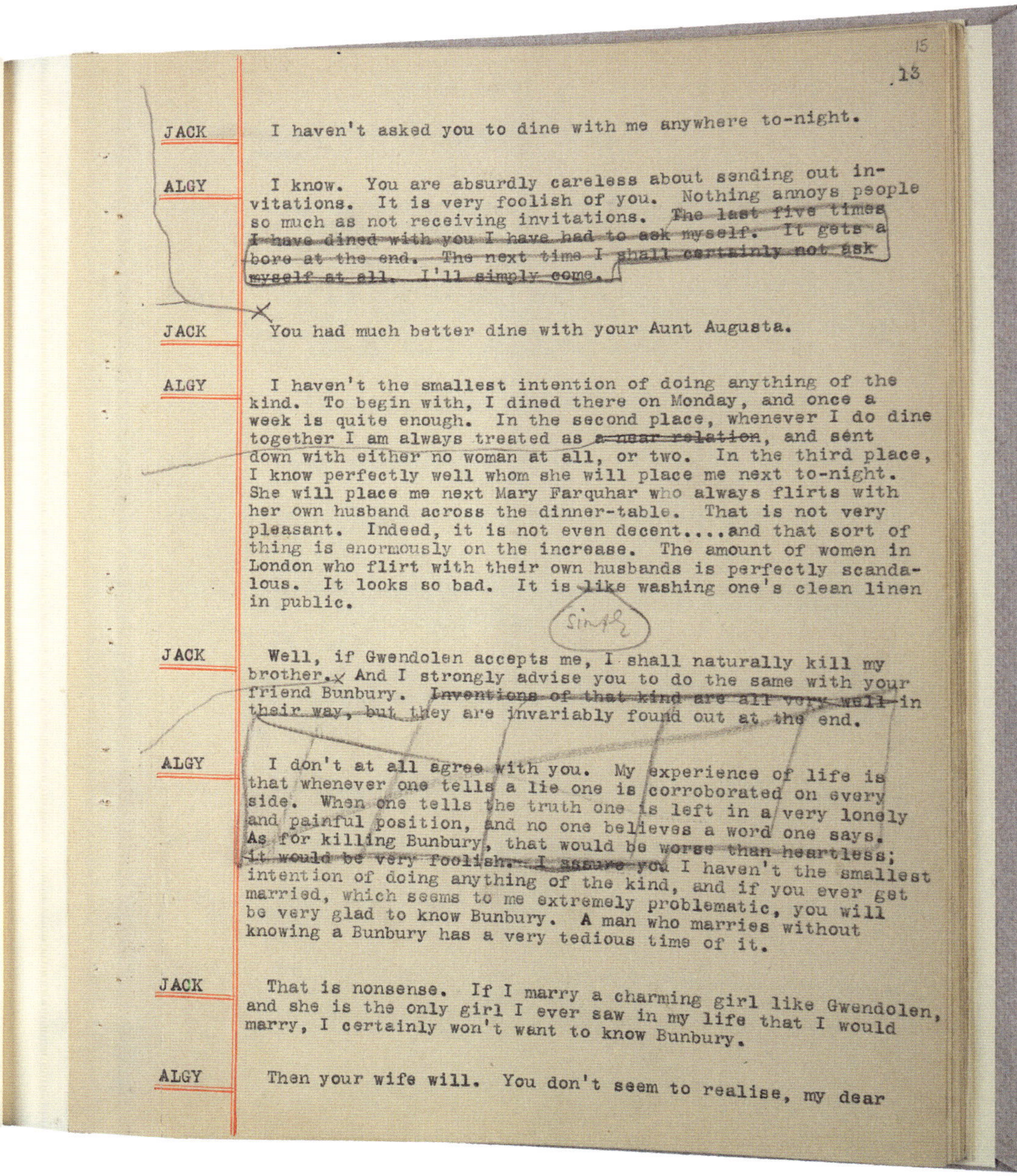

15

13

JACK I haven't asked you to dine with me anywhere to-night.

ALGY I know. You are absurdly careless about sending out invitations. It is very foolish of you. Nothing annoys people so much as not receiving invitations. ~~The last five times I have dined with you I have had to ask myself. It gets a bore at the end. The next time I shall certainly not ask myself at all. I'll simply come.~~

JACK You had much better dine with your Aunt Augusta.

ALGY I haven't the smallest intention of doing anything of the kind. To begin with, I dined there on Monday, and once a week is quite enough. In the second place, whenever I do dine together I am always treated as ~~a near relation~~, and sent down with either no woman at all, or two. In the third place, I know perfectly well whom she will place me next to-night. She will place me next Mary Farquhar who always flirts with her own husband across the dinner-table. That is not very pleasant. Indeed, it is not even decent....and that sort of thing is enormously on the increase. The amount of women in London who flirt with their own husbands is perfectly scandalous. It looks so bad. It is like washing one's clean linen in public.

JACK Well, if Gwendolen accepts me, I shall naturally kill my brother. And I strongly advise you to do the same with your friend Bunbury. ~~Inventions of that kind are all very well in their way, but they are invariably found out at the end.~~

ALGY I don't at all agree with you. My experience of life is that whenever one tells a lie one is corroborated on every side. When one tells the truth one is left in a very lonely and painful position, and no one believes a word one says. As for killing Bunbury, that would be ~~worse than heartless; it would be very foolish. I assure you~~ I haven't the smallest intention of doing anything of the kind, and if you ever get married, which seems to me extremely problematic, you will be very glad to know Bunbury. A man who marries without knowing a Bunbury has a very tedious time of it.

JACK That is nonsense. If I marry a charming girl like Gwendolen, and she is the only girl I ever saw in my life that I would marry, I certainly won't want to know Bunbury.

ALGY Then your wife will. You don't seem to realise, my dear

RADCLYFFE HALL

The novelist and poet Radclyffe Hall (1880–1943) became notorious in 1928 when her fifth novel, *The Well of Loneliness*, was published by Jonathan Cape, and, shortly after, she found herself prosecuted for obscenity and the novel banned in the UK. Hall, born Marguerite Radclyffe-Hall, referred to herself as an 'invert', a term used at the time to describe those who were sexually attracted to people of the same sex. She had been born into a wealthy family and had an independent income. In 1907 she met the singer Mabel Batten (1856–1916) who introduced her to a sophisticated group of intellectual and professional women, many of them lesbians. Batten encouraged Hall to publish her poetry, and she produced several volumes while she was in her twenties and thirties. Hall was given the nickname 'John' by friends at this time. From 1917, she lived with Una Vincenzo, Lady Troubridge (1887–1963), a sculptor and translator; Troubridge was to remain Hall's partner for the rest of her life. Hall's portrait by Charles Buchel (1872–1950; fig.83) was painted in 1918 and was later bequeathed to the National Portrait Gallery by Troubridge. It shows Hall with her hair cut short, wearing a masculine jacket, cravat and monocle along with a skirt. While this was not an uncommon fashion in the 1920s among intellectual and progressive women of all sexualities, after the publicity around *The Well of Loneliness* trial, it became particularly associated with lesbians.

It was in her forties that Hall turned to writing novels. Her fourth novel, *Adam's Breed* (1926), was a bestseller and won prestigious literary prizes. *The Well of Loneliness* was the only one of her eight novels to have an overtly lesbian theme. The book's protagonist, a woman called Stephen Gordon, is also an 'invert'. The narrative explores her struggles with her own self-hatred and the rejection and exclusion she experiences in society. Hall described her book as 'the first long and very serious novel entirely upon the subject of sexual inversion'.[12] It received a number of very positive reviews before its ban, including one from *Country Life* magazine, which commented that: 'The mature, the thoughtful and the open-minded will find in it much food for reflection, a window giving upon understanding, and a psychological study of profundity and pathos.'[13] Representations were made in favour of the book by many well-known writers of the time, including Virginia Woolf (1882–1941; see p.42).

The Chief Magistrate, Sir Chartres Biron (1863–1940), however, ruled on behalf of the London Public Morality Council (fig.84) that the book was

FIG.83
Radclyffe Hall
By Charles Buchel
(Karl August Büchel)
1918
Oil on canvas
National Portrait Gallery
NPG 4347

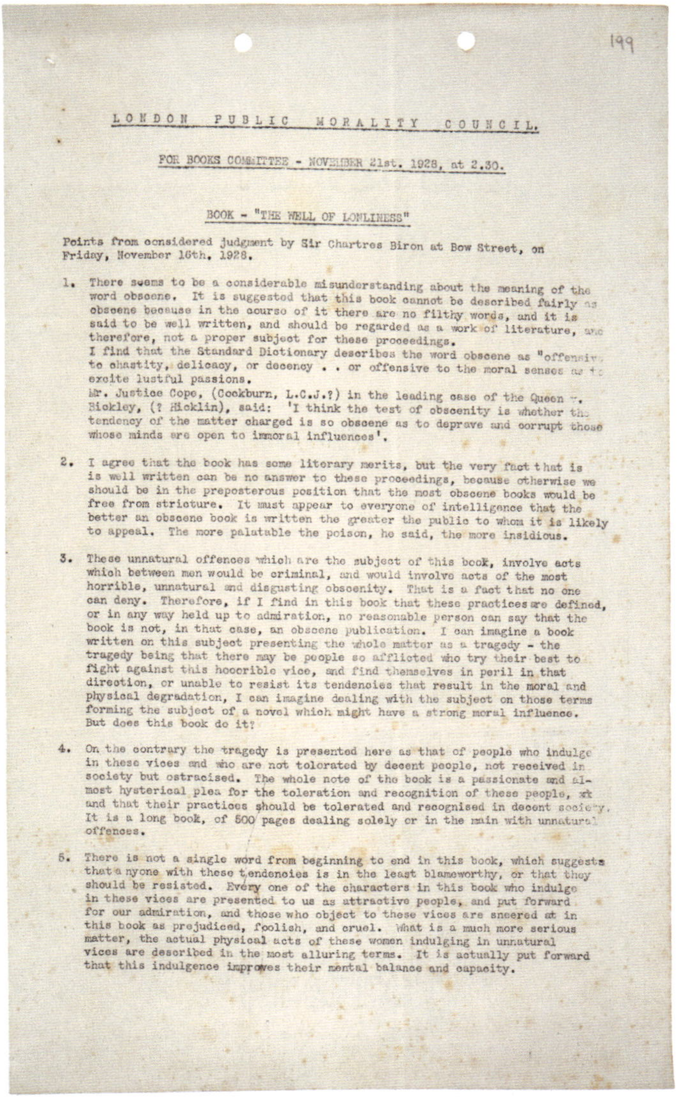

199

LONDON PUBLIC MORALITY COUNCIL.

FOR BOOKS COMMITTEE - NOVEMBER 21st. 1928, at 2.30.

BOOK - "THE WELL OF LONLINESS"

Points from considered judgment by Sir Chartres Biron at Bow Street, on Friday, November 16th. 1928.

1. There seems to be a considerable misunderstanding about the meaning of the word obscene. It is suggested that this book cannot be described fairly as obscene because in the course of it there are no filthy words, and it is said to be well written, and should be regarded as a work of literature, and therefore, not a proper subject for these proceedings.
I find that the Standard Dictionary describes the word obscene as "offensive to chastity, delicacy, or decency . . or offensive to the moral senses as to excite lustful passions.
Mr. Justice Cope, (Cockburn, L.C.J.?) in the leading case of the Queen v. Bickley, (? Hicklin), said: 'I think the test of obscenity is whether the tendency of the matter charged is so obscene as to deprave and corrupt those whose minds are open to immoral influences'.

2. I agree that the book has some literary merits, but the very fact that is is well written can be no answer to these proceedings, because otherwise we should be in the preposterous position that the most obscene books would be free from stricture. It must appear to everyone of intelligence that the better an obscene book is written the greater the public to whom it is likely to appeal. The more palatable the poison, he said, the more insidious.

3. These unnatural offences which are the subject of this book, involve acts which between men would be criminal, and would involve acts of the most horrible, unnatural and disgusting obscenity. That is a fact that no one can deny. Therefore, if I find in this book that these practices are defined, or in any way held up to admiration, no reasonable person can say that the book is not, in that case, an obscene publication. I can imagine a book written on this subject presenting the whole matter as a tragedy - the tragedy being that there may be people so afflicted who try their best to fight against this hoocrible vice, and find themselves in peril in that direction, or unable to resist its tendencies that result in the moral and physical degradation, I can imagine dealing with the subject on those terms forming the subject of a novel which might have a strong moral influence. But does this book do it?

4. On the contrary the tragedy is presented here as that of people who indulge in these vices and who are not tolerated by decent people, not received in society but ostracised. The whole note of the book is a passionate and almost hysterical plea for the toleration and recognition of these people, and that their practices should be tolerated and recognised in decent society. It is a long book, of 500 pages dealing solely or in the main with unnatural offences.

5. There is not a single word from beginning to end in this book, which suggests that anyone with these tendencies is in the least blameworthy, or that they should be resisted. Every one of the characters in this book who indulge in these vices are presented to us as attractive people, and put forward for our admiration, and those who object to these vices are sneered at in this book as prejudiced, foolish, and cruel. What is a much more serious matter, the actual physical acts of these women indulging in unnatural vices are described in the most alluring terms. It is actually put forward that this indulgence improves their mental balance and capacity.

FIG.84
Report regarding the *Well of Loneliness*
By the London Public Morality Council
20 November 1928
Typewritten on paper
British Library
Add MS 83659 B, f.199r

an 'obscene libel', not because it contained indecent language or explicit descriptions, but because: 'Unfortunately these women did exist ... and the book asked that their existence should be recognised and tolerated, instead of their being treated with condemnation as they were at present by all decent people.'[14] The quality of the writing made it even more likely that the book 'would tend to corrupt those into whose hands is should fall', and therefore it was condemned to be destroyed.[15] Ironically, the banning of the book brought the very existence of lesbianism much greater public recognition than it had previously had. The book also faced an obscenity trial in America, but ultimately the lack of sexually explicit material and differences in law meant that by 1929 it was cleared of obscenity and could be published in the US. It was finally republished in the UK in 1949. **CM**

JAMES JOYCE

Born and brought up in Dublin, James Joyce (1882–1941) was one of the most original, influential novelists of the twentieth century. He gained international recognition for the importance of his work during his lifetime, but like many innovative writers, he struggled with censorship. After attending university in Dublin, Joyce made half-hearted attempts to become a doctor and then a professional singer, before turning, in earnest, to writing. In June 1904 he met Nora Barnacle (1884–1951), a Dublin chambermaid, who was to become his muse throughout his life, and eventually also his wife. A few months later, Joyce and Barnacle left Dublin for Continental Europe, partly because the social difference between them made their relationship difficult in Ireland.

Joyce drew on his knowledge of and experiences in Ireland, and specifically Dublin, in all his writing, but spent almost all his adult life in Switzerland, Italy and France. He wrote slowly, which, combined with his often-dissolute lifestyle and the repeated censorship that he faced in the UK and the US meant that he was continuously in financial difficulties. However, a circle of friends and admirers, recognising the importance of his work, supported him throughout his working life, both financially and practically. This included other writers, and also journal editors and publishers, most notably the editor and publisher Harriet Shaw Weaver (1876–1961). *A Portrait of the Artist as a Young Man* was published in serial form and then as a novel, with Weaver's help, first in New York in 1916 and then in London in 1917.

The next book that Joyce wrote was *Ulysses* (1920), widely regarded as his masterpiece. It follows the lives and experiences of three people in Dublin over the course of one day in 1904. It is written using a rich variety of literary techniques, including, most famously a 'stream of consciousness', in which the characters' thoughts, feelings and sensations seem to pour unmediated onto the page. Joyce continually filled notebooks with thoughts, phrases, descriptions and observations, which he later extracted for use in his books. He used a different coloured crayon each time he went back to his notebooks, indicating what he'd taken from them at different times. The notes on these pages were used in Ulysses; the diagram charts the development of a human foetus and relates to an episode set in a maternity hospital (fig.85).

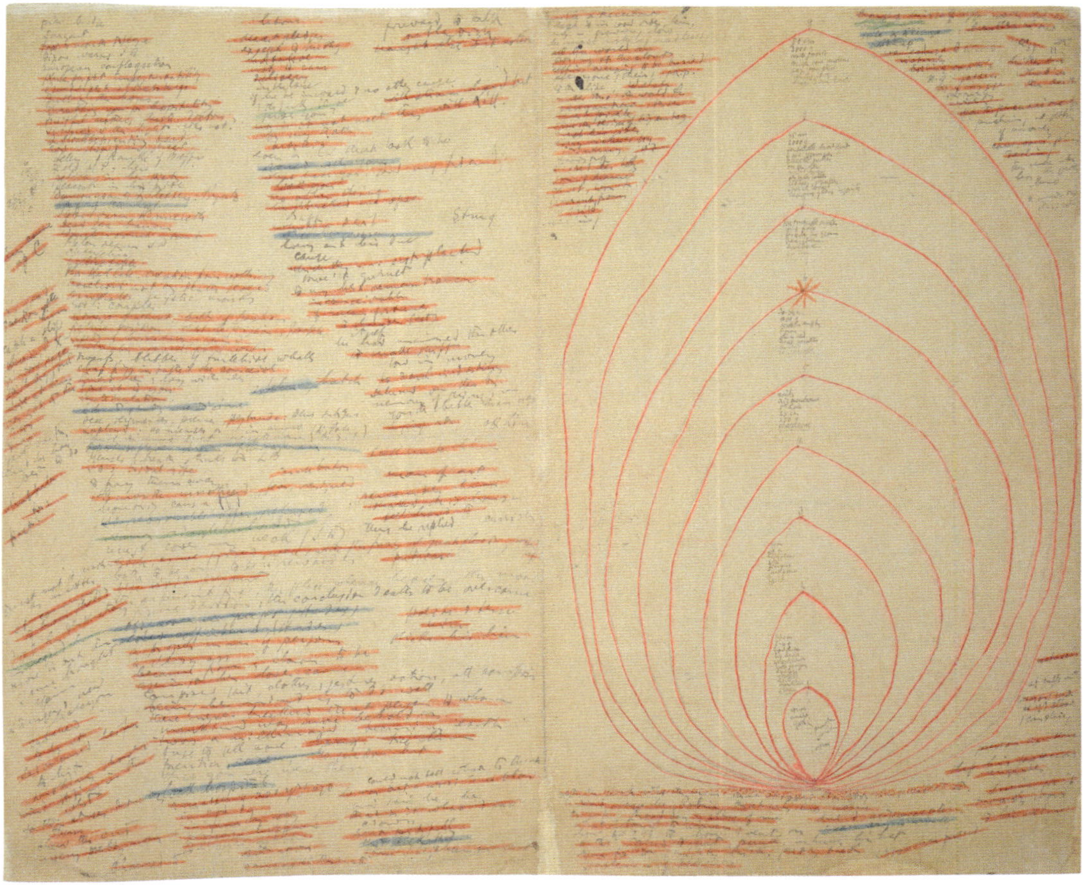

Like *A Portrait of the Artist*, Joyce published *Ulysses* initially in serial form, this time in the American literary journal *The Little Review*. Episodes were published from 1918 until 1920, when the New York Society for the Suppression of Vice instigated a prosecution for obscenity against the journal on the basis of the publication of the 'Nausicaa' episode in the April 1920 issue. Joyce's commitment to represent all of life in his novels, including the realities of bodily functions and of sex, found full expression in *Ulysses* and this was too much for the conservative establishment. The editors of the journal lost the court case and were fined, and as a result they stopped publishing the serials. In response to these events, Sylvia Beach (1887–1962), proprietor of the Paris bookshop Shakespeare and Company, decided to publish the full book in 1922. Weaver had a British edition printed in Paris for her Egoist Press, but many copies were seized by customs and the book was banned in the UK.

The French painter Jacques-Émile Blanche (1861–1942) was a largely self-taught but very successful portrait painter, working in Paris while Joyce was living there. He painted at least three portraits of the author in

FIG.85
Notes towards *Ulysses*
By James Joyce
*c.*1919–21
Pencil and black ink with green, blue, red and pink crayon on paper
British Library
Add MS 49975, f.11r

FIG.86
James Joyce
By Jacques-Émile Blanche
1935
Oil on canvas
National Portrait Gallery
NPG 3883

1934–5, of which this is one (fig.86). Joyce had suffered from eye problems and wore a bulging, magnifying lens over his left eye, about which Blanche recorded that Joyce was self-conscious. During this period Joyce was also suffering from periodic bouts of colitis and was deeply concerned about his daughter, Lucia, who was experiencing serious mental illness. He was working on his final book, *Finnegans Wake* (1939), at this time. However, better news was around the corner. The ban on *Ulysses* was lifted in the US in 1934, the judge having noted, memorably, that: 'In respect of the recurrent emergence of the theme of sex in the minds of [Joyce's] characters, it must always be remembered that his locale was Celtic and his season Spring.'[16] The UK ban was lifted two years later in 1936. **CM**

D. H. LAWRENCE

Born into a mining family in Nottinghamshire, England, the novelist David Herbert (D. H.) Lawrence (1885–1930) knew from an early age that he did not want to follow his father and uncles into the mines, and he was supported in his academic ambitions by his mother. After school, the obvious professional route for him at that time was into teaching; both his short-lived experiences of teaching and his mining background were to provide him with much material for his novels. His first novel, *The White Peacock,* was published in 1911, but it was with *Sons and Lovers* (1913) that he gained real literary admiration, although this did not translate into a high volume of sales. The book was completed while Lawrence was living on the Continent with Frieda Weekley (1879–1956), the wife of his professor from University College Nottingham. Weekley was to become Lawrence's wife in 1914 and was an important influence on his writing.

Lawrence's next novel saw a departure in his style from his previous work. This not only assured him a place in literary history as one of the great innovators of the twentieth century but also led – as such experimentation had for others – to censorship. The author had originally intended the work to be the first part of a single novel about three generations of one family, but he split his material into two books: *The Rainbow* (1915) and *Women in Love* (1920). Lawrence's approach in these books, influenced by contemporary work in psychology, psychoanalysis and philosophy, was to explore deeper aspects of the human psyche; these were often expressed through the physical experiences of his characters and by descriptions that made connections between his characters' emotional and psychological states and the countryside and nature around them.

The Rainbow was published by Methuen & Co. in September 1915, but received vicious reviews, mostly attacking its descriptions of sexual experiences. It was withdrawn from sale and, on 13 November after a trial at Bow Street Police Court, Methuen was ordered to destroy the remaining copies of the book on the grounds that it 'was a mass of obscenity of thought, ideas, and action throughout, wrapped up in language which he [the representative of the Commissioner of Police] supposed would be regarded in some quarters as an artistic and intellectual effort'.[17] The part seen as most offensive was probably the account of the character Ursula's lesbian affair with her teacher, but the book's strong anti-military views, in a time of war, were probably also a factor in the prosecution.

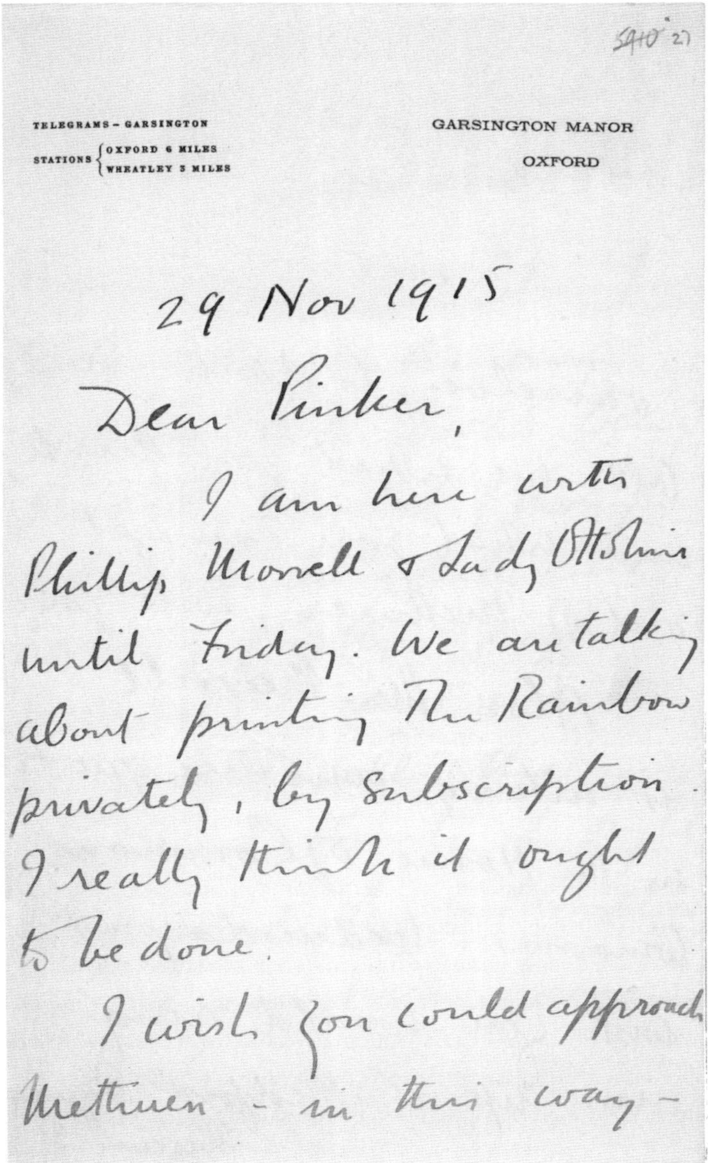
TELEGRAMS – GARSINGTON
STATIONS { OXFORD 6 MILES / WHEATLEY 3 MILES
GARSINGTON MANOR
OXFORD

29 Nov 1915

Dear Pinker,

I am here with Philip Morrell & Lady Ottoline until Friday. We are talking about printing The Rainbow privately, by subscription. I really think it ought to be done.

I wish you could approach Methuen – in this way –

FIG.87
Letter to James Brand Pinker
From D.H. Lawrence
29 November 1915
Black ink on letterhead paper
British Library
Add MS 74258, f.27r

The book was not banned in America but was published with significant cuts. However, Lawrence had not given up on the idea of publishing *The Rainbow* in Britain. As this letter to his literary agent James Brand Pinker (1863–1922) indicates (fig.87), he thought that printing it privately, paid for by subscription, might be the solution. In the event this did not happen, and it was unavailable in Britain for another 11 years. *Women in Love* was rejected by Lawrence's British publishers, Methuen, after the banning of *The Rainbow*, but was published in the US in 1920, and finally in London in 1921. By this time, the reception of *The Rainbow*, combined with despair about the war and what it reflected about his

FIG.88
D.H. Lawrence
By Jan Juta
1920
Oil on canvas
National Portrait Gallery
NPG 4036

fellow human beings, had deeply affected Lawrence's view of the world and he and Frieda had left England for good.

Lawrence and Frieda spent some time in Italy before moving away from Europe to Sri Lanka, Australia and later the US and Mexico. While they were in Italy they met a young South African artist, Jan Juta (1895–1990), who painted this portrait in Sicily in 1920 (fig.88), capturing the writer's intense expression and the reddish hair and beard that his contemporaries often commented on. Lawrence also used Juta's paintings of Sardinian life to illustrate his travel book, *Sea and Sardinia* (1921). After a period in the US and Mexico, Lawrence and Frieda settled finally in Italy. It was here that Lawrence wrote his final and most famous book, *Lady Chatterley's Lover* (1928), which he had printed in Florence and distributed privately through friends. The success of this book finally brought him the financial security that had previously evaded him. However, by this stage Lawrence was terminally ill with tuberculosis, and he died on 2 March 1930 at the age of 44. The book was banned in many countries. In England, the first unexpurgated edition of *Lady Chatterley's Lover* was published 1960 by Penguin Books. This led to a famous obscenity trial in London. Penguin was found not guilty, thereby liberalising British publishing and ushering in the 'permissive society' of the 1960s. **CM**

C. L. R. JAMES

Cyril Lionel Robert (C. L. R.) James (1901–1989) was an influential Marxist writer and political activist born in Trinidad, a British colony until it gained independence in 1962. During his education at the Queen's Royal College in Port of Spain, James became an accomplished cricketer and athlete, as well as starting to pursue a career in writing. On graduation, he began teaching and joined the Beacon Group, an anti-colonial circle of writers. At this time, he also drafted his only novel, *Minty Alley* (1936), and began campaigning for West Indian independence. In 1933 James moved to London where he discovered Marxism and joined pan-African and pan-Caribbean movements. Later, he visited Leon Trotsky (1879–1940) to discuss an independent Black movement.

In addition to his political activism, James helped uncover a hugely important yet significantly under-studied and ignored aspect of history: the Haitian Revolution. The Revolution began in August 1791 when enslaved peoples mounted a self-liberating insurrection against colonial rule. It was the only successful revolt of its kind in history and one that resulted not only in the colony's independence, but also a complete overhaul of the way in which Haiti was governed and run. That such a significant revolution, which began two years after the start of the French Revolution (1789), and only 26 years after the start of American Revolution (1765), was given very little attention was redressed by James in one book and two plays on the subject. Crucially, James told the story of the revolution from the perspective of the enslaved people, showing how they were agents in their own emancipation.

James wrote the play *Toussaint Louverture: The Story of the Only Successful Slave Revolt in History*, in 1934; it was staged in 1936. It was the first time a play written by a Black writer had been performed by professional Black actors in England. Toussaint Louverture (1743–1803), a formerly enslaved Haitian general, is considered the most significant leader of the Haitian Revolution. Using his wide-ranging political and military acumen and influence, Louverture sought to balance the economy and security of Haiti, restoring a plantation system using paid labour. Two years after James's play was first staged, he wrote the non-fiction work *The Black Jacobins: Toussaint L'Ouverture and the San Domingo Revolution*. In 1967 James went on to write a second play on the subject, *The Black Jacobins*, the playscript draft of which is in the British Library (fig.89).

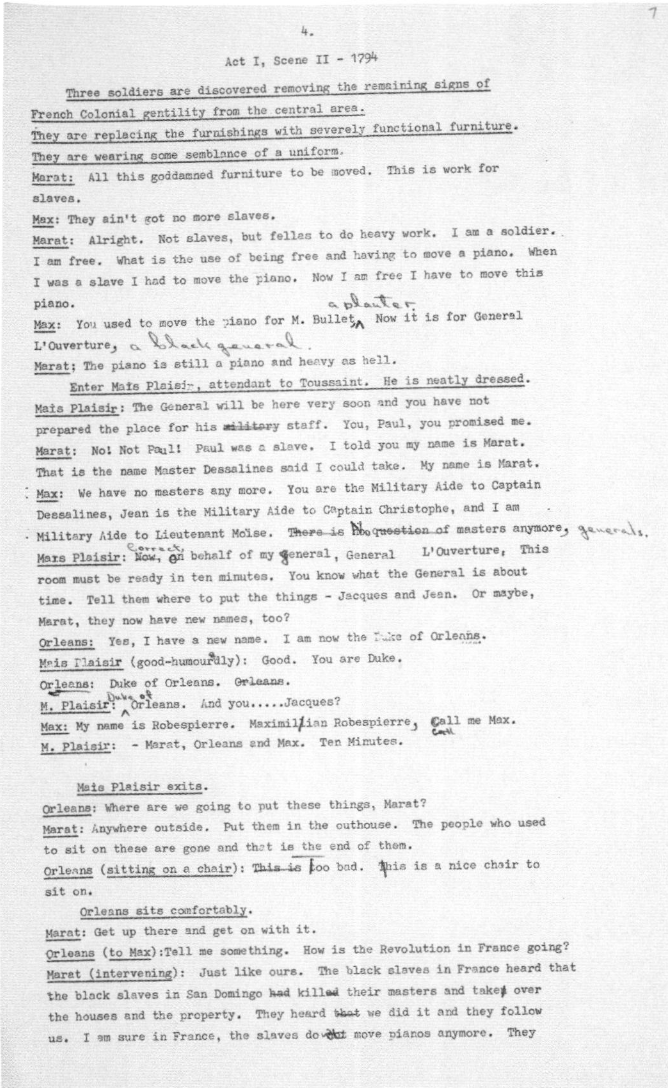

7

4.

Act I, Scene II - 1794

Three soldiers are discovered removing the remaining signs of French Colonial gentility from the central area. They are replacing the furnishings with severely functional furniture. They are wearing some semblance of a uniform.

Marat: All this goddamned furniture to be moved. This is work for slaves.

Max: They ain't got no more slaves.

Marat: Alright. Not slaves, but fellas to do heavy work. I am a soldier. I am free. What is the use of being free and having to move a piano. When I was a slave I had to move the piano. Now I am free I have to move this piano.

Max: You used to move the piano for M. Bullet, a planter. Now it is for General L'Ouverture, a black general.

Marat; The piano is still a piano and heavy as hell.

Enter Maîs Plaisir, attendant to Toussaint. He is neatly dressed.

Maîs Plaisir: The General will be here very soon and you have not prepared the place for his ~~military~~ staff. You, Paul, you promised me.

Marat: No! Not Paul! Paul was a slave. I told you my name is Marat. That is the name Master Dessalines said I could take. My name is Marat.

Max: We have no masters any more. You are the Military Aide to Captain Dessalines, Jean is the Military Aide to Captain Christophe, and I am Military Aide to Lieutenant Moïse. ~~There is no question of~~ No masters anymore, generals.

Mais Plaisir: ~~Now,~~ Correct, on behalf of my general, General L'Ouverture, This room must be ready in ten minutes. You know what the General is about time. Tell them where to put the things - Jacques and Jean. Or maybe, Marat, they now have new names, too?

Orleans: Yes, I have a new name. I am now the Duke of Orleans.

Mais Plaisir (good-humouredly): Good. You are Duke.

Orleans: Duke of Orleans. ~~Orleans~~.

M. Plaisir: Duke of Orleans. And you.....Jacques?

Max: My name is Robespierre. Maximilian Robespierre, call me Max.

M. Plaisir: - Marat, Orleans and Max. Ten Minutes.

Mais Plaisir exits.

Orleans: Where are we going to put these things, Marat?

Marat: Anywhere outside. Put them in the outhouse. The people who used to sit on these are gone and that is the end of them.

Orleans (sitting on a chair): ~~This is~~ Too bad. This is a nice chair to sit on.

Orleans sits comfortably.

Marat: Get up there and get on with it.

Orleans (to Max):Tell me something. How is the Revolution in France going?

Marat (intervening): Just like ours. The black slaves in France heard that the black slaves in San Domingo ~~had~~ kill their masters and take over the houses and the property. They heard ~~that~~ we did it and they follow us. I am sure in France, the slaves don't move pianos anymore. They

FIG.89

Draft playscript for *The Black Jacobins*

By C. L. R. James

1967

Typewritten and blue ink on paper

British Library

Add MS 89377/7/36, f.7r

James's two plays and book about Toussaint Louverture and the Haitian Revolution are key to making visible a moment when suppressed peoples were able to revolt with success. James explained the importance of telling the story of this fight for independence:

> 'Before Haiti, only one other nation had declared independence from a European power in the Americas. If this fact is startling to us the surprise stems from a very long history of making Haiti and the United States so unfathomably distant in their origins and histories, rather than two nations that broke away from European colonial powers within three decades of each other. The Haitian Revolution should not be so overshadowed.'[18]

FIG.90
C. L. R. James
By Val Wilmer for
Format Photographers
31 December 1975
Modern gelatin silver print
National Portrait Gallery
NPG x133130

When he visited Trinidad in 1962, his former pupil, Prime Minister Eric Williams (1911–1981), the first prime minister of independent Trinidad, banned James's books. James was placed under house arrest until a public outcry secured his release. He remained politically active throughout his life and was a leading figure in the Pan-African movement. Setting up the newspaper *We, the People*, James used the press to advocate for a new Trinidad based on an ancient Greek model of a city state.

This photograph of James was taken by Val Wilmer (b.1941) for Format Photographers (fig.90; see also p.112). In addition to photography, Wilmer is also a hugely influential writer specialising in jazz and British African-Caribbean music. Her work includes *Jazz People* (1970) and *As Serious as Your Life: Black Music and the Free Jazz Revolution* (1977), both of which were published by Allison & Busby, who were also publishers of C. L. R. James. **AA**

SAMUEL BECKETT

One of the most innovative and highly regarded of all playwrights, Samuel Beckett (1906–1989) was born in Dublin, Ireland, and studied modern European literature at Trinity College, Dublin, briefly trying teaching and taking up an academic post before turning to writing. With the interruption of a few periods in Ireland and London, Beckett spent much of the late 1920s and 1930s in Paris, where he became friends with James Joyce (1882–1941; see p.153), who was an influence on the younger writer. He worked on poems, novels and short stories during this time but had little success in publishing his work, which was often highly experimental and intellectual. During the Second World War, as an Irishman he was, in theory, neutral, but in fact he worked for the French Resistance and eventually had to flee Paris, escaping to rural France where he lived out the rest of the war with his partner and eventual wife, Suzanne Déchevaux-Dumesnil (1900–1989).

After the war, Beckett's writing underwent a marked stylistic change, with a clearer break from Joyce's influence. It became simpler but also darker, drawing on the uncertainty in his own inner consciousness rather than on external influences and information. Writing in French rather than English was an important part of letting go of his previously dense, layered linguistic approach. He was in financial penury at this time but was writing prolifically. Beckett wrote the play *Waiting for Godot* between October 1948 and January 1949; this was the work that was to make his reputation and literary career, and, still more significantly, was to transform the whole landscape of post-war theatre.

The play had run in Paris for two years when an application was made to stage it in London. Since 1737 all plays performed in Great Britain were required to be submitted to the office of the Lord Chamberlain, the most senior member of the Royal Household, for a licence. An official Examiner of Plays would read the plays, write a synopsis for each and recommend them – or not – for a licence, often also indicating where cuts should be made in order to make them acceptable. *Waiting for Godot* was read by Lieutenant-Colonel Sir Thomas St Vincent Wallace Troubridge (1895–1963), Assistant Examiner of Plays, who wrote his report on 18 March 1954 (fig.91).

Troubridge struggled to understand the play, as he freely admitted in his report:

FIG.91
Lord Chamberlain's report on *Waiting for Godot*
1954
Typewritten and blue ballpoint pen on paper
British Library
LCP Corr 1954/6597, f.1v

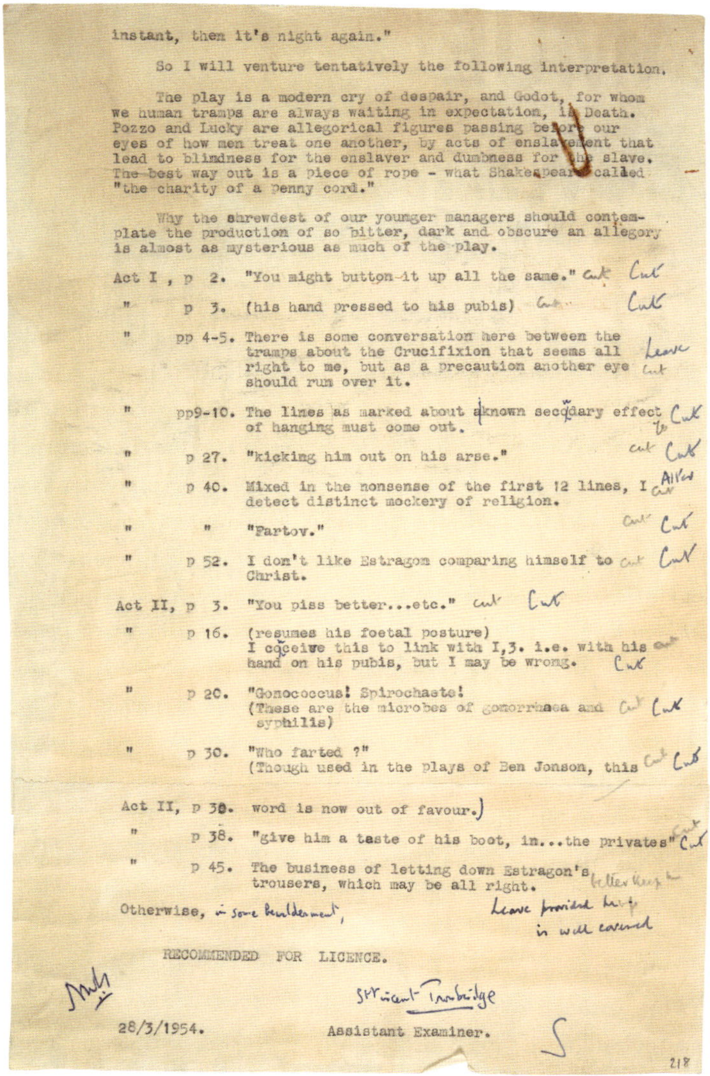

instant, then it's night again."

So I will venture tentatively the following interpretation.

The play is a modern cry of despair, and Godot, for whom we human tramps are always waiting in expectation, is Death. Pozzo and Lucky are allegorical figures passing before our eyes of how men treat one another, by acts of enslavement that lead to blindness for the enslaver and dumbness for the slave. The best way out is a piece of rope - what Shakespeare called "the charity of a penny cord."

Why the shrewdest of our younger managers should contemplate the production of so bitter, dark and obscure an allegory is almost as mysterious as much of the play.

Act I , p 2. "You might button it up all the same."

" p 3. (his hand pressed to his pubis)

" pp 4-5. There is some conversation here between the tramps about the Crucifixion that seems all right to me, but as a precaution another eye should run over it.

" pp9-10. The lines as marked about a known secondary effect of hanging must come out.

" p 27. "kicking him out on his arse."

" p 40. Mixed in the nonsense of the first 12 lines, I detect distinct mockery of religion.

" " "Partov."

" p 52. I don't like Estragon comparing himself to Christ.

Act II, p 3. "You piss better...etc."

" p 16. (resumes his foetal posture)
I conceive this to link with I,3. i.e. with his hand on his pubis, but I may be wrong.

" p 20. "Gonococcus! Spirochaete!
(These are the microbes of gonorrhaea and syphilis)

" p 30. "Who farted ?"
(Though used in the plays of Ben Jonson, this

Act II, p 30. word is now out of favour.)

" p 38. "give him a taste of his boot, in...the privates"

" p 45. The business of letting down Estragon's trousers, which may be all right.

Otherwise, in some bewilderment,

RECOMMENDED FOR LICENCE.

28/3/1954. Assistant Examiner.

> 'I can describe the simple happenings on the stage, and indicate for elimination the words and lines of Joycean grossness, but I can only offer the merest glimmer of a suggestion of what the author intends it all to mean.'[19]

Having described Beckett as 'a former Secretary of James Joyce', he blamed Joyce's influence for passages he felt were coarse. He suggested 15 lines or passages be cut from the play, of which three were in the end allowed to remain. Some of the cuts were to sexual references; others were to language that he had described as 'Joycean', including the line 'who farted?', where he noted, 'Though used in the plays of Ben Jonson, this word is now out of favour'.[20] He signed off, 'Otherwise, *in some bewilderment* [added in pen], RECOMMENDED FOR LICENCE'.

FIG.92
Samuel Beckett
By John Minihan
1985
Resin print
National Portrait Gallery
NPG x29006

Beckett was evidently furious about the suggested cuts, but in the end the play was staged at the Arts Theatre Club, London, in August 1955, directed by the then 24-year-old Peter Hall (1930–2017). Many audience members walked out, complaints were made to the Lord Chamberlain's office and there were bad reviews. However, two powerful, positive reviews – by Kenneth Tynan (1927–1980) for the *Observer* and Harold Hobson (1904–1992) for *The Sunday Times* – on 7 August, transformed both the critical and the popular view of the play. It became a huge critical and financial success and secured Beckett's reputation. Beckett went on to write other highly admired plays including *Endgame* (1957), *Krapp's Last Tape* (1958), and *Happy Days* (1961). In 1969 he won the Nobel Prize in Literature, 'for his writing, which – in new forms for the novel and drama – in the destitution of modern man acquires its elevation'.[21]

The photographer John Minihan (b.1946) took this evocative portrait of Beckett not long before the writer's eightieth birthday (fig.92). Minihan is a Dublin-born photographer who worked for the *Daily Mail* and the *Evening Standard* newspapers, before becoming a freelancer, specialising in photographing figures from the arts. He had photographed Beckett on previous occasions and in 1985 the author invited him to come to Paris. This photograph was taken in Beckett's local café in Montparnasse on a December afternoon, just as the light was fading. Minihan regards it as one of his best images, largely because the writer himself directed the scene. **CM**

ANDREW SALKEY, SAM SELVON AND JOHN LA ROSE

This photograph of Andrew Salkey (1928–1995), Sam Selvon (1923–1994) and John La Rose (1927–2006) was taken by Horace Ové (1939–2023), who called it *The Lime* (fig.93). The word 'liming' is a Caribbean term that describes relaxing with friends. Salkey, Selvon and La Rose were three writers who were part of the generation of people who emigrated from the Caribbean to England in the middle of the twentieth century, known as the Windrush generation. They wrote and talked about the racism they encountered and the barriers to publishing their works due to their nationalities and the colour of their skin.

FIG.93
***The Lime* (from left: Sam Selvon, John La Rose and Andrew Salkey)**
By Horace Ové
1974
Giclée print
National Portrait Gallery
NPG x126733

Part One CARIBBEA

Xaymaca

(i)

Caribbea,
knowledgeable,
patient,

raise your emancipated arms;
give your breasts,

maternal,
absolute,
elegant,
malachite eyes.

Caribbea,
moving in the morning,
shift your pearls;
bolster Xaymaca.

Our Sea,
prepare a path.

When the Doctor Breeze
and the Undertaker Wind
guess your age,
I see you wince;
I feel the shame you bear;
I, too, shudder,
knowing your age,
banded as the coconut palm.

I remember you aging like the coffee bean,
when the Arawaks screamed your name;
when, through the swift, slanting arbaletes
stinging the palpitating ground,
Port Maria bared her cocoa brown teeth
and Columbus found a wall of ghosts;
when, after scratches from lobster-claw,

FIG.94
Corrected typescript for 'Jamaica Symphony'
By Andrew Salkey
*c.*1955
Typewritten and pencil on paper
British Library
Add MS 89377/2/4, f.14r

Andrew Salkey was a Jamaican writer who moved to the UK in 1952. He became the main presenter of the Caribbean section at the BBC. The BBC broadcast a weekly programme called *Caribbean Voices*, which featured short stories and poems aimed at a Caribbean audience. In addition to Salkey, the programme gave voice to writers including Sam Selvon, Una Marson (1905–1965; see p.265) and George Lamming (1927–2022; see p.170). In 1966, along with John La Rose and Edward Kamau Brathwaite (1930–2020), Salkey founded the Caribbean Artists Movement, an initiative that helped foster the discussion and review of writing, music and theatre by Caribbean artists.

Salkey expanded on the importance of understanding his history and that of Jamaica:

> '... I really started learning about me and home and the history, because I damn well wanted to talk to Jamaicans about Jamaica in the long poem that I was hoping to write ... for the first time I began to realise myself as a colonial and us as a colony, and our history, and the way that we were forever at somebody else's beck and call. Our economy wasn't ours. Even our language wasn't really ours. We had to, at least I had to, relearn a great deal.'[22]

In 1973 Salkey published his epic poem, *Jamaica* (originally titled 'Jamaica Symphony'), dedicated to his mother and the people of his home country. Shown here is a page from part one of the poem, which Salkey has corrected (fig.94). When he first attempted to publish 'Jamaica Symphony' he was met with a number of rejections. A letter from the publishers New Authors on 17 November 1958 to Salkey suggests one of the reasons was because readers in Great Britain were unable to identify with the subject matter:

> 'We have carefully considered your typescript "Jamaica Symphony", but I am sorry to have to tell you that although we have read it with much interest we have decided against making an offer for publication ... one of our readers felt ... "though he's entitled to use exotic language when dealing with an exotic country he must relate it visually and mentally to our experience".'[23]

Like Salkey, Sam Selvon wrote about his experiences in England. He emigrated to London from Trinidad in 1950 and wrote television scripts, short stories, poetry and 11 novels. *The Lonely Londoners* (1956) is written in a Caribbean dialect and captures the hostility and isolation faced by Caribbean

FIG.95
The Lonely Londoners
By Samuel Selvon
(Allan Wingate, London, 1956)
British Library
RF.2013.a.2.

people living in London after the Second World War. This is a subject tackled later by Andrea Levy (1956–2019) in *Small Island* (see p.68). Shown here is the striking dust jacket for the first edition of the work by the artist Charles Mozley (1914–1991; fig.95) Selvon's story continues to resonate, with a theatrical adaptation staged at the Jermyn Street Theatre, London, in 2024.

Born in Trinidad, John La Rose was a writer and activist who founded New Beacon Books, the first specialist Caribbean publisher in the UK. La Rose later became chairman of the Institute of Race Relations and Towards Racial Justice, originally the vehicles for the publication of the *Race Today* journal. The poet Linton Kwesi Johnson (b.1952; see p.271) said in La Rose's obituary for the *Guardian* newspaper: 'John belongs to a Caribbean tradition of radical and revolutionary activism whose input has reverberated across continents.'[24]

Through New Beacon Books, La Rose was the driving force behind the establishment of the George Padmore Institute, an archive, educational research and information centre housing materials and documents relating mainly to Black communities of Caribbean, African and Asian descent in post-war Britain and Continental Europe. La Rose was good friends with Andrew Salkey and New Beacon published a number of Salkey's works. Shown here is a letter written in May 1974 by La Rose to Salkey, thanking him for his continued support and

FIG.96
Letter to Andrew Salkey
From John La Rose
4 May 1974
Typewritten and black ink on paper
British Library
Add MS 89377/7/41, f.21r

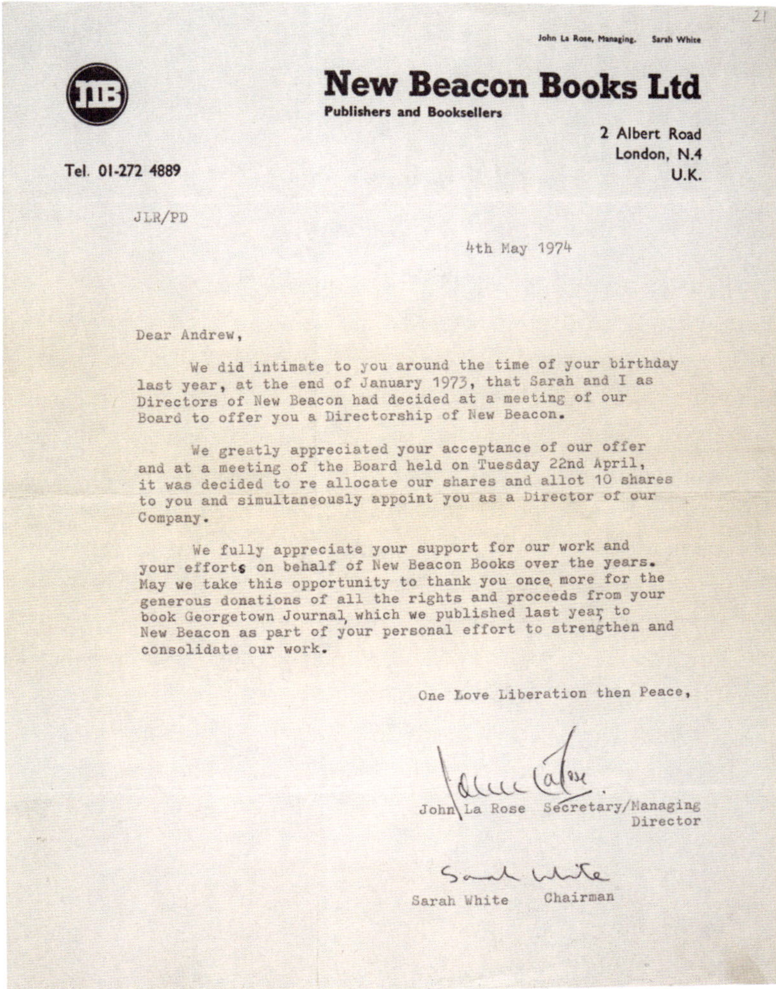

21

John La Rose, Managing. Sarah White

New Beacon Books Ltd
Publishers and Booksellers

2 Albert Road
London, N.4
U.K.

Tel. 01-272 4889

JLR/PD

4th May 1974

Dear Andrew,

We did intimate to you around the time of your birthday last year, at the end of January 1973, that Sarah and I as Directors of New Beacon had decided at a meeting of our Board to offer you a Directorship of New Beacon.

We greatly appreciated your acceptance of our offer and at a meeting of the Board held on Tuesday 22nd April, it was decided to re allocate our shares and allot 10 shares to you and simultaneously appoint you as a Director of our Company.

We fully appreciate your support for our work and your efforts on behalf of New Beacon Books over the years. May we take this opportunity to thank you once more for the generous donations of all the rights and proceeds from your book Georgetown Journal, which we published last year to New Beacon as part of your personal effort to strengthen and consolidate our work.

One Love Liberation then Peace,

John La Rose Secretary/Managing Director

Sarah White Chairman

confirming his appointment as a board director and shareholder of New Beacon Books (fig.96). Written under the New Beacon Books letterhead, La Rose acknowledges that Salkey donated the rights and proceeds from his book, *Georgetown Journal* (1972) to the publisher.

Another important achievement by La Rose was his organisation and joint directorship of the International Book Fair of Radical Black and Third World Books (1982–95). This was the first book fair of its kind and was intended to facilitate a 'new and expanding phase in the growth of the radical ideas and concepts and their expression in literature, politics, music, art and social life'.[25] Its purpose was to act as a vehicle through which many marginalised writers could promote their work.

La Rose published two books of his own poetry, *Foundations* (1966) and *Eyelets of Truth Within Me* (1992). Understanding the prejudice faced by Black writers and emigrants to Great Britain, La Rose was fond of saying 'we didn't come alive in Britain'.[26] **AA**

GEORGE LAMMING

The Barbadian writer and poet George Lamming (1927–2022) addressed the terrible prejudice and disillusionment faced by Caribbean emigrants who travelled to the UK after the Second World War. The author of four novels, his writing helps make visible the lives and experiences of many Caribbean people in England. In his essay 'Western Education and the Caribbean Intellectual', Lamming said: 'Subjugation and servitude became the logical instruments of social intercourse between Europe and all others.'[27] Lamming and the writer Sam Selvon (1923–1994; see p.165) had travelled to the UK together on the same boat, which Lamming described: 'This was a journey to an expectation, and between 1948 and 1960 every West Indian novelist of significance within their region made a similar journey.'[28]

While growing up in the Caribbean, writers like Lamming and Selvon believed that, as subjects of the British Empire, the UK was their home

FIG.97
The Emigrants
By George Lamming
(Michael Joseph, London, 1954)
British Library
NNN.5412.and
AAD/1995/8/31/433

FIG.98
George Lamming
By BHG Sampson
1952
Oil on board
National Portrait Gallery
NPG L281

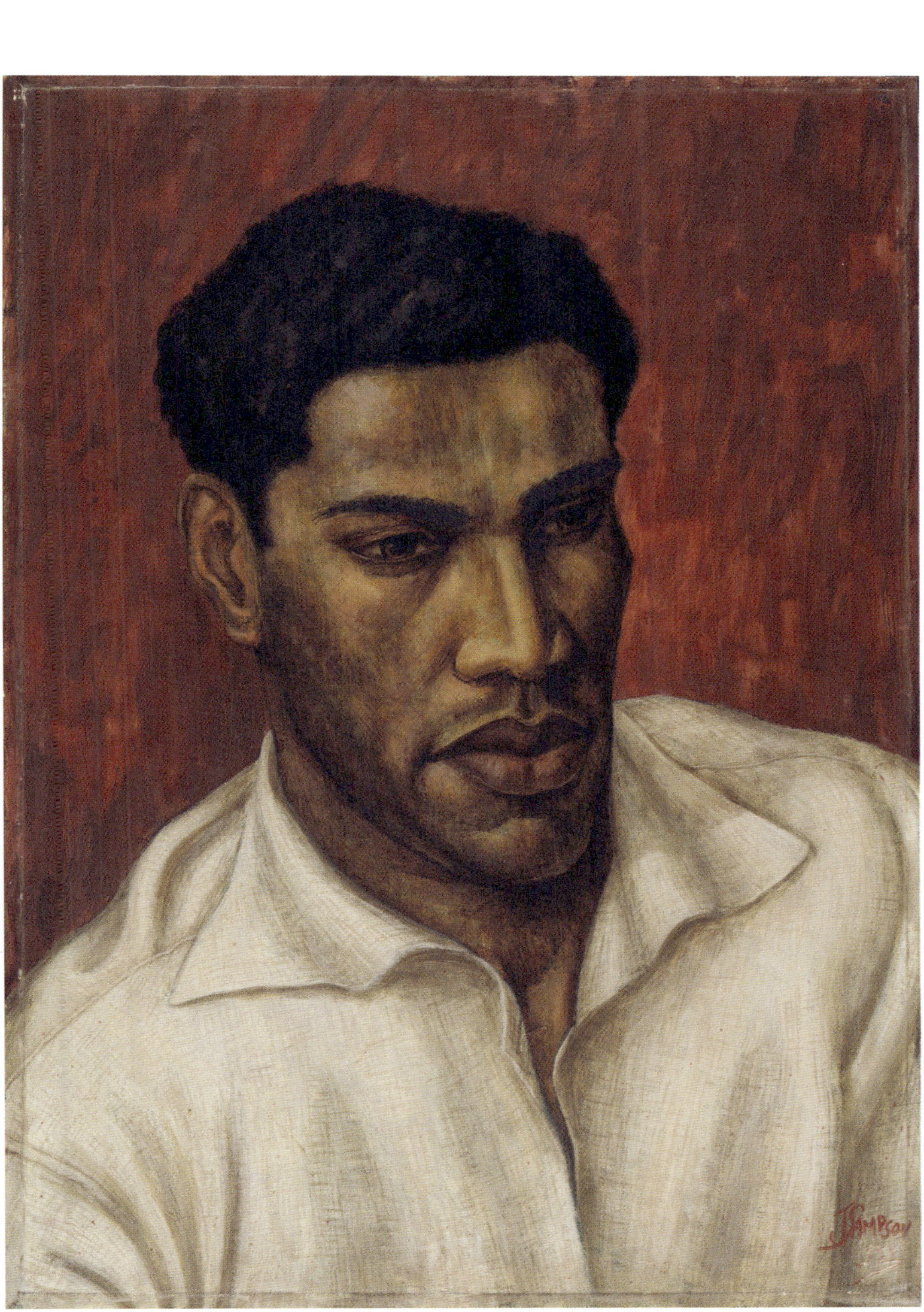

and that it represented an opportunity for a new life. Yet their dreams and beliefs were quickly quashed. Lamming stated:

> 'Migration was not a word I would have used to describe what I was doing when I moved with other West Indians to England in 1950. We easily thought we were going to an England that had been painted in our childhood consciousness as a heritage and a place of welcome. It is the measure of our innocence that neither the claim of heritage nor the expectation would have been seriously doubted ... Today I shudder to think how a country, so foreign to our own instincts, could have achieved the miracle of being called Mother.'[29]

In 1954 Lamming published *The Emigrants* as a sequel to his autobiographical work *In the Castle of My Skin* (1953), which describes the strategies of suppression of Caribbean people by colonial powers. *The Emigrants* charts the journey that many Caribbean people undertook, from Barbados to the UK, at first with hope and expectation, and then with realisation of the alienation and rejection they faced. Marginalisation due to colonialism is a theme that runs through this book and other published works by Lamming. Shown here is the first edition of *The Emigrants*, which features artwork and illustrations by the Guyanese artist Denis Williams (1923–1998; fig.97).

Painted two years before *The Emigrants* was published, this portrait by Bertonneux Harry George Sampson (1918–2005) shows Lamming shortly after he arrived in England (fig.98). The artist was a friend of Lamming, and he painted the portrait from life when the author was 25 years old. Sampson was a painter, photographer and ceramicist who was brought up on the Isle of Wight and studied at Camberwell College of Arts, London. Sampson's image is the only known portrait in oils of the author. **AA**

SALMAN RUSHDIE

Born in Bombay (now Mumbai), the acclaimed author Sir Salman Rushdie (b.1947) has been subject to one of the most notorious cases of censorship of modern times. He was educated in England and, after graduating from Oxford University, became a copywriter for the advertising agency Ogilvy & Mather. Here he came up with some memorable advertising strap lines including 'Naughty but nice' for cream cakes and 'That'll do nicely' for American Express. His first novel, *Grimus* (1975) was not well received nor a commercial success, but his second book, *Midnight's Children* (1981) won the Booker Prize and subsequently, in 1993 and 2008, won 'Best of the Bookers' on the occasions of the twenty-fifth and fortieth anniversaries of the prize. Like most of Rushdie's subsequent fiction, it features a protagonist of Indian origin and uses magic realism to create a complex and broad narrative, exploring interconnections and clashes between Eastern and Western cultures, and issues of identity in relation to nation, migration and postcolonialism. It has had immense influence on many subsequent writers, particularly those writing about postcolonial and immigrant experiences.

After the publication of *Midnight's Children*, Rushdie became an important spokesperson for Indian writers in Britain. He gave a lecture, 'The Indian Writer in England' (fig.99) at the Commonwealth Institute in July 1982 as part of the Festival of India in Britain, a state-sponsored celebration of historical and contemporary Indian culture in Britain. It appeared as a chapter in *The Eye of the Beholder: Indian Writing in English* edited by Maggie Butcher and published by the Commonwealth Institute, London, in 1983. On the page shown, Rushdie comments: 'Let me suggest that Indian writers in England have access to a second tradition ... It is the cultural and political history of the phenomenon of migration, displacement, life in a minority group.'

Rushdie's next novel was *Shame* (1983), which was also well received, followed by *The Satanic Verses* (1988). *The Satanic Verses* became the subject of one of the biggest literary controversies of the twentieth century. The book was perceived by many Muslims to be blasphemous in its treatment of the Prophet Muhammad, and it was banned in 13 countries with large Islamic communities. On 14 February 1989 the Supreme Leader of Iran, Ayatollah Ruhollah [Musavi] Khomeini (*c.*1900–1989), issued a *fatwa* (legal ruling in Islamic law) calling for Rushdie's execution. As a result,

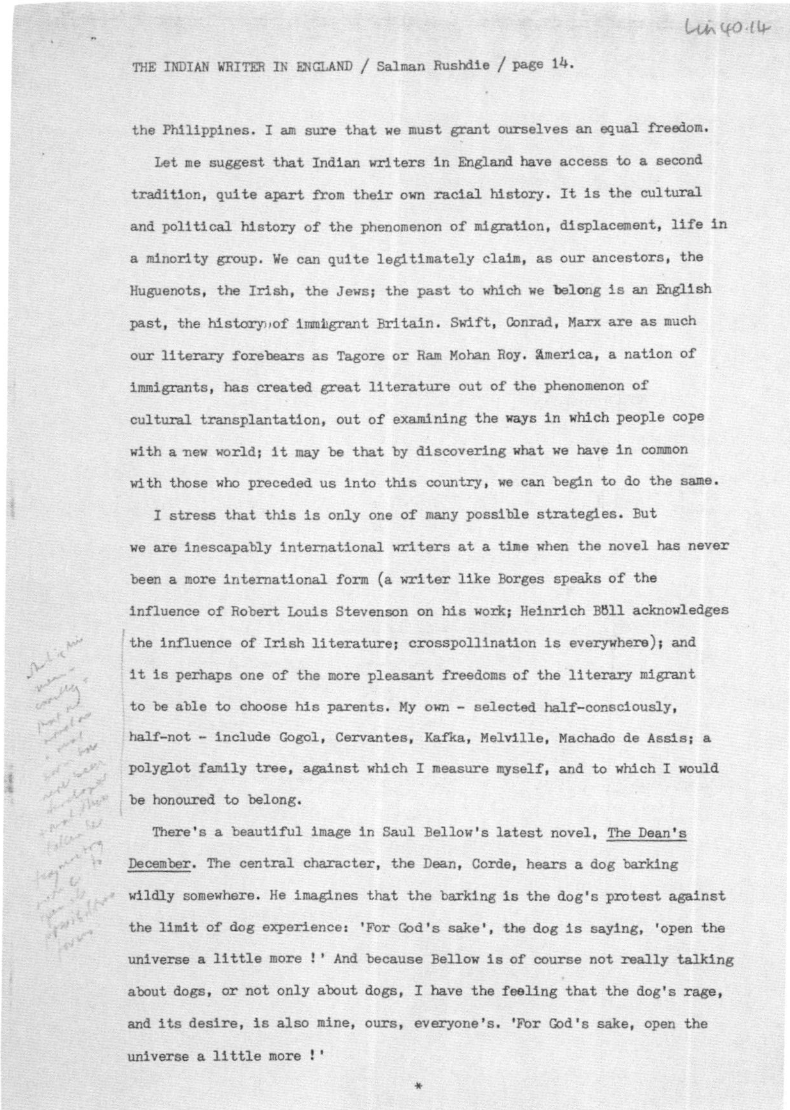

Lin 40.14

THE INDIAN WRITER IN ENGLAND / Salman Rushdie / page 14.

the Philippines. I am sure that we must grant ourselves an equal freedom.

Let me suggest that Indian writers in England have access to a second tradition, quite apart from their own racial history. It is the cultural and political history of the phenomenon of migration, displacement, life in a minority group. We can quite legitimately claim, as our ancestors, the Huguenots, the Irish, the Jews; the past to which we belong is an English past, the history of immigrant Britain. Swift, Conrad, Marx are as much our literary forebears as Tagore or Ram Mohan Roy. America, a nation of immigrants, has created great literature out of the phenomenon of cultural transplantation, out of examining the ways in which people cope with a new world; it may be that by discovering what we have in common with those who preceded us into this country, we can begin to do the same.

I stress that this is only one of many possible strategies. But we are inescapably international writers at a time when the novel has never been a more international form (a writer like Borges speaks of the influence of Robert Louis Stevenson on his work; Heinrich Böll acknowledges the influence of Irish literature; crosspollination is everywhere); and it is perhaps one of the more pleasant freedoms of the literary migrant to be able to choose his parents. My own – selected half-consciously, half-not – include Gogol, Cervantes, Kafka, Melville, Machado de Assis; a polyglot family tree, against which I measure myself, and to which I would be honoured to belong.

There's a beautiful image in Saul Bellow's latest novel, The Dean's December. The central character, the Dean, Corde, hears a dog barking wildly somewhere. He imagines that the barking is the dog's protest against the limit of dog experience: 'For God's sake', the dog is saying, 'open the universe a little more !' And because Bellow is of course not really talking about dogs, or not only about dogs, I have the feeling that the dog's rage, and its desire, is also mine, ours, everyone's. 'For God's sake, open the universe a little more !'

*

FIG.99
'The Indian Writer in England'
By Salman Rushdie
4 July 1982
Typewritten and pencil on paper
British Library
Deposit 11183L in 40 (Sept 1982) (Box 120)

FIG.100
Salman Rushdie ('The Moor')
By Bhupen Khakhar
1995
Oil on linen
National Portrait Gallery
NPG 6352

the author had to live in hiding for many years, before moving to the US in 2000 and living openly, in defiance of the continuing threat. In 2007 Rushdie was knighted in the Queen's Birthday Honours, which again stirred up international controversy, and in 2022 he survived a near-fatal stabbing attack when about to give a lecture in New York.

Bhupen Khakhar (1934–2003) painted Rushdie's portrait while the latter was still based in Britain, living in hiding (fig.100). Khakhar was a self-taught painter who became the best-known Indian artist of his generation in the West, and India's first openly gay artist. He had illustrated a privately printed volume by Rushdie, *Two Stories* (1989), with woodcuts and linocuts, and he appears as a character in *The Moor's Last Sigh* (1995) as an artist called 'the Accountant'. His portrait of Rushdie, painted in the year *The Moor's Last Sigh* was published, shows the author surrounded by scenes from the novel. Like other work by Khakhar, it combines Western and Eastern artistic influences from many different periods to create an image of the author that is appropriately wide-ranging and rich in reference and allusion. **CM**

FAME

Fame, frequently seen as a reward for success, can also be a problem for authors. In some cases, the popularity of a fictional character may exert unwanted control over a writer, dictating, to a greater or lesser extent, their future writing projects and publishing plans. In others, it has led to personality cults developing around authors, which have sometimes overshadowed their written output. This chapter explores the impact of popularity and fame on writers, their work and their public identities. It looks at authors' responses to their popularity, as well as considering short-lived and posthumous fame. It examines authors' attempts to break free of their most famous characters, the tensions between public and private identities and the ways that portraiture has reflected and responded to these struggles.

Some authors feel eclipsed by the fame of the protagonists they created. Such characters usually appear in more than one story, creating a following through successive volumes and often inspiring related products including films, toys and games, which further spread their fame. Examples include Lewis Carroll's Alice, Beatrix Potter's Peter Rabbit, A. A. Milne's Winnie-the-Pooh, J. K. Rowling's Harry Potter, Sir Arthur Conan Doyle's Sherlock Holmes and Bram Stoker's Dracula.

The success of such characters gives their authors financial security, but it has also, in many cases, circumscribed their ability to gain recognition in other areas. A. A. Milne was an accomplished playwright; Lewis Carroll wrote prolifically on other subjects including mathematics and logic; Beatrix Potter was a successful farmer and sheep breeder; Conan Doyle wanted to be remembered for his historical fiction as well as his support of spiritualism. Frustration with this situation has led to varying strategies. J. K. Rowling, for example, wrote her detective novels under a pseudonym because she wanted these works to be judged on their merits alone (although her identity was later uncovered).

For other authors, their personal fame has grown to overtake that of their writing. Sometimes the combination of highly admired work along with a relative lack of biographical information about the author has created a kind of mythology around their identity. This has fuelled a compulsion in readers to try to discover more about them, as is particularly the case with Shakespeare, whose identity has been continually questioned and whose likeness is persistently sought. Similarly, Jane Austen, who represents a distinct concept of 'Britishness' to many, remains a somewhat shadowy figure whose face is only known through one slight sketch.

Other authors in this chapter include Robert Burns, whose name has become synonymous with Scottish identity, and Charles Dickens, whose detailed depictions of both the best and the worst aspects of Victorian England have generated the adjective 'Dickensian'. Sometimes writers have, during their lifetimes, consciously taken on identities closely related to their writing, so that they become almost the personification of their art. Examples of this include Byron, whose portraits show him as the romantic hero of his own poetry, and Rabindranath Tagore who, in the context of huge international fame based on English translations of his Bengali poetry, created a distinctive new Indian visual style for himself, conveyed in his later portraits. Tagore, however, felt that the response of his readers and admirers had obscured rather than revealed the work of which he was most proud. For him, as for others, fame proved to be a mixed blessing.

WILLIAM SHAKESPEARE

Judged today by many to be one of the greatest ever writers, William Shakespeare (1564–1616) is arguably the most famous of all British authors. His plays and poetry, originally written in the language of Elizabethan and Jacobean England, have been translated into more than 100 written languages and have influenced almost every kind of popular and elite culture. Numerous lines from his texts have become everyday expressions. His plays have been quoted in support of nearly every kind of political movement and analysed with every type of critical theory. And his stories have been adapted into a multiplicity of cultural productions, ranging from 'authentic' performances in historic dress in reproduction Elizabethan theatres to strip cartoons.

In his own day, Shakespeare was a popular and well-known playwright, but probably not as popular and famous as his contemporary, Ben Jonson (1572–1637; see p.25). Born in Stratford-upon-Avon, the son of a relatively prosperous glove maker, Shakespeare is believed to have had a good education up to the age of about 15. In 1582, at the age of 18, he married Anne Hathaway (*c.*1555/56–1623) and they subsequently had three children. Much of the detail of Shakespeare's life is obscure, but it is clear that he worked first as an actor and then started writing plays, and that he spent most of his working life in London, while his family continued to be based in Stratford.

Shakespeare wrote at least 38 plays, two long narrative poems and 154 sonnets. The demand for plays in London was enormous at the time, with a frequent turnover of new shows and many play scripts being written collaboratively, rather like television scripts today. The texts were generally regarded as ephemeral and as belonging to the theatres for which they were written. Some of Shakespeare's plays survive in 'quarto' format, printed while he was alive. These were small, cheap objects, and very few remain today. Shown here is the first quarto of *Romeo and Juliet* (1597; fig.101). Although this quarto is one-fifth shorter than the second edition, it is an important source, showing how Shakespeare's plays were circulated and consumed during his lifetime. This particular quarto was owned by the Shakespearean actor David Garrick (1717–1779) who bequeathed it to the British Museum.

The posthumous publication of Shakespeare's collected plays in the First Folio (1623; p.8 and fig.102) was a milestone in the recognition of

FIG.101
First quarto of the *Tragedie of Romeo and Juliet*
By William Shakespeare (John Danter, London, 1597)
British Library C.34.k.55.

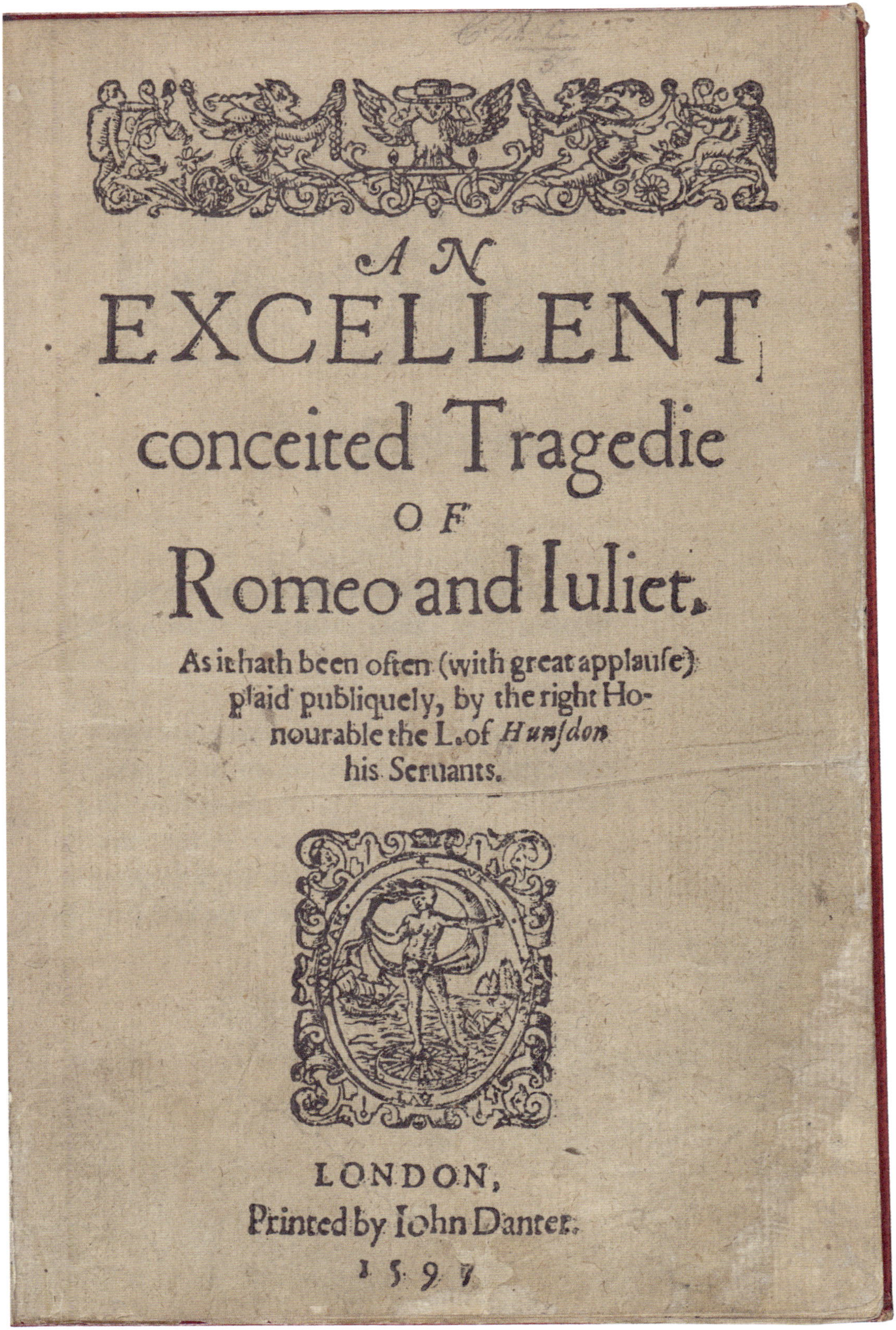

AN
EXCELLENT
conceited Tragedie
OF
Romeo and Iuliet.

As it hath been often (with great applause)
plaid publiquely, by the right Ho-
nourable the L. of *Hunsdon*
his Seruants.

LONDON,
Printed by Iohn Danter.
1597

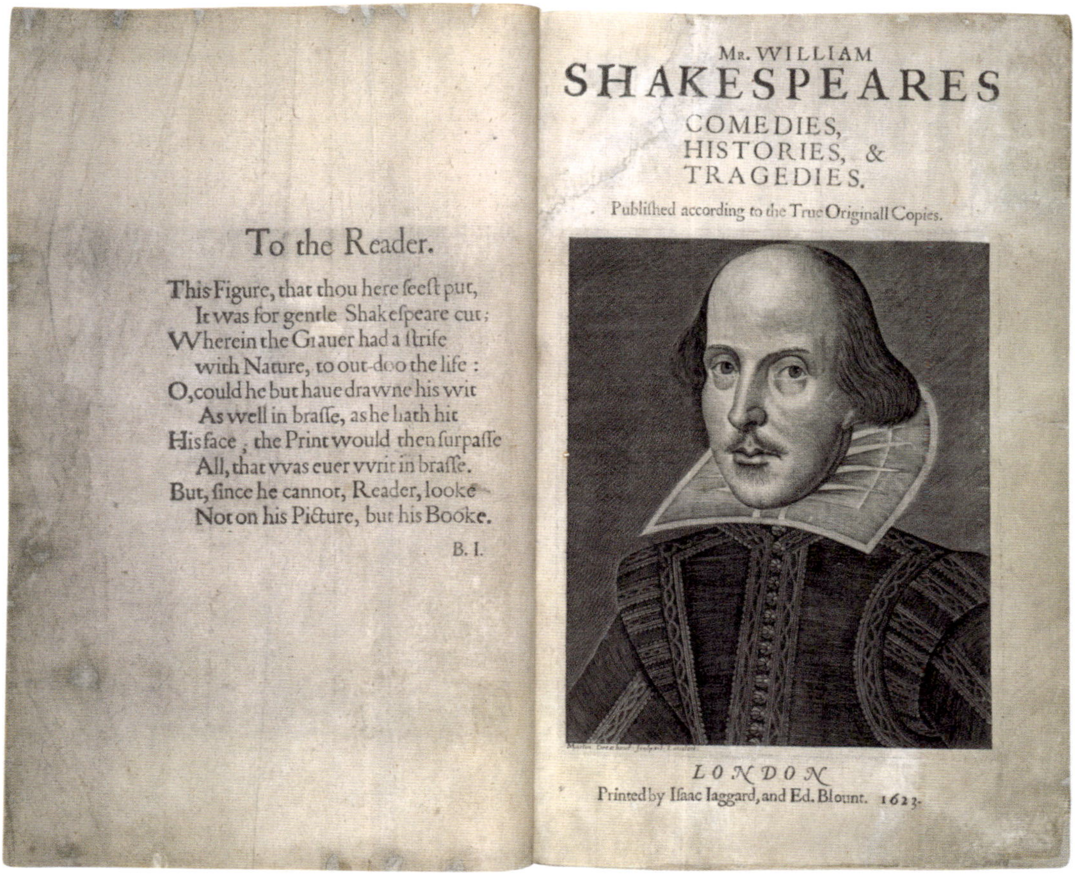

To the Reader.

This Figure, that thou here ſeeſt put,
It was for gentle Shakeſpeare cut;
Wherein the Grauer had a ſtrife
with Nature, to out-doo the life:
O, could he but haue drawne his wit
As well in braſſe, as he hath hit
His face; the Print would then ſurpaſſe
All, that vvas euer vvrit in braſſe.
But, ſince he cannot, Reader, looke
Not on his Picture, but his Booke.

B. I.

Mr. WILLIAM
SHAKESPEARES
COMEDIES,
HISTORIES, &
TRAGEDIES.
Publiſhed according to the True Originall Copies.

LONDON
Printed by Iſaac Iaggard, and Ed. Blount. 1623.

plays as potentially lasting, influential works of literature, although it was not until the eighteenth century that Shakespeare's fame and reputation really spread to international audiences. This copy of the First Folio features one of only four surviving first impressions of the frontispiece portrait engraving of Shakespeare by Martin Droeshout (1601–*c.*1650). The engraver later adjusted and improved some details, such as the area under Shakespeare's chin. It is therefore possible to conclude that this copy of the First Folio was one of the first to be printed. For many collectors and scholars, the First Folio is considered the most important source for documenting and understanding Shakespeare's literary output, even though it was made seven years after his death.

Of the 36 plays included in it, 18 had never been published before. It was expensively produced with around 750 copies originally made. Today, only 235 First Folios are known to survive. As Shakespeare's original

FIG. 102
***Mr. William Shakespeares Comedies, Histories, & Tragedies* ('First Folio')**
By William Shakespeare
(Isaac Jaggard and Edward Blount, London, 1623)
British Library
C.39.k.15.

FIG. 103
William Shakespeare
Associated with John Taylor
*c.*1610
Oil on canvas
National Portrait Gallery
NPG 1

manuscript playscripts are lost and probably destroyed, the First Folio and the quartos are the closest modern audiences and readers are able to get to the original texts by this most remarkable of writers.

By the mid-nineteenth century Shakespeare was so famous and so closely identified with British identity and literary achievement that it was felt appropriate that a portrait of him should be the founding gift to the National Portrait Gallery's collection (fig.103). The portrait – known as the 'Chandos' portrait after an earlier owner – was presented to the National Portrait Gallery in 1856 by Francis Egerton, 1st Earl of Ellesmere (1800–1857), and was the first portrait in the collection. It is the only portrait of Shakespeare that has a good claim to have been painted from life. In 1719 the antiquarian George Vertue (1684–1756) recorded a chain of ownership that included Shakespeare's godson Sir William Davenant (bap. 1606–1668); he also recorded that it was painted by 'one Taylor, a Player and painter'.[1] While this provenance has some uncertain elements, it is stronger than that associated with any other painted portrait claimed to be of Shakespeare. Two other works depict the author, but posthumously: the tomb monument of the author in Stratford-upon-Avon and Droeshout's frontispiece to the First Folio, both of which correspond reasonably well with the painting.

John Taylor (d.1651) was an important member of the Painter-Stainers' Company but few works by him are known. The painting is exactly the sort of relatively simple, modest work by a middle-ranking artist that was beginning to be produced to depict well-known authors. It should be remembered that the National Portrait Gallery portrait does not look as it would have done when first painted; the paint surface is very worn, the varnish darkened and the earring disproportionately prominent as the hard pigment in which it was painted has resisted the wear that has affected the rest of the painting. However, Shakespeare's fame and the relative lack of certain information about his life have led to a continuing quest for, and 'discovery' of, his portraits. The persistent pursuit of Shakespeare portraits speaks to a widespread and deep longing by readers and audiences for engagement not just on a literary, but also on a personal level with our most celebrated authors. **CM, AA**

ROBERT BURNS

Robert Burns (1759–1796) is recognised around the world as Scotland's national bard. He is a key symbol and mouthpiece of Scottish identity, a position he has held since his early death at the age of 37. In 1786 he wrote to his friend, the lawyer Gavin Hamilton (1751–1805):

> 'For my own affairs, I am in a fair way of becoming as eminent as Thomas à Kempis or John Bunyan; and you may expect henceforth to see my birthday inserted among the wonderful events in the poor Robin's and Aberdeen Almanacks, along with the black Monday and the battle of Bothwell Bridge.'[2]

He may have meant this with a degree of irony, but in retrospect it appears prophetic, as his birthday on 25 January is now celebrated annually as 'Burns Night', both in Scotland and around the world by Scottish diaspora communities.

Burns was born into a struggling farming family in the lowlands of Scotland, where he was brought up on a rich oral culture of folk songs and tales in the Scots dialect. He was also taught to read and write in English and Latin. As a teenager he began to write songs, often directed towards young women to whom he was attracted. He wrote both in formal English and in his native Lowland Scots language. After the 1707 Act of Union made England and Scotland into the single country of Great Britain, the perceived threat to a distinct Scottish identity stimulated a growing interest in indigenous Scots language and literature. Burns's poetry represents the apogee of this movement. He collected traditional songs and turned them into powerful and expressive poems, also writing new poetry drawn from folk traditions. His first major publication, *Poems, Chiefly in the Scottish Dialect* (1786), was presented and received – rather disingenuously – as the work of an uneducated ploughman poet writing songs about the rural world around him. The book was immediately popular, and its success was a factor in Burns abandoning plans to emigrate to Jamaica during a crisis in his personal life. In spite of this, however, Burns never made an adequate living through writing. He struggled to support himself, his wife and the many children he fathered with at least four different women, first through farming and then by collecting taxes as an exciseman.

FIG.104
'O my Luve's like a red, red rose'
By Robert Burns
Before 1794
Iron gall ink on laid paper
British Library
Add MS 22307, f.114r

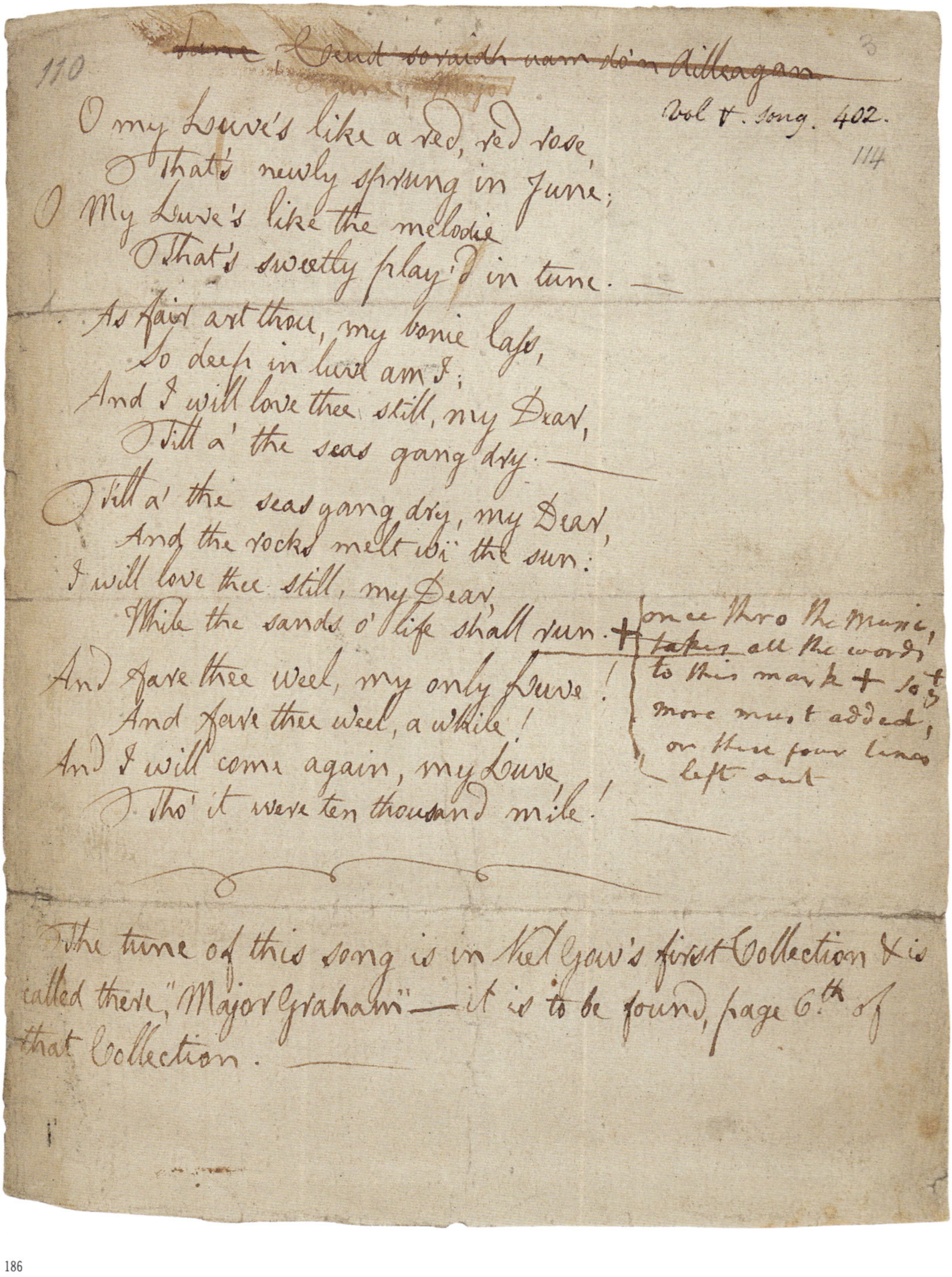
110

~~Tune, Cend soraidh uam do'n Ailleagan~~

Vol V. Song. 402.

114

O my Luve's like a red, red rose,
That's newly sprung in June;
O My Luve's like the melodie
That's sweetly play'd in tune. —
As fair art thou, my bonie lass,
So deep in luve am I;
And I will love thee still, my Dear,
Till a' the seas gang dry. —
Till a' the seas gang dry, my Dear,
And the rocks melt wi' the sun:
I will love thee still, my Dear,
While the sands o' life shall run. +
And fare thee weel, my only Luve!
And fare thee weel, a while!
And I will come again, my Luve,
Tho' it were ten thousand mile! —

once thro the music, ~~takes~~ all the words to this mark + so more must added, or these four lines left out

The tune of this song is in Niel Gow's first Collection & is called there, "Major Graham" — it is to be found, page 6th of that Collection. —

FIG. 105
Robert Burns
By Alexander Nasmyth
*c.*1821, based on a portrait
of 1787
Oil on canvas
National Portrait Gallery
NPG 46

The origins of Burns's poem, 'O my Luve's like a red, red rose' are obscure. Burns himself claimed that it was 'a simple old Scots song which I had pickt up in this country'.[3] Its words are similar to those in some folk songs, but Burns undoubtedly reworked them, as he did other songs. He contributed it, along with over 150 of his own poems and many others that he had collected and reworked, to a project by the engraver and publisher James Johnson (1753?–1811) to publish all Scots songs. Burns sent Johnson a copy of the poem (fig.104) along with the instruction to set it to a tune by Niel Gow (1727–1807) called 'Major Graham'. Johnson published it in the fifth volume of his *Scots Musical Museum* (1787–1803) shortly after Burns's death in 1796. In the same volume was Burns's even more well-known song 'Auld Lang Syne'. The song gained real popularity after it was set to a traditional tune, 'Low down in the broom', in 1821.

Burns's portrait in the National Portrait Gallery (fig.105) was painted for another publisher of traditional Scottish songs, George Thomson (1757–1851), to whom Burns had initially offered 'O my Luve', but who had not appreciated its merits. Thomson commissioned the artist Alexander Nasmyth (1758–1840) in 1820 to make a copy of the portrait Nasmyth had made of Burns 34 years earlier. The earlier portrait had been engraved for the 1787 edition of Burns's *Poems, Chiefly in the Scottish Dialect*, and then given to Burns's widow. Nasmyth was primarily a landscape painter, and he portrayed Burns in an evocative twilit landscape. The inclusion of the landscape in such a small-scale portrait is relatively unusual, and, while the specific location is not known (and may be imaginary) it underlines Burns's association with the natural world and particularly with the Scottish countryside. **CM**

JANE AUSTEN

Jane Austen (1775–1817) is one of the best loved writers in the English language. She is famous for her six completed novels, which, although set in specific and narrow social groups, reveal timeless and universal truths about human relations and emotions. She wrote modestly about her work, comparing the intricacy and scope of her writing to miniature painting – 'the little bit (two Inches wide) of Ivory on which I work with so fine a Brush' – in a letter to her nephew James Edward Austen-Leigh (1798–1874; fig.106).[4] However, while superficially the scope of her work

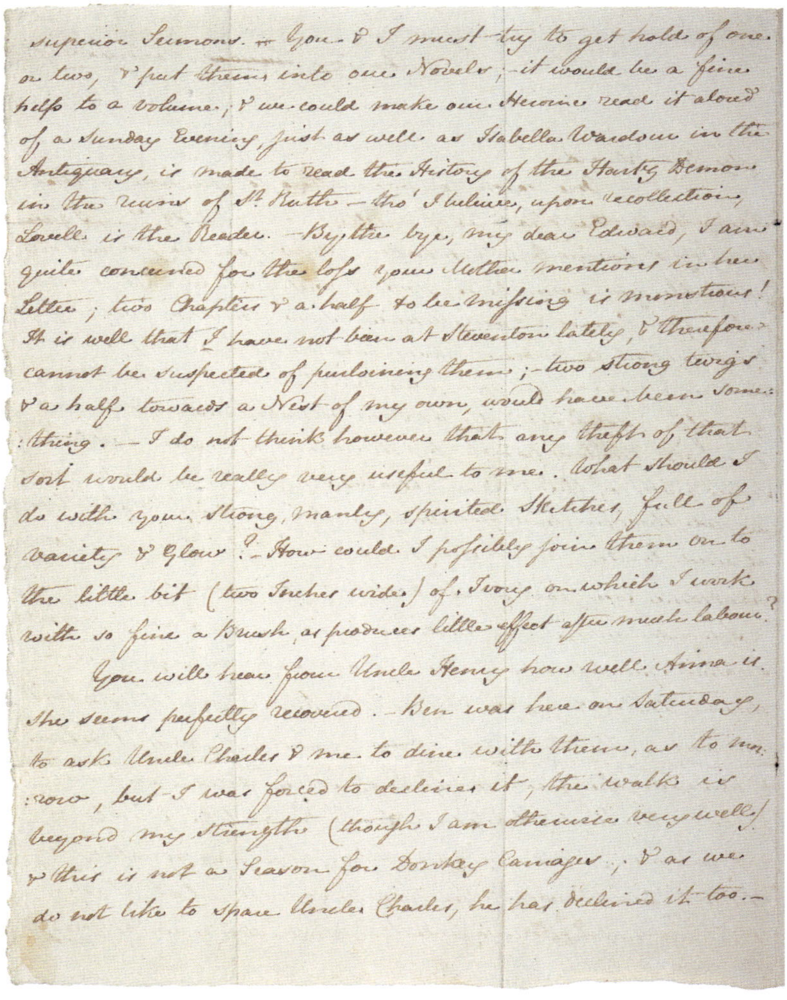

superior Sermons. — You & I must try to get hold of one
or two, & put them into our Novels; — it would be a fine
help to a volume; & we could make our Heroine read it aloud
of a Sunday Evening, just as well as Isabella Wardour in the
Antiquary, is made to read the History of the Hartz Demon
in the ruins of St Ruth — tho' I beleive, upon recollection,
Lovell is the Reader. — By the bye, my dear Edward, I am
quite concerned for the loss your Mother mentions in her
Letter; two Chapters & a half to be missing is monstrous!
It is well that I have not been at Steventon lately, & therefore
cannot be suspected of purloining them; — two strong twigs
& a half towards a Nest of my own, would have been some-
:thing. — I do not think however that any theft of that
sort would be really very useful to me. What should I
do with your strong, manly, spirited Sketches, full of
Variety & Glow? — How could I possibly join them on to
the little bit (two Inches wide) of Ivory on which I work
with so fine a Brush, as produces little effect after much labour?
You will hear from Uncle Henry how well Anna is.
She seems perfectly recovered. — Ben was here on Saturday,
to ask Uncle Charles & me to dine with them, as to mor-
:row, but I was forced to decline it, the walk is
beyond my strength (though I am otherwise very well)
& this is not a Season for Donkey Carriages; & as we
do not like to spare Uncle Charles, he has declined it too. —

FIG.106
Letter to James Edward Austen-Leigh
From Jane Austen
16 December 1816
Ink on wove paper
British Library
Add MS 89437, f.1v

may appear narrow, her insights into human nature and interactions, and her precise, elegant and witty prose have ensured enormous continuing popularity and admiration.

Growing up in a lively, middle-class household that hosted guests and staged amateur theatricals, Austen wrote playlets, novellas and sketches during her youth. She was particularly close to her older sister Cassandra (1773–1845). In about 1795 Austen had begun to write 'Elinor and Marianne', which would later become *Sense and Sensibility*. From 1796 she worked on *Pride and Prejudice*, originally titled 'First Impressions'. *Pride and Prejudice* was rejected at first by the publisher Thomas Cadell (1773–1836) in 1797, without his even seeing the manuscript. Austen returned to work on *Sense and Sensibility* and went on to write *Northanger Abbey*, originally called 'Susan'.

After the death of Austen's father in 1805, the writer, her sister and mother needed financial stability and a place to live. In 1809 the trio moved to Chawton, Hampshire, and it was at this point that Austen decided to focus entirely on her writing. Once established at Chawton, she published *Sense and Sensibility* anonymously in 1811, with only 1,000 copies produced; it sold out immediately. Following this, *Pride and Prejudice*, (1813), was a runaway success. *Mansfield Park* was the first novel to be written at Chawton and was published on 9 May 1814. All copies were sold by October of that year and Austen received over £320, the most she was ever to receive for any of her novels. Austen was shrewd in her dealing with publishers, acutely aware of the cost of paper and the intricacies of copyright. Additionally, she was aware of reviews of her works, which she wrote out by hand and retained. Shown here are the reviews of and opinions of *Mansfield Park*, which Austen collected and transcribed after the novel was published (fig.107).

The publication of *Emma* followed at the end of 1815, the last work to be published during the author's lifetime. Austen died in July 1817 after battling Addison's disease. In December 1817, her brother, Henry (1771–1850), had her last novel, *Persuasion*, published by John Murray (1778–1843), along with the much earlier *Northanger Abbey*. Henry's preface to the volumes acknowledged for the first time in print Austen's authorship of all six of her novels. Her previous anonymity in print meant that she received little fame or attention during her lifetime, but after her death, her reputation grew quickly. By the 1830s, all of her novels were available in an affordable format, which meant that more readers had access to her works.

In the context of her great popularity, Austen's nephew James wrote a *Memoir of Jane Austen* in 1869 (published 1870), and he searched

FIG.107
Opinions of *Mansfield Park*
By Jane Austen
After 1814
Ink on laid paper
British Library
Add MS 41253 A, f.5r

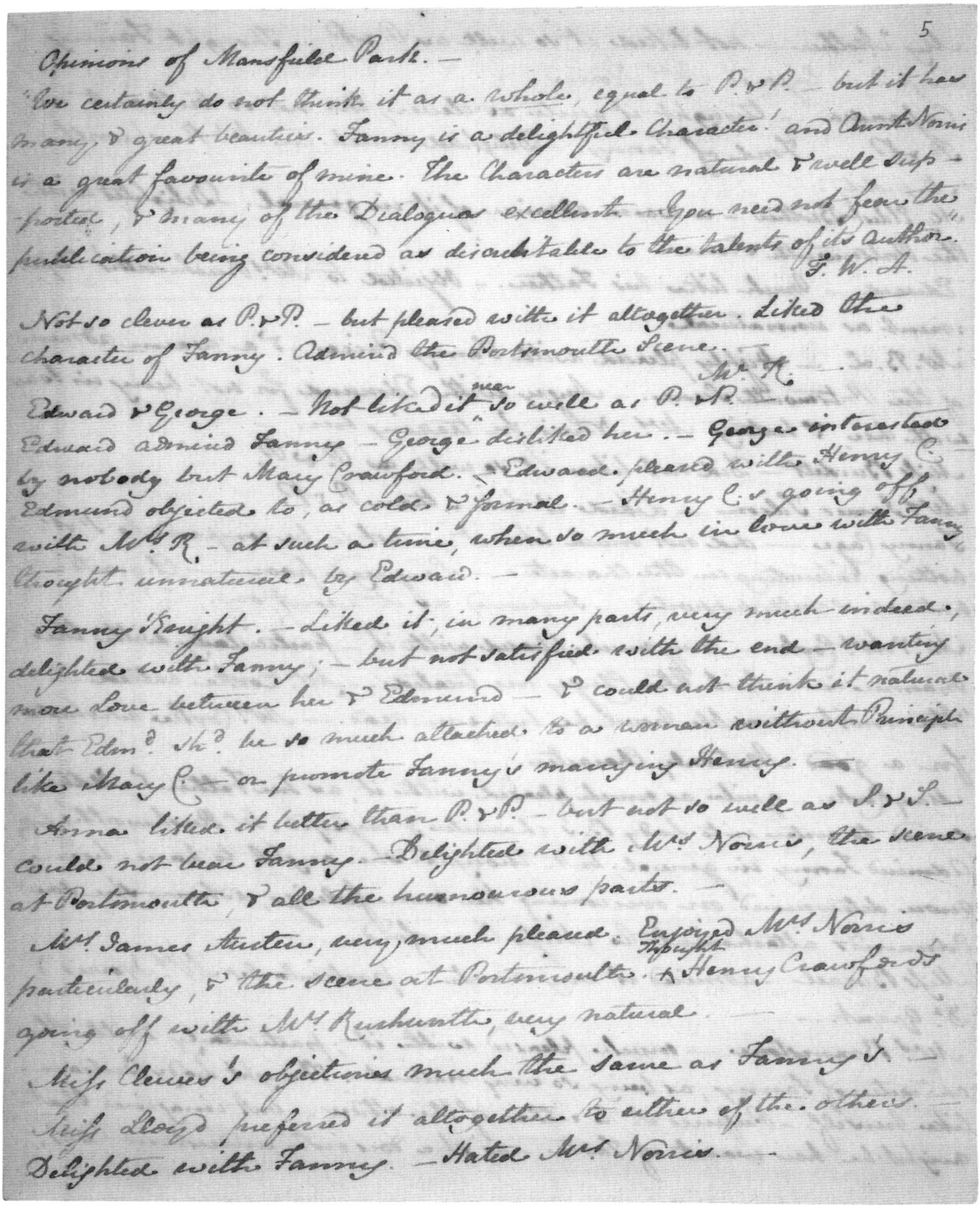
5

Opinions of Mansfield Park. —

We certainly do not think it as a whole, equal to P. & P. — but it has many, & great beauties. Fanny is a delightful Character! and Aunt Norris is a great favourite of mine. The Characters are natural & well supported, & many of the Dialogues excellent. — You need not fear the publication being considered as discreditable to the talents of it's Author. F. W. A.

Not so clever as P. & P. — but pleased with it altogether. Liked the character of Fanny. Admired the Portsmouth Scene. — Mr K. —

Edward & George. — Not liked it near so well as P. & P. — Edward admired Fanny — George disliked her. — George interested by nobody but Mary Crawford. — Edward pleased with Henry C. — Edmund objected to, as cold & formal. — Henry C.s going off with Mrs R. — at such a time, when so much in love with Fanny, thought unnatural by Edward. —

Fanny Knight. — Liked it, in many parts, very much indeed, delighted with Fanny; — but not satisfied with the end — wanting more Love between her & Edmund — & could not think it natural that Edm.d sh.d be so much attached to a woman without Principle like Mary C. — or promote Fanny's marrying Henry. —

Anna liked it better than P. & P. — but not so well as S. & S. — could not bear Fanny. — Delighted with Mrs Norris, the scene at Portsmouth, & all the humourous parts. —

Mrs James Austen, very much pleased. Enjoyed Mrs Norris particularly, & the scene at Portsmouth. Thought Henry Crawford's going off with Mrs Rushworth, very natural. —

Miss Clewes's objections much the same as Fanny's. —

Miss Lloyd preferred it altogether to either of the others. Delighted with Fanny. — Hated Mrs Norris. —

FIG.108
Jane Austen
By Cassandra Austen
1810
Pencil and watercolour
National Portrait Gallery
NPG 3630

among family papers and possessions for a portrait of the author to be engraved as a frontispiece. The only image he could find, apart from a drawing of her from behind, was a small, unfinished watercolour by her sister Cassandra (fig.108). Manuscript letters from surviving relatives record their scepticism about the likeness, including this comment from Austen's niece Caroline, 'there is a *look* which I recognise as *hers* – and though the general resemblance is *not* strong, yet as it represents a pleasing countenance it is so far a truth'.[5] This one certain – but slight – image of the author's face has ensured that as an individual she remains somewhat elusive, while continuing sales of her novels, numerous film and television adaptations, and societies and museums dedicated to her have ensured that her literary reputation thrives. **AA, CM**

LORD BYRON

In his lifetime George Gordon, Lord Byron (1788–1824) came to be seen as the epitome of the Romantic poet. His unconventional, nomadic lifestyle; handsome appearance; passionate, witty poetry and the mythology woven around him became inextricably merged and created an unprecedented level of celebrity. Allegedly described by Lady Caroline Lamb (1785–1828), one of his many lovers, as 'mad, bad and dangerous to know', the association with danger and degeneracy was an integral part of his appeal.[6] His poetry became popular not just because of its worth as literature but because it was created by him. In more recent times he has been seen as a figurehead for individuality and freedom of thought and action.

Born into a noble family, he was the only child of a doting, volatile mother and a profligate father, who abandoned his wife and son and died a year later. At the age of 10, Byron inherited his title and an estate from a great-uncle. Well-educated and well-read, he privately printed and then destroyed his first volume of poetry, *Fugitive Pieces*, in 1806. His first published volume was *Hours of Idleness*, which came out in 1807. A particularly negative review led Byron to write a vicious satirical poem *English Bards and Scotch Reviewers* (1809), in response to which he was challenged to a duel.

In the summer of 1809 Byron, a friend and three servants left England for a Grand Tour of Continental Europe, landing first in Lisbon, Portugal. Byron visited battlefields, admired dramatic scenery and contemplated the recent and ancient history of the countries he visited. He had a number of affairs, with both men and women, and he wrote poetry about his feelings and experiences. The most important poetic product of this journey was his long, narrative poem *Childe Harold's Pilgrimage*, a loosely autobiographical account of his travels. After his return to England in 1811 the first two sections or 'cantos' were published by John Murray (1778–1843) in early 1812. The initial print run was 500 copies, which sold out in three days. Ten editions were printed within three years. Byron later wrote, 'I awoke one morning and found myself famous'.[7] The poem seems to have been received immediately as a window onto Byron's own emotions, adventures and views, presenting the world with the original 'Byronic' hero, later described as 'a man proud, moody, cynical, with defiance on his brow, and misery in his heart; a scorner of his kind, implacable in revenge, yet capable of deep and strong affection'.[8]

In Albania Byron had been particularly struck by the appearance of the men in their local dress, describing them to his mother: 'The Albanians in their dresses (the most magnificent in the world, consisting of a long *white kilt*, gold worked cloak, crimson velvet gold laced jacket & waistcoat, silver mounted pistols & daggers)'.[9] He acquired a set of Albanian clothing, and in 1813 posed in it for a portrait by Thomas Phillips (1770–1845), probably at the request of his publisher, John Murray. Phillips painted at least three different versions of this portrait at different dates; the earliest was exhibited at the Royal Academy in 1814 where Byron's friends had mixed views about it as a likeness. Phillips painted the National Portrait Gallery version (fig.109) after Byron's death, in about 1835.

FIG.109
Lord Byron
By Thomas Phillips
*c.*1835, based on a work of 1813
Oil on canvas
National Portrait Gallery
NPG 142

Childe Harold had made Byron a celebrity, and from the time of its publication onwards, he wrote, published and sold poetry prolifically. But the work for which he is now most admired is his satirical, epic poem *Don Juan*, published in parts between 1819 and 1824. By this time Byron was living in Italy, having left England after his short-lived marriage to Annabella Milbanke (1792–1860) had ended in a maelstrom of scandal, rumour and debt in 1816. The poem took as its hero a figure from Spanish folklore, but completely reinvented him and described his adventures in Spain, Turkey, Russia and England. It examined the history of Europe across the end of the eighteenth and beginning of the nineteenth century, satirised various well-known living figures, including poets and politicians, and began with an ironic dedication to Robert Southey (1774–1843; p.32; fig.110), who was at that time Britain's Poet Laureate. It included the following lines:

'You, Bob! are rather insolent, you know,
At being disappointed in your wish
To supersede all warblers here below,
And be the only Blackbird in the dish;'[10]

Byron blamed Southey for circulating stories of incest with his half-sister Augusta Leigh (1783–1851) and 'promiscuous intercourse'.[11] Although Byron denied these accusations, other evidence suggested that they were true.

The first two cantos of *Don Juan* (1819) were received badly by critics as Byron was regarded as having gone too far in his treatment of recognisable individuals, and also in his descriptions of Don Juan's

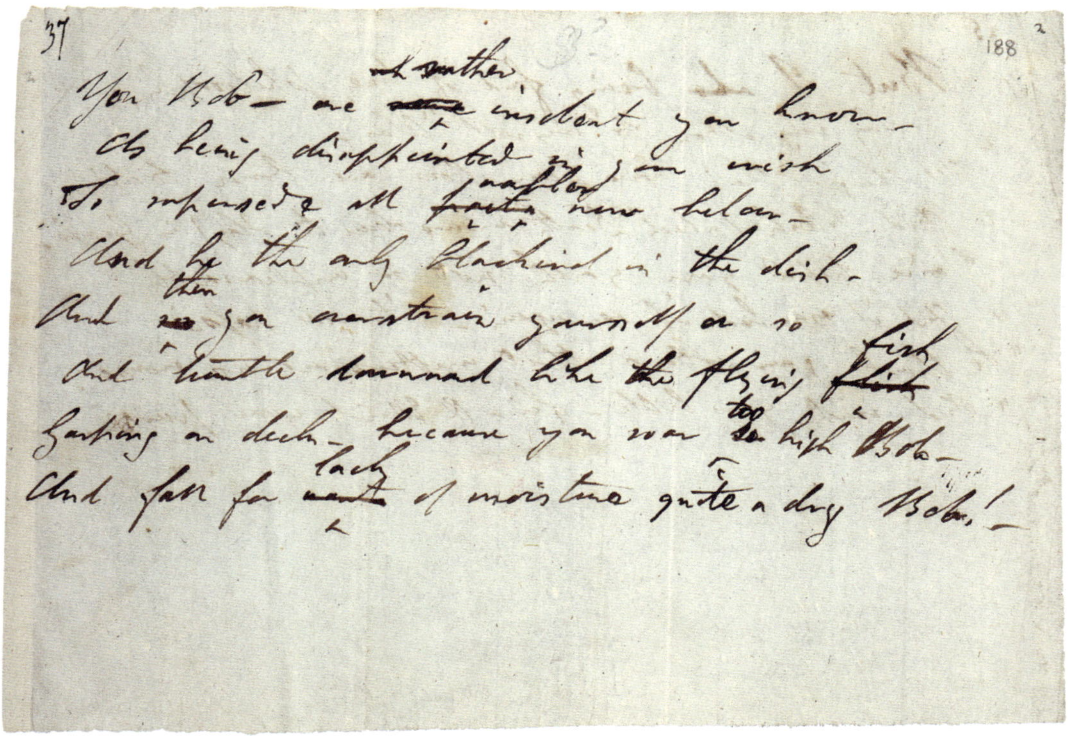
37 188

You Bob— are rather insolent you know—
At being disappointed in your wish
To supersede all warblers here below—
And be the only Blackbird in the dish—
And then you overstrain yourself or so
And tumble downward like the flying fish
Gasping on deck—because you soar too high Bob—
And fall for lack of moisture quite a dry Bob!—

sexual adventures. Byron continued writing the poem, however, and published the next three cantos with Murray in 1821. Subsequently, Murray refused to publish any more of the poem and the final 11 cantos were published by John Hunt (1775–1848). The poet Percy Bysshe Shelley (1792–1822) wrote of the work: 'Every word has the stamp of immortality ... It fulfils, in a certain degree, what I have long preached of producing – something wholly new and relative to the age, and yet surpassingly beautiful.'[12]

In 1823 Byron travelled to Greece to fight with the Greeks in their War of Independence against the Turkish Empire. There he became ill, and after less than a year he died in April 1824. In death, at the age of 36, having bravely joined what was largely seen as a noble cause, Byron became even more famous than in his lifetime. **CM**

FIG.110
Dedication and part of Canto I of *Don Juan*
By Lord Byron
1818
Iron gall ink on laid paper
British Library
Ashley MS A326, f.188r

CHARLES DICKENS

Charles Dickens (1812–1870) is one of the most famous of all British writers. The author of 15 novels, several plays and many short stories, Dickens wrote about contemporary life, injustice and society. Many of his powerfully drawn comic characters have become widely recognised symbols of human characteristics, like optimism (Mr Micawber) and miserliness (Scrooge). His highly detailed, evocative and often emotive descriptions of nineteenth-century life, especially at the margins of society, have influenced the way that the Victorian period is understood by global audiences.

Born in Portsmouth before moving to Chatham, the young Dickens experienced intense hardship when his father was sent to a debtors' prison. Dickens was forced to abandon his education and work in a shoe polish factory in London. Following this, he was employed as a clerk and then as a journalist at the *Morning Chronicle*, where he began writing 'Street Sketches', which were later published under his pen name, Boz, as *Sketches by Boz*. He made his name with *The Pickwick Papers* (1836–7), before writing *Oliver Twist* (serialised from 1837) about the maltreatment of orphans, child labour and violence and criminality in London. This story has been continually re-told, both on the stage and in film, adding to its persistent popularity and the fame of its author. Following *Oliver Twist*, Dickens wrote *The Life and Adventures of Nicholas Nickleby*, which was serialised between 1838 and 1839 before being published as a novel by Chapman & Hall. The story exposes the ill-treatment of young children in scam schools, a cause in which Dickens was personally invested. Shown here is his draft for Chapter 15 of *Nicholas Nickleby* (fig.111). Dickens usually made one draft, which he continually edited and crossed out before sending it to his printers. That this manuscript survived is miraculous; Dickens regarded manuscripts as working documents, used by printers to set text and to be discarded shortly afterwards. It was rescued by Charles Hicks (*c*.1799–1870), the foreman at the firm Bradbury & Evans, who printed the serialised version of *Nicholas Nickleby*.

At the same time that the reading public were finding themselves gripped by the serialised version of *Nicholas Nickleby*, Daniel Maclise (1806–1870) painted Dickens's portrait (fig.112). Artist and writer had become friends, and Dickens's publishers commissioned this portrait as the basis for an engraved version by William Finden (1787–1852) that

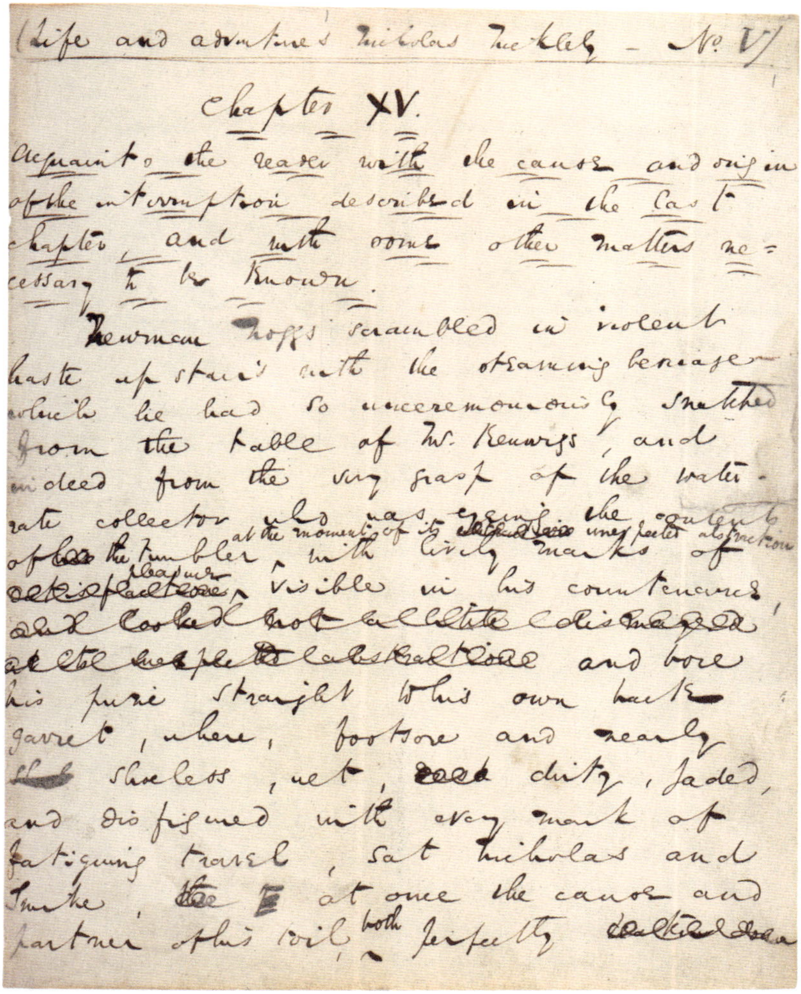

(Life and adventures of Nicholas Nickleby – No. V)

Chapter XV.

Acquaints the reader with the cause and origin of the interruption described in the last chapter, and with some other matters necessary to be known.

Newman Noggs scrambled in violent haste up stairs with the steaming beverage which he had so unceremoniously snatched from the table of Mr. Kenwigs, and indeed from the very grasp of the water-rate collector who was eyeing the contents of the tumbler at the moment of its unexpected abstraction, with lively marks of pleasure visible in his countenance, and bore his prize straight to his own back garret, where, footsore and nearly shoeless, wet, dirty, jaded, and disfigured with every mark of fatiguing travel, sat Nicholas and Smike, at once the cause and partner of his toil, both perfectly

FIG.111
Chapter 15 of *Nicholas Nickleby*
By Charles Dickens
*c.*1838
Black ink on wove paper
British Library
Add MS 57493, f.1r

FIG.112
Charles Dickens
By Daniel Maclise
1839
Oil on canvas
National Portrait Gallery
NPG 1172

could be used as the frontispiece for *Nicholas Nickleby*. Portrayed in elegant dress, Dickens assumes the role of a dandy and a writer. In a letter of 28 June 1839, he wrote: 'Maclise has made another face of me, which all people say is astonishing.'[13] The writer William Makepeace Thackeray (1811–1863) described the portrait as, 'a likeness perfectly amazing; a looking-glass could not render a better facsimile. Here we have the real identical man Dickens'.[14] The portrait was exhibited at the Royal Academy, which further served to increase the fame of the author.

Nicholas Nickleby was followed by many more novels and occasional pieces including *The Old Curiosity Shop* (1840–1), *A Christmas Carol* (1843), *Bleak House* (1852–3), *A Tale of Two Cities* (1859) and *Great Expectations* (1860–1). Such was Dickens's fame that he undertook reading tours in the US and the UK, and a wide range of memorabilia was produced, based on characters from his stories. **AA**

LEWIS CARROLL

The character of Alice has been persistently popular since she was first created by the author, mathematician and photographer Charles Lutwidge Dodgson, otherwise known as Lewis Carroll (1832–1898). First appearing in *Alice's Adventures in Wonderland* (1865) and *Through the Looking Glass and What Alice Found There* (1871), this quirky and charming figure has become internationally famous, inspiring films, popular songs, computer games, toys, dolls, figurines and even wallpaper and tiles. Yet the genesis of Alice was complicated and involved more than just the author's imagination.

Carroll matriculated in Mathematics at Christ Church, Oxford, in 1851 and became a mathematical lecturer there in 1855. One year later he purchased a camera and began taking photographs of a range of subjects including self-portraits, buildings and, most notably, children of families he knew. This self-portrait of 2 June 1857 shows a young Carroll, taken one year after he purchased his camera. It marks the point at which both his life and his writing were to change forever (fig.113). This is an albumen print, made using a technique that uses egg whites. Developed in 1847, it was the dominant type of photographic print during the second half of the nineteenth century.

It was through his photography that Carroll became friendly with Henry Liddell (1811–1898), Dean of Christ Church, and his young family, including their daughter Alice (1852–1934). Carroll took a number of images of the Liddell children, including Alice, whom he was to call his 'ideal child friend'.[15] Shown here is one of the images he made of Alice in 1860 (fig.114). In 1862, Carroll took a boat ride with some of the Liddell children and recounted the story of a girl called 'Alice' and her adventures in a magical land after she fell down a rabbit hole. The story proved so popular that Alice Liddell requested that Carroll commit the story to paper, resulting in the manuscript version of 'Alice's Adventures Underground', which Carroll illustrated himself in 1864.

While the eponymous heroine of the story shared a name with Alice Liddell, Carroll did not wholly base his character upon her, although this has been the popular assumption. Nevertheless, the friendship between Carroll and the young girl gave rise to the popular story, and indeed Carroll acknowledged her influence, writing to her, 'your adventures have had a marvellous success'.[16] There has been posthumous speculation about

FIG.113
Self-Portrait
By Lewis Carroll
1857
Albumen print
National Portrait Gallery
NPG P39

FIG.114
Alice Liddell
By Lewis Carroll
July 1860
Albumen print
National Portrait Gallery
NPG P991 (8)

FIG.115
Illustration to *Alice's Adventures in Wonderland* by Lewis Carroll
By Sir John Tenniel
(Macmillan & Co., 1866 [1865])
British Library
C.59.g.11., p.188

Carroll's motives for his images of children. Much has been published on this problematic question, although it appears that, whatever the truth, Carroll did not act upon any improper tendencies, perhaps because of the religious orders he had taken. At the same time Carroll gave the manuscript of 'Alice's Adventures Underground' to Alice, he also sent the story to his friend, the writer George MacDonald (1824–1905), whose own children adored the tale, and who persuaded Carroll to find a publisher. *Alice's Adventures in Wonderland* was published in 1865.

Carroll had a unique relationship with the publishers, Macmillan. While Macmillan took ten per cent of all profits and arranged for the printing and distribution of the books, Carroll was responsible for covering the costs of printing, advertising and illustrations, which meant he maintained control of the look of his books. The illustrator Sir John Tenniel (1820–1914) was

188 ALICE'S EVIDENCE.

At this the whole pack rose up into the air, and came flying down upon her; she gave a

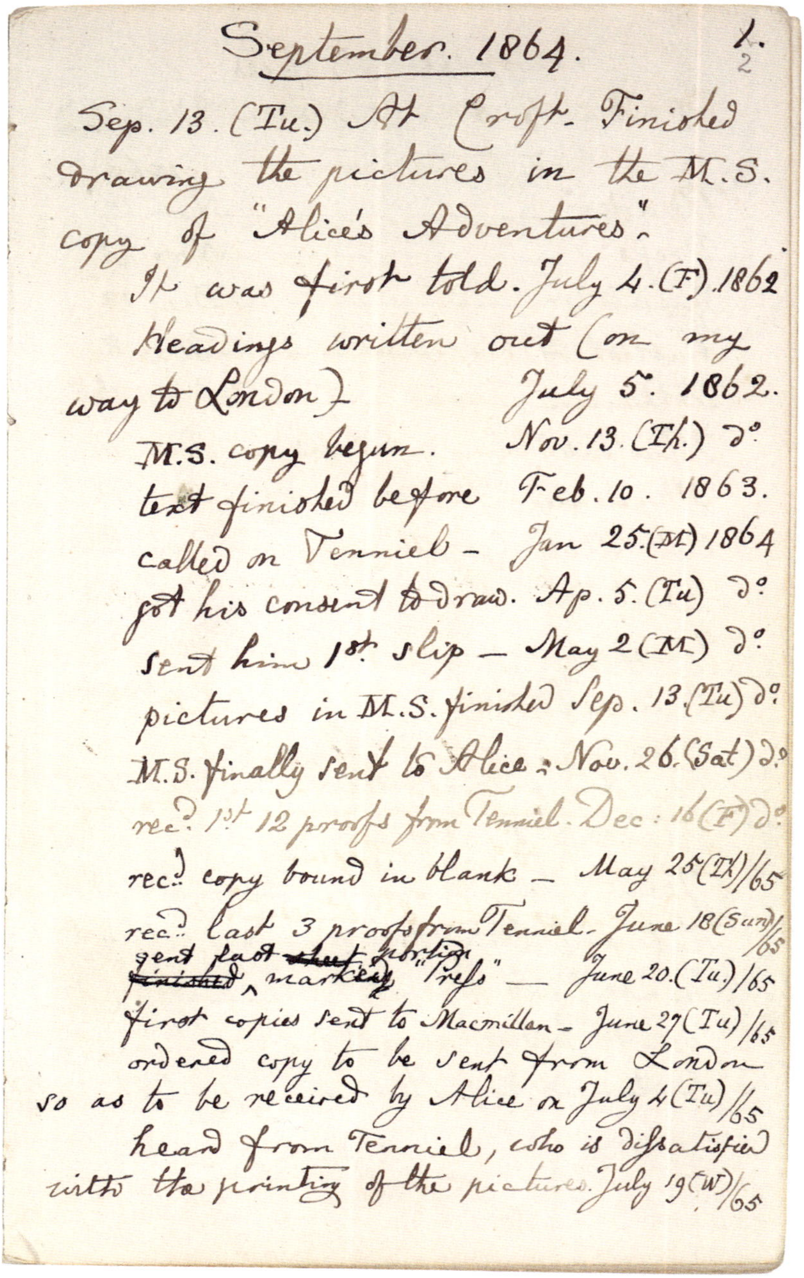
September. 1864. 1.
2
Sep. 13. (Tu.) At Croft. Finished drawing the pictures in the M.S. copy of "Alice's Adventures".
It was first told. July 4. (F.) 1862
Headings written out (on my way to London) July 5. 1862.
M.S. copy begun. Nov. 13. (Th.) do
text finished before Feb. 10. 1863.
called on Tenniel – Jan 25. (M.) 1864
got his consent to draw. Ap. 5. (Tu) do
sent him 1st slip – May 2 (M) do
pictures in M.S. finished Sep. 13. (Tu) do
M.S. finally sent to Alice: Nov. 26. (Sat) do
recd 1st 12 proofs from Tenniel. Dec: 16 (F) do
recd copy bound in blank – May 25 (Th)/65
recd last 3 proofs from Tenniel. June 18 (Sun)/65
sent last ~~sheet~~ portion ~~finished~~, marked "Press" – June 20. (Tu)/65
first copies sent to Macmillan – June 27 (Tu)/65
ordered copy to be sent from London so as to be received by Alice on July 4 (Tu)/65
heard from Tenniel, who is dissatisfied with the printing of the pictures. July 19 (W)/65

FIG.116
Private Journal No.9
By Lewis Carroll
13 September 1864–
24 January 1868
Black ink on laid paper
British Library
Add MS 54344, f.2r

hired to create 42 images, basing the pictures on Carroll's text and ideas (fig.115). Tenniel's job was not as independent artist, but to interpret and realise Carroll's vision. Carroll described the timeline of the *Alice* story in his diary, from when he first recounted it to Alice, to the meetings and proof stages with Tenniel (fig.116). It was this careful crafting of the illustrations, and ultimately the *image* of Alice, which continues to shape how we see this famous character today. **AA**

BRAM STOKER

Abraham (Bram) Stoker (1847–1912) was a writer and theatre manager best known for creating the character of Dracula. Born in Dublin, Ireland, and educated at Trinity College, Dublin, Stoker initially worked as a civil servant. From 1875 he began writing, publishing the novella 'The Primrose Path' in *The Shamrock* in 1875. Stoker found his career in the civil service unfulfilling and so volunteered, unpaid, to write theatre reviews for the *Daily Mail*. This led him into the path of the actor Sir Henry Irving (1838–1905). In 1878 Irving re-opened the Lyceum Theatre in London under his own management. He brought in Stoker as a business manager and the two worked together for 22 years, making the Lyceum a popular destination for Victorian theatregoers.

While working for Irving, Stoker continued his writing, publishing a book of fairy tales, a travel narrative and three adventure-romance novels between 1882 and 1895. From 1890, Stoker began developing a Gothic story about an Englishman who tracks down and kills a Hungarian vampire; this would become the basis of his story about Count Dracula. The story plays on fears of foreign invasion, shapeshifting, threat to ordinary people, subservience and masculine insecurity. During a holiday to the Yorkshire seaside town of Whitby, Stoker drafted the scene where Dracula arrives in England on a ghost ship. It is widely believed that Stoker based his fictional Dracula partly on the historical Vlad III of Wallachia (1428/31–1476/7), known as 'Vlad Dracula' or 'Vlad the Impaler' on account of his chosen means to display executed enemies. In addition, many of the captivating characteristics of Dracula were inspired by Henry Irving, whose physical and psychological presence was both mesmerising and controlling. Originally titled 'The Un-Dead', Stoker changed the name of the novel to *Dracula* shortly before publication in 1897.

Stoker, like many other authors at the time, sought to protect the copyright in his work. This could be achieved by ensuring the story was enacted on stage as a play, even if only for one performance. These were called 'copyright performances', and the audience was usually made up of invited guests rather than a wider paying public and the quality of the performance was of little importance. Thus, Stoker worked frantically to adapt his book into a play so that it could be performed, just once, to ensure the copyright was protected. He created a playscript, which was written afresh in parts, while elsewhere he simply cut and pasted large

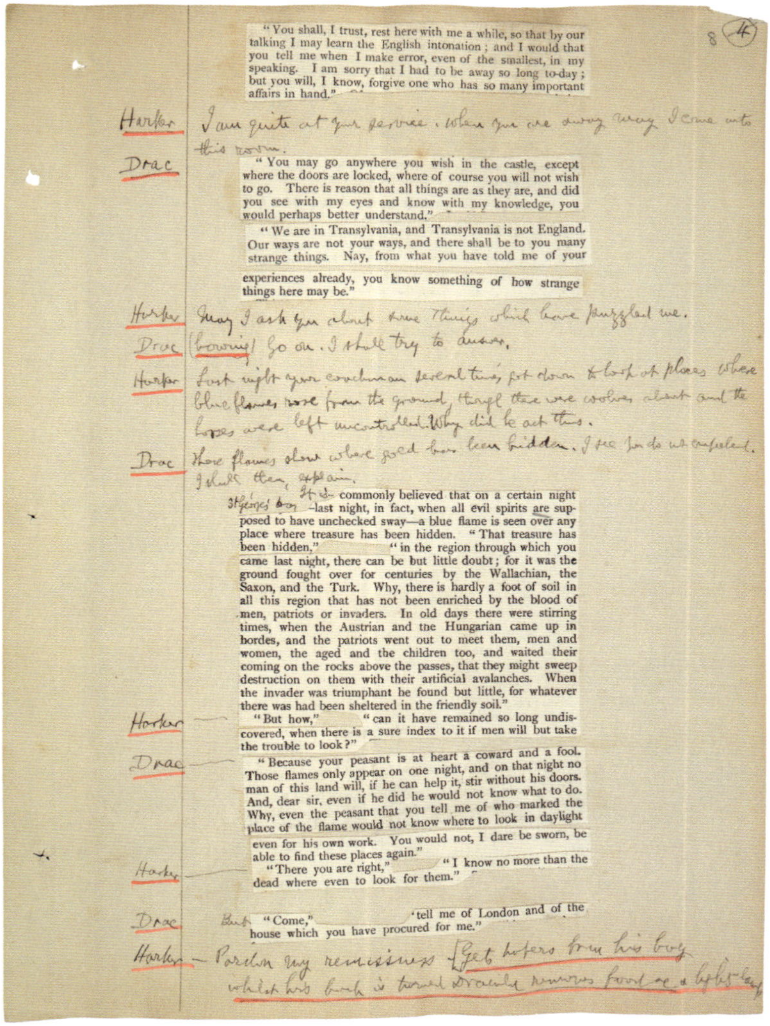
8 (4)

"You shall, I trust, rest here with me a while, so that by our talking I may learn the English intonation; and I would that you tell me when I make error, even of the smallest, in my speaking. I am sorry that I had to be away so long to-day; but you will, I know, forgive one who has so many important affairs in hand."

Harker | I am quite at your service. When you are away may I come into this room.

Drac | "You may go anywhere you wish in the castle, except where the doors are locked, where of course you will not wish to go. There is reason that all things are as they are, and did you see with my eyes and know with my knowledge, you would perhaps better understand."

"We are in Transylvania, and Transylvania is not England. Our ways are not your ways, and there shall be to you many strange things. Nay, from what you have told me of your experiences already, you know something of how strange things here may be."

Harker | May I ask you about some things which have puzzled me.

Drac | (bowing) Go on. I shall try to answer.

Harker | Last night your coachman several times got down to look at places where blue flames rose from the ground, though there were wolves about and the horses were left uncontrolled. Why did he act thus.

Drac | Those flames show where gold has been hidden. I see you do not understand. I shall then explain.

It is commonly believed that on a certain night St George's Eve — last night, in fact, when all evil spirits are supposed to have unchecked sway—a blue flame is seen over any place where treasure has been hidden. "That treasure has been hidden," "in the region through which you came last night, there can be but little doubt; for it was the ground fought over for centuries by the Wallachian, the Saxon, and the Turk. Why, there is hardly a foot of soil in all this region that has not been enriched by the blood of men, patriots or invaders. In old days there were stirring times, when the Austrian and tne Hungarian came up in hordes, and the patriots went out to meet them, men and women, the aged and the children too, and waited their coming on the rocks above the passes, that they might sweep destruction on them with their artificial avalanches. When the invader was triumphant he found but little, for whatever there was had been sheltered in the friendly soil."

Harker — "But how," "can it have remained so long undiscovered, when there is a sure index to it if men will but take the trouble to look?"

Drac — "Because your peasant is at heart a coward and a fool. Those flames only appear on one night, and on that night no man of this land will, if he can help it, stir without his doors. And, dear sir, even if he did he would not know what to do. Why, even the peasant that you tell me of who marked the place of the flame would not know where to look in daylight even for his own work. You would not, I dare be sworn, be able to find these places again."

Harker — "There you are right," "I know no more than the dead where even to look for them."

Drac | But "Come," 'tell me of London and of the house which you have procured for me."

Harker — Pardon my remissness {Get papers from his bag whilst his back is turned Dracula removes food &c a lighted lamp

FIG.117
Playscript for *Dracula*
By Bram Stoker
1897
Printed text, cut and pasted on paper, with red and black ink
British Library
Add MS 53630 F, f.8

chunks of text from his book making the play largely un-performable (fig.117). The play was staged on Tuesday 18 May 1897 at the Lyceum Theatre and the novel was published a week later. Much later, in 1927, the first authorised adaptation of *Dracula* was staged, although the script was not written by Stoker. Stoker went on to write other Gothic tales, but none matched the popularity of *Dracula*. Dracula is the most filmed literary character of all time and has been portrayed more than 500 times.

The Lyceum Theatre went into administration in 1902, and Irving died in 1905. Stoker wrote the *Personal Reminiscences of Henry Irving* in 1906, the same year he sat for the portrait photographers, W. & D. Downey, a firm with studios in Newcastle and London (fig.118). This was the first time Stoker sat for a formal portrait. This image is a photogravure – a photomechanical printing process based on a photograph – which could be reproduced in large numbers. The signature is also reproduced within

FIG. 118
Bram Stoker
By W. & D. Downey
1906
Photogravure
National Portrait Gallery
NPG x3769

the photogravure to give the impression that Stoker had personally signed the image.

Aside from the W. & D. Downey image, few portraits of Stoker exist. This is in stark contrast to other writers of Stoker's generation, such as Oscar Wilde (1854–1900; see p.145), who was photographed, sketched, painted and caricatured repeatedly throughout his lifetime. Comparison can also be made with Charles Dickens (1812–1870; see p.197) who has 95 portraits in the National Portrait Gallery, whereas Stoker has just one. It is remarkable that such an influential writer could remain so elusive. Here, Stoker's biography and life, as much as his likeness, are mere shadows of the powerful character he created. **AA**

ARTHUR CONAN DOYLE

Sir Arthur Conan Doyle (1859–1930) was the creator of the famous Sherlock Holmes, a character who dominated not only detective fiction, but also the life of the author himself. Together with his assistant Doctor Watson, Sherlock Holmes set about solving crimes and apprehending murderers from his residence at 221b Baker Street, London. Doyle was born in Scotland and studied medicine at Edinburgh University before becoming a professional author. While at medical school, he was taught by Joseph Bell (1837–1911) and Sir Patrick Heron Watson (1832–1907), who would later be used as models for Sherlock Holmes and Doctor Watson, respectively. During his studies, Doyle began writing fiction and his first short story, 'The Mystery of Sasassa Valley', was published in *Chambers's Edinburgh Journal* in 1879.

Doyle worked as a ship's doctor on a whaling boat in Greenland and on a steamer in West Africa before setting up a medical practice in Portsmouth, England. During this time, he amassed a significant portfolio of stories, many of which drew on his experiences on ships, including the Gothic short story 'The Captain of the Polestar', first published in the literary periodical *Temple Bar* (1883).

Doyle first introduced Sherlock Holmes and Doctor Watson in 'A Study in Scarlet', which was published in *Beeton's Christmas Annual* (1887), followed by 'The Sign of the Four' in *Lippincott's Monthly Magazine* (1890). At the same time, Doyle wrote *The White Company*, a medieval romance containing significant amounts of historical research, which was published in 1891. In that year Doyle moved his Sherlock stories to *The Strand Magazine* meaning that many more people had access to them. The Sherlock stories originally appeared in the very back of the magazine but proved so popular that they were soon moved to the front, causing subscription numbers to double. Following the success of the first series, *The Strand Magazine* requested another 18 stories. Demand for his stories meant that he had little time for his medical practice. Doyle feared he would only be known for his creation of Sherlock Holmes and thus invented the villain Professor Moriarty. He silenced both hero and villain through their mutual destruction at Reichenbach Falls in the short story 'The Final Problem', published in December 1893, leaving him free to write in other genres, especially historical fiction.

FIG.119
Sir Arthur Conan Doyle
By Sir Bernard Partridge
1926
Pencil, pen, ink and wash
National Portrait Gallery
NPG 3668

Bernard Partridge.

The 1926 drawing by Sir Bernard Partridge (1861–1945; fig.119), he chief cartoonist for *Punch* magazine, depicts Doyle literally chained to his character, Sherlock Holmes, who lurks behind him, blowing smoke from his pipe, which engulfs the author. He evidently changed his mind about how he wanted to depict Doyle's expression, as the head has been cut out of another piece of paper and pasted onto the rest of the drawing. Doyle's shackling to Sherlock was not resolved by 'The Final Problem', and the caricature, made 33 years after what was to be the last Holmes story, and published in *Punch* magazine, shows how the problem persisted.

Doyle published numerous stories and works that did not feature Holmes, but the death of the famous detective was short-lived. Between 1901 and 1902, he published *The Hound of the Baskervilles* as a serial, after the American *McClure's Magazine* offered him $45,000. The novel was published in 1902. Between 1903 and 1904, Doyle, claiming that Holmes had survived at Reichenbach, went on to publish another 13 stories in *The Strand Magazine* featuring the detective. The stories included 'The Adventure of the Retired Colourman' (fig.120), which appeared first in the US in *Liberty* (1926), and then in the UK in *The Strand Magazine* a year later. It was later published in the short story collection, *The Case-Book of Sherlock Holmes* (1927), and tells the story of the disappearance of the wife of an art supplier. The manuscript shows Doyle's neat handwriting with only a few corrections to the text. In his later years Doyle was devoted to Spiritualism, writing a number of works on the subject. In addition to historical fiction, he wrote a series of popular novels and short stories featuring the character Professor Challenger. Yet despite these, and other successes, Doyle was to be always primarily associated with his fictional hero, Sherlock Holmes. **AA**

FIG.120
'The Adventure of the Retired Colourman'
By Sir Arthur Conan Doyle
1926
Black ink on paper
British Library
Add MS 88924/2/10, f.1r

The Adventure of the Retired Colourman. 1

Sherlock Holmes was in a melancholy & philosophic mood that morning. His alert practical nature was subject to such reactions.

"Did you see him?" he asked.

"You mean the old fellow who has just gone out?"

"Precisely"

"Yes, I met him at the door."

"What did you think of him?"

"A pathetic futile broken creature"

"Exactly, Watson. Pathetic and futile. But is not all life pathetic & futile? Is not his story a microcosm of the whole? We reach. We grasp. And what is left in our hands at the end? A shadow. Or worse than a shadow — misery."

"Is he one of your clients?"

"Well, I suppose I may call him so. He has been sent on by the Yard. Just as medical men occasionally send their incurables to a quack. They argue that they can do nothing more and that whatever happens the patient can be no worse than he is."

"What is the matter?"

Holmes took a rather soiled card from the table. "Josiah Amberley". He says he was junior partner of Brickfall and Amberley who are manufacturers of artistic materials. You will see their names upon paint boxes. ~~provision merchants of note.~~ He made his little pile, retired from business at the age of ~~55~~ 61, bought a house at Lewisham, and settled down to rest after a life of ceaseless grind. One would think his future was tolerably assured"

"Yes indeed"

Holmes glanced over some notes which he had scribbled upon the back of an envelope.

"Retired in 1896, Watson. Early in 1897 he married a woman twenty years younger than himself — a good looking woman too if the photograph does not flatter. A competence, a wife, leisure — it seemed a straight road which lay before ~~him~~ him. And yet within two years he is, as you have seen ~~him~~, as broken & miserable a creature as crawls beneath the sun."

"But what has happened?"

"The old story, Watson. A treacherous friend and a fickle wife.

RABINDRANATH TAGORE

Rabindranath Tagore (1861–1941) was the first Indian writer to become world famous, having an enormous impact in his lifetime and beyond. Ironically it was only when he translated his work into English, the language of the imperial power that he opposed, that his international fame arrived. Recent work has done more to draw attention to the power and skill of the huge body of work he produced in Bengali that has never been satisfactorily translated.

Tagore was born into a wealthy and cultured Bengali family in Calcutta (Kolkata), at a time when Bengali culture was experiencing a renaissance focused in that city. Educated mainly at home, but also briefly at University College London, his first poem was published when he was a teenager. He became a prolific writer in Bengali, working in almost every literary genre. Over his lifetime he published over 60 books of poetry, wrote novels, plays, songs (including composing the music) and also painted prolifically. Tagore campaigned and spoke publicly about political and educational issues, occasionally clashing with his fellow anti-colonial nationalist, Mahatma Gandhi (1869–1948), although generally the two felt mutual admiration. By the time his writing was discovered by the wider world, Tagore was well-known and highly admired in Bengal and regarded by the British rulers of India as a political subversive.

The reach of Tagore's influence became dramatically wider after a visit to England in 1912. The English artist William Rothenstein (1872–1945) had become interested in Mughal art and was outraged by the assertion by leading figures in the British art world that Indian art had no value. Along with others, he founded the India Society in 1910, with the intention of promoting Indian arts of all kinds in Britain. Rothenstein travelled to India in 1910–11 and there he met Tagore. In turn, Tagore visited England with the purpose of publicising his educational work. He brought with him some translations of his poems that he had worked on while recovering from an illness, and during the voyage to England.

Rothenstein was so impressed by Tagore's poetry that he sent it to the Irish poet W. B. Yeats (1865–1939), and together they shared the work with literary London. In November 1912 the India Society published a collection of 103 translated poems under the title *Gitanjali* (Song Offerings) (fig.121), dedicated to Rothenstein and with an introduction by Yeats. In 1913 the poems were published again by Macmillan, and later that

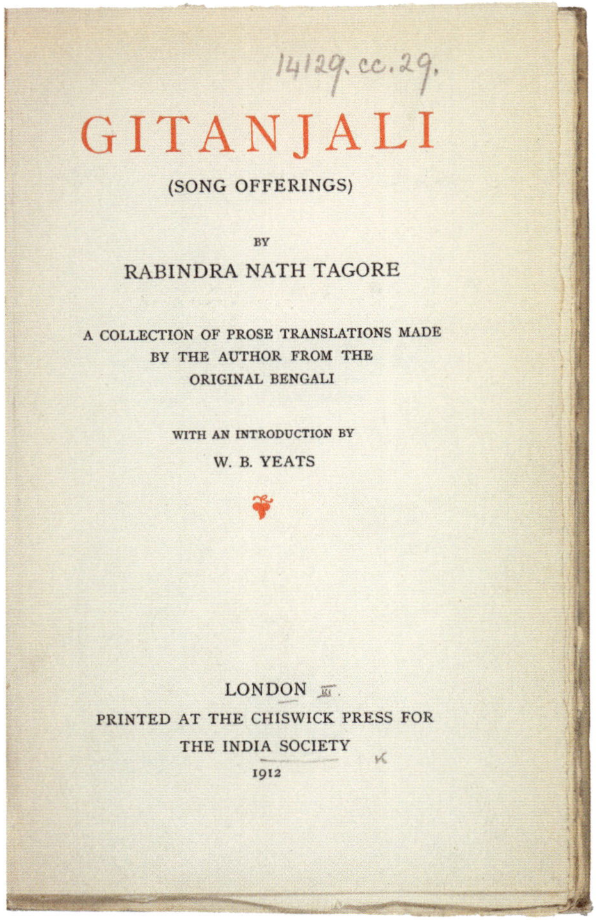

FIG.121
Gitanjali
By Rabindranath Tagore
(Chiswick, London, 1912)
British Library
14129.cc.29.

year Tagore was awarded the Nobel Prize in Literature, 'because of his profoundly sensitive, fresh and beautiful verse, by which, with consummate skill, he has made his poetic thought, expressed in his own English words, a part of the literature of the West'.[17] Tagore became an international literary star, and began a series of tours around Europe, America and Asia, raising money for the school, and later the university he founded in India, and promoting his views on education, politics and society. He was knighted in 1915 but returned the knighthood in 1919 in response to the massacre of protesters at Jallianwalla Bagh in Amritsar by the British Indian Army.

Rothenstein drew his friend Tagore many times. The artist's interest in Indian art influenced his own painting and drawing; the sinuous lines and near-profile pose in this portrait of Tagore seem to reflect this (fig.122). Tagore had, by this time, developed a distinctive visual image for himself, growing a long beard and wearing flowing robes. By the time this late portrait was drawn, Tagore had come to believe that it might have been better had he not translated his work and gained recognition through English versions of it. He wrote to Rothenstein on 26 November 1932:

FIG. 122
Rabindranath Tagore
By William Rothenstein
1930
Sanguine and black and white chalk
National Portrait Gallery
NPG 6697

> 'It was not at all necessary for my own reputation that I should find my place in the history of your literature. It was an accident for which you were also responsible and possibly most of all was Yeats. But yet sometimes I feel almost ashamed that I whose undoubted claim has been recognized by my countrymen to a sovereignty in our own world of letters should not have waited till it was discovered by the outside world in its own true majesty and environment.'[18]

The translations of Tagore's work, particularly of those volumes published after *Gítanjali*, have been recognised more recently as an inadequate representation of his huge literary achievement, reflecting neither the breadth, nor the quality of his work in Bengali. These translations ensured him enormous fame and influence during his lifetime, although that fame waned subsequently. The cultural importance of his work in his own country, however, is reflected in, among many other things, the adoption of two of his songs as the national anthems of India and Bangladesh. **CM**

BEATRIX POTTER

The children's author Beatrix Potter (1866–1943) became a famous name around the world for her character Peter Rabbit. First created in a letter to a child, Peter eventually found his way into a book. Potter had not originally intended to be an author, and her initial attempts to publish her creations met with rejection, but persistence, a clear concept of the kind of book she wanted, and the benefit of private wealth eventually led to success.

The child of wealthy parents who were interested in art, Potter was educated by governesses at home and encouraged to draw and paint. A rather isolated childhood in London was punctuated by summer holidays first to Scotland and then to the Lake District, England, where Potter and her younger brother Bertram (1872–1918) developed a love for nature and for animals. Potter's Lake District explorations were supplemented by visits to London museums, including the Natural History Museum, where she studied plants and animals, and the South Kensington Museum (later renamed the Victoria and Albert Museum) where she studied art. She and her brother also kept numerous creatures as pets in their school room, including mice, frogs and rabbits.

As an adult, Potter continued drawing and painting her pets, and she produced humorous Christmas cards for her family featuring animals dressed in clothes. These were greatly admired, and Potter was encouraged to submit them to a publisher to be turned into commercial greetings cards. Several designs were purchased and published as cards by Hildesheimer & Faulkner in 1890. The genesis of her books, however, was in letters to the children of her former governess, Annie Moore (b.1863/4), when in September 1893, Potter wrote a story about a rabbit called Peter in a letter to Moore's son Noel, who was recovering from an illness. She then wrote a story about a frog in a letter to Noel's brother Eric and another story about a squirrel to their sister Norah. Some years later, in about 1900, she borrowed the letters back and copied the drawings and story from Noel's letter to make a little book. This was submitted to various publishers, but Potter struggled to come to an agreement about the nature of the book. She felt strongly that the book should be small and inexpensive, so that children could buy it easily. In the end she printed the book herself, in a limited edition of 250, with black and white illustrations and a coloured frontispiece showing Peter's mother giving him camomile tea in bed.

FIG.123
The Tale of Peter Rabbit
By Beatrix Potter
(Frederick Warne & Co., London, 1902)
British Library
Cup.402.a.4.

FIG.124
Beatrix Potter
By Delmar Banner
1938
Oil on canvas
National Portrait Gallery
NPG 3635

The book was popular among Potter's extended family and friends, and she paid for a second printing in February 1902. At this point the publishers Frederick Warne & Co., one of the firms that had originally turned down the publication, expressed an interest and convinced her to shorten the book slightly and re-illustrate it entirely in colour. The first commercial edition of 8,000 copies was published by Frederick Warne & Co. in October 1902 (fig.123) and was an immediate success. This was the first of 23 books she was to publish with the company. Potter worked mainly with the editor Norman Warne (1868–1905), and their close working relationship became a romantic one, with Warne proposing to Potter in 1905. Tragically, only a month later, he died of leukaemia. While Potter continued to write after this and to publish books with Frederick Warne & Co., she spent increasing amounts of time in the Lake District and began to turn her attentions to farming.

Potter had bought Hill Top Farm in Near Sawrey, in the Lake District, with royalties from her books in 1905. While continuing to add to her landholdings she met a local solicitor, William Heelis (1871–1945), whom she married in 1913. Focusing increasingly on country life, she bought more and more land in the Lake District in an effort to save it from building developers. She became a prize-winning breeder of the local Herdwick breed of sheep and was frequently a judge at agricultural shows. It is in this role that she was painted in 1938 by Delmar Banner (1896–1983; fig.124), with notebook in hand and sheep in the background.

Banner was a German-born artist who studied and lived in Britain and who specialised in landscapes of the Lake District and portraiture. He was a friend and neighbour of Potter, and he gave the portrait to the National Portrait Gallery after the author's death. By the time she died in 1943 at the age of 77, Potter had accumulated many farms and a huge amount of land in the Lake District, using her inheritance, as well as the proceeds from her books and related merchandise, to preserve the landscape and ensure the continued breeding of her beloved Herdwick sheep. **CM**

A. A. MILNE

Winnie-the-Pooh is one of the twentieth century's most loved characters from children's literature. Originally created by Alan Alexander (A. A.) Milne (1882–1956), the bear featured in the eponymous story of 1926 and *The House at Pooh Corner* of 1928. Within these two books, Milne created a world based around the 'Hundred Acre Wood' that featured the bear, his other animal friends and the young boy, Christopher Robin. Boy and bear were based on Milne's son, Christopher Robin Milne (1920–1996), and his toy teddy bear, Edward, given to him on his first birthday. This 1926 photograph of Milne, his son Christopher and Edward the bear, by Howard Coster (1885–1959), was taken at Milne's home in the same year that *Winnie-the-Pooh* was published (fig.125). Coster was a leading portrait photographer, with a studio in central London. He photographed many prominent men of the day in the worlds of the arts, literature and politics.

Milne chose E. H. Shepard (1879–1976) to illustrate *Winnie-the-Pooh* and *The House at Pooh Corner*. Shepard was a popular artist who created

FIG.125
A.A. Milne and Christopher Robin Milne
By Howard Coster
1926
Sepia-toned gelatin silver print
National Portrait Gallery
NPG P715

FIG.126
Letter to Thomas Anstey Guthrie
From Christopher Milne
*c.*1930
Black ink on paper bearing printed illustrations from 'The King's Breakfast'
British Library
Add MS 72705, f.15r

15

THE KING'S BREAKFAST

The King asked
The Queen, and
The Queen asked
The Dairymaid:
"Could we have some butter for
The Royal slice of bread?"

Dear Uncle Anstey,
I do thank you for the picture you sent me. it looks ever so nice hanging up with your other two. I do hope you are well.
With love from
Christopher Robin Milne

I *only* want
A little bit
Of butter for
My bread!"

FIG.127
Letter to Marie Stopes
From E.H. Shepard
1934
Pen and black ink on
letterhead paper
British Library
Add MS 58542, f.48r

FIG.128
Letter to Thomas Anstey Guthrie
From A.A. Milne
14 February 1930
Pen and black ink on
letterhead paper
British Library
Add MS 72705, f.11r

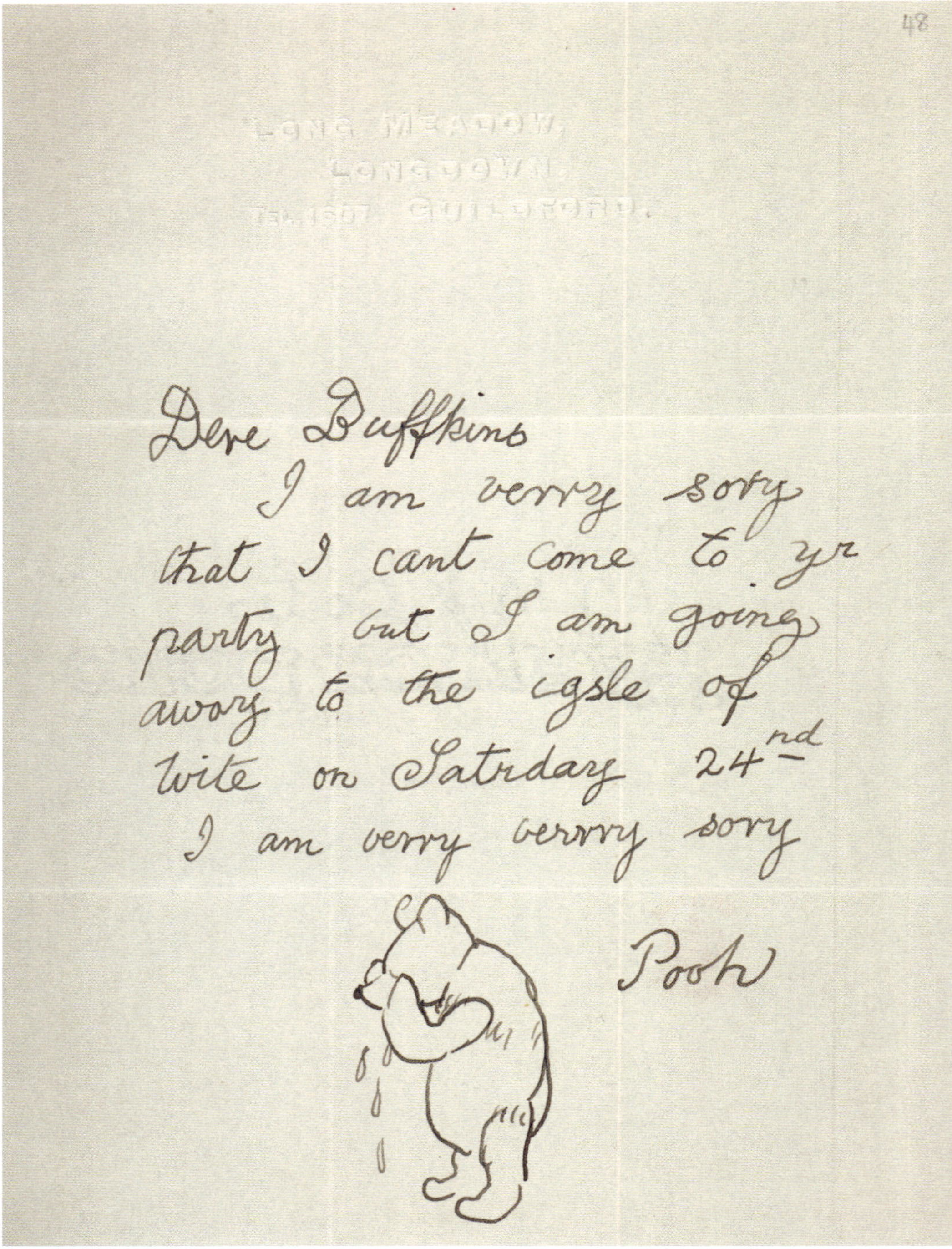

48

LONG MEADOW,
LONGDOWN,
TEL. 1507 GUILDFORD.

Dere Buffkins
I am verry sory
that I cant come to yr
party but I am going
away to the igsle of
wite on Satrday 24nd
I am verry verrry sory

Pooh

HOTEL-PENSION SCHWEIZERHOF

1057 Meter über Meer
Sommer- und Winterkurort

GRINDELWALD

AD. ANNELER
propr.

Feb. 14 [1930]

Dear [illegible],

Of course I like your congratulations. I don't feel a play of mine has really come on until you have been to see it. I am so glad you think Michael & Mary my best play. We both do, very strongly. It is a really huge success; sold out at every performance. I wrote to the Manager to say that I wanted a box for my Father at a matinée next week, and he said that I couldn't have that for a long time!

We are here for another week

illustrations for magazines such as *Punch*. Milne wrote a number of other works that featured illustrations by Shepard including *Now We Are Six* (1927)and 'The Kings Breakfast', which featured in the poetry anthology *When We Were Very Young* (1924). Illustrations from the latter can be seen in a letter from the young Christopher Milne to his godfather, the author Thomas Anstey Guthrie (1856–1934)(fig.126). Milne realised Shepard's illustrations were key to the success of *Winnie-the-Pooh* and arranged for the artist to have a share of the book's royalties. He inscribed a copy of the book to Shepard, saying:

> 'When I am gone,
> Let Shepard decorate my tomb,
> And put (if there is room)
> Two pictures on the stone:
> Piglet from page a hundred and eleven,
> And Pooh and Piglet walking (157) ...
> And Peter, thinking that they are my own,
> Will welcome me to Heaven.'[19]

When Shepard drew Winnie-the-Pooh he based his image on a bear owned by his own son, Graham. Shown in fig.127 is a sketch of Pooh by Shepard, in a letter to the author and campaigner Marie Stopes (1880–1958), in which he adopts the voice of the bear when declining an invitation to a party. Yet Shepard began to resent his work for Milne, saying his images for *Winnie-the-Pooh* dominated his career and overshadowed his other artistic work. Similarly, Christopher Milne came to dislike his association with Winnie-the-Pooh, once saying: 'It seemed to me almost that my father had got to where he was by climbing upon my infant shoulders, that he had filched from me my good name and had left me with the empty fame of being his son.'[20] A. A. Milne also lived in Pooh's shadow, his career eclipsed by the bear. Milne was also a successful essayist, author of detective fiction and a popular playwright. Shown here is a letter from Milne to Thomas Anstey Guthrie about his play 'Michael and Mary', which was staged between 1929 and 1930 in New York and London (fig.128). Yet despite Milne's broad creative output, he is best remembered for Winnie-the-Pooh. **AA**

J. K. ROWLING

One of the most internationally famous of all fictional characters, the boy wizard Harry Potter is the creation of Joanne (J. K.) Rowling (b.1965). As well as her immensely popular *Harry Potter* series of novels for children and young people, Rowling has written adult novels, including the *Strike* series of detective fiction and screenplays for films (2013–23). She is one of the world's highest earning authors, largely due to the international success of the *Harry Potter* series. The character and the world Rowling created around him have also inspired a huge range of related products, including toys, games and theme parks. Rowling has used her money and her high social profile to establish charities, support causes she believes in and to raise awareness of social and political issues. In recent times, her views on transgender issues have caused controversy.

Born near Bristol in England, Rowling grew up in Gloucestershire and Wales and studied French and Classics at Exeter University. She conceived the idea for the *Harry Potter* series while on a train from Manchester to London and developed the first story, *Harry Potter and the Philosopher's Stone*, while living in Portugal and working as a teacher of English as a foreign language. Returning to the UK with her baby daughter, she completed the book while living in Edinburgh, famously working in cafés and struggling in difficult financial circumstances. After having been turned down by 12 publishers, her book was published by Bloomsbury in June 1997. The publishers suggested using initials rather than her full name so as not to deter boy readers. They also changed the title to *Harry Potter and the Sorcerer's Stone* for the American edition the following year; both are decisions that Rowling says she now regrets.

Harry Potter and the Philosopher's Stone quickly became a bestseller and won major children's book prizes including the Nestlé Smarties Book Prize. The second book, *Harry Potter and the Chamber of Secrets* was published in 1998, and the rest of the series followed in rapid succession. Shown here is a first edition paperback copy of *The Chamber of Secrets,* with a cover illustration by Cliff Wright (b.1963) showing Harry, with his distinctive lightning-shaped scar, accompanied by his pet owl Hedwig and his friend Ron Weasley in a magical flying car (fig.129). The final book, *Harry Potter and the Deathly Hallows* (2007), became the fastest selling book of all time, with 2,650,000 copies selling in the UK within the first 24 hours of publication.

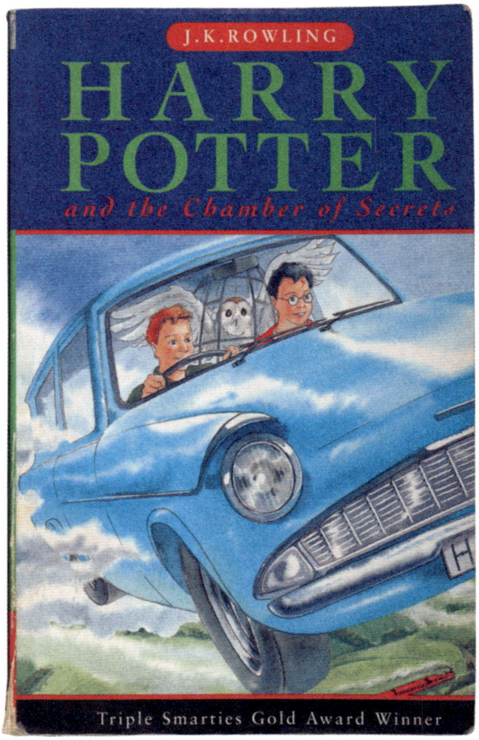

FIG.129
Harry Potter and the Chamber of Secrets
By J.K. Rowling
(Bloomsbury, London, 1998)
Private collection

FIG.130
J.K. Rowling
By Stuart Pearson Wright
2005
Charcoal on paper
National Portrait Gallery
NPG 6745(12)

The books follow a group of young wizards through their school years, with their adventures becoming progressively darker as the protagonists, and their readers, get older. Traditional elements from children's literature, such as a boarding school setting and narratives in which the underdog triumphs, are combined with richly detailed, imaginative fantasy and humour. This mix has proved enduringly successful, and the creation of a film series based on the books has ensured even wider reach and greater popularity for the stories.

The artist Stuart Pearson Wright (b.1975) won the National Portrait Gallery's Portrait Award in 2001 and was commissioned to produce a portrait of Rowling. He travelled to Edinburgh where he took photographs and made drawings as preparation for a painting. The drawings were made in Rowling's office and also in a café where she sometimes worked. In this drawing (fig.130), Wright's meticulous graphic technique captures the focus and concentration with which she works, apparently oblivious to the world around her, writing with a fountain pen on paper. Rowling was writing the sixth Harry Potter book, *Harry Potter and the Half-Blood Prince* (2005). Wright's slight elongation of her features adds a touch of melancholy, characteristic of his portraiture. The completed painting is a small oil portrait, in a three-dimensional structure like a toy theatre. It is full of references to Rowling's life, but this drawing is particularly effective and unusual among portraits of authors in actually showing the writer writing. **CM**

WRITING TO CHANGE THE WORLD

5

For some authors, writing and publishing their work is driven by an ambition to change the world around them. This chapter focuses on writers who have sought to create social and political change through prose fiction, poetry and autobiography. It explores the work of oppressed groups and their advocates, whose goals included the abolition of slavery and the emancipation of women, examining how authorial identity, communicated both through text and portraiture, has been used as a tool in these campaigns.

Writing, especially if it reaches wide audiences, has always had the power to incite social and political change. The earliest author in this book is the sixteenth-century writer Sir Thomas More, whose vision of an alternative society, for which he coined the word *Utopia* (1516), provided inspiration to countless other writers seeking change. More carefully ensured that there was enough ambiguity in his book to protect him from accusations of treason in his own, dangerous times. Later writers, including Andrew Marvell and Percy Bysshe Shelley, addressed the political issues of their times in a more direct way, although sometimes anonymously. In more recent times, campaigning against war has been an important area of political protest through literary means and here Wilfred Owen and Siegfried Sassoon were key figures.

The position of women in society has always been a source of debate and concern. As literacy among women has grown over the centuries, traditional limitations on their roles have increasingly been questioned in prose fiction, poetry and drama, as well as in polemical texts. In some cases, female authors have challenged society through their lifestyles as well as their writing. George Eliot's unconventional life with a married man, as well as the content of her novels, highlighted the restrictions and prejudices that women could suffer as a result of the marriage laws and conventions of the day. Sylvia Pankhurst's whole life was focused on campaigning and writing, not just for women's rights but also against war, fascism and racism. Author and journalist Angela Carter was an important voice in the rapidly growing feminist movement of the late twentieth century.

Legal and social equality for those whose sexual preferences, sexuality and/or gender identity have not conformed to the social mores of the day has been a focus for other writers. Often, simply the publication of poems and stories with protagonists from what is now recognised as the LGBTQ+ community has had a powerful effect, inspiring others to be more open about who they are and creating empathy and understanding among the wider reading public. W. H. Auden exemplifies this kind of writing.

Another important subject for authors who have sought change has been racial equality. In the eighteenth and nineteenth centuries this centred on the campaign for the abolition of slavery. Ignatius Sancho and Olaudah Equiano, both enslaved people who were freed, were important advocates against enslavement, both through their actions and their writing. Elizabeth Barrett Browning, a well-known white, English poet, joined a growing group of campaigners using fiction and poetry to make powerful statements against slavery. Since the nineteenth century, ongoing inequalities and prejudices – especially in relation to Britain's colonial past – continue to be highlighted and increasingly addressed. In the twentieth and twenty-first centuries, powerful writing on the subject has been produced by authors including Una Marson, Linton Kwesi Johnson, Benjamin Zephaniah and Bernardine Evaristo.

THOMAS MORE

Over 500 years ago, the scholar, lawyer, statesman, philosopher and writer Sir Thomas More (1478–1535) penned one of the most influential books in Western literature, and one that created a new word and defined a new concept: *Utopia* (1516). Born into a wealthy merchant family, More excelled academically from an early age. After leaving university, he trained as a lawyer, but also translated classical literature, studied theology and became part of an international scholastic community that included the Dutch scholar Desiderius Erasmus (*c.*1466–1536). More's intellectual interests led him towards political work and in May 1515 he was sent by Henry VIII (1491–1547) as an ambassador to Bruges, Belgium. While visiting nearby Antwerp, he met Erasmus's friend Pieter Gillis (1486–1533), the town clerk of Antwerp, and he began to formulate *Utopia.* The book, originally written in Latin, was half finished by the time More returned to England in the autumn of 1515 and published the following year, immediately becoming a literary sensation.

Utopia is written in two parts, the first taking the form of a conversation between More, Gillis and a fictional traveller called Raphael Hythloday, and the second being Hythloday's description of the apparently ideal island of Utopia. More's clever blend of fact and fiction enabled him to make the work both topical and to protect himself from direct personal association with the ideas of social and political change that he explores. The context in Antwerp reflects More's actual visit and various real characters appear in the conversation. The book was undoubtedly written to encourage political reform, but its use of satire and irony creates ambiguities that have led to widely varying interpretations. The word 'Utopia' derives from two Greek words that, combined by More, literally mean 'no place', but it is also a pun on the Greek word 'eutopia', meaning 'good place'. The island is run on broadly communist principles: all property is held in common, there is a national system of education open to both men and women and access for all to free healthcare. Different forms of religion are tolerated but punishments are harsh, and slavery is part of the system. The wide range of issues the book raises in relation to how societies could or should be run has ensured its popularity and influence ever since.

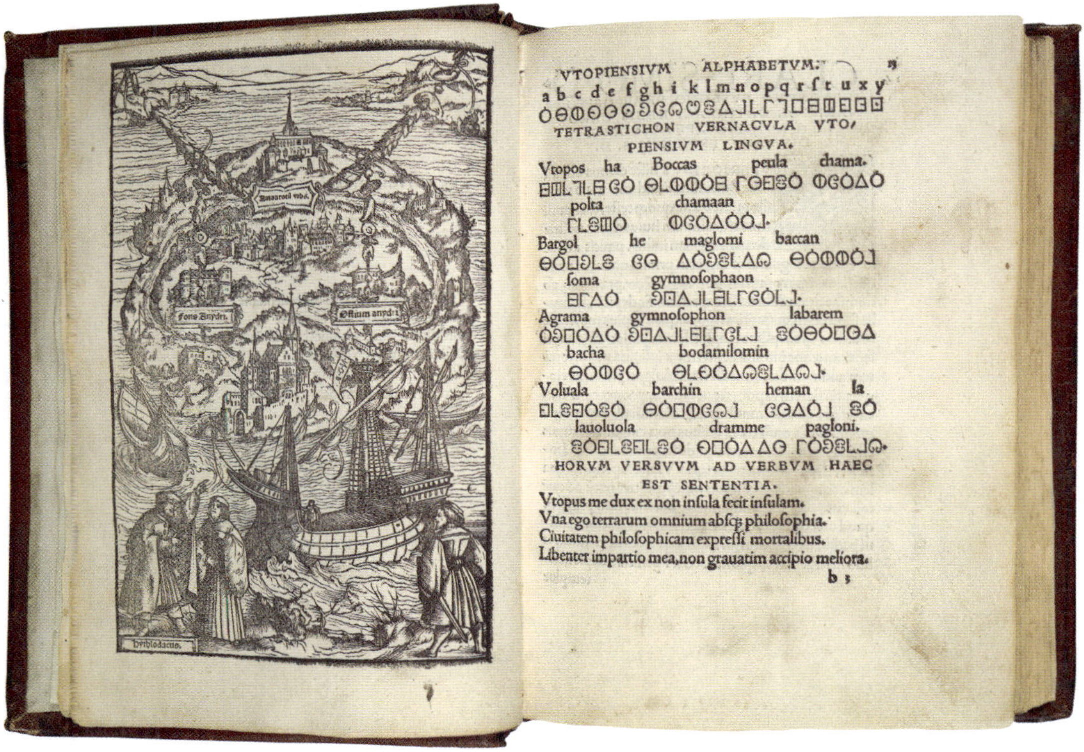

FIG.131
Utopia
By Thomas More
(Johannes Froben, Basel, December 1518)
British Library
C.67.d.8.

The edition of *Utopia* shown here is the third edition of 1518, printed in Basel. The printer, Johannes Froben (*c*.1460–1527) used a border design that had been supplied to him by the artist Hans Holbein the Younger (*c*.1497/8–1543). Holbein's brother Ambrosius (*c*.1494–*c*.1519) designed the map of Utopia (fig.131). In the foreground, at left, he shows Hythloday describing the island to More; on the right is Peter Gillis. The facing page shows the imaginary Utopian language. *Utopia* went through several more editions in the 1520s, and was translated from Latin into German in 1524, but was not translated into English until 1551, some time after the author's death.

In 1518 More became part of Henry VIII's council, and from then on rose progressively in favour with the king and in political power until in 1529 he was made Lord Chancellor, one of the most powerful positions

FIG.132
Sir Thomas More
After Hans Holbein the Younger
Late sixteenth century, based on a work of 1527
Oil on panel
National Portrait Gallery
NPG 3543

at court. During this time, he maintained his intellectual interests and writing, as well as his close friendship with Erasmus. In 1526 Holbein arrived in England with an introduction from Erasmus to More. Erasmus had met and had been painted by the artist in his native Basel; Holbein's visit to England was in search of work and More seems to have put him up in his household. Here he painted a portrait of More, now in The Frick Collection, New York; this was much copied (fig.132), especially during the later sixteenth century, when More became revered as a Catholic martyr after his death. In the painting, More is presented as a loyal courtier and statesman, wearing a Collar of Esses, denoting loyalty to Henry VIII.

More's relationship with the king was severely tested and eventually broken by Henry's relationship with Anne Boleyn (*c.*1501/7–1536) and the subsequent English Reformation – the move of the English Church from Catholicism into Protestantism. Finally, in 1532, More felt compelled to resign his chancellorship, and in 1534 refused to swear to the Act of Succession because it rejected the authority of the Pope. Henry, by this time implacably opposed to his former friend, had More imprisoned, tried and, in July 1535, executed. However, the consistent popularity of *Utopia*, and its translation into many languages, has ensured More's continuing influence. **CM**

ANDREW MARVELL

Known today mainly as a metaphysical poet, the author of such lyrical works as 'To His Coy Mistress' and 'The Garden', Andrew Marvell (1621–1678) was known in his own day, and for centuries afterwards, primarily for his satirical political writing, both in poetry and prose. The son of a prosperous clergyman in Yorkshire, England, Marvell was well educated and, from the age of 19, had an independent income following the death of his father. He spent four years travelling on the Continent during the first English Civil War (1642–6). Like many of his contemporaries, his political position shifted over time. Initially a royalist, in 1650 he wrote 'An Horatian Ode upon Cromwell's Return from Ireland' about the Parliamentarian leader Oliver Cromwell (1599–1658). It appears to be supportive of Cromwell but Marvell's exact political position in it has been much debated. Later poetry supported Cromwell more unequivocally.

In 1657 Marvell took up a position as Latin secretary in the office of John Thurloe (1616–1668), who was secretary to the Council of State and the head of the government's intelligence service. In this position, he wrote letters to heads of state, translated documents and undertook other clerical and diplomatic work. He was elected MP for Kingston upon Hull in 1659 and supported the restoration of Charles II (1630–1685) to the throne in 1660. Marvell's travels on the Continent and work for Thurloe put him in a good position to undertake a number of diplomatic missions for Charles in the early 1660s. However, his support for the monarch turned quickly to scepticism. The poem 'Instructions to a Painter' (1666) by Edmund Waller (1606–1687), in praise of the actions of the king and of James, Duke of York (later James II; 1633–1701) in the Dutch wars brought about a satirical response from Marvell, with his 'Last Instructions to a Painter' (1667). Marvell probably also wrote the anonymously published satirical 'Second' and 'Third Advice to a Painter' poems (1666). In addition to their obvious social and political subject matter, these poems implicitly address the theme of whether painting or poetry can best reflect the realities of life and, specifically, the internal truths of people's characters. The fact that the poet advises the painter suggests that word is superior to image.

Marvell's political satire was not limited to poetry; he also wrote and circulated a number of prose works anonymously. By the 1670s he was lampooning, in prose and poetry, the king's bad decisions, his lifestyle,

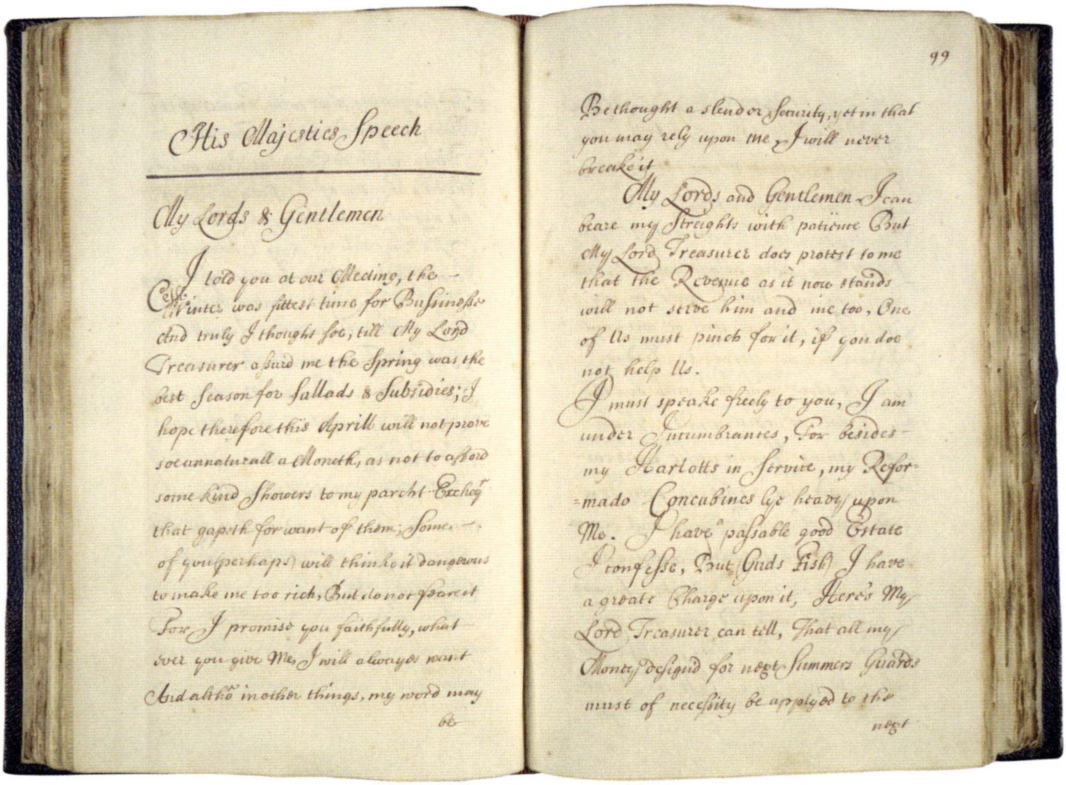

His Majesties Speech

My Lords & Gentlemen

I told you at our Meeting, the Winter was fittest time for Businesse And truly I thought soe, till My Lord Treasurer assured me the Spring was the best Season for Sallads & Subsidies; I hope therefore this Aprill will not prove soe unnaturall a Moneth, as not to afford some kind Showers to my parcht Excheqr that gapeth for want of them; Some of you perhaps will think it dangerous to make me too rich, But do not feare it For I promise you faithfully, what ever you give Me, I will alwayes want And altho in other things, my word may be

99

Be thought a slender Security, yet in that you may rely upon me, I will never breake it

My Lords and Gentlemen I can beare my Streights with patience But My Lord Treasurer does protest to me that the Revenue as it now stands will not serve him and me too, One of Us must pinch for it, if you doe not help Us.

I must speake freely to you, I am under Incumbrances, For besides my Harlotts in Service, my Reformado Concubines lye heavy upon Me. I have a passable good Estate I confesse, But Gods Fish I have a great Charge upon it, Here's My Lord Treasurer can tell, That all my Money design'd for next Summers Guards must of necessity be applyed to the next

FIG. 133
'His Majesties Speech'
By Andrew Marvell
*c.*1703
In scribal hand; iron gall ink on laid paper
British Library
Harley MS 7315, f.98v–99r

the vulnerability of the country's security, the power of the bishops and what he saw as the king's unrestricted power. 'His Majesties Speech' (fig.133) is a mock speech purportedly made by the king at the opening of Parliament on 13 April 1675. It has been copied out by a scribe in this manuscript volume, which dates to about 1703. The poem imagines the king asking for money, beginning:

> 'My Lords and Gentlemen,—I told you at our meeting, the winter was fittest time for business, and truly I thought soe, till my Lord Treasurer assured me the spring was the best season for sallads and subsidies ... For I promise you faithfully, whatever you give Me I will always want And altho in other things, my word may be thought a slender security, yet in that, you may rely upon me, I will never breake it.'[1]

It also contains references to Charles's mistresses and illegitimate children:

> 'I must speak freely to you, I am under Incumbrances, for besides my Harlotts in Service, my Reformado Concubines lye heavy upon

FIG.134
Andrew Marvell
By an unknown artist
*c.*1655–60
Oil on canvas
National Portrait Gallery
NPG 554

> Me. I have a passable good Estate I confesse, But Gods Fish ... all my Money design'd for next Summers Guards must of necessity be applyed to the next year's cradles and swadling-cloths. What shall we do for ships then?'[2]

Marvell died in 1678 and in 1681 a volume, *Miscellaneous Poems,* was published with a prefatory note by Marvell's wife. This included a frontispiece engraving of his portrait. The engraving is close to, and probably based on, the National Portrait Gallery painting (fig.134), which, along with the painting's provenance in the Marvell family, confirms it as the most securely identified portrait of the poet. *Miscellaneous Poems* included much of Marvell's writing, previously unknown to most of the public, but it excluded the political satires; these were only printed with attributions to Marvell after the political context had changed completely with the revolution of 1688. From that time until the nineteenth century, Marvell was known and celebrated for his political satire; it was only in the nineteenth and then more particularly in the twentieth century that his complex and evocative lyrical poetry, by which he is largely known today, came into prominence. **CM**

IGNATIUS SANCHO

The writer and musical composer Ignatius Sancho (*c*.1729–1780) was a campaigner for the abolition of the transatlantic slave trade and the first person of African heritage to vote in a British parliamentary election. Information about Sancho's early life is almost entirely based on *Life of Ignatius Sancho* by Joseph Jekyll (1754–1837), which was prefixed to the publication of Sancho's letters in 1782. According to Jekyll, Sancho was born on a slave ship crossing the Atlantic Ocean travelling to the West Indies and his mother died shortly after docking in the Spanish colony of New Granada. Jekyll states that Sancho was sent to England where he was enslaved to three unmarried women in Greenwich, London. John Montagu, 2nd Duke of Montagu (1690–1749), lived nearby and gave the young boy access to books in his library. Jekyll suggests that following the duke's death, Sancho fled from the three sisters, seeking refuge with Montagu's widow, Mary, Duchess of Montagu, née Lady Mary Churchill (1689–1751), who employed him as her butler. On the death of the duchess, Sancho was left an annuity, and her son-in-law George, the newly created 1st Duke of Montagu (1712–1790), employed him as a personal attendant from 1766. Sancho's letters confirm that he was in fact born in Africa, and while documentary evidence shows that he certainly worked for the Montagus, the details of the writer's early life remain unclear.

With the help of the Montagus, Sancho and his wife Anne, née Osborne, (1733–1817) set up a grocery shop in London in 1774. At the time, only males who owned freehold property with a rentable value of 40 shillings per year were allowed to vote in elections. Sancho was therefore able to vote in parliamentary elections in 1774 and 1780. He and his wife had seven children, one of whom was Elizabeth Sancho (1766–1837), whose manuscript letters survive.

From the 1760s, Sancho had begun publishing musical compositions, many of which were dedicated to members of the aristocracy. He also wrote newspaper articles and was a prolific letter writer, corresponding with a range of individuals including the vicar and writer Laurence Sterne (1713–1768; see p.88). In 1776 Sancho wrote poignantly about slavery in his correspondence with Sterne, encouraging the writer to take up the campaign: 'Consider slavery—what it is—how bitter a draught—and how many millions are made to drink it.'[3]

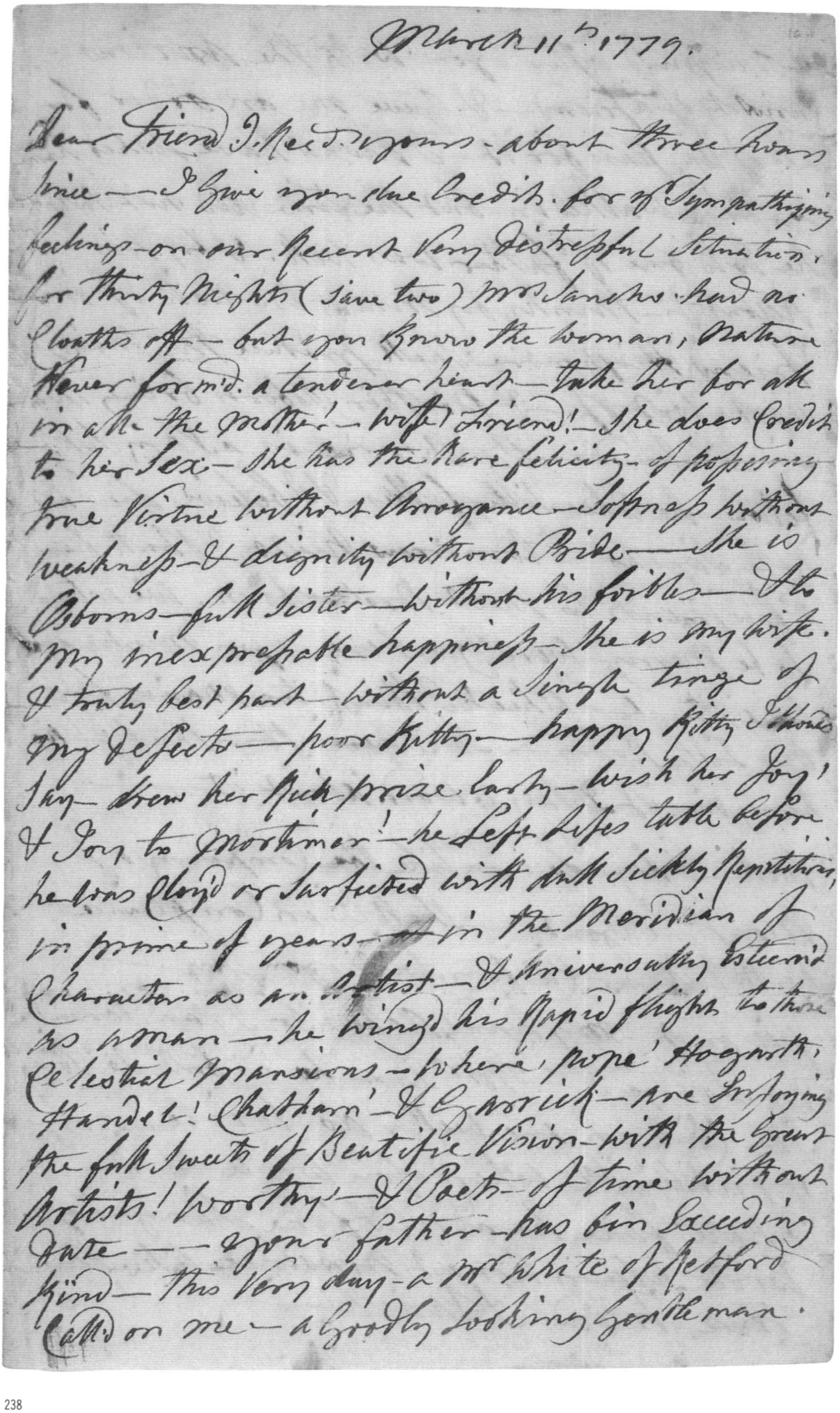
March 11th 1779.

Dear Friend I Rec'd yours about three hours since — I give you due Credit for ye Sympathizing feelings on our Recent very distressful Situation. for thirty Nights (save two) Mrs Sancho had no Cloaths off — but you know the woman, Nature Never form'd a tenderer heart — take her for all in all the Mother! — Wife! Friend! — She does Credit to her Sex — She has the Rare felicity of possessing true Virtue without Arrogance — Softness without weakness — & dignity without Pride — She is Osborns full Sister — without his foibles — She is my inexpressable happiness — She is my wife, & truly best part — without a single tinge of my defects — poor Kitty — happy Kitty I should say — drew her Rich prize lately — wish her Joy! & Joy to Mortimer! — he left Life's table before he was Cloy'd or Surfeited with dull Sickly Repetition, in prime of years — in the Meridian of Character as an Artist — & universally esteem'd as a man — he wing'd his Rapid flight to those Celestial Mansions — where Pope! Hogarth! Handel! Chatham! & Garrick — are Enjoying the full Sweets of Beatific Vision — with the Great Artists! Worthys — & Poets — of time without date — your father has bin Exceeding kind — this very day — a Mr White of Retford Call'd on me — a goodly looking Gentleman.

FIG. 135
Letter to William Stevenson
From Ignatius Sancho
11 March 1779
Iron gall ink on laid paper
British Library
Add MS 89077, f.16r

FIG. 136
Ignatius Sancho
By Francesco Bartolozzi, after Thomas Gainsborough in *Letters of the Late Ignatius Sancho, an African* (5th edition, William Leach Sancho, London, 1803)
1781
Stipple engraving
British Library
Add MS 89077

Writing in 1778 to Jack Wingrave (1757–1797), the son of a friend, Sancho was even more explicit about his feelings about the perpetrators of the slave trade:

> '[Y]our country's conduct has been uniformly wicked in the East – West Indies – and even on the coast of Guinea. –The grand object of English navigators – indeed of all Christian navigators – is money – money – money.'[4]

Sancho's letters were published after his death in 1782. Remarkably, a number of the original manuscript letters written to the printer and journalist William Stevenson (1741–1821) survive, found folded within Stevenson's own copy of the published letters. In a letter dated 26 November 1776, Sancho shared his thoughts on writing with Stevenson: 'simplicity is the characteristic of good writing – which I heave learnt'.[5] In another letter, dated 11 March 1779, Sancho talks about the death of the artist John Hamilton Mortimer (1740–1779), demonstrating his wide social knowledge and his literary style (fig.135):

> '[H]e left life's table ... in prime of years – in the meridian of character as an artist – & universally Esteem'd as a man – he wing'd his rapid flight to those Celestial mansions – where Pope! Hogarth! Handel! Chatham! – & Garrick-are enjoying the full sweets of Beatific Vision—with the great Artists! Worthys—& Poets-of time without date.'[6]

In other letters, Sancho talks about his domestic life and family trips to the theatre and to watch fireworks, writing in a humane, amusing and tender way.

When the 1st Duke of Montagu's portrait was painted by Thomas Gainsborough (1727–1788), so too was Sancho's. The portrait was apparently painted in under two hours. Gainsborough's portrait of Sancho was later engraved by Francesco Bartolozzi (1727–1815) as the frontispiece to the volume of Sancho's letters (fig.136). Like this copy of the book, Gainsborough's painting was at one time owned by William Stevenson, to whom it had been given by Sancho's daughter, Elizabeth. Stevenson has written beneath the image 'The original by Gainsborough is in my possession'. The portrait shows Sancho dressed as a prosperous gentleman, emphasising his role in society. Sancho's powerful words, and life story, were used by opponents of the slave trade, providing fuel to the argument that finally led to the Slave Trade Act of 1807. **AA**

OLAUDAH EQUIANO

Olaudah Equiano (*c.*1745–1797), known for much of his life as Gustavus Vasa, was an important figure in the anti-slavery movement and whose writing contributed to the growing calls for its abolition. A contemporary of Ignatius Sancho (1729–1780; see p.237), Equiano was born in southern Nigeria. He was kidnapped, along with his sister, at the age of eight, before being sold into slavery and shipped across the Atlantic to Barbados and then Virginia in North America. Repeatedly sold to different owners, Equiano spent a long period at sea with the Royal Navy officer, Lieutenant Michael Pascal (d.1786). Equiano travelled the oceans with Pascal for eight years, during which time he learned to read and write. He was later sold to the merchant Robert King (b. before 1735). It was while working for King that Equiano earned enough money through trading that he was able to purchase his own freedom. After travelling the world for 20 years, he settled in London where he became involved in the movement to end slavery. A member of the Sons of Africa group, Britain's first Black resistance movement, Equiano published his autobiography, *The Interesting Narrative of the Life of Olaudah Equiano* in 1789.

The autobiography details Equiano's life as an enslaved person, and recounts times when he was forced to watch horrific acts of violence against Black people, as well as their continual maltreatment and abuse. Like Sancho's writings, the book helped strengthen support for abolitionists in Britain, and it remains powerful in its message. Shown here is the frontispiece to Equiano's book, which depicts the author, like Sancho, in fashionable British clothing (fig.137). The portrait is a stipple engraving by Daniel Orme (1766–1837) based on a work by William Denton (*fl.*1792–1795). The whereabouts of the portrait by Denton is unknown and so Orme's engraving is the only known likeness of Equiano. In the image, Equiano holds the Bible open at Acts, Chapter 4, Verse 12, presenting himself as a Christian, the religion to which he converted in 1759. It has been argued that by using Acts, which is about Christian community, Equiano found an additional way to garner support for the abolition of slavery. The title page includes the lines from another book of the Bible, Isaiah, Chapter 12, Verses 2–4, which begins 'Behold, God is my Salvation', showing the extent to which the author identified with his faith. Contemporary readers in Britain would have been familiar with these passages from the Bible and would have understood their meaning. The image of Equiano is complex and powerful: a writer, once enslaved, embracing Christian salvation and dressed in fine clothes. His image suggests parallels between himself and the viewer, which sets up a framework for empathy and understanding. Quickly, viewer becomes reader and on turning the page is confronted with the barbarities of the slavery and the purpose behind his book:

> '[T]he chief design of which is to excite in your august assemblies a sense of compassion for the miseries which the Slave-Trade has entailed on my unfortunate countrymen. By the horrors of that trade I was first torn away from all tender connections that were naturally dear to my heart.'[7] **AA**

FIG.137
The Interesting Narrative of the Life of Olaudah Equiano
By Olaudah Equiano
(T. Wilkins, London, 1789)
British Library
10605.aaa.5.

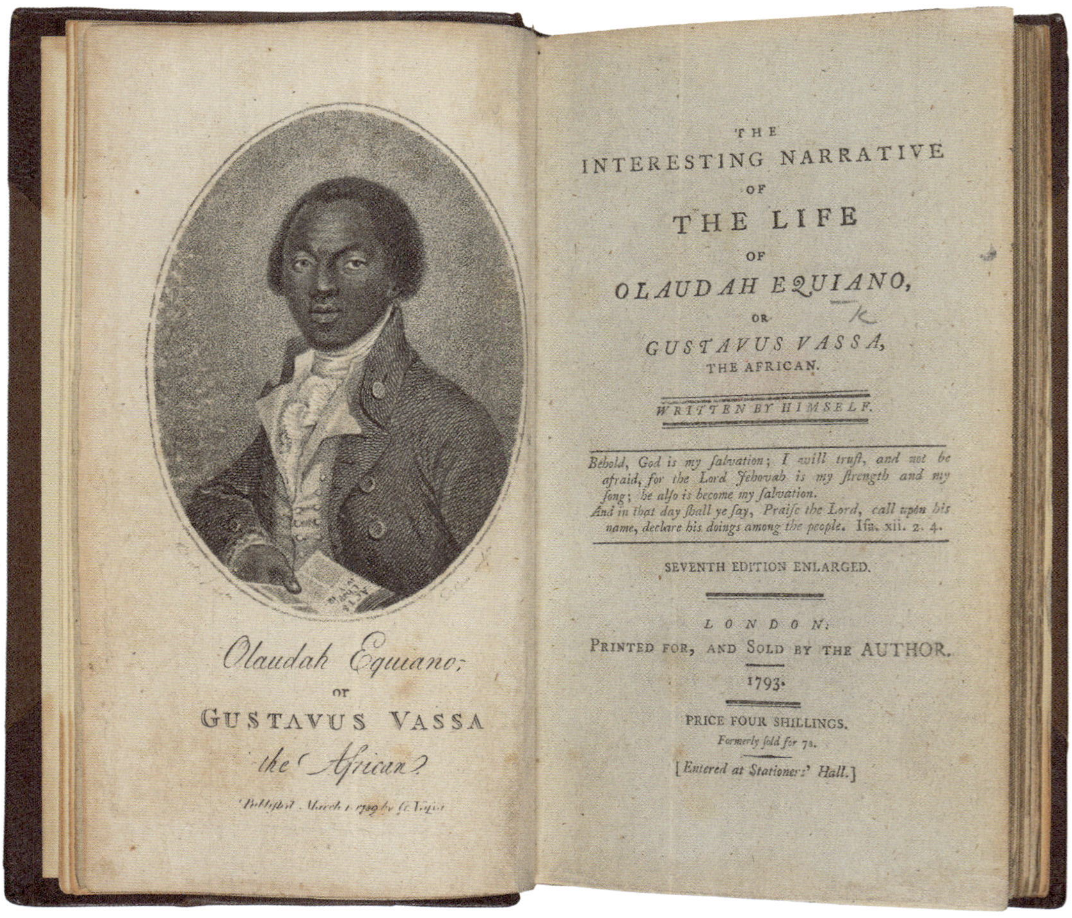

WILLIAM BLAKE

Writer and artist William Blake (1757–1827) was born in London to a family of shopkeepers and artisans. Exhibiting visionary tendencies from a young age, Blake apparently saw 'a tree filled with angels' at the age of seven or eight and 'the Prophet Ezekiel under a Tree in the Fields'.[8] In 1772, he was apprenticed to the printmaker James Basire (1730–1802), assisting him with engravings for the Society of Antiquaries and the Royal Society in London. Blake joined the Royal Academy Schools in 1779 in order to pursue a career as an artist. He also wrote poetry from the age of 12, some of which was published in *Poetical Sketches* (1783). The death of his brother, Robert (1762–1787), led to visions of his sibling that directed him to create poetry and illustrations in the form of relief etching. Blake developed this unusual process so that he could merge word and image on a single plane, rather than needing to combine expensive letterpress text with etched or engraved images. His first book of illuminated poems was *Songs of Innocence* (1789).

Both Blake's politics and his religious outlook were radical. From 1790 he printed *The Marriage of Heaven and Hell*, which rejected the Church of England and called for a complete overhaul of religious and secular tyrannies. A supporter of the French and American Revolutions, Blake operated outside of convention, creating imaginary worlds in his work. In around 1797 he began work on an epic poem, originally called 'Vala' but later changed to 'The Four Zoas'. Divided into 'Nights', the poem addresses themes of life, humanity, sexual freedom, redemption through a reformed Christianity, and death and immortality, set in a mythological universe of Blake's creation. Comprising over 4,000 lines of text, the vast project was eventually abandoned by Blake by 1807, and it was never published. Shown here is the first 'Night' together with Blake's handwritten text and original illustration. Blake drafted some of the text in pencil and then amended or wrote over it in black ink. A number of the sections have been crossed out in ink (fig.138).

Blake's visionary outlook can also be seen in his correspondence. Writing to the Reverend John Trusler (1735–1820) on 16 August 1799 he said: 'I find more and more that my style of designing is a species by itself, and in this which I send you have been compelled by my genius or angel to follow where he led.'[9] In another letter to Trusler on 23 August 1799 Blake wrote: 'I know that this world is a world of imagination and vision

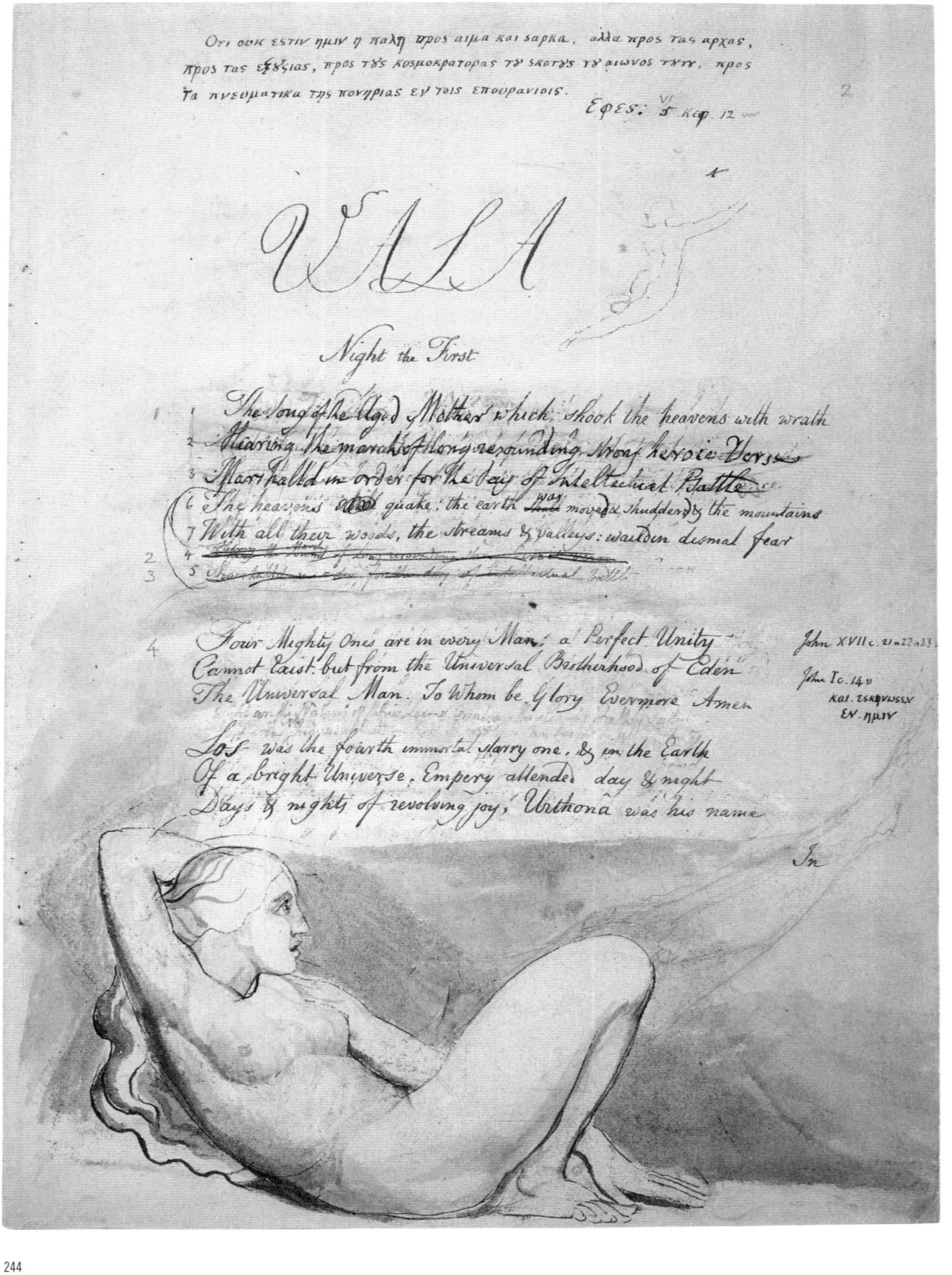
VALA
Night the First
The Song of the Aged Mother which shook the heavens with wrath
Hearing the march of long resounding strong heroic Verse
Marshalld in order for the day of Intellectual Battle
The heavens quake: the earth was moved & shudderd & the mountains
With all their woods, the streams & valleys: waild in dismal fear
Four Mighty Ones are in every Man; a Perfect Unity
Cannot Exist. but from the Universal Brotherhood of Eden
The Universal Man. To Whom be Glory Evermore Amen
Los was the fourth immortal starry one, & in the Earth
Of a bright Universe, Empery attended day & night
Days & nights of revolving joy, Urthona was his name
John XVII c. 21 & 22 & 23
John I c. 14 v
In

FIG.138
'Vala' or 'The Four Zoas'
By William Blake
1797
Black ink and pencil with grey and blue wash on paper
British Library
Add MS 39764, f.2r

FIG.139
William Blake
By Thomas Phillips
1807
Oil on canvas
National Portrait Gallery
NPG 212

... To me this world is all one continued vision of fancy or imagination. I see everything I paint in this world.'[10]

When Thomas Phillips (1770–1845) painted Blake at the age of 50 in 1807, he chose to depict him as artist, writer and visionary (fig.139). Apparently 'the rapt poetic expression' was conjured up by Phillips's luring Blake to talk about his friendship with the Archangel Gabriel.[11] Seated on a wooden bench, Blake is seen holding a pen or engraving tool, looking above the viewer and into the distance, as if focused on something far away. Blake's radical outlook and experimental artistic output have influenced many other writers, artists and musicians seeking to change or reinterpret the world in which they live. **AA**

PERCY BYSSHE SHELLEY

Public fascination with Percy Bysshe Shelley (1792–1822) has always revolved as much around his unconventional and tragic life as it has around his poetry, but the fact that a strong driving force in both his life and work was his political and social campaigning is perhaps sometimes overlooked. From a prosperous background, he went to Oxford University at the age of 18, in 1810. His studies were brief, as he was expelled in March 1811 for co-writing and publishing a pamphlet, *The Necessity of Atheism,* with his friend Thomas Jefferson Hogg (1792–1862). Later in the same year he eloped with the 16-year-old Harriet Westbrook (1795–1816), in spite of having philosophical objections to the institution of marriage. Shortly after this, Shelley began corresponding with the philosopher William Godwin (1756–1836), who had a profound and lasting impact on Shelley's social and political outlook. During this time Shelley published political and philosophical pamphlets, and two substantial poems with political themes, 'The Devil's Walk' (1812) and *Queen Mab* (1813).

Shelley's contact with Godwin was to have other consequences. By 1814 his marriage to Harriet was in difficulties and, in the summer of 1814, he fell in love with Mary (1797–1851), Godwin's daughter. Shelley and Mary Godwin travelled to the Continent with Mary's stepsister, Claire Clairmont (1798–1879) in July 1814. They returned to London in September 1814, to much public and familial disapproval.

Shelley, Mary and Claire spent the summer of 1816 in Switzerland with the poet George Gordon, Lord Byron (1788–1824; see p.193), who was having an affair with Clairmont. This was a productive, creative time for the group. Shelley wrote poetry, including 'Mont Blanc' and Mary famously began to write her novel *Frankenstein* (1818). However, the year was to end with tragedy, with the suicides of first Mary's half-sister Fanny Imlay (1794–1816), and then of Shelley's estranged wife Harriet, who was heavily pregnant. After Harriet's death, Shelley and Mary married and in 1818 he, Mary, their children and Claire left England for Italy. Shelley was never to return to England.

Shelley continued to write and took a keen interest in political events in Britain. In 1819, a month after the event, Shelley heard about the Peterloo Massacre. In response to a severe economic slump, which had hit the north of England particularly hard, a mass rally had been organised by the Manchester Patriotic Union in St Peter's Field, Manchester to demand

FIG. 140
'The Masque of Anarchy'
By Percy Bysshe Shelley
1819
Iron gall ink and pencil on wove paper
British Library
Ashley MS 4086, f.1r

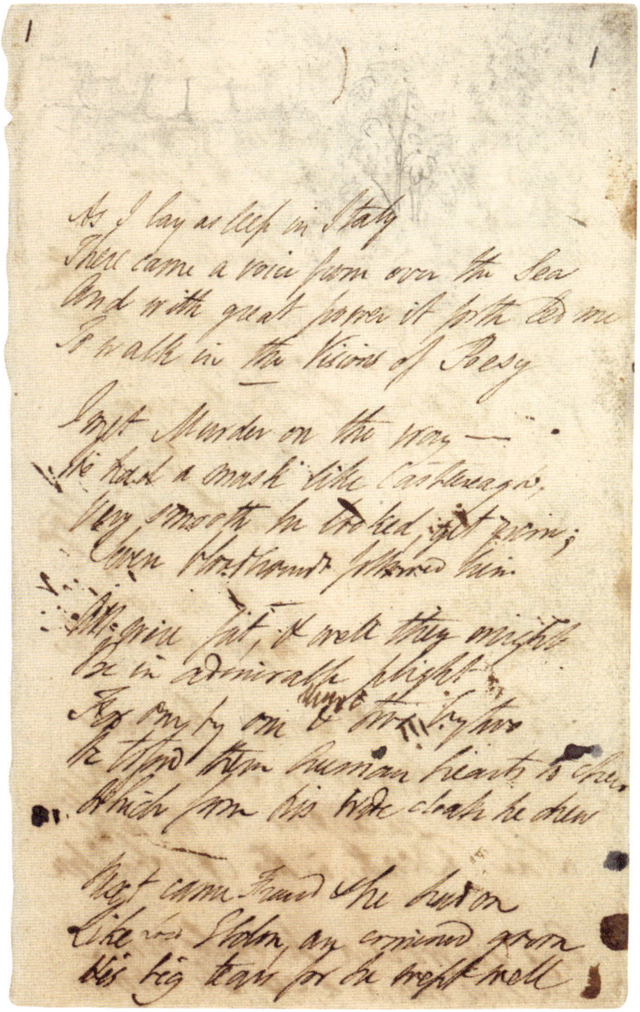
As I lay asleep in Italy
There came a voice from over the Sea
And with great power it forth led me
To walk in the Visions of Poesy

I met Murder on the way —
He had a mask like Castlereagh,
Very smooth he looked yet grim;
Seven bloodhounds followed him.

All were fat, & well they might
Be in admirable plight
For one by one & two by two
He tossed them human hearts to chew
Which from his wide cloak he drew

Next came Fraud & he had on
Like Lord Eldon an ermined gown
His big tears for he wept well

parliamentary reform. The rally was peaceful, but a cavalry regiment was ordered to charge the crowd with drawn sabres; at least a dozen people were killed and hundreds more were injured. In response, Shelley wrote 'The Masque of Anarchy' (fig.140), the first English poem to call for non-violent resistance to oppression. Shown here is the first page in which the lines 'I met murder on the way / He had a face like Castlereagh' appear. Robert Stewart, Viscount Castlereagh (1769–1822) was the Leader of the House of Commons at the time and was blamed by many for the government's harsh policies. Shelley sent the poem to his friend Leigh Hunt (1784–1859) in England, for publication in Hunt's weekly journal *The Examiner*, but Hunt judged that the public was not ready for Shelley's uncompromising attacks on powerful politicians, and the perpetrators of the attack had by then been exonerated. It was not published until 1832, since when it continues to be an inspiration to many political movements and protest campaigns.

FIG.141
Percy Bysshe Shelley
By Amelia Curran
1819
Oil on canvas
National Portrait Gallery
NPG 1234

During the last years of his life, Shelley continued to write and to move around Italy with his extended family. In July 1822 he and a friend, Edward Ellerker Williams (1793–1822), were sailing from Livorno back to his house near Lerici when a sudden storm blew up. The boat capsized and both men drowned. Shelley was 29 years old but had experienced – and written – more than most in his short life.

During their time in Rome in 1819, the Shelleys had by chance met Amelia Curran (1775–1847), a childhood friend of Mary and Claire, who was studying art. She painted Shelley's portrait (fig.141), as well as those of Mary, Claire and the Shelleys' son William. After Shelley's death, Mary wrote to Curran to ask for the portrait of Percy. Curran was not happy with the painting, describing it as 'ill done', and had nearly destroyed it, but after repeated requests from Mary, she finally sent it to her in 1826.[12] Mary was delighted, exclaiming 'unlike aught earthly wert thou ever, and art now!'[13] She maintained that it was the best portrait of Shelley, and her daughter-in-law bequeathed it to the National Portrait Gallery in 1899. **CM**

ELIZABETH BARRETT BROWNING

Elizabeth Barrett Browning (1806–1861) was a poet who regularly tackled societal injustice in her works. Born in the north of England, Barrett Browning was the daughter of Edward Barrett Moulton Barrett (1785–1857), a plantation owner. The Barrett family had resided in Jamaica for centuries, owning sugar plantations on which enslaved people were forced to work. Barrett Browning was the first child in her family to be born in England in over 200 years. Suffering from ill health and mourning the deaths of her mother and brother, Barrett Browning lived a reclusive existence, spending time reading and writing alone in her room. Educated at home, she showed an early interest in literature, reading passages from John Milton's (1608–1674) *Paradise Lost* (see p.76) and *Othello* and *The Tempest* by William Shakespeare (1564–1616; see p.180). In 1838 Barrett Browning published *The Seraphim and Other Poems*, which cemented her reputation in literary circles in England and North America.

In 1844 Barrett Browning published *Poems* in two volumes, which made her a literary celebrity. *Poems* was read and admired by the poet Robert Browning (1812–1889). The two poets began a correspondence, which ultimately led to marriage in 1846. During this time, Barrett Browning wrote *Sonnets from the Portuguese* (later published in *Poems*, 1850), which included 'How do I love thee? Let me count the ways'. The couple went on to live in Italy, during which time Barrett Browning developed an interest in Italian politics. Supporting the Unification of Italy, she penned *Casa Guidi Windows* (1851), which documented the country's struggle for political autonomy.

The topic of slavery had previously been addressed by Barrett Browning in the poem 'The Runaway Slave at Pilgrim's Point'. Much of this work had been composed in Pisa in 1846 and it was published two years later in the anti-slavery magazine, *The Liberty Bell*, in Boston, US. Slavery had been abolished in the UK and its colonies by 1838, whereas the campaign continued in the US until abolition in 1865. Barrett Browning's manuscript is a partial draft of the poem, which contains stanzas 14–26 and which differs significantly from parts of the published text (fig.143). Robert Browning's comments can be seen in pencil on some of the folios. The poem is spoken by an enslaved woman who was separated from

FIG. 142
Elizabeth Barrett Browning
By Michele Gordigiani
1858
Oil on canvas
National Portrait Gallery
NPG 1899

FIG. 143
'The Runaway Slave at Pilgrim's Point'
By Elizabeth Barrett Browning
1846
Black ink on wove paper
British Library
Ashley MS A2517, f.5r

the man she loved and raped by her white master, resulting in the birth of her son. The protagonist is tormented by the whiteness of the child and suffocates him, which leads to her punishment by whipping. This deeply harrowing poem was designed to shock Victorian readers, as much as it impacts readers today. 'Pilgrim's Point' is thought to reference the landing of the Pilgrim Fathers from the ship *Mayflower* at Plymouth Rock in Massachusetts, in 1620. While this event has been seen as the moment of the founding of the United States, Barrett Browning links the white settlement in North America to the enslavement of men and women.

In 1857, after two decades of writing, Barrett Browning published *Aurora Leigh*, a narrative poem that deals with education, the treatment of marginalised women, societal imbalance, sexual violence and prostitution. The year after *Aurora Leigh* was published, this portrait of Barrett Browning was painted by Michele Gordigiani (1835–1909; fig.142) for Sophia May Eckley (1823–1874), the American poet and spiritualist medium, with whom Barrett Browning had a close friendship during their time in Italy. The portrait is one of a pair with a portrait of Robert Browning, also commissioned by Eckley. Robert Browning felt Gordigiani's painting was the best depiction of his wife, and it seems to convey both her reticence and her determination. **AA**

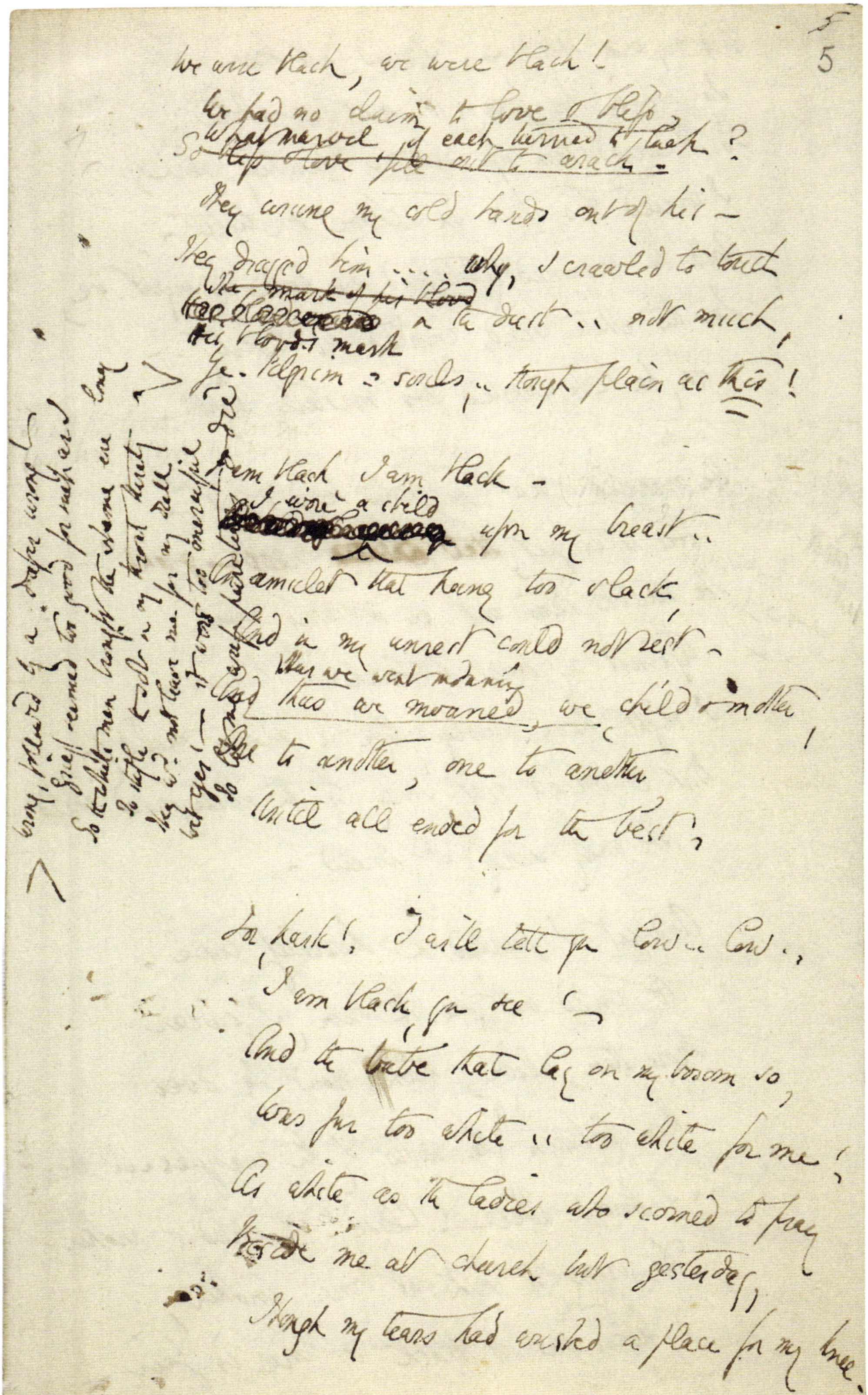
5

We were black, we were black!
We had no claim to love & bliss
What marvel if each turned to lack?
They wrung my cold hands out of his –
They dragged him .. why, I crawled to touch
His blood's mark in the dust .. not much,
Ye pilgrim-souls,.. though plain as this!

I am black, I am black –
I wore a child upon my breast..
An amulet that hung too slack,
And in my unrest could not rest –
Thus we went moaning, we child & mother,
One to another, one to another
Until all ended for the best;

For hark!, I will tell you low .. low ..,
I am black you see, –
And the babe that lay on my bosom so,
Was far too white .. too white for me!
As white as the ladies who scorned to pray
Beside me at church but yesterday,
Though my tears had washed a place for my knee.

GEORGE ELIOT

George Eliot (1819–1880) was regarded both during her lifetime and since as one of the greatest novelists of the nineteenth century. Her unconventional life and challenging but popular writing posed questions that ultimately inspired changes in society. Among the themes she explored were political and social reform; the role of women in society and in marriage; the nature and impact of religious belief; the role of education; the nature of Jewish experiences in nineteenth-century Britain and the desire for a Jewish homeland.

Eliot was born Mary Anne Evans, the daughter of an estate manager near Nuneaton in Warwickshire. She was educated in a number of schools – at which she achieved academic distinction – but at the age of 16 the terminal illness of her mother brought her home. After her mother's death she worked as housekeeper for her father until his death in 1849. At that point – unmarried, nearly 30, well-read, intellectually ambitious and self-conscious about her appearance (which was regarded as 'plain') – she began an independent life and career.

Eliot and her father had moved to Coventry in 1841 and there she became friends with a progressive and intellectual family, the Brays. In the summer of 1849 Eliot was invited by the Brays to travel with them to Switzerland and Italy. When the Brays returned home to Coventry, Eliot remained in Geneva, lodging with the family of the painter François D'Albert-Durade (1804–1886) for the winter. D'Albert-Durade painted Eliot's portrait in February 1850. She wrote to a friend that the portrait was the artist's idea, not hers: 'The idea of making a study of my visage is droll enough.'[14] D'Albert-Durade produced a sympathetic image of Eliot, with whom he maintained a long friendship, later translating some of her novels into French. The National Portrait Gallery's portrait is the second of two versions painted by him (fig.144), and one of a very few portraits of the writer, most of which are in the Gallery's collection. Eliot was particularly uncomfortable about portrait photography, perhaps because the potentially unlimited reproducibility of the photograph could subject her to the gaze of so many people.

On her return to England, Eliot decided, very much against the conventions of the day, to move to London to pursue a career as a journalist. She lodged in the home and workplace of John Chapman

FIG. 144
George Eliot
Replica by François D'Albert-Durade
After 1850, based on a work of 1850
Oil on canvas
National Portrait Gallery
NPG 1405

(1821–1894), the owner of the radical paper the *Westminster Review*. She worked for Chapman, becoming in effect the managing editor, although she was not credited as such. She also produced articles and reviews under her own name, which she had changed to Marian Evans. One of her fellow lodgers at this time later recalled her unconventional character: 'She was really one of the most sceptical, unusual creatures I ever knew, and it was this side of her character which was to me the most attractive.'[15] During this time she met the writer George Henry Lewes (1817–1878), who was to become her life's companion. Lewes was in a very unhappy, open marriage, but having registered two of his wife's four children with another man as his own, he could not by law divorce her on grounds of adultery.

Lewes and Eliot fell in love and decided – in defiance of society – to live together openly as man and wife. From this time, Eliot called herself Mrs Lewes or Marian Evans Lewes, regarding their relationship as a true marriage. They began this period of their lives with a trip to Germany in the summer of 1854. On their return to England, Eliot found that she – although not Lewes – was shunned by respectable society. But with Lewes's encouragement, Eliot began to write fiction: first, *Scenes of Clerical Life* (1857), and then *Adam Bede* (1859), which was an instant critical success and a bestseller. Eliot had chosen to publish both works under a pseudonym, 'George Eliot', partly because of her reputation as a woman living with a married man, and partly because of her natural shyness and wish to avoid attention. After two years of public speculation about who George Eliot was, however, including the increasing assertion that the author was a Warwickshire man called Joseph Liggins, Mary Anne Evans Lewes felt compelled to reveal her identity.

These works were admired for their warmth and humanity, and for their moral compass. The revelation that their author was a woman, who was considered by many to be an immoral, atheistic radical, forced George Eliot's readers to reassess some of their assumptions and judgements. Eliot herself found the experience excruciatingly painful but, with Lewes's encouragement, she continued to write and, in 1860, published her next novel, *The Mill on the Floss*, again to enormous popular and critical acclaim. Literary success, and recognition from much-admired contemporaries like Charles Dickens (1812–1870; see p.197), eventually brought a degree of social acceptance. Queen Victoria (1819–1901) read and admired her novels, and in 1877 Eliot met the queen's daughter, Princess Louise (1848–1939).

Middlemarch, A Study of Provincial Life (fig.145) was Eliot's sixth novel. Longer than her previous works, it was published initially in eight parts in two-monthly intervals by Blackwood, from December 1871 to December 1872, and then as four volumes. Shown here is the beginning of Chapter 1 of Part 1, which introduces the main character, Dorothea Brooke, in the novel. This was the manuscript that was sent to the printers, and it contains inky fingerprints from the typesetters throughout, as well as some late amendments made by Eliot. *Middlemarch* sold very well but received mixed reviews. Subsequently, however, it came to be recognised as one of the greatest works of English fiction, famously described by Virginia Woolf (1882–1941; see p.42) as 'one of the few English novels written for grown-up people'.[16] **CM**

FIG.145
Middlemarch
By George Eliot
1871–2
Black ink on wove paper
British Library
Add MS 34034, f.5r

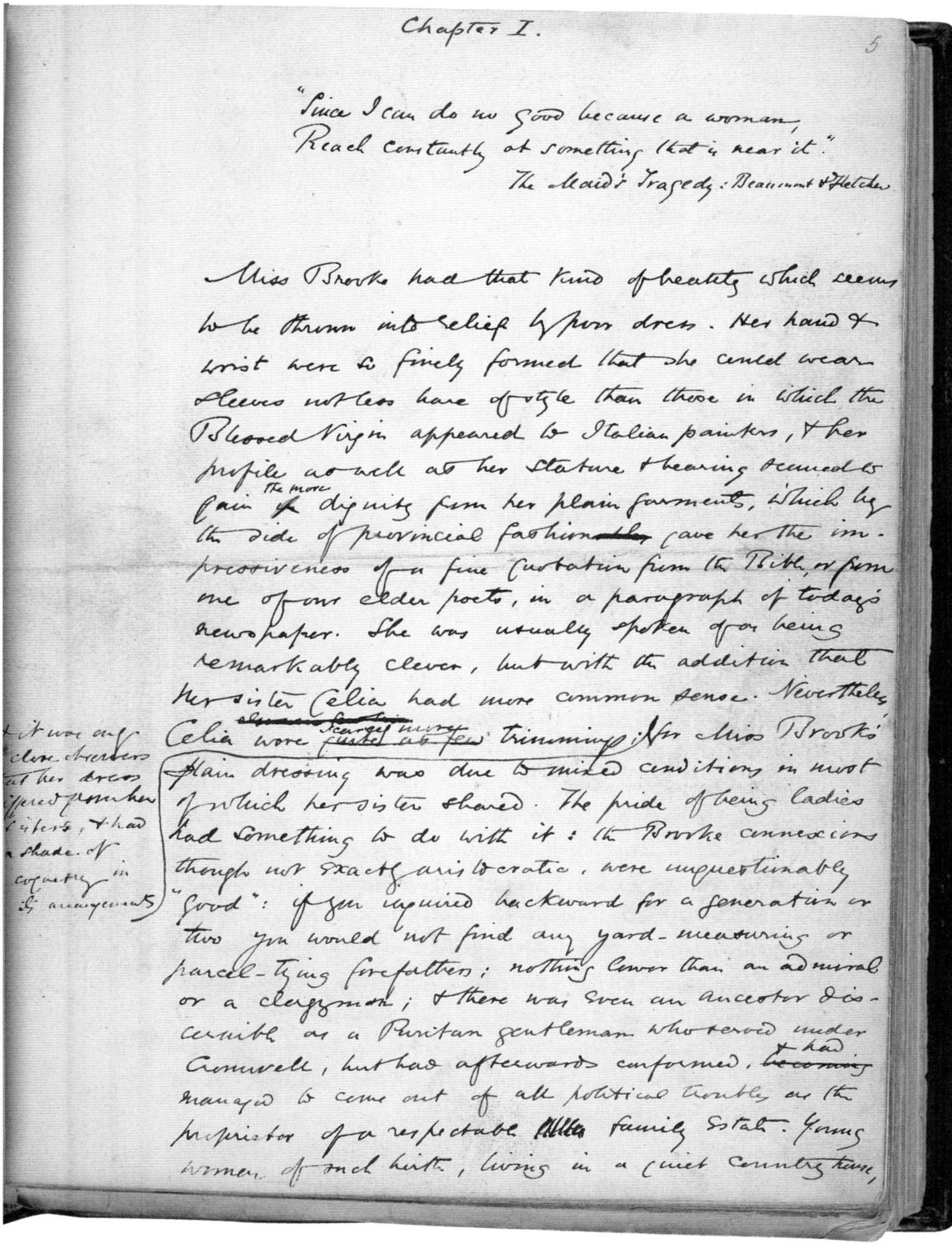

Chapter I. 5

"Since I can do no good because a woman,
Reach constantly at something that is near it."
The Maid's Tragedy: Beaumont & Fletcher

Miss Brooke had that kind of beauty which seems to be thrown into relief by poor dress. Her hand & wrist were so finely formed that she could wear sleeves not less bare of style than those in which the Blessed Virgin appeared to Italian painters, & her profile as well as her stature & bearing seemed to gain the more dignity from her plain garments, which by the side of provincial fashion gave her the impressiveness of a fine quotation from the Bible, or from one of our elder poets, in a paragraph of today's newspaper. She was usually spoken of as being remarkably clever, but with the addition that her sister Celia had more common sense. Nevertheless Celia wore scarcely more trimmings; & it was only close observers that her dress differed from her sister's, & had a shade of coquetry in its arrangements. Her Miss Brooke's plain dressing was due to mixed conditions in most of which her sister shared. The pride of being ladies had something to do with it: the Brooke connexions though not exactly aristocratic, were unquestionably "good": if you inquired backward for a generation or two you would not find any yard-measuring or parcel-tying forefathers; nothing lower than an admiral or a clergyman; & there was even an ancestor discernible as a Puritan gentleman who served under Cromwell, but had afterwards conformed, & had managed to come out of all political troubles as the proprietor of a respectable family estate. Young women of such birth, living in a quiet country house,

SYLVIA PANKHURST

Activist, writer and artist Sylvia Pankhurst (1882–1960) was a campaigner who fought for social reform as well as workers' and women's rights. A daughter of the suffragette Emmeline Pankhurst (1858–1928), Sylvia Pankhurst's childhood was spent surrounded by political activism and campaign. She trained as an artist, first studying at Manchester School of Art and then the Royal College of Art in London. In 1903 her mother and sister Christabel (1880–1958) established the Women's Social and Political Union (WSPU). From 1906 Sylvia gave up her studies in order to support the work of the WSPU and she was imprisoned that same year for protesting in court over a trial at which women were not allowed to speak in their own defence. From this point onwards, she was involved in numerous campaigns, seeing women's suffrage as part of wider societal issues that required reform. Shown here is a portrait of Pankhurst taken by the American photographer George Grantham Bain (1865–1944) in the first decade of the twentieth century (fig.146). The Bain News Service was one of the first news agencies providing images of international events to newspapers worldwide. It photographed suffragettes on a number of occasions, taking individual portraits and documenting protests and arrests. This photograph of Pankhurst is one of a group of many images of suffragettes that appeared in the press.

In 1913 Pankhurst established the East London Federation of Suffragettes (ELFS), which organised demonstrations and protests. Arrested and sent to prison eight times between 1913 and 1914, Pankhurst engaged in hunger strikes as well as physical resistance to arrest. In addition to women's rights, the ELFS supported trade unions and the rights of workers. Pankhurst established and edited the newspaper the *Woman's Dreadnought*, which she used as a means to protest against conflict at the outset of the First World War. In 1917 she renamed her newspaper the *Workers' Dreadnought* to reflect the revolutionary sentiment her campaigning had adopted. She worked on behalf of the 'Hands Off Russia' campaign, at one point travelling to Russia to meet Vladmir Lenin (1870–1924). In 1920 she published an article in her newspaper based on reports from an English sailor, which alleged unrest on an unnamed British battleship and urged sailors to support the Russian navy. The article led to Pankhurst's arrest as she

FIG.146
Sylvia Pankhurst
By George Grantham Bain
1910s
Gelatin silver print
National Portrait Gallery
NPG x194305

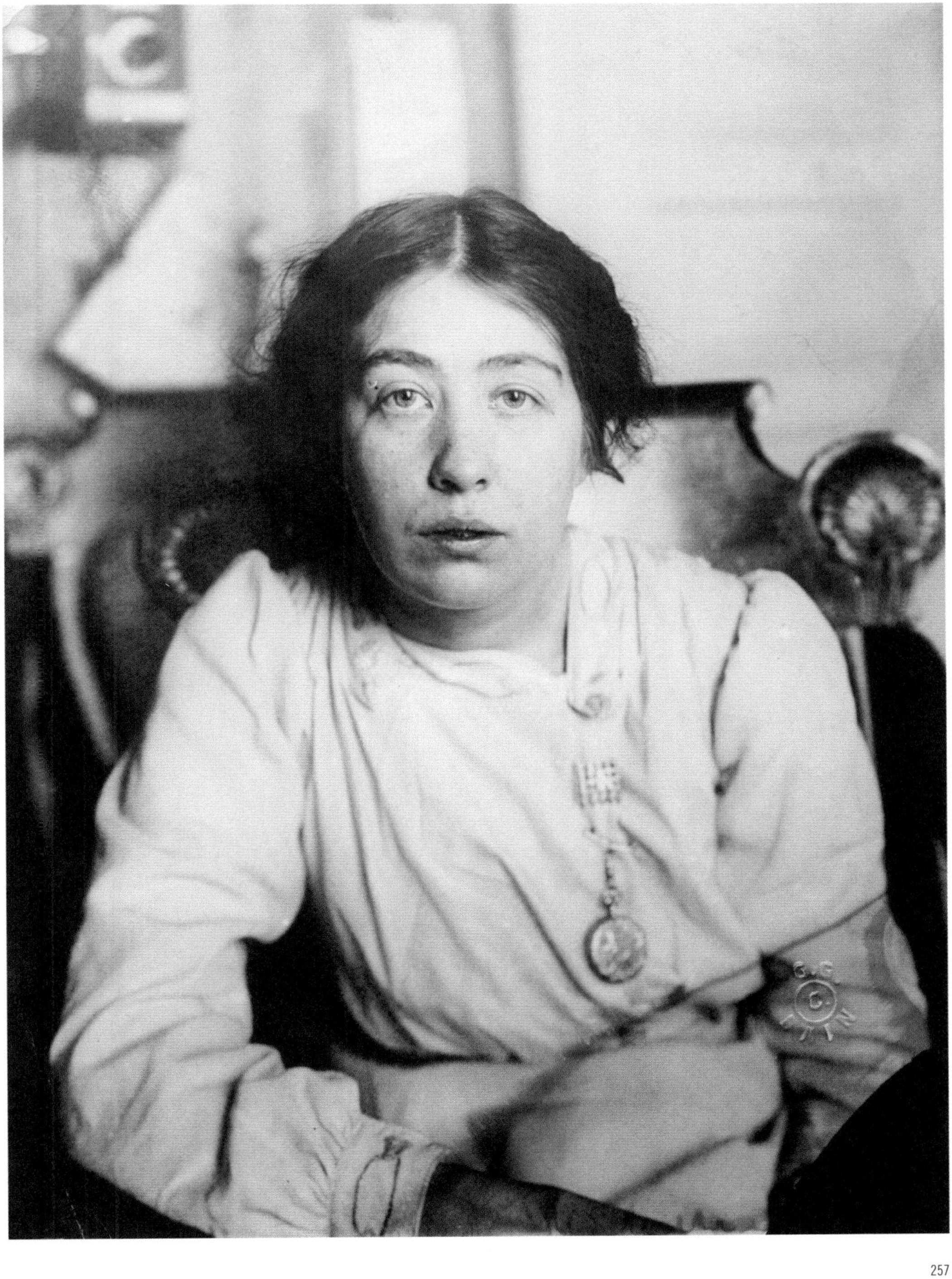

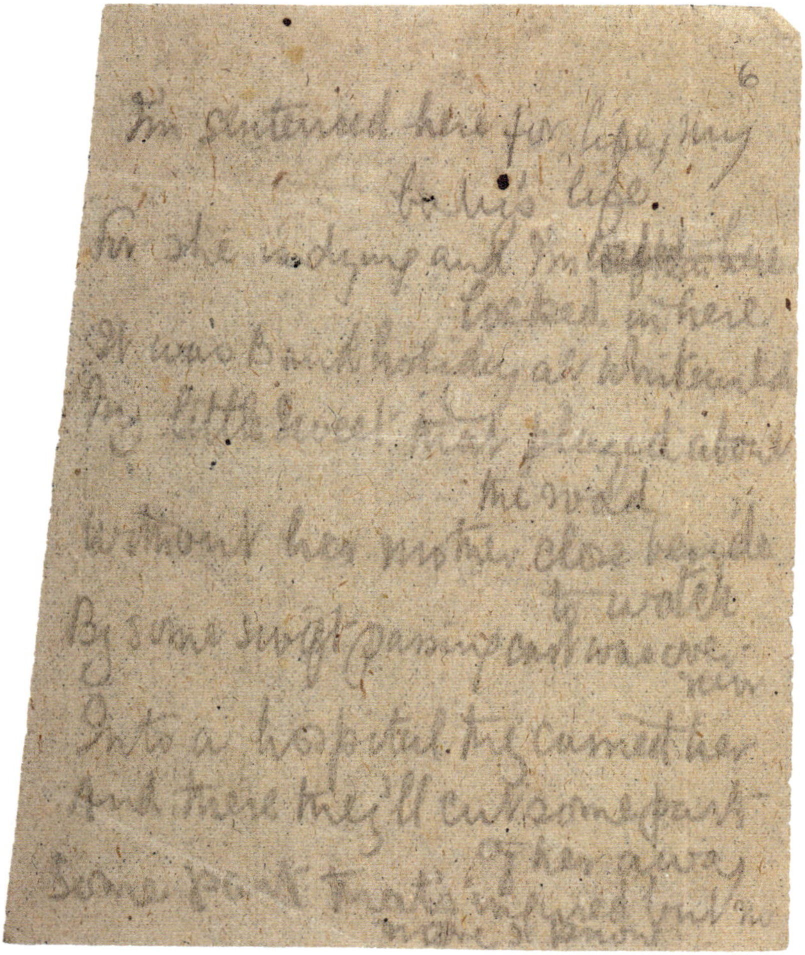

6

I'm sentenced here for life, my
baby's life.
For she is dying and I'm locked in here
It was Bank holiday at Whitsuntide
My little sweet one played about the road
without her mother close beside to watch
By some swift passing cart was overrun
Into a hospital they carried her
And there they'll cut some part of her away
Some part that's injured but I'm not to know

FIG.147
Untitled poem
By Sylvia Pankhurst
1921
Pencil on toilet paper
British Library
Add MS 88925/1/1, f.6r

would not name the sources she relied on for information. Spending five months in Holloway Prison, London, Pankhurst used the time to write using a small slate and chalk. She transcribed her writing using a contraband pencil on prison toilet paper and hid it in her undergarments until it could be smuggled out of prison by her friends. Shown here is one of a number of untitled poems by Pankhurst (fig.147). The start of the poem references the harshness of prison for women incarcerated and separated from their children: 'I'm sentenced here for life, my baby's life / For she is dying and I'm locked in here.'[17]

After the 1920s, Pankhurst concentrated her efforts on fighting for peace and against the Fascist movement. She later focused on Ethiopian independence and supporting refugees who had been displaced after the 1935–6 Italian invasion of Abyssinia (modern-day Ethiopia). Pankhurst's entire life was devoted to campaign and reform and her work contributed to the movement to allow greater freedoms not just to women but to marginalised and oppressed peoples throughout the world. **AA**

WILFRED OWEN AND SIEGFRIED SASSOON

The chance meeting of two young poets in a military hospital during the First World War led to some of the most powerful anti-war poetry that has ever been written. In April 1917, Siegfried Sassoon (1886–1967) was wounded in France and returned to England to convalesce. In June 1917, at the age of 30 and already a published poet, he wrote a forceful statement against the war, which was read out in the House of Commons and printed in *The Times* in July. It began: 'I am making this statement as an act of wilful defiance of military authority, because I believe that the war is being deliberately prolonged by those who have the power to end it.'[18] The result of this statement was that Sassoon was declared to be suffering from shell shock and was sent to Craiglockhart War Hospital, near Edinburgh. Here he met Wilfred Owen (1893–1918), aged 24, who had also been sent back from the front, diagnosed with shell shock.

Owen was seven years younger than Sassoon, less well-educated and from a less privileged background, and it took him several weeks to pluck up the courage to introduce himself. He had been writing (unpublished) poetry for some time and had been editing the hospital's journal *Hydra*. He had also read Sassoon's recently published *The Old Huntsman* (1917) and was in awe of the older man. He eventually went to Sassoon's room, knocked on his door and asked him to sign some copies of *The Old Huntsman* for himself and some friends. A close friendship began, which was to change both their lives. Sassoon's encouragement and advice transformed Owen's poetry, and eventually Sassoon came to believe that Owen was the greater talent. Among the poems that Owen wrote during the months at Craiglockhart in 1917 were his most famous works, including 'Anthem for Doomed Youth' and 'Dulce et Decorum est' (fig.148). Owen then reworked these poems several times with the help of Sassoon's editorial suggestions. This is a late draft, close to the final, 1920 published version of the poem.

Owen planned a volume of poems that, following Sassoon's example, exposed the horror of the experience of war. He drafted a preface that famously described:

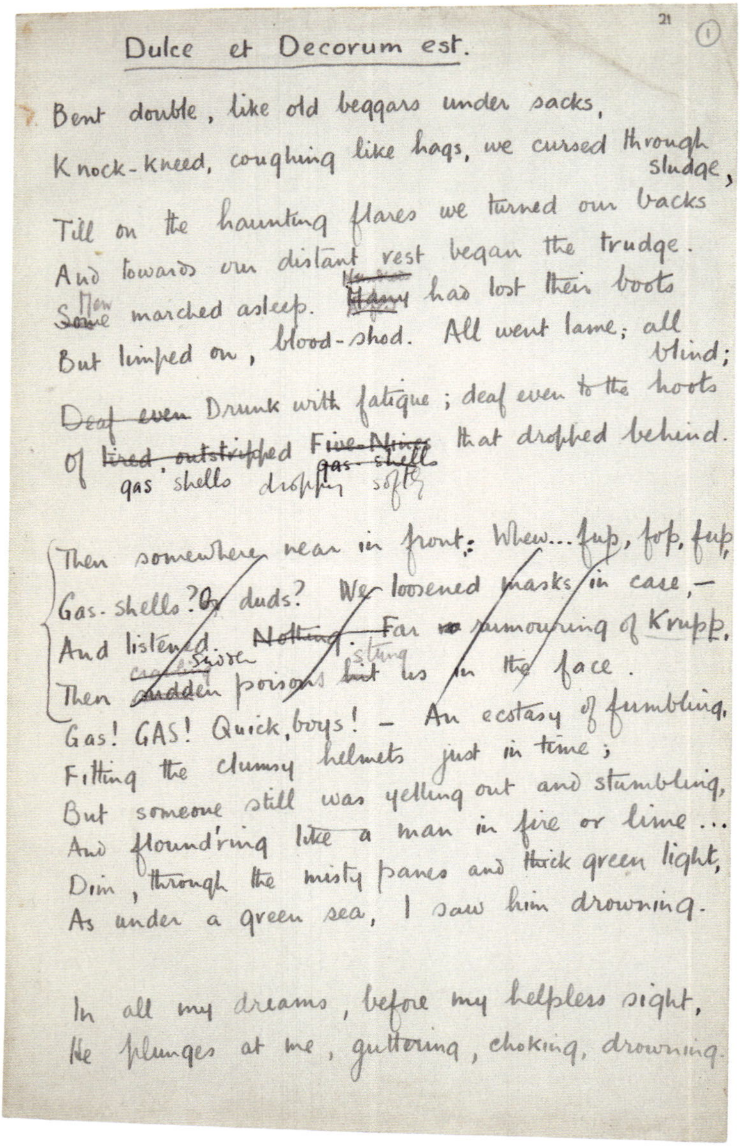
21 ①

Dulce et Decorum est.

Bent double, like old beggars under sacks,
Knock-kneed, coughing like hags, we cursed through sludge,
Till on the haunting flares we turned our backs
And towards our distant rest began the trudge.
~~Some~~ Men marched asleep. ~~Many~~ had lost their boots
But limped on, blood-shod. All went lame; all blind;
~~Deaf even~~ Drunk with fatigue; deaf even to the hoots
Of ~~tired, outstripped~~ ~~Five-Nines~~ gas-shells that dropped behind.
gas shells dropping softly

Then somewhere near in front: Whew... fup, fop, fup,
Gas-shells? Or duds? We loosened masks in case,—
And listened. ~~Nothing~~. Far rumouring of Krupp.
Then ~~sudden~~ poisons hit us in the face.
Gas! GAS! Quick, boys! — An ecstasy of fumbling,
Fitting the clumsy helmets just in time;
But someone still was yelling out and stumbling,
And flound'ring like a man in fire or lime...
Dim, through the misty panes and thick green light,
As under a green sea, I saw him drowning.

In all my dreams, before my helpless sight,
He plunges at me, guttering, choking, drowning.

FIG. 148
'Dulce et Decorum Est'
By Wilfred Owen
with annotations by
Siegfried Sassoon
1917
Ink and pencil on paper
British Library
Add MS 43720, f.21r

'This book is not about heroes ...
My subject is War, and the pity of War.
The Poetry is in the pity.'[19]

In 1918 Owen was declared fit and returned to the front. He fought bravely and was awarded the Military Cross, but on 4 November 1918 he was killed near the village of Ors in northern France, one week before the war ended. Sassoon also returned to the war but survived. He subsequently edited and wrote the introduction to the first collection of Owen's poems, which was published in 1920. Sassoon went on to publish several more volumes of his own poetry during this decade, and it was

FIG.149
Siegfried Sasson
By Cecil Beaton
Late 1920s
Gelatin silver print
National Portrait Gallery
NPG x40357

also at this time that his photograph was taken by Cecil Beaton (1904–1980; fig.149), one of the most celebrated British photographers of the twentieth century. The composition and lack of focus on Sassoon creates a sense of instability and restlessness in the sitter.

Sassoon continued to write poetry on a range of subjects, as well as prose; he won literary prizes and was awarded a CBE and the Queen's Gold Medal for Poetry. However, it is for the friendship between Sassoon and Owen, their literary influence on one another and their resulting war poems, that both men are remembered most widely today. Owen, who hero worshipped Sassoon, had written to him: 'I held you as Keats + Christ + Elijah + my Colonel + my father-confessor + Amenophis IV in profile.'[20] Sassoon later wrote: 'I count it among my most satisfactory performances that I was able to be of service to his genius.'[21] **CM**

W. H. AUDEN

Wystan Hugh (W. H.) Auden (1907–1973) was struck by the revelation that he would become a poet at the age of 15. Auden's first pamphlet, entitled *Poems,* was published by his friend, the writer Stephen Spender (1909–1995), in 1928. A year later, T. S. Eliot (1888–1965; see p.45) published a dramatic sketch by Auden in his literary magazine *The Criterion*, and in 1930 Eliot published at Faber & Faber the first commercially available book of Auden's poems, again called *Poems*. In this work, Auden had developed a new, modernist style that seemed to capture the atmosphere of England at the time. This portrait of Auden, taken by the British portrait and fashion photographer Cecil Beaton (1904–1980), dates from the same year (fig.150). It was the first of three sittings that Auden had with Beaton during his lifetime, and one of several images that show the poet in a mirror image. Auden emerges from the darkness, with his reflection appearing like a shadowy twin. Both he and his twin stare directly at the viewer. The dividing and mirroring of Auden's face and body forces the viewer to consider the poet in a series of opposing parts: public and private, illuminated and shadowed, hidden and revealed. In a 1962 article for *Vogue*, 'Mirror: A set of notes by W. H. Auden', the poet explored the notion of the self and its reflection, writing: 'Every man carries with him through life a mirror, as unique and impossible to get rid of as his shadow.'[22]

Aware he was homosexual from an early age, Auden at one point underwent therapy in an alleged attempt to 'cure' him of his sexuality. Although briefly engaged to a woman, he called off the union in 1929, deciding to accept his homosexuality. His friend, Michael Yates (1919–2001), inspired love poems including 'The Dream', and 'Lullaby', written in the late 1930s. At this time Auden also wrote the now famous 'Funeral Blues', also known as 'Stop All the Clocks', which was set to music by his friend Benjamin Britten (1913–1976).

In the face of unrest in Germany in the late 1920s, Auden had begun writing poems that considered societal change and adopted a politically socialist outlook. He volunteered as a medical worker for the Spanish Republic during the civil war and gave the profits of his propagandist poem 'Spain' (1937) to medical organisations that aided the Spanish republic. Following this, in 1938 Auden was commissioned to co-author a book on the Sino-Japanese War, and he visited China and Japan, before

FIG.150
W. H. Auden
By Cecil Beaton
1930
Gelatin silver print on white card mount
National Portrait Gallery
NPG P859(3)

travelling to New York in 1939. Auden's time in New York was to cement a life-long connection with North America, and he eventually applied for American citizenship in 1946.

In April 1939 he met the poet and librettist Chester Simon Kallman (1921–1975) with whom he was to have a relationship, which he regarded as a marriage. Auden wrote his 1939 poems 'The Prophets' and 'Like a Vocation' about the experience of falling in love with Kallman. In 1940 Auden completed his book of poems, *The Double Man*, which recorded his return to Christianity.

In 1957 Auden purchased a small farmhouse in Austria. This was the first house he had ever owned, and it inspired his volume *About the House* (1965). The prologue for *About the House* was entitled 'The Birth of Architecture'. Auden drafted the poem in a notebook that also contained prose and musical drafts dating between 1946 and 1965 (fig.151). The poem begins: 'From gallery-grave and the hunt of a wren king',

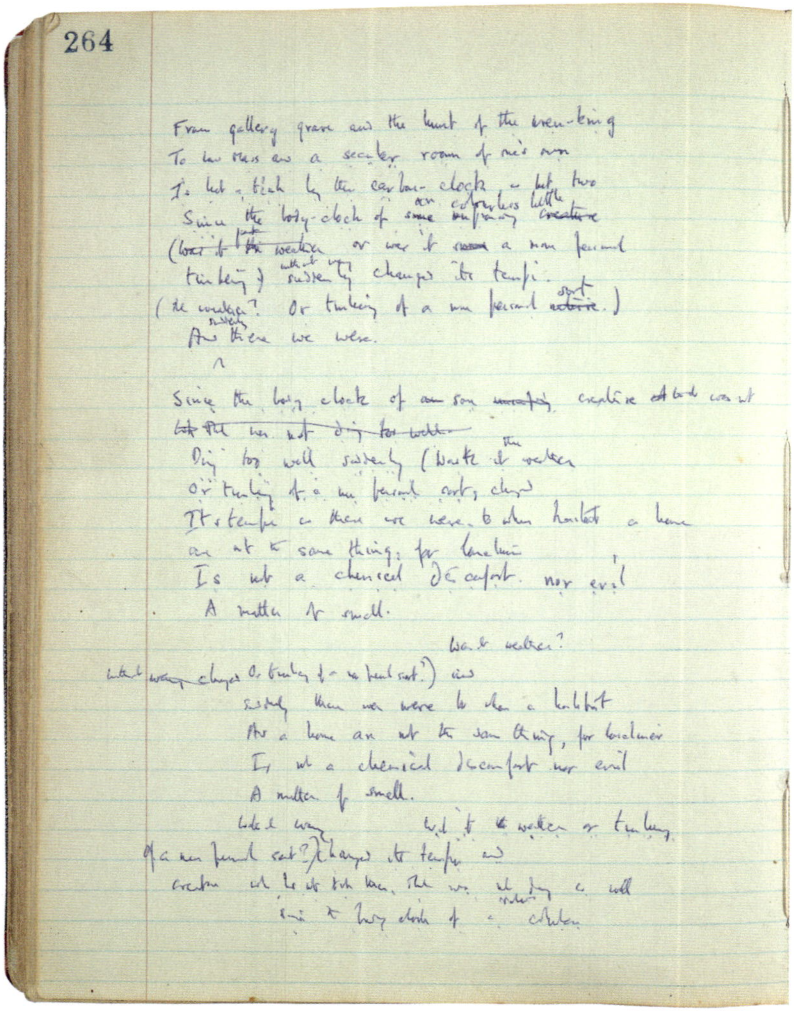

FIG. 151
Draft of 'Prologue: The Birth of Architecture'
By W.H. Auden
*c.*1962–5
Blue ballpoint pen on lined paper
British Library
Add MS 53772, f.132v

referencing a pre-historic time that is swiftly pulled into the present day by 'low mass and a secular room of one's own' in the second line. Auden changed this line in the published poem to read 'low mass and trailer camp'. The poem takes the reader through structures including Stonehenge, the Acropolis, Chartres Cathedral and Blenheim Palace, through to the 'Immortal Commonwealth'. The rest of the manuscript poem is both different and unfinished, and clearly shows the poet at work, considering both word and rhythm. The 'Postscript' to 'The Birth of Architecture' as printed is more comical and makes the reader consider the relationship between the human body and the home. In the published volume *About the House*, Auden's writing is tied to his close friends and lovers, set within a domestic, physical, space. His skill in this collection is to make the exploration of his home a personal and bodily process, which he shares with the reader. **AA**

UNA MARSON

Una Marson (1905–1965) was a playwright, poet, journalist, campaigner, radio producer and presenter. Her extraordinary career involved many 'firsts'. Born in Jamaica, she worked initially as a typist but by the age of 23 she had started the magazine *The Cosmopolitan*, becoming the first Jamaican woman to edit her own publication. Four years later, in 1932, she staged her own play, *At What a Price*, which was a great success. With the profits from this she travelled to London. Here she became actively involved with the League of Coloured Peoples (LCP), a civil-rights organisation that campaigned for racial equality around the world, but particularly in Britain. She contributed to and eventually became the editor of its quarterly magazine, *The Keys*.

During this first period in London, Marson staged *At What a Price* at the YWCA in December 1933 (fig.152), and then at the Scala Theatre in January 1934. The cast was taken entirely from members of the LCP, and it was the first play to be performed in the UK with an entirely Black cast. Una herself played the lead role, Ruth Maitland. Harold Moody (1882–1947), an influential Jamaican-born doctor working in London who was the founder of the League, played her character's father, James Maitland. Despite the play's popularity it was not published, and this is the only surviving copy of the script. This is the copy that was submitted to the Lord Chamberlain's office for approval, a legal requirement for plays performed in Britain until 1968. The first page records that the play was by Marson in collaboration with the Jamaican author Horace D. Vaz (1911–1964), and that it was performed at the Scala Theatre on 15 January [1934]. It features the beginning of Act 1, which is a conversation between Ruth Maitland's parents about their daughter.

In 1935 Marson travelled to Turkey as the first Black representative at the Congress of the International Alliance of Women for Suffrage and Equal Citizenship. Also during this year, she was the first Black woman to attend the League of Nations. In 1936, in the context of war between Italy and Ethiopia, she acted as secretary to the Ethiopian Emperor Haile Selassie (1892–1975) during his negotiations with the League of Nations. Returning to Jamaica after this, she worked as a journalist, published more poetry and wrote and staged at least two more plays, including *Pocomania* (1938), which was described at the time as marking the beginning of a Jamaican school of drama. She also founded the Jamaican branch of the Save the Children Fund.

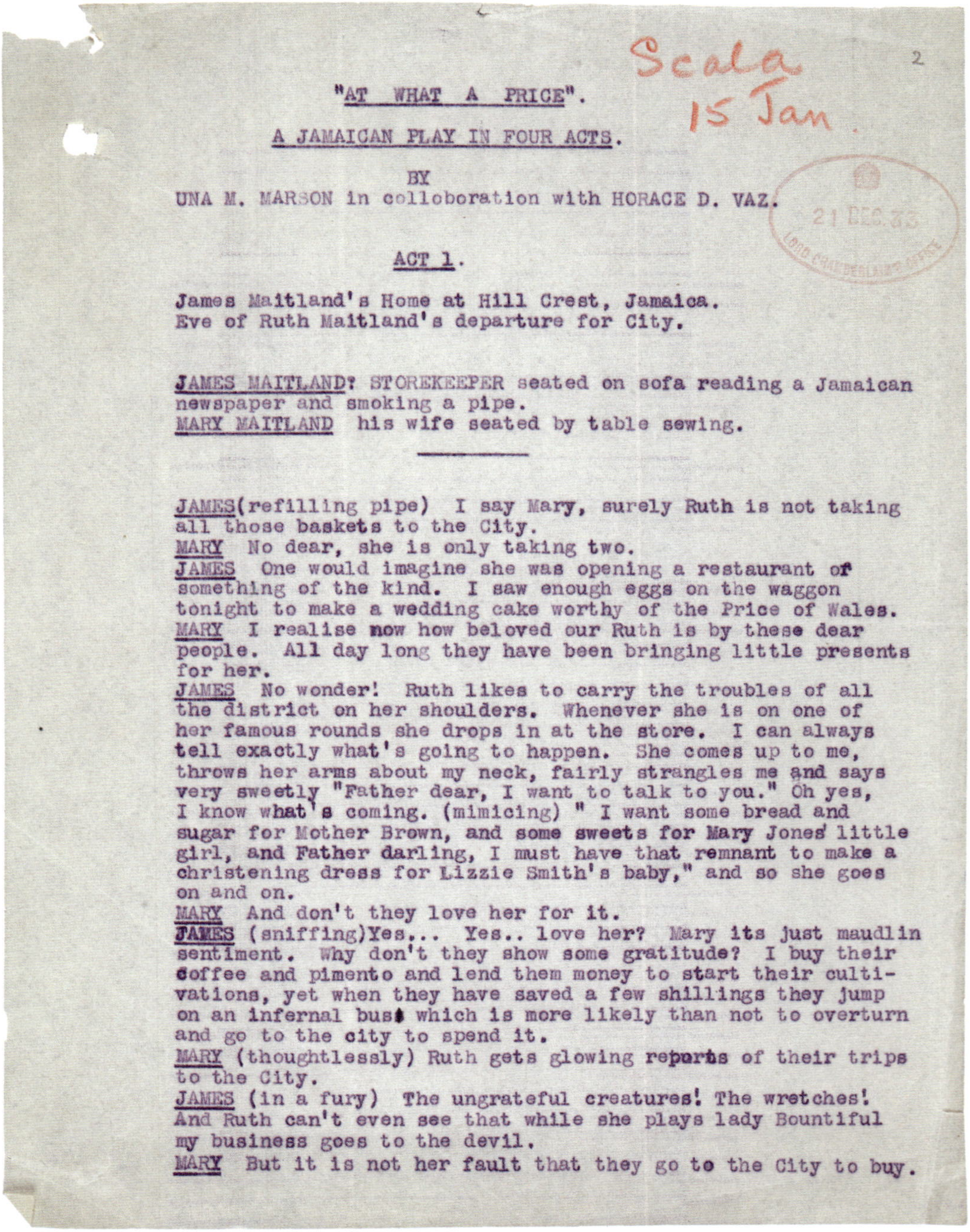

Scala
15 Jan.

2

"AT WHAT A PRICE".

A JAMAICAN PLAY IN FOUR ACTS.

BY
UNA M. MARSON in colloboration with HORACE D. VAZ.

21 DEC 33
LORD CHAMBERLAIN'S OFFICE

ACT 1.

James Maitland's Home at Hill Crest, Jamaica.
Eve of Ruth Maitland's departure for City.

JAMES MAITLAND? STOREKEEPER seated on sofa reading a Jamaican newspaper and smoking a pipe.
MARY MAITLAND his wife seated by table sewing.

JAMES(refilling pipe) I say Mary, surely Ruth is not taking all those baskets to the City.
MARY No dear, she is only taking two.
JAMES One would imagine she was opening a restaurant or something of the kind. I saw enough eggs on the waggon tonight to make a wedding cake worthy of the Price of Wales.
MARY I realise now how beloved our Ruth is by these dear people. All day long they have been bringing little presents for her.
JAMES No wonder! Ruth likes to carry the troubles of all the district on her shoulders. Whenever she is on one of her famous rounds she drops in at the store. I can always tell exactly what's going to happen. She comes up to me, throws her arms about my neck, fairly strangles me and says very sweetly "Father dear, I want to talk to you." Oh yes, I know what's coming. (mimicing) " I want some bread and sugar for Mother Brown, and some sweets for Mary Jones' little girl, and Father darling, I must have that remnant to make a christening dress for Lizzie Smith's baby," and so she goes on and on.
MARY And don't they love her for it.
JAMES (sniffing)Yes... Yes.. love her? Mary its just maudlin sentiment. Why don't they show some gratitude? I buy their coffee and pimento and lend them money to start their cultivations, yet when they have saved a few shillings they jump on an infernal bus which is more likely than not to overturn and go to the city to spend it.
MARY (thoughtlessly) Ruth gets glowing reports of their trips to the City.
JAMES (in a fury) The ungrateful creatures! The wretches! And Ruth can't even see that while she plays lady Bountiful my business goes to the devil.
MARY But it is not her fault that they go to the City to buy.

Moving back to Britain in 1938, Marson worked initially as a freelance journalist for the BBC and then in 1941 was appointed a producer in the Empire Department. She thus became the first Black woman producer at the BBC. However, an internal BBC memo confirming her appointment, dated 28 January 1941, reveals that although the BBC was keen to appoint 'a coloured British subject', they felt that her probationary period should

FIG.152
Playscript for 'At What a Price'
By Una Marson with Horace D. Vaz
1933
Typewritten with graphite and red pencil on paper
British Library
Add MS 66878 D, f.2r

FIG.153
Una Marson
By an unknown photographer for the BBC
10 March 1941, printed 2023
Modern gelatin silver print
National Portrait Gallery
NPG x202627

be taken particularly seriously and that she should be appointed initially at a lower grade than the post merited, being regraded after her probation.[23] While at the BBC, Marson made talks and programmes for the *Calling the West Indies* series, including a new strand, *Caribbean Voices*, which provided a platform for new poetry and short stories by Caribbean writers working in Britain. Marson was also involved in other radio series, in which she worked with high-profile literary figures of the day. Marson is shown in this photograph (fig.153) during the time she worked for the BBC.

In 1945 she returned to Jamaica. Her physical and mental health were affected by the enormous amount of work she had undertaken and by pressure she faced inside the BBC. After a long period of recuperation, she seems to have returned to publishing, writing and campaigning. She lived in the US from 1952 until 1960 and was briefly married to an African American dentist. Working in Israel in 1965 at an education centre for women, the Mount Carmel Training Centre in Haifa, she became ill. Marson returned again to Jamaica and died of a heart attack at the age of 60. Marson not only blazed a trail with her own literary and campaigning work, but also facilitated the careers and literary production of many other writers of colour, not just in her own lifetime but into the future. **CM**

ANGELA CARTER

The most famous work by the feminist writer and journalist Angela Carter (1940–1992) re-imagined the helpless heroines of fairy tales as strong, assertive women seizing their own destinies, or helped by other women. Born during the Second World War in London, Carter spent much of her early childhood in Yorkshire, England, with her grandmother. After academic success at school in south London, she worked briefly as a reporter for the *Croydon Advertiser*. Carter married at the age of 20 and after her marriage she read English at Bristol University. Here she discovered a love for medieval literature, and she began writing. Her first novel, *Shadow Dance* (1966), was written while she was at university and published shortly after she graduated. Other novels followed rapidly, and she won the literary prize, the Somerset Maugham Award, with *Several Perceptions* (1968), using the prize money to leave her husband and travel to Japan.

Carter's writing was strongly influenced by her love of medieval romance and Gothic fantasy, but with a more explicit element of sexual menace and violence, and a deep interest in imagery reflecting the unconscious mind. The work for which she is probably best known and most admired is her collection of fairy tales, *The Bloody Chamber and Other Stories* (1979; fig.154). Shown here is the first page of the manuscript. Although it is typewritten Carter has corrected extensively in black and blue ballpoint pen; she revisited the text at least three times on this draft. Carter's stories, based on traditional fairy tales, are full of Gothic horror and dark fantasy; in them, sexually liberated heroines surprise both villains and heroes with their actions. Carter herself explained that: 'My intention was not to do "versions" or, as the American edition of the book said, horribly, "adult" fairy tales, but to extract the latent content from the traditional stories.'[24] The author Neil Gaiman (b.1960) has said:

> '*The Bloody Chamber* is such an important book to me ... Angela Carter, for me, is still the one who said: "You see these fairy stories, these things that are sitting at the back of the nursery shelves? Actually, each one of them is a loaded gun. Each of them is a bomb. Watch: if you turn it right it will blow up."'[25]

The London-born photographer Sally Soames (1937–2019) photographed Carter for *The Sunday Times* in 1981 (fig.155). Soames

FIG. 154
Draft of *The Bloody Chamber*
By Angela Carter
*c.*1979
Typewritten with black and blue ballpoint pen
British Library
Add MS 88899/1/33, f.50r

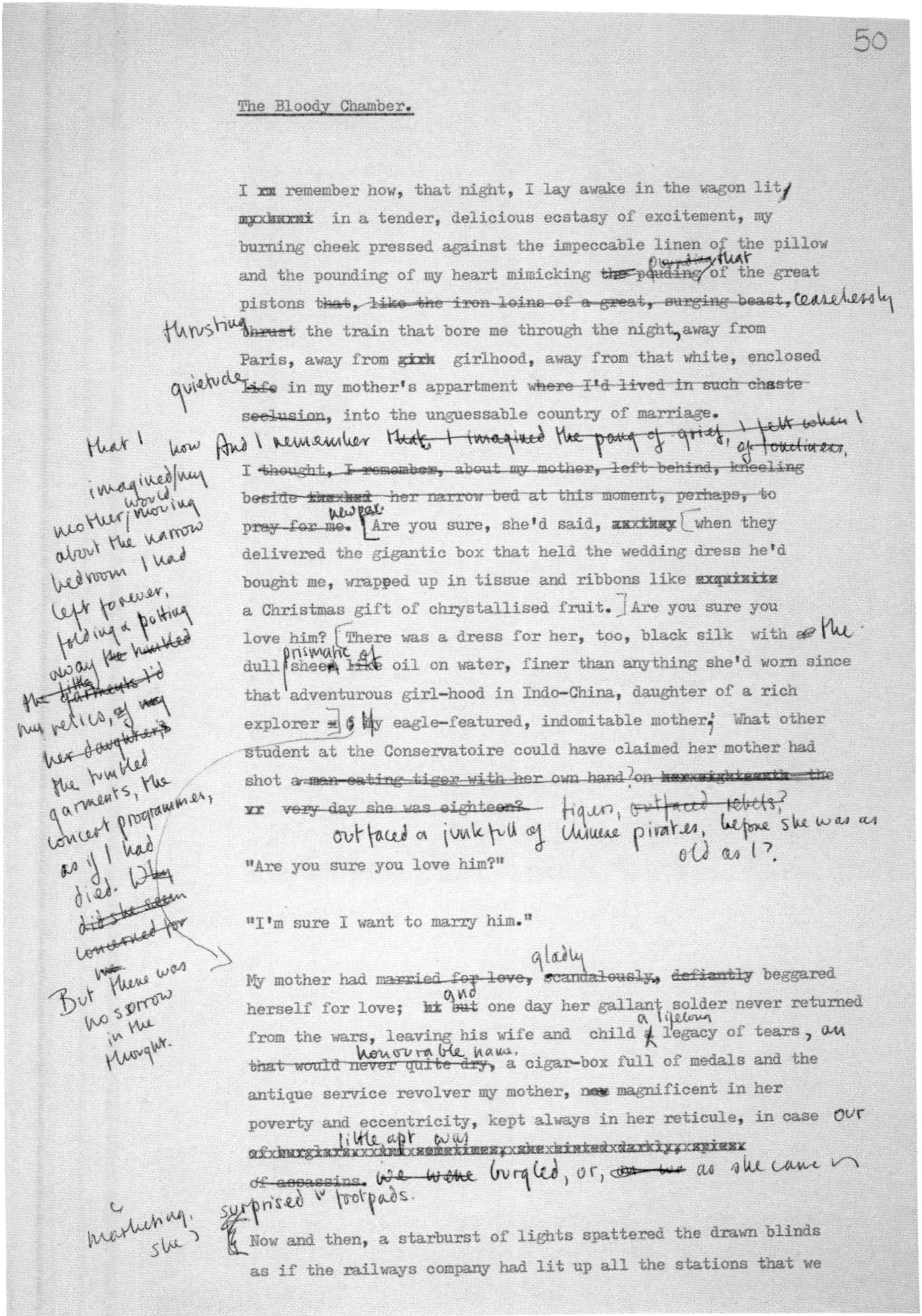

50

The Bloody Chamber.

I xx remember how, that night, I lay awake in the wagon lit myxbxxxi in a tender, delicious ecstasy of excitement, my burning cheek pressed against the impeccable linen of the pillow and the pounding of my heart mimicking the pouding of the great pistons that, like the iron loins of a great, surging beast, thrust the train that bore me through the night, away from Paris, away from girh girlhood, away from that white, enclosed life in my mother's appartment where I'd lived in such chaste seclusion, into the unguessable country of marriage.

I thought, I remember, about my mother, left behind, kneeling beside thexbed her narrow bed at this moment, perhaps, to pray for me. Are you sure, she'd said, axxthey when they delivered the gigantic box that held the wedding dress he'd bought me, wrapped up in tissue and ribbons like exquisite a Christmas gift of chrystallised fruit. Are you sure you love him? There was a dress for her, too, black silk with a dull sheen like oil on water, finer than anything she'd worn since that adventurous girl-hood in Indo-China, daughter of a rich explorer x of my eagle-featured, indomitable mother. What other student at the Conservatoire could have claimed her mother had shot a man-eating tiger with her own hand on her eighteenth the xx very day she was eighteen?

"Are you sure you love him?"

"I'm sure I want to marry him."

My mother had married for love, scandalously, defiantly beggared herself for love; bx but one day her gallant solder never returned from the wars, leaving his wife and child a legacy of tears that would never quite dry, a cigar-box full of medals and the antique service revolver my mother, now magnificent in her poverty and eccentricity, kept always in her reticule, in case ofxburglarsxxxandxsometimesxxshexhintedxdarklyxxspiesx of assassins.

Now and then, a starburst of lights spattered the drawn blinds as if the railways company had lit up all the stations that we

FIG. 155
Angela Carter
By Sally Soames
1981
Gelatin silver print
National Portrait Gallery
NPG P637

was one of the few female photographers of her generation working on Fleet Street, and she was renowned for her fearlessness, which was particularly apparent when she covered the 1973 Arab–Israeli war. She always worked in black and white, preferring to use natural light for her photographs, and often enhanced the black areas of her images to emphasise the faces of her sitters. She spent time talking to her subjects before photographing them, aiming to get them to forget momentarily that they were being photographed; this image of Carter appears to capture just such a moment. **CM**

LINTON KWESI JOHNSON

The Reggae poet Linton Kwesi Johnson (b.1952) was born in Jamaica and has lived in England since 1963, when he emigrated to join his mother. She had arrived three years earlier as part of the generation of immigrants from the Caribbean who arrived in Britain on HMT *Empire Windrush*, and other ships, invited by the government to help build post-war Britain. Living in Brixton, London, and later studying sociology at Goldsmiths, University of London, Johnson became a poet, activist, musician and writer, dedicating his career to documenting the Black British experience. Johnson was friends with older writers, including Andrew Salkey (1928–1995; see p.165), with whom he often shared news and examples of his work. The difficulties faced by the Windrush generation were felt by the next generation too, and Johnson said he started to write poetry in his late teens as a way to express how he felt growing up in a racially hostile environment. Johnson belonged to a group within the political Black Panther Movement who were interested in literature and read poems to one another, and who believed class struggles deserved attention in addition to struggles of race.

Johnson began performing his signature London–Jamaican Patois over dub reggae. He recited his poem 'Inglan is a Bitch' in 1980 on the BBC. Writer Gary Younge (b.1969) said of the performance: 'I didn't know you could do that ... effectively say what you're thinking about racism in Britain out loud in public and still work again.'[26] Shown here is the cover of *Inglan is a Bitch*, a collection of poems that were first published by the Race Today Collective in 1980 (fig.156). The Race Today Collective was a leading instrument in Black politics in the 1970s and 1980s and used journalism and direct action to fight against racism.

Johnson said he saw his verse 'as a way of chronicling Black British history as it was being made'.[27] His poems reflected his 'deep sense of alienation and rejection'.[28] He said:

> 'In Jamaica we were schooled to be British, to wave the flag when the Queen came, but when we came here we were *othered* by the rest of British society. That kind of estrangement was profound and it is one reason why reggae was so important to us. It gave us a sense of independent identity that was all our own.'[29]

FIG.156
Inglan is a Bitch
By Linton Kwesi Johnson
(Race Today Publications, London, 1980)
British Library
YD.2007.a.9088

FIG.157
Linton Kwesi Johnson
By Norman McBeath
August 2002
Inkjet print
National Portrait Gallery
NPG x137966

Johnson is only the second living poet, and the only Black poet, to have a Penguin anthology dedicated to his work. His portrait by Norman McBeath (b.1952; fig.157) shows him at the age of 50, making eye contact with the viewer. Johnson adopts the confident, steady and calm gaze of a sitter unafraid to challenge societal wrongs and call out injustice. Edinburgh-based McBeath is a photographer and printmaker interested in capturing the individual in his portraiture and is known for his collaborations with poets. **AA**

BENJAMIN ZEPHANIAH

Benjamin Zephaniah (1958–2023) was a dub poet, animal rights activist, writer, actor and musician who was born to Jamaican parents in a part of Birmingham that Zephaniah called the Jamaican capital of England. By the age of 15, Zephaniah's poetry was known among Afro-Caribbean communities, but he decided, after spending time in prison for burglary, that he wanted his work to reach wider audiences. Converting to Rastafarianism at the age of 17, Zephaniah later said that the religion, 'gave me pride in being Black and, most importantly, it taught me that there is nothing wrong with seeing God through Black spectacles – from the perspective of a Black person.'[30]

Moving to London at the age of 22, Zephaniah was assaulted during the Brixton Riots, which he documented in the album *Rasta* (1982). At the time, Zephaniah regularly experienced racism, saying 'it was in your face ... the police were also very racist'.[31] Rejecting an Order of the British Empire (OBE) award in 2004, Zephaniah said the word 'Empire' reminded him of slavery.

In 1993 an 18-year-old student, Stephen Lawrence (1974–1993), was murdered while waiting for a bus in London in a racially motivated attack by a group of white youths. Six people were arrested but none were charged. Despite witnesses, no convictions were secured. An investigation found that the police were institutionally racist and that, because of this, the case had not been adequately handled. It was not until 2012, when the law was changed, that a retrial was permitted and even then, only two of the perpetrators were convicted of murder. Zephaniah wrote the poem 'What Stephen Lawrence Has Taught Us' in 1999 (fig.158). He said in 2022:

> 'I have suffered injustice, and I have seen a lot of injustice in my time. But as a Black man growing up in Britain, it's frustrating, and infuriating, when you seek justice, then find it not forthcoming because of legal technicalities. This, I believe, is how Black people in Britain felt after Stephen Lawrence was murdered in 1993. We all knew who killed Stephen. They were secretly filmed boasting about how they could beat Black people up. They mocked us. They hated us. They were proud of their racist views. When I wrote this poem, I was confident. This is why in the poem I don't just say, "I know who the killers are", I say "*we* know who the killers are"

FIG.158
'What Stephen Lawrence Has Taught Us'
By Benjamin Zephaniah
15 May 2016, first published 24 February 1999
Ballpoint pen on letterhead paper
British Library
Add MS 89636, f.1r

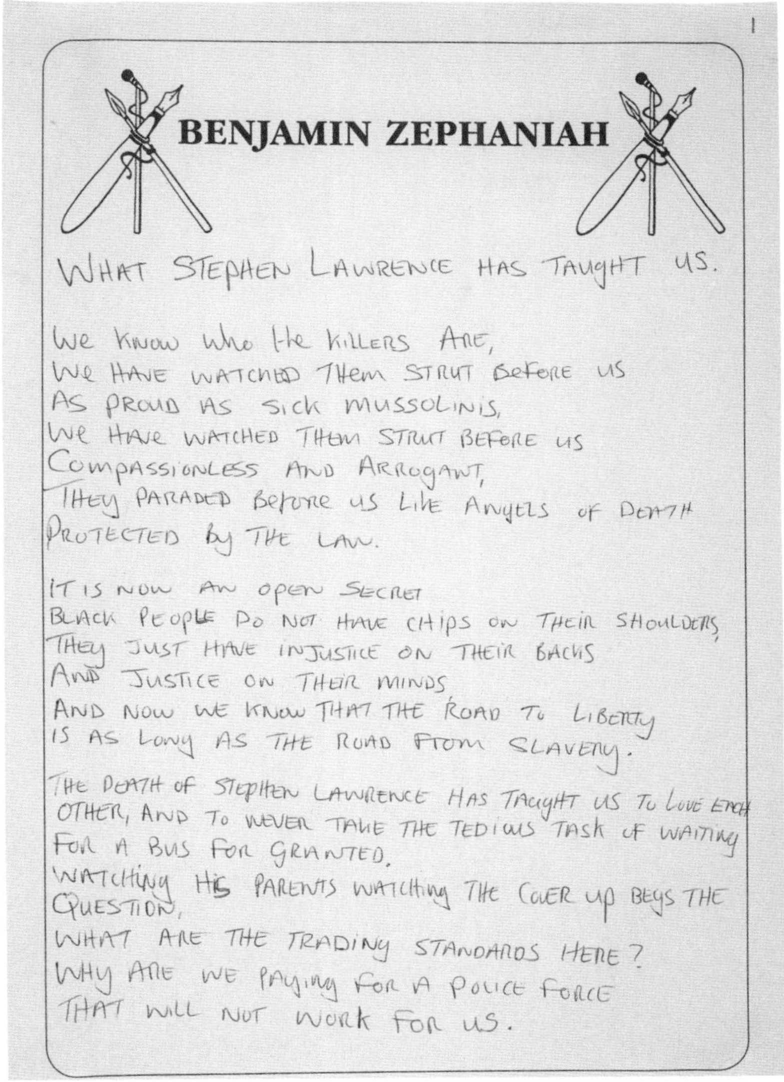

1

BENJAMIN ZEPHANIAH

WHAT STEPHEN LAWRENCE HAS TAUGHT US.

We know who the killers are,
We have watched them strut before us
As proud as sick mussolinis,
We have watched them strut before us
Compassionless and arrogant,
They paraded before us like angels of death
Protected by the law.

It is now an open secret
Black people do not have chips on their shoulders,
They just have injustice on their backs
And justice on their minds
And now we know that the road to liberty
Is as long as the road from slavery.

The death of Stephen Lawrence has taught us to love each other, and to never take the tedious task of waiting for a bus for granted.
Watching his parents watching the cover up begs the question,
What are the trading standards here?
Why are we paying for a police force
That will not work for us.

... In January 2012 two people were sent to prison for the killing of Stephen, but we know there are more who are guilty of this murder. So, in fact, we are still waiting for justice, even though we still know who the killers are.'[32]

Zephaniah said he did not keep his manuscript drafts, but he wrote this fair copy of the poem in May 2016, which he donated to the British Library.

This portrait of Zephaniah by Donald MacLellan (b.1967; fig.159) was taken just three years after Stephen Lawrence was murdered, and another six years before any form of conviction for the murder took place. The photograph, with Zephaniah's face off-centre emerging from the surrounding darkness, and his intense almost confrontational expression, seems to convey both the energy and courage with which

the poet campaigned against societal injustice. Here, only a small part of Zephaniah's dreadlocks are visible, an important aspect of his identity that closely linked him to his Rastafarian religion. MacLellan is a Scottish photographer, whose first show, *Black Power,* was held at the National Portrait Gallery in 1998. **AA**

FIG.159
Benjamin Zephaniah
By Donald MacLellan
29 August 1996
Toned gelatin silver print
National Portrait Gallery
NPG x88746

BERNARDINE EVARISTO

A multi-award-winning novelist, poet, critic and playwright, Bernardine Evaristo (b.1959) is also a long-standing advocate for increasing the representation of people of colour in the arts in the UK. Born to a white English mother and a Nigerian father, she grew up in south-east London, in an area that was then predominantly white, and in her own words, 'my family were seen as rank outsiders and vilified because of it. This has been instrumental in shaping my creative choices as a writer all my adult life, and I wouldn't change it for the world because it made me the writer I am'.[33] She attended Rose Bruford College of Speech and Drama, graduating in 1982. In 2013 she was awarded a doctorate in creative writing from Goldsmiths, University of London.

Evaristo's first published book was a collection of poems, *Island of Abraham*, in 1994. This was followed by the semi-autobiographical verse novel *Lara* in 1997 and *The Emperor's Babe*, another novel written in verse, in 2001. Both novels won awards as did subsequent works, including *Mr. Loverman* (2013), which won the Jerwood Fiction Uncovered Prize. In 2019 Evaristo won the Booker Prize, for *Girl, Woman, Other* (fig.161). The novel tells the stories of 12 different people, mainly Black women, across a wide span of time and has been described as 'a gloriously new kind of history for this old country'.[34] Evaristo was the first Black woman and the first Black British person to win the prize. Much of her work is experimental in form and dissolves the boundaries of traditional literary genres, including her use of verse-fiction. She explores sexuality as well as the African diaspora and ideas of post-nationalism, looking at the way that the histories of individuals, as well as countries, are formed by migrations and global movements.

Advocacy for writers of colour has gone alongside Evaristo's writing throughout her career. After graduation from Rose Bruford College, she and two friends founded the Theatre of Black Women, Britain's first Black women's theatre company. She also organised the first major conference on Black theatre in Britain, held at the South Bank Centre in 1995, and the first conference on Black British writing, held at the Museum of London in 1997. In 2012 Evaristo founded the Brunel International African Poetry Prize in order to help stimulate the writing of African poetry, and to provide a means by which African poets could publish their work. In 2022 this was renamed the Evaristo African Poetry

FIG.160
Bernardine Evaristo
By Ruth Ossai
2020
Inkjet print
National Portrait Gallery
NPG x203027

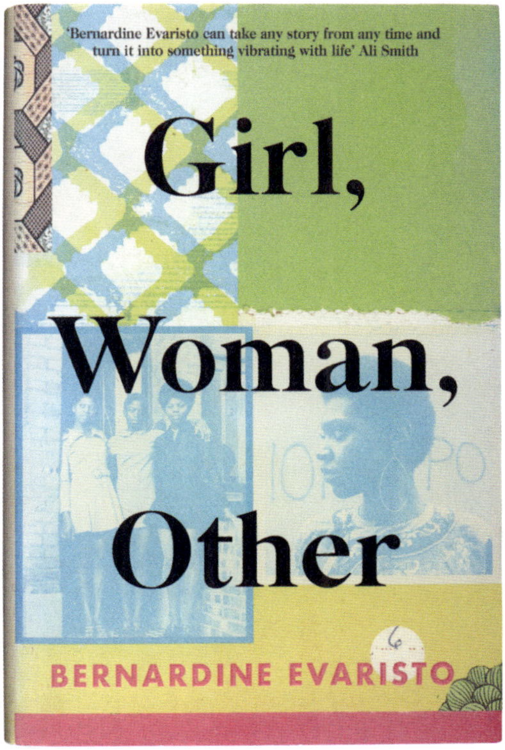

FIG.161
Girl, Woman, Other
By Bernardine Evaristo
(Hamish Hamilton, London, 2019)
British Library

Prize and taken over by the African Poetry Book Fund at the University of Nebraska. She has also selected the books and written the introductions for the 'Black Britain: Writing Back' series, which re-publishes pioneering out of print books about Black Britain. Evaristo was awarded an OBE for services to literature in 2020. She has taught creative writing since 1994 and is Professor of Creative Writing at Brunel University. Since 2021 she has also been President of the Royal Society of Literature, the second woman and the first person of colour to hold this post.

This photograph of Evaristo (fig.160) by Ruth Ossai (b.1991) was taken as part of a photoshoot for *The Sunday Times Style* magazine on 26 July 2020; the issue was guest edited by Evaristo. Ossai was born in Eastern Nigeria but is based in West Yorkshire in the UK. Her work is influenced by traditional Nigerian studio photography and celebrates African, and particularly Nigerian, identity. She is known for her bold use of colour, often using striking backdrops and flooring. Her joyful image seems to convey the strength and positivity with which Evaristo has approached both her writing and her advocacy. **CM**

NOTES

INTRODUCTION

1 William Shakespeare, *Mr. William Shakespeares Comedies, Histories, & Tragedies* (Isaac Jaggard and Edward Blount, London, 1623), front matter.
2 Ibid.

IN SEARCH OF THE AUTHOR

1 Will of John Donne, 13 December 1630. Donne described the picture as the 'picture of myne w[hi]ch is taken in the shaddowes'. Reproduced in R. C. Bald, *John Donne: A Life* (Clarendon Press, Oxford, 1970), p.567. The original is held at The National Archives, Kew, PROB 11/159/426.
2 British Library, London, c.12.e.17.
3 Ben Jonson, 'My Picture left in Scotland', line 17, Martin Butler et al., *The Cambridge Edition of the Works of Ben Jonson* (Cambridge University Press, Cambridge, 2012), Vol. VII, p.103.
4 Joseph Cottle, *Early Recollections; Chiefly Relating to the late Samuel Taylor Coleridge* (Longman, Rees & Co. and Adams, Hamilton & Co., 1837), xxxi.
5 Letter from John Keats to George and Georgiana Keats, 14 February 1819, http://www.john-keats.com/briefe/140219.htm [accessed 14 August 2024].
6 Letter from Joseph Severn to George Scharf, 22 December, 1858, National Portrait Gallery, London (RP 58, NPG Archive).
7 Paul Lewis, 'Censoring *The New Magdalen*: Wilkie's Brushes with the Lord Chamberlain', *The Wilkie Collins Society*, July 2019. Lewis cites a letter from Pinero to Walter de la Mare, written in the 1920s or early 1930s, quoted by Walter de la Mare in his essay 'The Early Novels of Wilkie Collins' in *The Eighteen Sixties: Essays by the Fellows of the Royal Society of Literature*, by John Drinkwater (Cambridge University Press, Cambridge, 1932), pp.68–9.
8 British Library, London, Add MS 71002, f.53r.
9 British Library, London, Add MS 71003, f.36r.
10 Tarnya Cooper (ed.), *National Portrait Gallery: A Portrait of Britain* (National Portrait Gallery, London, 2014), p.219.
11 Humphrey Carpenter, *The Letters of J. R. R. Tolkien* (George Allen & Unwin, London, 1981), letter 144, to Naomi Mitchison, 25 April 1954.
12 Snowdon, *Snowdon: Personal View* (Weidenfeld & Nicolson, London, in association with Condé Nast, 1979), p.76.
13 Carpenter, *The Letters of J. R. R. Tolkien*, op. cit., letter 443, to Dorothy Wood, 26 May 1971.
14 Mervyn Peake, 'Illustration, 1911–1968', https://www.mervynpeake.org/illustrator.html [accessed 17 April 2024].
15 Maeve Gilmore and Sebastian Peake, *Mervyn Peake: Two Lives* (Vintage, London, 1999), p.11.
16 Rab MacGibbon and Tanya Bentley (eds), *Icons and Identities* (National Portrait Gallery, London, 2021), p.25.
17 Letter from Dylan Thomas to Vernon Watkins, British Library, London, Add MS 52612, f.169r.
18 Jan Morris, email to Sarah Howgate, 16 January 2004, National Portrait Gallery, London (RP 6722, NPG Archive).
19 Jan Morris, letter to Sandy Nairne, 3 July 2005, National Portrait Gallery, London (RP 6722, NPG Archive).
20 Irene Lacher, 'No Fear He May Offend', *Los Angeles Times*, 25 May 1990, https://www.latimes.com/archives/la-xpm-1990-05-25-vw-326-story.html [accessed 7 August 2024].
21 Hanif Kureishi, 'There Were No Books About People Like Me', *Guardian*, 25 April 2020, https://www.theguardian.com/books/2020/apr/25/there-were-no-books-about-people-like-me-so-i-wrote-one-myself-hanif-kureishi-on-the-buddha-of-suburbia [accessed 7 August 2024].
22 Ibid.
23 *100 Photographs* (National Portrait Gallery, London, 2018), p.111.
24 Kureishi, 'There Were No Books About People Like Me', op. cit.

THE JOURNEY TO SUCCESS

1 Bodleian Library, Oxford, MS. Aubrey 8, f.63r.
2 Aphra Behn, *Sir Patient Fancy* (E. Flesher for Richard Tonson and Jacob Tonson, London, 1678), Preface.
3 Virginia Woolf, *A Room of One's Own* (Hogarth Press, London, 1929), p.65.
4 Alexander Pope, *The Second Epistle of the Second Book of Horace* (Robert Dodsley, London 1737), p.6.
5 Christopher Fanning, 'Sterne and Print Culture', *The Cambridge Companion to Laurence Sterne* (Cambridge University Press, Cambridge, 2009), pp.125–41.
6 Melvyn New and Peter de Voogd (eds), *The Letters of Laurence Sterne: Part 1, 1739–1764* (University Press of Florida, Florida, 2009), pp.129–30.
7 *The London Chronicle*, 19–22 April 1760, Burney Collection, Gale Document Numbers: Z2001657872, Z2001671391.
8 Letter to Henry Crabb Robinson in Ernest de Selincourt and Alan G. Hill (eds), *The Letters of Dorothy and William Wordsworth: the Later Years 1821–1853*, Vol 7 (Oxford University Press, Oxford, 1988), pp.106–7.
9 British Library, London, Add MS 54923, f.3r.
10 *The Personal Notebooks of Thomas Hardy* (Macmillan, London, 1978), p.75.
11 *Evening Standard*, 7 April 1932.
12 Kipling published three of the stories in the children's journal *St Nicholas Magazine*, Vol. XXXV, no.2, December 1897, p.89.
13 The Nobel Prize in Literature 2005, The Nobel Prize, nobelprize.org [accessed 14 August 2024].
14 Harold Pinter, Award ceremony speech, The Nobel Prize in Literature 2005, The Nobel Prize, nobelprize.org [accessed 14 August 2024].
15 'Arts Diary', *Guardian*, 22 November 2006.
16 *Independent on Sunday*, 25 April 1999.

17 The Nobel Prize in Literature 1992, The Nobel Prize, nobelprize.org [accessed 15 July 2024].

18 British Library, London, Add MS 52594, ff.32–41.

19 The Poetry Foundation, https://www.poetryfoundation.org/poets/sylvia-plath [accessed 7 August 2024].

20 Wole Soyinka, 'The Power of Words', *Alumni feature: Wole Soyinka*, The University of Leeds, https://spotlight.leeds.ac.uk/the-power-of-words/index.html [accessed 17 May 2024].

21 Email from Maggie Murray to Clare Freestone, 8 April 2024, National Portrait Gallery, London (RP NPG x202638, NPG Archive).

22 Interviewed 2008–9 for Authors' Lives, C1276/18, British Library, London.

23 'Fine art graduate Nick Lord unveils painting of Booker Prize-winning author Hilary Mantel in British Library following Sky Arts Portrait Artist of the Year win', Kingston University London, 24 February 2014, https://www.kingston.ac.uk/news/article/1252/24-feb-2014-fine-art-graduate-nick-lord-unveils-painting-of-booker-prizewinning-author-hilary-mantel-in-british/ [accessed 18 April 2024].

24 Peter Edwards interview on NPG soundguide, National Portrait Gallery, London (RP 6322, NPG Archive).

25 *Independent on Sunday*, 24 October 1999.

26 'Kazuo Ishiguro', The Nobel Prize, nobelprize.org [accessed 18 April 2024].

27 Lisa Appignanesi Archive, British Library, London, Deposit 11141.

SUPPRESSION, CENSORSHIP & SECRECY

1 Ludovico Ariosto, *Orlando furioso in English heroicall verse*, trans. John Harington (Richard Field, London, 1591), Preface, A.

2 Ibid., p.225.

3 British Library, London, Harley MS 7003, ff.262–3.

4 J. Treglown (ed.), *The Letters of John Wilmot, Earl of Rochester* (The Shakespeare Head Press, Oxford, 1980), p.232.

5 R. Parsons, *A sermon preached at the funeral of the Rt Honorable John Earl of Rochester, who died at Woodstock-Park, July 26. 1680, and was buried at Spilsbury in Oxford-shire, Aug. 9* (Richard Davis & Thomas Bowman, Oxford, 1680), pp.28–9.

6 *Poems by the most deservedly admired Mrs Katherine Philips, the matchless Orinda* [...] (printed by J. M. for H. Herringman, London, 1667), Preface.

7 John Gibson Lockhart, editor of the *Quarterly Review*. Letter quoted in James Wise and John Alexander Symington, *The Brontes: Their Lives, Friendships and Correspondence* (Blackwell, Oxford, 1980), Vol. 2, p.169.

8 British Library, London, Add MS 39763, ff.10r–10v.

9 British Library, London, Ashley MS 166, ff.1–2.

10 Elizabeth Gaskell, *The Life of Charlotte Brontë* (2nd edition, Smith, Elder & Co., London, 1857), pp.144–5.

11 Roy Morris Jr, *Declaring his Genius: Oscar Wilde in North America* (Harvard University Press, Cambridge, MA, 2013), p.1.

12 Laura Doan, *Fashioning Sapphism: The Origins of a Modern English Lesbian Culture* (Columbia University Press, New York, 2001), p.2.

13 V. H. F., 'Review of *The Well of Loneliness*', *Country Life*, Vol. LXIV, 25 August 1928, p.257.

14 Report regarding *The Well of Loneliness*, the London Public Morality Council, 20 November 1928, British Library, London, Add MS 83659 B, f.199r.

15 Ibid.

16 'United States v. One Book Entitled *Ulysses* by James Joyce', 5, *Federal Supplement*, 184, Southern District of New York, 1933.

17 *The Times*, 15 November 1915.

18 C. L. R. James, *The Black Jacobins* (Penguin, London, 2002), ix.

19 Lord Chamberlain's report on *Waiting for Godot*, 18 March 1954, British Library, London, LCP Corr 1954/6597, f.1r.

20 Ibid., f.1v.

21 The Nobel Prize in Literature 1969. nobelprize.org [accessed 8 September 2024].

22 Anne Walmsley, *The Caribbean Artists Movement 1966–1972* (New Beacon, London, 1992), p.45.

23 British Library, London, Add MS 89377/2/2.

24 Linton Kwesi Johnson, 'Obituary for John La Rose', *Guardian*, 4 March 2006.

25 Ibid.

26 Ibid.

27 George Lamming, *Coming, Coming Home: Conversations II* (House of Nehesi, New York, 2000), p.6.

28 George Lamming, 'Sea of Stories', *Guardian*, 24 October 2002.

29 Ibid.

FAME

1 Notebooks of George Vertue 1713–23, British Library, London, Add MS 21111, ff.30r–31v.

2 J. Logie Robertson, *The Letters of Robert Burns*, XXXIV, 7 December 1786 , pp.40–1.

3 Letter from Robert Burns to Alexander Cunningham, autumn 1794 in Maurice Lindsay, *The Burns Encyclopedia, 'Pietro Urbani'* (St Martin's Press: New York, 1980), pp.366–7.

4 British Library, London, Add MS 89437, f.1v.

5 Copy of a letter from Caroline Austen not dated but probably shortly after publication of the Memoir in 1870, National Portrait Gallery, London (RP 3630, NPG Archive).

6 Paul Douglass, *Lady Caroline Lamb: A Biography* (Palgrave Macmillan: New York and London, 2004), p.104.

7 Thomas Moore, *Letters and Journals of Lord Byron* (John Murray, London, 1830), Vol. II, letter 228 to Lord Holland, note 1.

8 Lord Macaulay, *Critical, Historical and Miscellaneous Essays*, 6 Vols (Sheldon & Co., New York, 1860), Vol. II, p.359.
9 Letter from Byron to Catherine Gordon Byron, 12 November 1809, L. A. Marchand (ed.), *Byron's letter and journals*, 12 Vols (John Murray, London, 1973–82; suppl.1994), Vol. I, p.227.
10 British Library, London, BL Ashley MS A326, f.188r.
11 Letter from Byron to John Murray, 15 May 1819, British Library, London, Ashley MS 4740.
12. Letter from Percy Shelley to Mary Shelley, 10 August 1821, Oxford, Bodleian Libraries, MS Shelley c.1.ff 445–8.
13 Georgina Hogarth and Mamie Dickens (eds), *The Letters of Charles Dickens* (Chapman and Hall, London, 1882), Vol. I, p.29.
14 Frederick G. Kitton, *Charles Dickens* (T. C. & E. C. Jack, London, 1908), p.67.
15 Morton N. Cohen and Roger Lancelyn Green (eds), *The Letters of Lewis Carroll* (Macmillan, London, 1979), p.561.
16 Ibid.
17 'All Nobel Prizes in Literature', The Nobel Prize, nobelprize.org [accessed 24 April 2024].
18 M. M. Lago (ed.), *Imperfect Encounter: Letters of William Rothenstein and Rabindranath Tagore, 1911–1941* (Harvard University Press, Cambridge, MA, 1972), p.346.
19 Presentation copy of A. A. Milne's *Winnie-The Pooh* (E. P. Dutton and Company, London, 1926) from A. A. Milne to E. H. Shepard. Sotheby's, London, 17 December 2008, Lot 2.
20 'Obituary: Christopher Milne', *Independent*, 23 April 1996.

WRITING TO CHANGE THE WORLD

1 British Library, London, Harley MS 7315, ff.98v–99r.
2 Ibid.
3 Ignatius Sancho, *Letters of the Late Ignatius Sancho* (William Sancho, London, 1803), p.71.
4 Ibid., p.149.
5 British Library, London, Add MS 89077 f.1r.
6 Ibid., f.16r
7 Olaudah Equiano, *The Interesting Narrative of the Life of Olaudah Equiano* (T. Wilkins, London, 1789), p.1.
8 Alexander Gilchrist, *Life and Works of William Blake* (Macmillan, London, 1880), Vol. I, p.7; G. E. Bentley Jr, *Blake Records* (The Clarendon Press, Oxford, 1969), p.519.
9 British Library, London, Add MS 36498, f.324r.
10 Ibid., f.328v.
11 Allan Cunningham, *Cunningham's Cabinet Gallery of Pictures* (Hodgson & Graves, London, 1836), Vol. I, p.11.
12 Letter from Amelia Curran to Mary Shelley, 6 October 1822 in Betty T. Bennett (ed.), *The Letters of Mary Wollstonecraft Shelley* (Johns Hopkins University Press, Baltimore, 1980), Vol. I, p.241.
13 Richard Walker, *Regency Portraits* (National Portrait Gallery: London, 1985), https://www.npg.org.uk/collections/search/portraitExtended/mw05763/Percy-Bysshe-Shelley [accessed 8 August 2024].
14 Letter from George Eliot to Charles and Cara Bray, 15 February 1850, G. S. Haight (ed.), *The George Eliot Letters*, 9 Vols (Yale University Press and Oxford University Press, New Haven and London, 1954–78), Vol. I, p.330.
15 William Hale White, 'Literary Gossip', *Athenaeum*, Vol. 3031, 28 November 1885, p.702.
16 Virginia Woolf, 'Modern Novels', *The Times Literary Supplement*, 10 April 1919, reprinted in *The Common Reader*, 1925.
17 British Library, London, Add MS 88925/1/1, f.6.r.
18 *The Times*, 31 July 1917.
19 First published in Wilfred Owen, *Poems* (Chatto & Windus, London, 1920), p.vii.
20 Letter from Wilfred Owen to Siegfried Sassoon, 5 November 1917, in Wilfred Owen, *Collected Letters*, Harold Owen and John Bell (eds) (Oxford University Press, Oxford, 1967), p.505.
21 'Lives of the First World War', Imperial War Museums, https://livesofthefirstworldwar.iwm.org.uk/story/78962 [accessed 8 August 2024].
22 W. H. Auden, 'Mirror: A Set of Notes by W. H. Auden', *Vogue*, December 1962.
23 'Una Marson: Appointment Memo', BBC/Science Museum Group, https://canvas-story.bbcrewind.co.uk/100objects/unamarsonletter/ [accessed 21 May 2024].
24 John Haffenden, *'Angela Carter', Novelists in Interview* (Methuen Press, New York, 1885), p.80.
25 *Daily Telegraph*, 20 November 2014.
26 Sean O'Hagan, 'Interview with Linton Kwesi Johnson', *Guardian*, 31 July 2022.
27 Ibid.
28 Ibid.
29 Ibid.
30 Benjamin Zephaniah, 'I am a Rastafarian', Fortress Press handout, https://ms.fortresspress.com/downloads/9780800699703_Handout_Rastafarian.pdf [accessed 21 May 2024].
31 'Benjamin Zephaniah on Nelson Mandela, Bob Marley and race riots in London', *Dunmow Broadcast*, 29 October 2019.
32 Alexandra Ault and Laura Walker, *Poems in Progress: Drafts from Master Poets* (British Library Publishing, London, 2022), p.139.
33 Bernardine Evaristo, 'These Stories We Tell', 1 October 2019, *Arvon*, https://www.arvon.org/bernardine-evaristo-the-stories-we-tell/ [accessed 8 August 2024].
34 Booker Prize website, https://thebookerprizes.com/the-booker-library/books/girl-woman-other [accessed 8 August 2024].

FURTHER READING

If you would like to learn more about the collections of the National Portrait Gallery and British Library, here is a list of further reading:

100 Writers
Edited by Catharine MacLeod (National Portrait Gallery, London, 2019)

Icons and Identities
Edited by Rab MacGibbon and Tanya Bentley (National Portrait Gallery, London, 2021)

Inspirational Women: Rediscovering Stories in Art, Science and Social Reform
Edited by Lydia Miller, with an introduction by Samira Ahmed (National Portrait Gallery, London, 2021)

Love Stories: Art, Passion & Tragedy
Edited by Lucy Peltz and Louise Stewart (National Portrait Gallery, London, 2020)

National Portrait Gallery: The Collection
Edited by Rab MacGibbon (National Portrait Gallery, London, 2023)

The Bloomsbury Group
By Frances Spalding (National Portrait Gallery, London, 2021)

Women at Work: 1900 to Now
Edited by Flavia Frigeri, with contributions by Emma Chapman, and Alice Rawsthorn (National Portrait Gallery, London, 2023)

Poems in Progress: Drafts from Master Poets
Edited by Alexandra Ault and Laura Walker (British Library Publishing, London, 2022)

Shelf Life: Writers on Books and Reading
Edited by Alex Johnson (British Library Publishing, London, 2018)

Swallowed by a Whale: How to Survive the Writing Life
By Huw Lewis-Jones (British Library Publishing, London, 2020)

The Book by Design: The Remarkable Story of the World's Greatest Invention
Edited by P. J. M. Marks and Stephen Parkin (British Library Publishing, London, 2023)

The Book Lover's Bucket List: A Tour of Great British Literature
Edited by Caroline Taggart with a foreword by Tracy Chevalier (British Library Publishing, London, 2021)

PICTURE CREDITS

The National Portrait Gallery and The British Library would like to thank the copyright holders for granting permission to reproduce works illustrated in this book. Every effort has been made to contact the holders of copyright material, and any omissions will be corrected in future editions if the publisher is notified in writing.

p.2 Purchased, 1914. © National Portrait Gallery, London.
p.6 Purchased with help from the Contemporary Art Society, 1965. © Patrick Heron/DACS 2024.
p.19 Collection: British Library. Public domain.
p.20 Purchased, 1936. © National Portrait Gallery, London.
p.22 Purchased with help from the National Heritage Memorial Fund, the Art Fund, Lord Harris of Peckham, L. L. Brownrigg, the Portrait Fund, Sir Harry Djanogly, the Headley Trust, the Eva & Hans K. Rausing Trust, The Pidem Fund, Mr O. Damgaard-Nielsen, Sir David and Lady Scholey and numerous Gallery visitors and supporters, 2006. © National Portrait Gallery, London.
p.23 Acquisition made possible with a grant from the National Heritage Memorial Fund and with funding from the Friends of the National Libraries, the British Library Collections Trust, the T. S. Blakeney Fund, the Bridgewater Fund, and the American Trust for the British Library with thanks to Paul Chrzanowski and Patrick Donovan. Collection: British Library. Public domain.
p.26 Collection: British Library. Public domain.
p.27 Collection: British Library. Public domain.
p.28 Purchased, 1935. © National Portrait Gallery, London.
p.30 Collection: British Library. Public domain.
p.31 Purchased with help from the Art Fund, 1933. © National Portrait Gallery, London.
p.33 Purchased, 1877. © National Portrait Gallery, London.
p.34 Collection: British Library. Reproduced by kind permission of Priscilla Coleridge Cassam.
p.36 Collection: British Library. © Reserved.
p.37 Given by S. Smith Travers, 1859. © National Portrait Gallery, London.
p.39 Purchased, 1894. © National Portrait Gallery, London.
p.41 Collection: British Library. Reproduced by permission of Faith Clarke, great-granddaughter of Wilkie Collins.
p.43 Purchased, 1983. © National Portrait Gallery, London.
p.44 Collection: British Library. Reproduced by permission of The Society of Authors as the Literary Representative of the Estate of Virginia Woolf.
p.46 Collection: British Library. Reproduced by permission of Faber & Faber Ltd.
p.47 Collection: British Library. Reproduced by permission of Faber & Faber Ltd.
p.49 Purchased with help from the Contemporary Art Society, 1965. © Patrick Heron/DACS 2024.
p.51 Collection: British Library. © The Tolkien Estate Ltd, 2025.
p.52. Collection: British Library. © The Tolkien Estate Ltd, 2025.
p.53 Purchased, 2000. © Armstrong Jones.
p.55 Given by the Estate of Mervyn Peake, 2019. © Estate of Mervyn Peake/National Portrait Gallery, London.
p.56 Collection: British Library. Reproduced by permission of the Estate of Mervyn Peake.
p.58 Purchased with support from the Art Fund (with a contribution from the Wolfson Foundation), the National Heritage Memorial Fund and The Thompson Family Charitable Trust, 2018. © Estate of Augustus John/Bridgeman Images.
p.59 Collection: British Library. © The Dylan Thomas Trust. Reprinted by permission of David Higham Associates.
p.60 Collection: British Library. Reproduced by permission of Faber & Faber Ltd.
p.61 Commissioned, 2005. © National Portrait Gallery, London.
p.63 Purchased, 1994. Photograph © National Portrait Gallery, London.
p.64 Collection: British Library. © Ted Hughes Estate.
p.66 Collection: British Library. Second draft of Buddha of Suburbia © Hanif Kureishi, used by permission of The Wylie Agency (UK) Limited.
p.67 Purchased, 1990. © Jillian Edelstein/Camera Press.
p.69 Collection: British Library. © Andrea Levy Estate.
p.71 Purchased, 2004. © Mary Dunkin.
p.77 Purchased, 1961. © National Portrait Gallery, London.
p.78 Collection: British Library. Public domain.
p.80 Collection: British Library. Public domain.
p.81 Purchased with help from L. L. Brownrigg, the Art Fund, the Lerner Gift and Lewis Golden, 2008. © National Portrait Gallery, London.
p.83 Collection: British Library. Public domain.
p.84 Purchased with help from the Friends of the National Libraries and the Pilgrim Trust, 1966. © National Portrait Gallery, London.
p.85 Collection: British Library. Public domain.
p.86 Collection: British Library. Public domain.
p.87 © National Portrait Gallery, London.
p.89 Purchased with help from Mr and Mrs Lewis Golden, the Art Fund, the Pilgrim Trust, H. M. Government and the results of a public appeal, 1975. © National Portrait Gallery, London.
p.90 Collection: British Library. Public domain.
p.92 Collection: British Library. Reproduction courtesy of the Wordsworth Trust.
p.93 Bequeathed by John Fisher Wordsworth, 1920. © National Portrait Gallery, London.
p.95 (above) Collection: British Library. © The Estate of Thomas Hardy, courtesy Dorset Natural History and Archaeological Society.
p.95 (below) Collection: British Library. © The Estate of Thomas Hardy, courtesy Dorset Natural History and Archaeological Society.
p.96 Purchased, 1931. © National Portrait Gallery, London.
p.98 Bequeathed by Mrs Elsie Bambridge, 14 December 1976. Collection: British Library. Public domain.
p.99 Collection: British Library. Public domain.
p.101 Bequeathed by the artist's mother, 1920. © National Portrait Gallery, London.
p.103 Purchased with support of the National Heritage Memorial Fund, Friends of the British Library, Friends of the National Libraries and contributions from other generous donors, 2007. The cataloguing project was supported by the Gladys Krieble Delmas Foundation. Collection: British Library. © Fpinter Limited. *The Homecoming* is published by Faber and Faber Ltd; Excerpt from *The Homecoming* by Harold Pinter, © 1965, 1966 by H. Pinter Ltd. Used by permission of Grove/Atlantic, Inc.
p.104 Commissioned as part of the First Prize, 1991 BP Portrait Award, 1992. © National Portrait Gallery, London.
p.106 Collection: British Library. "Lampfall" from THE CASTAWAY AND OTHER POEMS by Derek Walcott. © 1965 by Derek Walcott. Reprinted by permission of Farrar, Straus and Giroux. All Rights Reserved.
p.107 Purchased, 2004. © Horace Ové/National Portrait Gallery, London.
p.109 Given by Rosalie Thorne McKenna Foundation, 2011. © Rosalie Thorne McKenna Foundation. Courtesy of the Center for Creative Photography, University of Arizona Foundation.
p.110 Collection: British Library. Reproduced by permission of Faber & Faber Ltd.
p.112 © Maggie Murray/Format Photographers Archive.
p.113 Collection: British Library. © Wole Soyinka. Courtesy of Melanie Jackson.
p.115 Presented to the British Library on behalf of Sky Arts and Storyvault Films, 2013. Collection: British Library. Artwork by Nick Lord for Sky Arts and Storyvault Films.
p.116 Collection: British Library. Reprinted by permission of Penguin Books Limited.
p.118 Collection: British Library. © Kazuo Ishiguro. Reproduced by permission of the Author c/o Rogers, Coleridge & White Ltd., 20 Powis Mews, London W11 1JN.
p.119 Commissioned as part of the First Prize, 1994 BP Portrait Award, 1995. © National Portrait Gallery, London.
p.122 Collection: British Library. © Zadie Smith. Reproduced by permission of the Author c/o Rogers, Coleridge & White Ltd., 20 Powis Mews, London W11 1JN.
p.123 Given by Roderick Field, 2000. © Roderick Field.
p.129 Collection: British Library. Public domain.
p.130 Collection: British Library. Public domain.
p.131 Purchased, 1942. © National Portrait Gallery, London.
p.133 Collection: British Library. Public domain.
p.135 Purchased, 1888. © National Portrait Gallery, London.
p.137 Collection: British Library. Public domain.
p.138 Acquired, 1939. © National Portrait Gallery, London.
p.140 Collection: British Library. Public domain.
p.141 Collection: British Library. Public domain.
p.143 Purchased, 1914 © National Portrait Gallery, London.
p.147 Part of the Eccles Bequest, formed by Mary, Viscountess Eccles, a book collector, philanthropist and member of the American Friends of the British Library. Collection: British Library. Public domain.

pp.148–9 Part of the Eccles Bequest, formed by Mary, Viscountess Eccles, a book collector, philanthropist and member of the American Friends of the British Library. Collection: British Library. Reproduced by kind permission of the Estate of Oscar Wilde.
p.151 Bequeathed by Una Elena Vincenzo (née Taylor), Lady Troubridge, 1963. © National Portrait Gallery, London.
p.152 Collection: British Library. Public domain.
p.154 Presented by Miss Harriet Shaw Weaver. Collection: British Library. © the Estate of James Joyce.
p.155 Purchased, 1953. © National Portrait Gallery, London.
p.157 Collection: British Library. Reproduced by permission of Paper Lion Ltd and the Estate of Frieda Lawrence Ravagli. © Estate of Frieda Lawrence Ravagli.
p.158 Purchased, 1957. National Portrait Gallery, London. © Reserved.
p.160 The Eccles Centre for American Studies supported cataloguing and engagement around the Salkey Archive. Collection: British Library. Reproduced by permission of Curtis Brown Ltd, London, on behalf of the Estate of C. L. R. James. © C. L. R. James.
p.161 Purchased, 2009. © Val Wilmer.
p.163 Collection: British Library. Public domain.
p.164 Given by John Minihan, 1988, in conjunction with the exhibition *In Close Up: Samuel Beckett*. © John Minihan/National Portrait Gallery, London.
p.165 Purchased, 2004. © Horace Ové/National Portrait Gallery, London.
p.166 The Eccles Centre for American Studies supported cataloguing and engagement around the Salkey Archive. Collection: British Library. By permission of the Estate of Andrew Salkey.
p.168 Collection: British Library. Published by Allan Wingate, London, 1956.
p.169 The Eccles Centre for American Studies supported cataloguing and engagement around the Salkey Archive. Collection: British Library. © The Estate of John La Rose.
p.170 Collection: British Library. Published by Michael Joseph, London, 1954. Cover illustration by Denis Williams.
p.171 Lent by a Private Collection, 2023.
p.174 Collection: British Library Lecture to the Commonwealth Institute Seminar on Indian Writing in English delivered by Salman Rushdie. © Salman Rushdie, used by permission of The Wylie Agency (UK) Ltd.
p.175 Purchased, 1995. © Estate of Bhupen Khakhar.
p.181 Collection: British Library. Public domain.
p.182 Collection: British Library. Public domain.
p.183 Given by Francis Egerton, 1st Earl of Ellesmere, 1856. © National Portrait Gallery, London.
p.186 Collection: British Library. Public domain.
p.187 Given by John Dillon, 1858. © National Portrait Gallery, London.
p.189 Purchased with the assistance of the Collections Trust. Collection: British Library. Public domain.
p.191 Collection: British Library. Public domain.
p.192 Purchased with help from the Friends of the National Libraries, 1948. © National Portrait Gallery, London.
p.195 Purchased, 1862. © National Portrait Gallery, London.
p.196 Collection: British Library. © The Estate of Lord Byron
p.198 Collection: British Library. Reproduced by kind permission of Mark Charles Dickens.
p.199 Transferred from Tate Gallery, 2015. © National Portrait Gallery, London.
p.201 Purchased, 1977. © National Portrait Gallery, London.
p.202 Purchased jointly with the National Science and Media Museum, Bradford, with help from the Art Fund and the National Heritage Memorial Fund, 2002. © National Portrait Gallery, London and the National Media Museum (part of the Science Museum Group, London).
p.203 Collection: British Library. Public domain.
p.204 Collection: British Library. © C. L. Dodgson Estate.
p.206 Collection: British Library. © 2025 Noel Dobbs. Reproduced by permission of the Bram Stoker Estate Collection. www.bramstokerestate.com Bram Stoker LLC.
p.207 Purchased, 1977. © National Portrait Gallery, London.
p.209 Purchased, 1949. © National Portrait Gallery, London.
p.211 Collection: British Library. Grateful acknowledgement is made to the Conan Doyle Estate Ltd.
p.213 Collection: British Library. Public domain.
p.214 Accepted in lieu of tax by H. M. Government and allocated to the Gallery, 2005. © National Portrait Gallery, London.
p.216 Collection: British Library. Public domain.
p.217 Given by Delmar Banner, 1948. © National Portrait Gallery, London.
p.218 Given by the Estate of Howard Coster, 1959. © National Portrait Gallery, London.
p.219 Collection: British Library. Reproduced with permission of Curtis Brown Ltd, London, on behalf of The Estate of the late Lesley Milne Ltd. Copyright © The Estate of the late Lesley Milne Ltd.
p.220 Bequeathed by Dr M. C. C. Stopes and incorporated in May 1975. Collection: British Library. Reproduced by permission of Curtis Brown Ltd, London, on behalf of the Estate of E. H. Shepard. © E. H. Shepard.
p. 221 Collection: British Library. Reproduced with permission of Curtis Brown Ltd, London, on behalf of The Estate of the late Lesley Milne Ltd. Copyright © The Estate of the late Lesley Milne Ltd.
p.224 Private Collection. J K. Rowling, *Harry Potter and the Chamber of Secrets*, Bloomsbury Publishing, London: 1998. © Cover illustration Cliff Wright 1997.
p. 225 Purchased, 2005. © National Portrait Gallery, London.
p.231 Collection: British Library. Public domain.
p.232 Purchased, 1947. © National Portrait Gallery, London.
p.235 Collection: British Library. Public domain.
p.236 Transferred from the British Museum, London, 1879. © National Portrait Gallery, London.
p.238 Collection: British Library. Public domain.
p.239 Collection: British Library. Public domain.
p.242 Collection: British Library. Public domain.
p.244 Collection: British Library. Public domain.
p.245 Purchased, 1866. © National Portrait Gallery, London.
p.247 Collection: British Library.
p.248 Bequeathed by the sitter's daughter-in-law, Jane, Lady Shelley, 1899. © National Portrait Gallery, London.
p.250 Given by Florence L. Barclay (Florence Louisa Barclay (née Charlesworth)), 1921. © National Portrait Gallery, London.
p.251 Collection: British Library. Reproduced by permission of the Provost and Fellows of Eton College.
p.253 Purchased, 1905. © National Portrait Gallery, London.
p.255 Presented by the author. Collection: British Library. Reproduced by permission of the literary representative of George Eliot.
p.257 Given by Terence Pepper, 2014. © National Portrait Gallery, London.
p.258 Presented by Professor Richard Pankhurst in August 2003. Collection: British Library. Reproduced by permission of Helen Pankhurst.
p.260 Presented by the Friends of the National Libraries with the help of various subscribers. Collection: British Library. © Siegfried Sassoon by kind permission of the Estate of George Sassoon.
p.261 Accepted in lieu of tax by H. M. Government and allocated to the Gallery, 1991. © Cecil Beaton Archive/Condé Nast.
p.263 Accepted in lieu of tax by H. M. Government and allocated to the Gallery, 1991. © Cecil Beaton Archive/Condé Nast.
p.264 Collection: British Library. © 1962 by The Estate of W.H. Auden. Reprinted by permission of Curtis Brown, Ltd. All rights reserved. 'Prologue: The Birth of Architecture', copyright © 1965 by W.H. Auden; from COLLECTED POEMS by W.H. Auden, edited by Edward Mendelson. Used by permission of Random House, an imprint and division of Penguin Random House LLC. All rights reserved.
p.266 Collection: British Library. © Estate of Una Marson
p.267 Purchased, 2023. © BBC Photo Library.
p.269 Collection: British Library. Copyright © Angela Carter. Reproduced by permission of the Estate c/o Rogers, Coleridge & White Ltd., 20 Powis Mews, London W11 1JN.
p.270 Purchased, 1995. © News International Newspapers Ltd.
p.272 Collection: British Library. Linton Kwesi Johnson, *Inglan is a Bitch*, London: Race Today Publications, 1980, front cover design by Fay Chang. © LKJ Music Publishers.
p.273 Given by Norman McBeath, 2013. © Norman McBeath/National Portrait Gallery, London.
p.275 Collection: British Library. Benjamin Zephaniah, *Too Black, Too Strong* (Bloodaxe Books, 2001) Reproduced with permission of Bloodaxe Books. www.bloodaxebooks.com.
p.276 Given by Donald MacLellan, 1998. © Donald MacLellan.
p.278 © Ruth Ossai.
p.279 Collection: British Library. Published by Hamish Hamilton, London, 2019. Reprinted by permission of Penguin Books Limited.

DIRECTORS' ACKNOWLEDGEMENTS

This book and exhibition brings together, for the first time, two great national collections to explore some of the most celebrated writers in the English language. In uniting author portraits, original literary manuscripts and rare first editions, we are presented with new opportunities to examine writers and their works from the last 500 years. Our desire to step closer into the lives of those whose words have impacted us is persistent, and it is our hope that the juxtaposition of these often unique objects will allow audiences and readers to do just this. While the content of this book and exhibition celebrates literary achievement, it also asks us to consider the lives, complete with successes and challenges, of the writers represented. By uniting word and image, portrait and draft, writers are truly revealed, often in surprising ways.

Colleagues across both institutions have worked closely to draw together objects that yield rich stories about the writers represented. Paintings, photographs and drawings, together with manuscripts, sound recordings, printed books and letters, have been curated thematically, allowing different narratives about each writer to emerge. It is important to acknowledge the vision of the people from both institutions who have been involved in conceiving this project. The National Portrait Gallery's former Director, Dr Nicolas Cullinan OBE, and Head of International Programmes, Melanie Pilbrow, were instrumental in the development of this project as were the British Library's former Head of Western Heritage Collections, Scot McKendrick, who championed this project alongside William Frame, Head of Modern Archives and Manuscripts, and Conrad Bodman, Head of Cultural Programmes.

Particular credit should be given to the exhibition's curators who have co-authored this publication and devised the exhibition it accompanies. Alexandra Ault, Lead Curator Modern Archives and Manuscripts, selected the items from the British Library's collection and Catharine MacLeod, Senior Curator of 17th-Century Collections, selected the portraits from the National Portrait Gallery. We also extend our thanks to the other curators at both institutions who have contributed to this project. It would not have been possible without the expertise of the staff at both the National Portrait Gallery and British Library, particularly within the exhibition, interpretation and conservation teams and loan registry. Our thanks go to all our colleagues, past and present.

We are grateful to our publishing teams at both institutions including, at the National Portrait Gallery: Kara Green, Senior Publishing Manager; Priti Kothary, Production Manager; Katie Anderson, Picture Research and Rights Clearance Coordinator; Tom Love, former Project Editor; and especially Taylor Bentley, Project Editor, and at the British Library: Rebecca Nuotio, Head of Commercial Brand Development and Sales and John Lee, Publisher. Externally we would like to thank Lizzy Silverton for her diligent copy-editing and layout editing, Anjali Bulley for proofreading and Daniela Rocha for her thoughtful design of the book.

We are extremely grateful for the support of our touring venue partners, who have enabled us to showcase our collections internationally. In particular, our thanks go to the team at HOTA, Home of the Arts, Gold Coast, Australia, including Susi Muddiman, Director, Gallery and Visual Arts, David Don, Exhibitions and Collections Manager, Sam Creyton, Curatorial and Engagement Manager and Sarah Harper, Registration Coordinator.

Victoria Siddall
Director, National Portrait Gallery

Sir Roly Keating CBE
CEO, British Library

CURATORS' ACKNOWLEDGEMENTS

Neither the British Library nor the National Portrait Gallery could have developed a book and exhibition of this kind alone but together we have been able to create a project with richness and depth, highlighting the work of some of the most significant writers represented in two national collections.

Many curators at both institutions have contributed invaluable expertise on the objects included. At the British Library these include Mercedes Aguirre, Catherine Angerson, Alison Bailey, Greg Buzwell, Andrea Clarke, Steve Cleary, Victoria Devenport, Adrian Edwards, Michael Erdman, William Frame, Catriona Gourlay, Tanya Kirk, Karen Limper-Herz, Helen Melody, Valentina Mirabella, Nicole-Rachelle Moore, Lucy Rowland, Malini Roy, Mary Stewart, Laura Walker, Matthew Waters and Alice Zamboni. At the National Portrait Gallery, Louise Stewart, former Cross-Collections Curator, began the process of assembling the exhibition; further advice and expertise has been given by Georgia Atienza, Charlotte Bolland, Rosie Broadley, Clare Freestone, Sarah Howgate, Sarah Moulden, Lucy Peltz and Alison Smith. Consultants Maria Blyzinsky and Susan Dymond have helped to shape the exhibition and its interpretation.

The project was developed by the following staff at the National Portrait Gallery: Emily Green, International Programmes Assistant; Imogen Haines, former International Projects Manager; Charlie King, International Projects Manager; Ted McDonald-Toone, former Head of International Programmes; Melanie Pilbrow, Head of International Programmes; Aleksandra Shevchenko, former International Programmes Assistant; Pauline Velge, International Partnerships Manager. Many staff from the British Library have also contributed including: Ellie Alexander, Touring Exhibitions and Partnerships Manager; Amy Dillmann, former Touring Exhibitions and Partnerships Manager; Hannah Kaufmann, former Touring Exhibitions and Partnerships Manager; Helen Richardson, Senior Exhibitions and Touring Manager and especially Stella Yeung, Exhibitions Coordinator.

Thanks to the conservation and digitization teams and loans registry at the British Library including Rick Browne, Antonio Falzone, Tony Grant, Elizabeth Hunter, Jenny Snowdon, Lesley Thomas and Alex White; conservation and collections staff at the National Portrait Gallery, including Marta Capelli, Emmanuelle Largeteau, Katherine Robson and Polly Saltmarsh and to many other staff at both institutions who have contributed. Externally, we are most grateful to David Yates for his support.

As co-authors of the book and co-curators of the exhibition it has been a huge pleasure and privilege to work together, to learn more about the treasures of one another's institutions, and to delve deeper into the lives, images and writings of authors who have produced some of the greatest works of literature in English.

Finally, we would like to thank our families for their support while writing this book and developing the exhibition.

Catharine MacLeod
Senior Curator of 17th-Century Collections, National Portrait Gallery

Alexandra Ault
Lead Curator Modern Archives and Manuscripts, British Library

Published in Great Britain by National Portrait Gallery Publications, in collaboration with The British Library
National Portrait Gallery
St Martin's Place
London WC2H 0HW

Published to accompany the exhibition:
Writers Revealed: Treasures from the British Library and the National Portrait Gallery, London
HOTA, Home of the Arts, Gold Coast, Australia
12 April to 3 August 2025

This exhibition has been made possible as a result of the Government Indemnity Scheme. The National Portrait Gallery, London, would like to thank HM Government for providing indemnity and the Department for Culture, Media and Sport and Arts Council England for arranging the indemnity.

Every purchase supports the National Portrait Gallery, London. For a complete catalogue of current publications, please visit our website at www.npg.org.uk/publications

ISBN 978-1-85514-599-3

A catalogue record for this book is available from the British Library

10 9 8 7 6 5 4 3 2 1

Director of Commercial: Anna Starling
Senior Publishing Manager: Kara Green
Project Editor: Taylor Bentley
Picture Research: Katie Anderson
Production Manager: Priti Kothary
Publishing Assistant: Jemma Jacobs
Copy-editor: Lizzy Silverton
Proofreader: Anjali Bulley
Design: Daniela Rocha

Printed and bound in Italy by Graphicom
Reproduction by DL Imaging

FSC www.fsc.org MIX Paper | Supporting responsible forestry FSC® C013123

Front cover:
Bernardine Evaristo
By Ruth Ossai, 2020
National Portrait Gallery, London, NPG x203027
(see p.278)

Back cover:
Letter to William Stevenson
From Ignatius Sancho, 11 March 1779
British Library, London, Add MS 89077, f.16r
(see p.238)

Endpaper:
Letter to James Edward Austen-Leigh
From Jane Austen, 16 December 1816
British Library, London, Add MS 89437, f.1v
(see p.189)

Page 2:
Charlotte, Emily and Anne Brontë
By Branwell Brontë, *c.*1834
National Portrait Gallery, London, NPG 1725
(see p.143)

Page 6:
T. S. Eliot
By Patrick Heron, 1949
National Portrait Gallery, London, NPG 4467
(see p.49)

must try to get hold of one
Novels; - it would be a fine
ke our Heroine read it aloud
e as Isabella Wardour in the
History of the Hartz Demon
' I believe, upon recollection,
bye, my dear Edward, I am
ur Mother mentions in her
o be missing is monstrous!
at Steventon lately, & therefore
ng them; - two strong twigs
own, would have been some
er that any theft of that
ful to me. What should I
spirited Sketches, full of
I possibly join them on to
... which I work

superior Sermons. # You &

or two, & put them into ou

help to a volume; & we could

of a Sunday Evening, just as

Antiquary, is made to read t

in the ruins of St. Ruth —

Lovell is the Reader. — By the

quite concerned for the loss

Letter; two Chapters & a half

It is well that I have not bee

cannot be suspected of purlo

& a half towards a Nest of

:thing. — I do not think how

sort would be really very

do with your strong, manly

variety & Glow? — How coul